Researching Society *and* Culture

Researching Society *and* Culture

Edited by
Clive Seale

SAGE Publications
London · Thousand Oaks · New Delhi

First published 1998

 SAGE Publications Ltd
6 Bonhill Street
London EC2A 4PU

SAGE Publications Inc.
2455 Teller Road
Thousand Oaks, California 91320

SAGE Publications India Pvt Ltd
32, M-Block Market
Greater Kailash – I
New Delhi 110 048

British Library Cataloguing in Publication data

A catalogue record for this book is available from the British Library

ISBN 0 7619 5276 4
ISBN 0 7619 5277 2 (pbk)

Library of Congress catalog card number 97-062309

Typeset by Type Study, Scarborough
Printed in Great Britain by The Cromwell Press Ltd, Trowbridge, Wiltshire

Contents

Notes on contributors

Les Back is a Senior Lecturer at Goldsmiths. His research interests span the areas of racism, popular culture, social identity and local politics. He is the author of *New Ethnicities and Urban Culture* (UCL Press, 1996), and co-author with Professor John Solomos of *Race, Politics and Social Change* (Routledge, 1995) and *Racism and Society* (Macmillan, 1996). He has also edited with Anoop Nayak a collection of essays entitled *Invisible Europeans: Black People in the New Europe* (AFFOR, 1993). His current ESRC-funded research focuses on the cultures of racism in football.

Heather Brunskell is a Visiting Tutor of Sociology at Goldsmiths. She is currently completing a doctorate thesis on Foucault and modern feminism. Her research interests are in post-structuralism and modern/post-modern feminist theory.

Paul Filmer is Co-ordinator of Taught Postgraduate Studies in Sociology at Goldsmiths. His main research interests are in the sociology of art and he has published work in sociological theory, sociology of literature, sociology of craft and sociology of dance.

Anne-Marie Fortier is a Postdoctoral Research Fellow at the Centre for Research on Citizenship and Social Transformation at Concordia University, Montreal. She is working on a study of Italian diaspora politics of identity in Montreal, Toronto and New York. Apart from her forthcoming book on gender and ethnicity in London Italian identity formation, she has published and given talks and lectures on social theories of 'race' and ethnicity, reflexive social science, and Italian emigration. Prior to her current work she completed a PhD in Sociology at Goldsmiths.

Chris Jenks is Professor of Sociology and Pro-Warden (Research) at Goldsmiths. His most recent publications are *The Sociology of Childhood* (Gregg, 1992), *Cultural Reproduction* (Routledge, 1992), *Culture* (Routledge, 1993), *Visual Culture* (Routledge, 1995), *Childhood* (Routledge, 1996) and *Theorizing Culture* with A. James and A. Prout (Polity, 1997), and he awaits publication of *Subculture* (Sage, 1998).

Moira Kelly is now a Research Manager at the Health Education Authority, London. Primarily a health researcher, she has been involved in clinical research in psychiatry and palliative care. Prior to moving to health promotion, she worked with Clive Seale at Goldsmiths on a study comparing hospice and hospital care for people dying from cancer.

David Lazar is Senior Lecturer at the Department of Sociology in the University of the Witwatersrand, having previously worked in Goldsmiths as a Lecturer. His major interests are in the sociology of economic life and in developments in economic policy in South Africa after apartheid. His most recent publication is 'Competing ideologies in South Africa's economic debate' (*British Journal of Sociology*, December 1996).

Josep Llobera is Visiting Professor of Anthropology at University College, London and at the Universitat Pompeu Fabra (Barcelona). Between 1980 and 1996 he lectured at Goldsmiths, and was appointed Reader in 1994. He has published in the areas of the history of the social sciences, the anthropology of Europe and nationalism. An important recent publication is *The God of Modernity: The Development of Nationalism in Western Europe* (Berg, 1994).

Clive Seale is Senior Lecturer at Goldsmiths. His research interests are in the field of death and dying, particularly hospice care and euthanasia. He is author of (with Ann Cartwright) *The Year Before Death* (Avebury, 1994) and of *The Natural History of a Survey* (King's Fund, 1990) and has written and contributed to books in the Open University series 'Health and Disease'. His forthcoming publications include *Constructing Death: The Sociology of Dying and Bereavement* (Cambridge University Press).

David Silverman is Professor of Sociology at Goldsmiths. His research interests are focused on professional–client interaction, medicine and counselling and qualitative research methods. He is the author of *Interpreting Qualitative Data: Methods for Analysing Talk, Text and Interaction* (Sage, 1993) and of *Discourses of Counselling: HIV Counselling as Social Interaction* (Sage, 1996) and editor of *Qualitative Research: Theory, Method and Practice* (Sage, 1997). He is also the author of *Harvey Sacks and Conversation Analysis* (Polity, 1998).

Don Slater is a Lecturer in Sociology at Goldsmiths. His research interests include theories of consumer culture, sociology of the Internet, economic sociology, and photography. Recent publications include *Consumer Culture and Modernity* (Polity, 1997).

Fran Tonkiss is Lecturer in Sociology at Goldsmiths, and has lectured in Philosophy of Social Research at City University, London. Her research is in the fields of economic sociology and urban studies.

David Walsh is Senior Lecturer in Sociology at Goldsmiths. He is author (with P. Filmer, M. Phillipson and D. Silverman) of *New Directions in Sociological Theory* (Collier-Macmillan, 1972), and has published in the areas of sociological theory, the sociology of science and the sociology of culture. He is currently embarked upon a book on the film and stage musical with P. Filmer and V. Rimmer.

Acknowledgements

The Durkheim example in Chapter 2 was originally developed by Dr Norman Stockman (University of Aberdeen). Paul Acourt (Goldsmiths) gave helpful comments on Chapter 9. Tony Coxon (University of Essex) gave permission for use of the material in Figure 11.3. Marion Garnett (Goldsmiths) supplied a data extract from her study used in Chapter 12. John Seidel (Qualis Research) gave permission for the extract used in Figure 12.4. Patricia Taraborelli (University of Wales) gave permission for the use of the diagram in Figure 12.5. Basiro Davey (Open University) gave permission for use of the interview material used in Exercises 12.2 and 16.2. Table 14.1 is adapted from an original developed for teaching purposes by George Brown (Royal Holloway). Sara Arber (University of Surrey) gave permission for use of the material in Tables 15.1 and 15.2. Workshop Exercise 15.1 was developed in part from materials created by Lionel Sims (University of East London). Caroline Ramazanoglu (Goldsmiths) supplied guidelines for Exercise 16.3. Exercise 17.1 is adapted from an original by David Kelleher (Guildhall University). Daniel Miller (University College, London) supplied the material for Exercise 17.3. Vikki Bell (Goldsmiths) provided the idea for Exercise 19.1. We would like to thank all these people for allowing their ideas to be used in this book. In Chapter 20, the section on 'Elements of conversation analysis' closely follows Sacks et al. (1974). Mari Shullaw gave generously towards the development of the book in its early stages. Chris Rojek and Robert Rojek have supported the book in its writing and production. We would like to thank Isabelle Seale and Karen Catling for helping with the typing.

1

Introduction

Clive Seale

Researching Society and Culture provides, in a single volume, theoretically informed guidance to practising the key social research methods for investigating society and culture. It is a text in both methods and methodology, in which the importance of understanding the historical, theoretical and institutional context in which particular methods have developed is stressed. The contributors, all of whom are (or have been) members of the Sociology Department in Goldsmiths College, share a belief that social researchers do not just apply a set of neutral techniques to the issues which they investigate. Research is part of a dynamic, reflexive engagement with social and cultural worlds, and the way in which students learn 'methods' requires a continual awareness of this.

Many existing textbooks imply a 'toolbox' approach to research. This originated at a time when researchers were primarily committed to an idea of a social science modelled on the approach of natural sciences. Under this scheme, a view of methods as neutral tools for the objective investigation of social and cultural life is uncontroversial. Classically, this has been the approach of texts describing social survey work, the method primarily associated with a positivist social science. But, it seems, undergraduate and even some postgraduate courses, as well as publishing houses, have taken some time to shake off this legacy of the toolbox approach, in spite of the revolutions in social theory and methodology that have successfully challenged the once dominant, quantitatively oriented social survey approach. Existing textbooks, even where they describe qualitative approaches, often reflect an uncomfortable degree of separation between the philosophy of social science, social theory and the actual practice of social and cultural research.

As well as presenting approaches in which the links between these areas are stressed, we wish in this book to help students to break free from divisive and stultifying disputes between rival camps associated with particular approaches. Divisions have often been over-emphasized as researchers have struggled to find the institutional and intellectual space to develop distinctive new approaches. A variety of theoretically informed qualitative approaches to social and cultural research have resulted from struggles with the old quantitative orthodoxy. Yet some of the most keenly defended distinctions and disputes have developed between those advocating different varieties of qualitative methodology. We believe that a considerable amount can now be done to bring these different traditions together, emphasizing the need for practising researchers to find what is of value in each approach.

Social and cultural research can be understood as proceeding as a series of *genres*. An analogy with schools of painting may help explain this. Convention has it that impressionism, cubism, fauvism, post-impressionism and so on describe particular approaches to fine art around the early years of the twentieth century. No one now tries to claim that one of these is more 'true' than another. At most, this is a matter of taste; beauty is a more dominant criterion than truth. Can we understand schools of social and cultural research in this way? Is a preference for numbers, for ethnography, interviews, discourse analysis, ethnomethodology or semiotic analysis simply a matter of taste? At one level, this is so. Nobody is forced to 'belong' to a particular school of social research, and aesthetic taste certainly enters the picture in explaining why some individuals come to be committed to particular approaches.

Yet there are also differences between fine art and research. Avoiding some of the furthest extremes of post-modern thought, some commitment to truth as well as beauty seems right to most practising social researchers (Silverman, 1997). A text reporting on a research project can be ugly or inelegant but nevertheless be true to the social or cultural world being analysed. Even with this modified position, though, the *genre* analogy holds some force. The greatest painters have made it their business to practise in a variety of genres during their careers, then breaking free from existing divisions and using their creative powers to generate new forms from the old ones. This is also true of the innovators in social and cultural research who draw upon a variety of influences, using their thorough familiarity with existing approaches, to deal with new research problems in creative ways. If this book can convey something of this spirit it will have succeeded.

This book outlines in a concise way the standard methods that a student beginning to learn how to do research will need to know: the conduct of social surveys, interviews (both qualitative and quantitative), participant observation, coding and the basic procedures of statistical and qualitative data analysis, the writing of research proposals. However, the book is also more ambitious as it seeks to bring to a student readership knowledge and practice in methods hitherto the preserve of more advanced texts. Thus, there are chapters on discourse analysis, on the semiotic analysis of images, historical methods, the analysis of literature and conversation analysis. Several of these have arisen from revolutions in social theory that have occurred over the past 20–30 years. It is also our belief that one can only fully understand methods if one has an understanding of the historical and theoretical context from which they arise. To this end, there are chapters on the history and theoretical context of methods towards the beginning of the book.

Additionally, this is a book about **methodology** as well as methods. That is to say, it is a book which encourages you to think about the political, theoretical and philosophical implications of making particular choices of method when doing a research project. To this end, there are chapters on the relationship between research and social policy, research and social theory, the philosophy of social science and feminist methodology. If the revolutions in social theory that have transformed our understanding of research methods have a common direction, it is towards an interest in the role of language in representing and creating social realities. Importantly, therefore, the book ends with a chapter analysing the writing of social research itself. A heightened awareness of the rhetorical strategies used in social research writing enhances the **reflexivity** of social researchers; that is, their capacity to reflect upon what they are doing, and to recognize that social research is itself a form of intervention in the social and cultural world.

Although all the contributors are, or have been, members of the Department of Sociology at Goldsmiths, the book is not solely addressed to sociologists. This is in part because of the nature of the department at Goldsmiths, which contains groupings of staff with backgrounds and interests in disciplines other than sociology: cultural studies, philosophy, literature, history, geography and anthropology for example. But it is also because the old divisions between academic subjects that once were a guide to associated divisions in methods have now been broken down. Increasingly it is the case that sociologists have become interested in historical and cross-cultural perspectives, out of a belief that this is a valuable way to understand the present. Sociology, in some respects, has become a 'history of the present' just as anthropologists have become more interested in making their *own* cultures anthropologically strange. Additionally, anthropologists, geographers, students of cultural and media studies, historians, people involved in health studies, sociologists and others have increasingly come to recognize common interests and influences in social theory, and therefore in methods for investigating social and cultural life.

ORGANIZATION OF THE BOOK

At a more mundane level, this book addresses the practical constraint of undergraduate student finances at a time when it is unrealistic to expect all students to buy three or four texts for each of the courses they may study during a typical year. Under one cover, *Researching Society and Culture* offers the opportunity to learn how to practise the main varieties of method used by social and cultural researchers today. To this end, the final part contains a variety of practical exercises designed for use in workshops and discussion groups, all of which have been tried and tested with students by the contributors to this book. At the end of each chapter there is guidance on further reading which will allow a deeper understanding of the topic to develop. **Key terms** are shown in **bold** type where a definition of the term is given in the text. Wherever possible, this occurs when the term is first used and sometimes such terms are defined more than once in the text, occurring in bold on each occasion. Every such occurrence of a key term is indexed at the end of the book, so that you can look up the definitions. Additionally, many of the more important key terms are explained in a separate glossary towards the end of the book. *Italic* type is used for emphasis and on some occasions where key terms are used, but not defined. If you need to know what these italicized words mean, you can use the index and glossary to find out.

However, it is inevitably the case that a book like this contains some variability in the level of language used in the chapters. Although both the contributors and the editor have tried to assume no previous familiarity with the topics discussed, learning this material is always going to feel a little like learning a new language. This variability is in part due to the fact that some of the ideas are more abstract and difficult than others, and this is especially so when the approach is explicitly seeking to generate a novel view of the social and cultural world, breaking with common-sense ideas. People sometimes express their feeling of strangeness about the language of social research by saying that it feels 'too technical', or that there is 'jargon' involved. We hope that you will find these feelings of strangeness reduce, as you gain familiarity with the topics of the book.

The book is divided into four parts. Part I contains chapters on the philosophy of social science, developments in social theory, feminist methodology, the history of quantitative methods in social science, and an account of the historical and comparative method. This part is designed to give a broad background of the ideas and developments that either exercise an influence over, or are implied in the practice of, social and cultural research. Additionally this part contains a case study (Chapter 5) showing the influence of theoretical and political issues on a particular research project. The case study also demonstrates application of the ethnographic method, and so is relevant to a later chapter on this subject. All of the contributors to this volume have used examples from actual research studies that they or others have carried out, and in some cases chapters end with extended 'case study' sections.

Part II explores considerations of importance at the beginning of a research project, showing how careful thought about the relationships with social policy and social theory can influence the formulation of research problems and the subsequent conduct of research. The writing of research proposals is also discussed.

Part III contains chapters covering a full range of the methods in use by social and cultural researchers, ranging from statistical and survey work to a variety of qualitative approaches, and ending with a chapter on reading and writing research. These chapters give practical guidance on how to apply the methods in research projects, coupled with a continual awareness of the theoretical implications of methodological decisions.

The book ends with the workshop and discussion exercises of Part IV, which will help students become theoretically aware research practitioners.

Part I

PHILOSOPHY, METHODOLOGY AND HISTORY

Selected issues in the philosophy of social science

David Lazar

CONTENTS

Firstly in this chapter I will consider how we might gain knowledge of social life and what should count as knowledge in the social sciences. One approach for social researchers is to examine the possible implications of competing philosophies of natural science (for example, physics, chemistry, biology) for the social sciences. The arguments here are between those who claim that only *scientific* methods produce knowledge and those who claim that such methods are irrelevant to the subject matter of the social sciences. The former are **naturalists**, who argue that the methods of natural science are models for social science, and the latter are **interpretivists** (or *interpretive* social scientists), who claim that there is a sharp disjunction between the methodology appropriate in the two realms. Indeed, many of the latter group deny that what I am calling social science should be called 'science' at all. Naturalists argue that basic methodological principles (for instance, models of explanation) are shared between natural and social sciences, while interpretivists emphasize the *meaningfulness* of social life and the alleged irrelevance of natural scientists' modes of analysis and explanation. On this issue the philosopher Roy Bhaskar writes: 'Without exaggerating, I think one could call this question the primal problem of the philosophy of the social sciences' (1989: 66).

Secondly I shall consider whether the particular social sciences (economics, sociology, psychology, politics, anthropology) produce anything which is true knowledge of some objective reality, rather than, say, ephemeral notions merely dictated by fashion or subjective pictures of social, psychological or economic reality. This problem is often referred to as the problem of **objectivity**. Because it is about the *status* of social scientific 'knowledge', it is one which no social scientist can avoid. For even if we try to avoid the issue, others in wider society will raise it and thereby question the validity of our methods and conclusions.

A sensitivity to the philosophical issues discussed in this chapter is essential for anyone who wishes to be able to evaluate social research results thoroughly. I have already said that we need to think about how we might gain knowledge and about the status of the results produced by research. The problem is that, all too often, researchers and readers of research reports are unconscious of the fact that any approach to research is based on often contentious philosophical assumptions about these matters. This chapter will enable you to discern such underlying assumptions, even when authors fail to make them explicit or are themselves unaware that they have made methodological decisions by default. It will also provide you with some explanations of key ideas to which other chapters frequently refer.

PHILOSOPHIES OF NATURAL SCIENCES AND THE SOCIAL SCIENCES

What is science, and is there an identifiable scientific method? What implications (if any) do the successes (and failures) of the natural sciences have for social science methodology? By **methodology**, I refer to the fundamental or regulative principles which underlie any discipline (for example, its conception of its subject matter and how that subject matter might be investigated). There are no straightforward answers to these questions. Major philosophers of science (for example, Kuhn, Popper, Feyerabend) have debated whether science is a *distinctive* kind of activity and their contributions are discussed below. However, for many social scientists in the interpretive (or humanistic) tradition, the agreements or disagreements of philosophers about the nature of science and scientific method are of no relevance. For such theorists, the essential point of social science is to grasp *meanings* and complexes of meanings. We can, therefore, say that there are basically three streams in social science with respect to the above questions: **naturalists** who advocate the adoption of some preferred conception of science and scientific method as a model for the social sciences; *interpretive* social scientists who reject the scientific model because they believe that the nature of human social life is not appropriately grasped by scientific methods and *reconcilers* who wish to bridge the divide between naturalism and humanism. In sociology, the work of Max Weber (1864–1920) is an example of such reconciliation. His ideas are discussed in more depth in Chapter 3.

Competing philosophies of science: Karl Popper

The examination of philosophies of science will enable us to understand the complex relationships between theory and observation and what it might mean for a social science to be modelled on the natural sciences. I will begin with the ideas of Karl Popper (1902–94) and then describe the rival views of Kuhn and Feyerabend.

Firstly, Popper rejected **inductivist empiricism**. This is a view which claims that scientific theory has validity because it is rigorously derived from repeated observations. The **empiricist** view is that knowledge must be derived from observation. Accordingly, scientific knowledge is thought to be valid because it is a complex product of such innumerable, systematic and repeated observations. Scientific theories are claimed to be derived from observation by a process called **induction**. Inductive logic is believed by such theorists to enable us to move from the particular to the general, that is, from many observations to some kind of universal statement. But Popper argues both that inductive inference is an invalid form of inference and that scientific theories are not in fact derived from observation. Popper preferred a view of science based on *critical rationalism*, and argued that science consisted of conjectures and refutations.

His claim (Popper, 1963: Chapter 1) that induction is not a logically valid method for deriving theories from observations is supported by his argument that theories are general and refer to all occurrences of a phenomenon in the past, present and future. But observation is always finite and we can never know whether the instances we have not observed (or which have not yet occurred) will resemble those we have. Therefore, induction cannot be a valid form of inference because even one counter-instance would refute the theory. Instead, Popper states, scientific progress is made possible because scientists seek theory with a greater scope and truth content, replacing empirically or theoretically discredited theories with better ones. For Popper what is crucial is that, although theories cannot be proved, they can be refuted, and the refutability of scientific theories is what demarcates real sciences from what he calls pseudo-sciences (for example, astrology).

His view that actually theories are not derived from observation is supported by his argument that theorizing is *prior* to observation. Popper believed that we cannot observe without theories. Incidentally, this is a common assumption of what Hesse (1972: 10–11) refers to as a 'post-empiricist' philosophy of science. It is a view, for example, which underlies the post-structuralist and post-modernist theories explained in Chapter 3. Sciences, Popper contended, are particularly sophisticated forms of theory but like all theory are problem-solving enterprises, that is, driven by speculative solutions to problems rather than by fact gathering. At this point, you need to under-stand that an **epistemology** is a specific theory of knowledge or, in the words of Williams and May, an answer to the question 'Where does our knowledge come from and how reliable is it?' (1996: 5). Popper advocates a **rationalist epistemology**, that is, he believes that knowledge is a product of mind actively organizing and making sense of our experience of the world. This is in contrast to an **empiricist epistemology** which claims that knowledge and scientific theories of the world are derivable solely from empirical sense experience or observation.

We can understand why observation cannot be prior to theory by examining Popper's (1963: 44–5) argument about judgements of similarity. Popper contends that any generalization (and theories are very abstract generalizations) depends upon judgements of similarity. Say we wish to formulate a generalization about the connection between events of type A and events of type B. How do we know that particular events are all examples of As and others are all Bs? Only because we have theories (however low level) which tell us which characteristics matter. That is, judgements of similarity are not possible purely on the basis of observation.

Popper is also a rationalist in a second sense in that he believed that theory choice in science can be *rationally justified* by reference to a universal set of criteria. As Newton-Smith states:

> A rational model [of scientific change] involves two ingredients. First, one specifies something as the goal of science. That is, scientists are taken as aiming at the production of theories of some particular kind. For example, it might be said as Popper would that the goal of science is the production of true explanatory theories ... Second, some principle or set of principles is specified for comparing rival theories against a given evidential background. (1981: 4)

The principles Newton-Smith is referring to are, for instance, accuracy, explanatory scope, absence of internal contradictions or contradictions of other accepted theories, simplicity and fruitfulness in terms of new research findings.

In fact this led Popper to believe in the *unity of science* and he proposed a single model on which he felt scientific explanations could rest: the **hypo-thetico-deductive scheme** (Popper, 1957). Some philosophers of science (for example, Hempel, 1966) refer to this as the *covering law model of explanation*. According to this view, explanations consist of two elements, one general and one more specific. Together these elements form an explanation of what has to be explained. More precisely, one can **deduce** a statement describing the matter to be explained from the statements which form the explanation. This is shown in Figure 2.1. You explain an event by showing that it can be

```
LAW
(a generalization or theory which covers events and phenomena of this type)


INITIAL CONDITIONS
(statements which describe the circumstances in which the events take place)


EVENT(S) TO BE EXPLAINED
(statement describing what is to be explained)
```

Figure 2.1   *Hypothetico-deductive scheme*

deduced from a general *law* (or generalization or theory) together with *initial conditions*, these being statements which describe the relevant antecedent events. Let us examine a well-known sociological example to see whether this idea of a common scheme of explanation for all sciences is at all relevant to the social sciences.

Durkheim's Suicide (1897): a sociologist uses the hypothetico-deductive scheme

Émile Durkheim (1858–1917) set himself the task of providing a sociological explanation for the wide variations in suicide rates in different sections of the population, revealed in official statistics. In particular, he found that Catholics showed lower suicide rates than Protestants. For Durkheim, suicide was a **social fact**, that is, a property of society rather than an aggregate of individual actions. He distinguished between types of suicide and I shall look at his explanation of one of these, *egoistic suicide*. Durkheim contended that certain states of religious society, of domestic life, and of political society more effectively bind individuals to a group. For instance, he said that Catholicism was associated with greater social cohesion than was Protestantism. Durkheim claimed that egoistic suicide was the result of an excessive detachment of the individual from the group, writing: 'So we reach the

```
LAW
(Suicide varies inversely with the degree of integration of the social groups of which
the individual forms a part)


INITIAL CONDITIONS
(Catholicism binds the individual into a more socially cohesive community than
does Protestantism)


EVENT TO BE EXPLAINED
(The suicide rate for Catholics is lower than that for Protestants)
```

Figure 2.2   *Durkheim's use of the hypothetico-deductive scheme*

general conclusion: suicide varies inversely with the degree of integration of the social groups of which the individual forms a part' (1970: 209). Greater social cohesion (argued to be provided by Catholicism) led to a lower suicide rate, and lower cohesion led to a higher suicide rate (argued to be characteristic of Protestantism). Figure 2.2 is an attempt to cast Durkheim's explanation of the phenomenon of the suicide rate for egoistic suicide in terms of the hypothetico-deductive scheme.

Competing philosophies of science: Thomas Kuhn

Kuhn differs from Popper in rejecting the rationalist view of scientific development: he does not accept that there is a set of (rationally justifiable) principles for the comparison of, and choice between, competing theories. He argues instead that mature sciences are characterized by **paradigms**. Scientific development is only possible if practitioners of the particular discipline share a whole way of working and an overall conception of what it is they are studying. Kuhn distinguishes two basic meanings of the term: 'paradigms [are] the entire constellation of beliefs, values, techniques, and so on shared by members of a given [scientific] community' (1970: 175) and they are a concrete puzzle solution or exemplar of how to solve a scientific problem.

He emphasizes that the paradigm is a shared view of the discipline and the world it seeks to investigate, as well as a set of methods for such an investigation. Thus for Kuhn, everyday science is *normal science* or science as it is practised within the confines of a paradigm. Normal science involves puzzle-solving activity within the disciplinary cognitive world of the paradigm. Characteristically, according to Kuhn, a lack of fit between the theory and the facts is a puzzle to be solved by developing a theory (or, if you like, articulating the paradigm) or reinterpreting the facts. Kuhn (1970: 146–7) therefore differs from Popper in claiming that everyday science is not, in practice, continuously critical of the paradigm.

Normal science is only possible when puzzle solving that stays within the boundaries of the paradigm is still feasible. But, ultimately, certain recalcitrant and significant anomalies appear which are not resolvable within these boundaries. If they are too important to be ignored by practitioners, the paradigm is in crisis. Kuhn believes that normal science is largely uncritical of basic assumptions within the relevant paradigm. It is only during a crisis of the paradigm that new, competing theories get the attention of the scientific community. There is then felt by some to be a need for a *paradigm shift*, a time of fundamental change. Change of paradigm can be so fundamental as to be thought of as **scientific revolution** (for instance, change from Ptolemy's earth-centred astronomy to Copernicus's sun-centred astronomy). Indeed, the book in which Kuhn explains these ideas is called *The Structure of Scientific Revolutions* (1970).

For Kuhn, the essential feature of a scientific revolution is that the new paradigm and the old are *incommensurable*. Incommensurability means that there is no shared set of criteria of evaluation and there is a qualitative break between successive paradigms. Successive paradigms conceptualize the world which the discipline studies in starkly different ways and there is *no* universal set of principles which are accepted by adherents of both as criteria of evaluation applicable to each. This is why Kuhn sees scientific revolutions as being like a conversion experience rather than a rational process (as Popper would). It is an exchange of *belief* systems. The new paradigm becomes the conceptual and methodological basis of everyday scientific practice. Because of this, Kuhn might be said to reject the rationalist view of science. Indeed, some have accused him of **relativism**, that is, a belief that the terms 'truth' and 'falsity' have meaning only within a paradigm and that there is no reality outside the paradigm (relativism is also discussed later in the chapter).

In criticism, it should be noted that Kuhn's notion of the paradigm seems to deny that theoretical diversity is a feature of everyday science. Indeed, the theoretically disputatious state of all social sciences, despite the self-proclaimed scientific nature of certain perspectives in psychology and economics, would probably lead Kuhn to refer to such disciplines as inherently inferior because they are pre-paradigmatic. Other criticisms have been made by Paul Feyerabend whom we shall examine below. Feyerabend is scathing about Kuhn's idea of normal science. He argues: 'Was there ever a period of normal science in the history of thought? No – and I challenge anyone to prove the contrary' (1981: 160). Like Popper, despite their disagreements, he believes that science is intrinsically disputatious.

Paul Feyerabend: the rejection of method

We have been trying so far to identify the characteristics of science and scientific method. Both Popper and Kuhn, despite their deep differences, believe wholeheartedly in the value of science. But Feyerabend has a deeply critical view of science.

Feyerabend claims that the history of science shows that there is no single scientific method. For him, however, a lack of rules is a matter for celebration rather than concern. In large measure, he is concerned to nourish the conditions for individual, as well as intellectual and theoretical, diversity. He develops a powerful **epistemological** argument for using a diversity of methods to gain knowledge. (An epistemological argument is a claim about how we might gain true knowledge of the world.) Feyerabend opposes the notion that there is one supreme method for doing this:

> the world we want to explore is a largely unknown entity. We must, therefore, keep our options open ... Epistemological prescriptions may look splendid when compared with other epistemological prescriptions ... but who can guarantee that they are the best way to discover, not just a few isolated 'facts', but also some deep-lying secrets of nature? (1975: 20)

Feyerabend denies that the growth of science has, in fact, depended on one particular method: 'All methodologies have their limitations and the only

"rule" that survives is "anything goes" ' (1975: 296). Epistemological pluralism, or in his terms *epistemological anarchism*, he argues, is essential for
science. He recommends that we might advance science by proceeding
counter-inductively. This means, firstly, that it is often fruitful to adopt
hypotheses which *contradict* well-established theories. He justifies this
recommendation by stating that no theory ever 'agrees with all the known
facts in its domain' (1975: 31). He argues that we are more likely to maximize
the empirical content of scientific theories if we stand outside those which
are widely accepted.

Feyerabend contends that it is a myth that science is characterized by
scepticism and openness (as, for instance, argued by Popper). Science has, in
his view, overpowered its opponents: '*But science still reigns supreme ... its
practitioners are unable to understand*, and *unwilling to condone*, different
ideologies, because they have the *power* to enforce their wishes' (1975: 298).
As I mentioned earlier, Feyerabend wishes to encourage diversity of
thought: 'Science does not excel because of its method for there is no method;
and it does not excel because of its results; we know what science *does*, but
we have not the faintest idea whether other traditions could not do *much
better*. So we must find out' (1978: 106).

The fundamental question for social and cultural researchers, however,
concerns the value of these ideas of Popper, Kuhn and Feyerabend about
natural sciences for philosophical understanding of the social sciences, and it
is to this matter that we now turn. Should the social sciences seek laws (if
such exist) of social development and of social life? Is the investigation of
social life in its myriad forms (economic action and institutions, cultural
production, political action and systems and so on) analogous to the study of
the natural world, or is there fundamental discontinuity between these
worlds?

MEANING AND THE SOCIAL SCIENCES

What primarily distinguishes human beings from organic and inorganic
matter is that they consciously act and what they do has *meaning* for them. In
social science there are those, for instance Durkheim, Parsons and Merton,
who advocate a natural scientific approach to investigation in their disciplines (they are *naturalists*), and those, like Geertz, Taylor and Schutz, who
are deeply critical of this idea of a science of society because they focus on the
meaningfulness of the subject matter of the social sciences (they are *anti-
naturalists* or *interpretivists*). Max Weber attempted to reconcile the two
positions but, despite this, can be considered as the founder of *interpretive*
social science because of the central importance he gave to the interpretive
understanding of subjective meaning.

Let us start with the naturalists. Émile Durkheim argued that the study of
social life could and should be scientific. For Durkheim, sociology was the
study of **social facts**. He used this term to refer to a wide range of regularities of

social life, for instance, to 'religious beliefs and practices, the rules of morality and the innumerable precepts of law' (1972: 73). Social facts, in Durkheim's view, could be identified by certain characteristics: they constrain individuals, are general throughout society and are independent of their individual manifestations. In *The Rules of Sociological Method* (1982: Chapter 2), Durkheim outlined rules for the observation of social facts. He argued: 'The first and most basic rule is *to consider social facts as things*' (1982: 60). He was claiming *not* that social facts were no different from natural facts but rather that the sociological attitude should be like that of the natural scientist. In his view, social science ought to be a rigorously empirical discipline. Thus he wrote:

> He [the social scientist] must embark upon the study of social facts by adopting the principle that he is in complete ignorance of what they are, and that the properties characteristic of them are totally unknown to him, as are the causes upon which these latter depend. (1982: 245–7)

Durkheim contended that to achieve this empirical attitude, it was necessary to eradicate the influence of values and preconceptions and to observe what was there rather than substitute our prior notions for the thing we should be observing.

We now turn to an examination of the approach which emphasizes the *meaningfulness* of the subject matter of social science. Clifford Geertz characterizes this approach by emphasizing the centrality of *interpretation* rather than the methods appropriate to the natural sciences. He states in relation to the study of culture:

> Believing, with Max Weber, that man is an animal suspended in webs of significance he himself has spun, I take culture to be those webs, and the analysis of it to be therefore not an experimental science in search of law but an interpretive one in search of meaning. (1973: 3)

Similarly, Charles Taylor argues that interpretation is essential in the social sciences. He rejects the notion of the empiricist tradition that 'tries to reconstruct social reality as consisting of brute data alone' (1994: 181–211). Brute data are those which can (allegedly) be observed independently of interpretations. They are, therefore, according to the view Taylor criticizes, empirically established. To this view Taylor counterposes a conception of 'social reality as characterized by intersubjective and common meanings' (1994: 199). He states:

> Common meanings are the basis of community. Intersubjective meaning gives a people a common language to talk about social reality and a common understanding of certain norms, but only with common meanings does this common reference world contain significant common actions, celebrations, and feelings. These are the objects in the world that everybody shares. This is what makes community. (1994: 197)

This demonstrates how the social sciences are inextricably bound up with interpretation because social science needs to be able to make sense of this subject matter. Now the problem with this for naturalists, who believe social sciences should be methodologically like natural sciences, is how one might test any purportedly valid interpretation.

Finally, let us briefly look at the views of Alfred Schutz (1899–1959). Schutz contends in his classic paper 'Concept and theory formation in the social sciences' that:

> The primary goal of the social sciences is to obtain organised knowledge of social reality. By the term 'social reality' I wish to understand the sum total of objects and occurrences within the social cultural world as experienced by the common sense of men living their daily lives among their fellow-men, connected with them in manifold relations of interaction. (1970: 5)

He criticizes those I have referred to as *naturalists* for not analysing basic features of the social world: 'Intersubjectivity, interaction, intercommunication and language are simply presupposed as the unclarified foundation of these theories' (1970: 6). For Schutz, *interpretive understanding* or **verstehen** (the German word for this) is not just a method in social science but the way in which everyday participants in the social world understand each other.

Weber's reconciliation of naturalism and the interpretive tradition

Weber makes clear that he wishes the study of social life to be *both* scientific and interpretive. He is emphatic that persuasive interpretation of social action is necessary but not sufficient:

> Every interpretation attempts to attain clarity and certainty, but no matter how clear an interpretation as such appears to be from the point of view of meaning, it cannot on this account claim to be the causally valid interpretation. On this level it must remain only a peculiarly plausible hypothesis. (1978, Volume 1: 9)

Accordingly, he asserts: 'verification of subjective interpretation by comparison with the concrete course of events is, as in the case of all hypotheses, indispensable' (1978, Volume 1: 10). Weber states clearly that both interpretation and scientific verification are essential:

> A correct causal interpretation of typical action means that the process which is claimed to be typical is shown to be both adequately grasped on the level of meaning and at the same time the interpretation is to some degree causally adequate. If adequacy in respect of meaning is lacking, then no matter how high the uniformity and how precisely its probability can be numerically determined, it is still an incomprehensible statistical probability ... On the other hand, even the most perfect adequacy on the level of meaning has causal significance from a sociological point of view only insofar as there is some kind of proof for the

existence of a probability that action in fact normally takes the course which has been held to be meaningful. (1978, Volume 1: 12)

The interpretive tradition has informed several approaches to social research, about which more will be found in Chapter 3. Broadly speaking interpretivists tend to favour **qualitative** rather than **quantitative** methods. This is because, on the whole, researchers find that people's words provide greater access to their subjective meaning than do statistical trends. Weber's perspective, though, opens up possibilities for using both quantitative and qualitative methods in pursuing explanations adequate at the levels of both cause and meaning.

CAN SOCIAL SCIENCE PRODUCE OBJECTIVE KNOWLEDGE?

Social scientists, whatever their theoretical perspectives, are individuals with personal characteristics, are situated in a certain class, ethnic group, gender, religious group and live in a particular historical period. How, when each researcher is embedded in prejudices, values and specific cognitive frameworks, can we move, however tentatively, towards something which might be called *objectivity*? Both Weber and Durkheim were, although in different ways, convinced that a scientific way of studying social and cultural life could be constructed which would generate objective results, that is, conclusions which were not merely valid within a particular school of theory.

I will consider four basic positions about the implications of initial value commitments and subjectivity for the achievement of objectivity. Firstly, there is the view that it is possible to eradicate the effect of values *either* through a rigorous detachment on the part of the social scientist *or* by means of the critical role of the scientific community which independently evaluates research. Secondly, I shall consider the view that values have a positive, albeit strictly limited, role in research. Thirdly, there is the view that values and personal experience are the fundamental resource out of which we can fashion disciplines which truly reflect what social life is like for those who live it. Here the researcher's own emotions play an important role. Lastly, I shall consider **relativism**, which is the view that different theories construct their *own* conception of reality as well as criteria for evaluating claims to knowledge.

Eradicating values: Durkheim's scientific approach

Durkheim wrote in *The Rules of Sociological Method* that:

> reflective thought precedes science, which merely employs it more methodically. Man cannot live among things without forming ideas about them ... because these notions are closer to us and more within our mental grasp than the realities to

which they correspond, we naturally tend to substitute them for the realities, concentrating our speculations upon them. Instead of a science which deals with realities, we carry out no more than an ideological analysis. (1982: 60)

He was aware that our ideas are powerful influences on us because of the sentiments we attach to them. Our political, religious and other ideas, for instance, are connected to our fundamental values and moral notions. Therefore, between us and the reality which we seek to know stands a whole host of assumptions, preconceptions, ideologies and beliefs. This is true of natural science but even more so in social science. Durkheim believed that empirical detachment is a precondition for scientific knowledge: 'social phenomena are things and should be treated as such ... they are the social *datum* afforded the sociologist. A thing is in effect all that is given, all that is offered, or rather forces itself upon our observation. To treat phenomena as things is to treat them as *data*, and this constitutes the starting point for science' (1982: 69).

Durkheim formulated rules which would help social scientists to achieve this goal. Firstly, he described a *negative* rule: '*One must systematically discard all preconceptions*' (emphasis in original). The social scientist 'must resolutely deny himself the use of those concepts formed outside science and for needs entirely unscientific' (1982: 73). Secondly, he added a *positive* rule: we must attend to the 'inherent properties' of the phenomena. Initially, the only properties to which we have access are the external features, these are all we know of reality. He readily admits that such external properties may be insignificant but in this way we start correctly: our point of departure is the *real* rather than our ideas. Thus social scientists should attempt, through the rigorous application of these methodological procedures, coupled with the demand to expose their methods and findings to a critical scientific community, to achieve objectivity.

Values have a positive but limited role: Weber on facts, values and objectivity

Weber's starting point was that reality is infinitely complex and that what we see and know represents a specific way of organizing and selecting from an infinite number of sense impressions. Underlying human thought then is a *selective* standpoint. Therefore, the notion that we can construct an objective science of society merely on the basis of observation is inconceivable for Weber.

According to Weber, we live in a world of irreconcilable values. There is no rational or empirical way to choose between values. How is science possible in a world of conflicting values? For Weber, the key point is to distinguish between determining the facts and making judgements of value: 'An empirical science cannot tell anyone what he *should* do – but rather what he *can* do' (1949: 54). There is no way to demonstrate the validity of values, even the value of science itself. The scientist must concern herself or himself with what *is* (what are the facts) rather than what may, from her or his point of view, be desirable. Weber knew that it was no easy matter to discard values and merely determine the facts. He contended that we cannot help but structure what we see according to our values. How, then, can Weber believe that anything objective can be produced by people studying social life? The answer is that he distinguishes between *relevance for value* and **value freedom**. He accepts that we study what has 'cultural significance' for us: this is relevance for value. Consequently, what we study and the concepts we use incorporate our values. But, and this is what makes objective social science possible, once we have decided on our topic and framework of analysis, it is the social scientist's responsibility to determine the facts in a value-free manner. (Chapter 8 elaborates the application of Weber's ideas in the practice of social research.)

The uses of emotion

Stanley and Wise are feminist social researchers who examine 'the place of the personal within research' (1993: 150). They reject the notion of 'research as orderly, coherent and logically organised' (1993: 152). The researcher's self cannot be left behind when doing research. The conventional view treats theory as superior to experience but, in their view, researchers should not 'mistrust experience' (1993: 153) and should, indeed, challenge the 'power relationship between theory and experience' (1993: 162). Feminists contend the personal is political: 'We suggest that this insistence on the crucial importance of the personal must also include an insistence on the importance, and also the presence, of the personal *within research experiences* as much as within other experiences' (1993: 157). Accordingly, they reject the goal of seeking objective descriptions based on the separation of researcher and researched. The researcher is a 'person' and, if one wishes to understand the oppression of women, one should start from 'the point of view of women's reality' (1993: 161). They assert that objectivity is 'an excuse for a power relationship every bit as obscene as the power relationship that leads to women being sexually assaulted, murdered, and otherwise treated as objects' (1993: 167).

This point of view might seem like a species of relativism in that Stanley and Wise (1993: 171) work with the notion of 'partial' truths and many realities. In fact, though, Stanley and Wise give a privileged position to their versions of truth and reality. That is, that oppressed women's experiences and the theory derived from them are considered to be true and that andro-centric (male-centred) theory and data collection distort reality.

Renato Rosaldo also rejects the idea that social scientists should cultivate detachment. Rosaldo (1989) discusses Weber's conception of value freedom and claims that the idea has been transformed since Weber from a 'demanding ethic' into an orthodoxy. Weber's notion of research is that research is driven by passion and yet the researcher needs to be cool-headed, but Rosaldo says that contemporary researchers take detachment to extremes. He tries to show how the emotional feelings of researchers about their subject of study are *resources* of knowledge. For instance, Rosaldo refers to the work of Briggs on the Eskimos. Briggs, according to Rosaldo, 'used her own feelings, particularly depression, frustration, rage, and humiliation, as sources of insight into the emotional life among members of an Eskimo group' (1989: 176). He states: 'My argument is that social analysis can be done – differently, but quite validly – either from close up or from a distance, either from within or from the outside' (1989: 188). Chapter 4, on feminist methodology, explores some of these arguments in greater depth.

Relativism: truths not truth

The **relativist** position is that there are only *truths* and no universal *truth*, versions of reality but no one reality. The point of departure is the well-known fact that cultures are diverse. We shall concentrate on *conceptual relativism*. In Daniel Little's words this means that

> Different cultures employ radically different conceptual schemes defining what exists in the world, how things are organized in time and space, what sorts of relation obtain among things, and how some things influence others ... [from this standpoint] it is not possible to give rational grounds for concluding that one such scheme is more congruent to reality than another. (1991: 203)

Peter Winch exemplifies a particularly radical version of conceptual relativism. He rejects the notion that science tells us what exists. He claims that 'the check of the independently real is not peculiar to science' (1970: 81). And he states in respect of the idea of God: 'The point is that it is *within* the religious use of language that the conception of God's reality has its place, though, I repeat, this does not mean that it is at the mercy of what anyone cares to say: if this were so, God would have no reality' (1970: 82). Like all relativists, Winch does not accept that reality exists outside cultures and languages: 'Reality is not what gives language sense ... both the distinction between the real and the unreal and the concept of agreement with reality themselves belong to our language' (1970: 82). Goodman (1982), another radical relativist, makes a similar point in arguing that social science can produce no single 'right' view of the world, but only one of many possible 'versions'.

However, *rationalists* – in the second sense of this term, referring to a belief in universal principles of theory choice, as introduced earlier in the discussion on Popper – reject conceptual relativism. Popper refers to the 'myth of the framework', this being the view that 'a rational and fruitful discussion is impossible unless the participants share a common framework of basic assumptions or, at least, unless they have agreed on such a framework for the purpose of the discussion' (1994: 34–5). Popper contends that it is in fact *differences* between frameworks which lead to fruitful dialogue. The opposite belief that frameworks are incommensurable is one he wholeheartedly criticizes: 'The proponents of relativism put before us standards of mutual understanding which are unrealistically high. And when we fail to meet those standards, they claim that understanding is impossible' (1994: 33–4). Dialogue will be fruitful but we must not expect final agreement for that would be too much (1994: 37). Dialogue takes the form of mutual *criticism* from which both sides learn.

To resolve these problems Popper (1972) distinguishes three worlds: a world of physical objects; a world of states of consciousness; and a *third* world, the world of **objective knowledge**. This third world consists, for instance, of theoretical systems, problems and problem situations and critical arguments. This world effectively exists autonomously of individual scientists (1972: 111). This suggests, I think, that a focus on the people who produce knowledge might be inappropriate. Popper distinguishes his view from traditional epistemology, that is, traditional theories of knowledge. Traditional epistemology has studied knowledge and thought in the 'subjective sense', that is, from the point of view of an individual subject (1972: 108). Popper is claiming that knowledge, problem situations, criticism are 'out there' and develop effectively a momentum independent of individuals because the community of scientists (science being for him the most important form of knowledge) develops a world independent of the wishes of particular individuals. For instance, new problems which emerge from a theory are not 'generally intentionally created by us' (1972: 119). Thus a problem leads to a tentative theory, which in turn leads to a process of error elimination, so that we are left with a new problem. The new problem is not intentionally created but emerges in the third world. Popper argues 'that the study of the products is vastly more important than the study of the production of [knowledge]' (1972: 114). If one looks at knowledge this way, it is possible to believe in the feasibility of objectivity in a world of clashing theories.

CONCLUSION

If we wish to decide whether social sciences might learn from the successes (and failures) of natural sciences, we must ask both what is science and what is scientific method. We, therefore, examined three competing views of science. Popper is a rationalist in two senses. Firstly he stresses the priority of theory over observation and secondly he believes that theories share a common goal of seeking true explanations *and* universal criteria for the evaluation of opposed theories. Kuhn is a moderate relativist. He takes for granted the value of science but takes a relativist position about the incommensurability of paradigms which makes it difficult to see the history of science as rational progress towards truth. Feyerabend takes a radically relativist position, claiming that there is no one scientific method: epistemologically and methodologically, anything goes.

Popper argues that the common model of explanation for all sciences is the *hypothetico-deductive scheme*. But the key question is this: should social scientists gear research to a search for laws? Or, to put it differently, are humans and their institutions governed by laws in the way many naturalists would claim? Do social scientists find the idea of a methodological unity of science, that is a common model of explanation for all sciences, helpful? Does, rather, the notion of a single model of explanation deny the validity of a rich variety of methods and associated theories which is, after all, the reality with which we are all familiar?

The interpretive tradition contends that the *meaningfulness* of the social world makes the application of scientific methods such as explanation by laws and causes inappropriate. Instead, the social sciences should seek to grasp the meanings which individuals and social groups give to their actions and institutions.

The possibility of objectivity was discussed from the point of view of those who believe that the influence of values and preconceptions can be eradicated from research. The Weberian tradition is associated with the idea that values play a positive role in determining what it is worth investigating. However, there is a fundamental distinction in this tradition between stating value judgements and determining the facts. For feminists, values and experience are not something to be excluded from research or controlled but are, instead, a fundamental resource. Finally, relativism rejects the notion of a common objective reality and counterposes to the idea of truth the notion of truths, there being (allegedly) no rational basis for choosing one version of truth as the truth.

Further reading

Martin and McIntyre (1994) is a treasury of important articles in the philosophy of science. Hollis (1994) is an exceptionally good introductory text. Williams and May (1996) is a good introductory book with a useful final chapter on contemporary developments.

Developments in social theory

Paul Filmer, Chris Jenks, Clive Seale and David Walsh

CONTENTS

This chapter reviews the main ideas of a variety of social theories that seek to explain the distinguishing characteristics of social and cultural life, and which can guide the practising social researcher in formulating research problems and deciding on methods. The chapter reviews a variety of competing perspectives which have variously influenced social scientists over time. It will appear, at first, that Kuhn's depiction of social science as 'pre-paradigmatic', which you saw in Chapter 2, is fully justified. You may find that the differences between perspectives seem impossible to reconcile. Yet it is the key message of the final theoretical perspective reviewed in this chapter, *post-modernism*, that the very search for a single, unifying model of social and cultural life may be inappropriate. The notion of researchers pursuing a variety of *genres* (explained more fully in Chapter 1) may be more appropriate.

It will become clear, too, as you read this chapter that social theories, and the methods that can be located within them, are human products, with an institutional history and micro-politics of their own. 'Theory' can sometimes look as if it has a life independent of human agency, with the objective hardness of a *thing*, enshrined in textbooks that appear to give it a solid, fixed quality. Theories and models (the difference between which is explained in Chapter 9), then, are 'handed down' to new generations of students, who learn the truths of rival camps, and come to recognize familiar disputes. But social theory, if perceived to be the creation of particular human individuals, struggling to generate their own visions of the social world against the traditions 'handed down' to them in their time, is in fact much more fluid than this, and should be used and shaped by practising researchers, rather than mechanically determining their actions.

For example, it is sometimes put about that a particular philosophical position, theory or model (say, *positivism* or *functionalism*) inevitably entails the use of a particular set of methods (for example, statistical approaches). While such stereotypes always hold a kernel of truth, this book will help you see that these are links from which creative researchers often break free. Indeed, the logical connections between areas of theory (such as *symbolic interactionism*) and particular methods (such as ethnography) are often more a matter of appearance than reality, encouraged by the tendency of researchers to increase the legitimacy of their work by publicly avowing its theoretical location (see Hammersley, 1992 for an extended discussion of this feature of social research). In Chapter 9 of this book a more flexible approach to the use of social theory in thinking about research problems is outlined.

If there is one key development that stands out above all others in more recent trends in social theory, it is the change that has occurred in the view of language. Broadly speaking, there has been a shift from seeing language as *referential* (that is, that it refers to a reality existing beyond language) to seeing it as *representational* and *constructive* of reality. That is to say, the perception has increased that language is the means by which humans *socially construct* their worlds. This interest in the play of language runs through some of the more recent conceptions of ethnography (Chapters 17 and 22), and wholly informs the approaches of semiotics, discourse analysis and conversation analysis (Chapters 18–20). One of our key messages, though, is that language is clearly *both* referential and representational; it describes the world, and is limited in its possible descriptions by an externally existing reality, as well as generating new realities. This means that methods which often (though not always) draw upon the more common-sensical view of language as referential, such as classical social surveys and certain types of ethnography and interviewing, have a valuable role in investigating social and cultural life.

This is not just an abstract issue, or a matter of preference, but a political issue as well, and goes to the heart of the position of social and cultural researchers in society. This is illustrated by the issues raised in feminist thought (Chapter 4), where it is sometimes claimed that the realities of oppression and disadvantage are belittled by an approach to the social world that says all is a social construction, potentially to be swept away by some alternative construction. The case of illness and suffering (with which some social researchers are concerned) also reminds us that the material conditions of our bodily existence give us a basic grounding in a reality that exists prior to language, and suggests a (literally) solid foundation for the existence of human need.

Finally then, it is appropriate to note that social theory is often linguistically difficult material. Indeed, difficulty appears to have increased as the turn to language has advanced. Concepts can sometimes appear infuriatingly inconsistent in their definition, or lack any grounding in recognizable social reality. The reasons for this are complex, sometimes lying in the writers' personal confusion or their need to look impressive, at other times in the sheer novelty of the ideas themselves. If you are new to social theory you will find that this chapter will be easier to understand if you have first read Chapter 2, which explains many of the ideas underlying the theories reviewed. We have also done our best to explain words that are new, and to maintain a reasonable degree of linkage with more concrete phenomena to which concepts refer.

THE ENLIGHTENMENT LEGACY

The idea of a science of society can be said to have emerged in the eighteenth century **Enlightenment**, a period in European history characterized by intellectual innovations, ranging across the arts, literature, science and engineering. The spirit of these times can be characterized as *progressive*, in that there existed faith in the power of reason and rationality to order and improve human affairs. Revolutions in France and America, and striking evidence of the power of science to transform the physical conditions of people's existence, combined to generate this sense of optimism, which was also associated with a growing rejection of religious authority.

Thinkers like Saint-Simon (1760–1825), Comte (1798–1857) and Spencer (1820–1903) developed this positive spirit in their social theories, to conceive of a social science that might guide the evolution of societies towards utopian forms, in which social affairs were regulated by the principles of reason. (Chapter 7 discusses the ideas of these thinkers in greater detail.)

Comte coined the term **positivism** or 'the positive philosophy' to indicate the broad direction of his views. As a philosophy of science, positivism is identified with **empiricism**, which, as was shown in Chapter 2, is a belief in the importance of observation and the collection of facts, assumed to exist prior to theories. Positivism is also a **naturalist** approach (in the sense used in Chapter 2), in that the methods of the social sciences are seen as appropriately modelled on that of the natural sciences. The aim was to discover 'laws' of society, that operate in a manner similar to the laws of nature, so that just as technology successfully manipulated the physical world, a social technology could engineer rational changes in the social world.

Because the subject matter of social science was not distinguished from that of natural science, this new science paid little attention to the inner lives, the thoughts and feelings, of people (their **subjectivity**). Just as it made no sense for physicists to inquire into the inner thoughts of molecules, it made no sense for positivist social scientists to consider subjectivity. With the advent of Durkheim, subjectivity came to be of greater interest to social science, though in a particular, **deterministic**, way. Thus his study of suicide (described in Chapter 2) envisioned people's subjectivities (the emotions that led to suicide) as being determined in a law-like way by their degree of integration into larger social structures. It should be noted, however, that Durkheim's thought is by no means as simple as this brief outline suggests, and his writings on the meanings of religion (Durkheim, 1915) suggest a conception of the relationship between humans and their society that varies substantially from the 'overdeterminism' of which he has sometimes been accused. While he was by no means a straightforward positivist, he shared Comte's vision of the social scientist as potential social engineer, and his statements on method stress the discovery of causal laws and the use of statistical data.

Durkheim is also associated with the theory of **functionalism**, which involves the idea that society is a system of interrelated forces, all of which tend to combine to produce social stability. When used to explain particular social phenomena, functionalism can lead to some surprises, such as Durkheim's idea that a certain level of criminal behaviour was necessary for the maintenance of social order, a view that made him enemies in the French establishment of his time. Functionalism influenced both anthropologists and sociologists, but shares with Comte's positivism a tendency towards an overdeterministic view of people, which underplays their capacity to formulate their own plans of action independent of the influence of 'society'. Functionalism is most often associated with conservative thinkers such as Parsons, who stress the value of consensus and social order. However, it is possible to understand Marxism as a type of functionalism, except that social forces (which similarly determine human subjectivity) lead to conflict, revolution and change.

The research methods that have often been associated with these theories are quantitative and statistical. In part this is because such methods are easily cast in a mould that imitates the natural sciences, generating *hypotheses*, measuring *social facts* and discovering the causes of events so that laws are generated. However, this is not exclusively so. Durkheim drew extensively on the qualitative research of early anthropologists for his study of religion, and functionalist anthropologists straightforwardly used the ethnographic method.

Additionally, the mere fact of quantification does not imply an adherence to all the tenets of positivism or functionalism. Counting regularities and their statistical analysis is, in practice, done by social researchers using the whole range of methods described in this book.

REALISM AND IDEALISM

Returning briefly to concepts in the philosophy of science, it is helpful at this point to distinguish between **realism** and **idealism**. Realism is the view that the world has an existence that is independent of our perceptions of it, so that science is an attempt to explain in thought the things that act independently of thought. Realism is not the same as empiricism, but it has some similarities. Idealism, on the other hand, is the view that the world exists only in so far as people think it exists. If our thoughts change, then so does the world. Idealism entered social science primarily through the work of Kant (1724–1804). For Kant, mind introduces an order into sensory experiences, establishing their objective character. He proceeded further to argue that the mind also contained a world of values and freedom of action, distinct from the world of (mind-ordered) facts. Values were the determinants of human life which was ordered on the basis of reason and purposive actions.

Taking up Kant's idealist position, social science developed the **interpretive** tradition which argues that the social world is distinguished from the natural world. It is an **intersubjective** world of culture, consciousness and purposive action, in which relationships are organized through the ideas, values and interests of members of society, producing human action and interaction. With this comes a politics of critical, relativistic enquiry into society rather than a politics of social engineering.

ACTION THEORY

Weber (1864–1920) primarily established the interpretive tradition in social science, and his contemporary Simmel (1858–1918) developed it specifically in the analysis of culture. Weber focused on the place of subjectivity, consciousness and culture in social life because, he argued, the social world consists of the subjectively meaningful action of individuals, as opposed to the intrinsically meaningless world of objects which is nature. Precisely because individuals give meaning to their actions they have a purposive character, so he constructed an **action theory** of society. Weber was drawing here on the legacy of nineteenth century political liberalism, based on the supremacy of the individual.

For Weber action becomes social – and through it society is produced – when individual actors orient their actions to one another, acknowledging shared beliefs, values and interests. Social institutions are reducible to interactions of this kind. Social research, then, involves interpretation, and social life cannot be reduced to explanation solely in terms of laws. Action cannot be understood by external observation; the researcher must achieve a degree of empathy with the actor to get at its meaning. This is achieved not through an identification with the actor (in which the researcher tries to become the actor) but by grasping the actor's meaning. It is the latter that is crucial for the method of understanding, which Weber called **verstehen**, because it provides rational understanding as opposed to the emotional understanding which identification would produce. Such rational understanding is capable of empirical verification and therefore objective. And in this way it creates the possibility of a *science* of action.

Famously Weber (1930) brought interpretive understanding to an analysis of the origins of modern industrial capitalism. He sees this as typified by the highly rationalized organization of economic activity, depending on the calculative use of human and material resources to produce and sell commodities on a free market for profit. But, he argued, the rationalism and instrumentalism of capitalist economic activity was dependent on the emergence of particular cultural values, which Weber called the 'spirit of capitalism'. Protestantism, specifically its Calvinist Nonconformist form, introduced a new theology based on the doctrines of a calling, predestination and asceticism. Religious duty was a task to be performed through adherence to a work ethic as its moral foundation. Success in this, as measured by profit, was then seen as a sign of God's favour. Asceticism prevented the use of profit for enjoyment so it could only be ploughed back into economic activity. So Calvinism promoted the spirit of capitalism. Weber demonstrated this through an analysis of historical materials, statistical data and theological and economic texts written by Calvinist theologians and capitalist businessmen. Although he used statistical data they were insufficient on their own for his analysis. They had value for the explanation of social life only when translated into meanings. For this he engaged in the qualitative analysis of texts.

Simmel moved action theory on into a more specifically cultural analysis of social life. Primarily he demonstrated, in studies of a variety of topics taken from economic life, and aspects of the city in the modern world, how cultural organization influenced social consciousness, experience and identity. Thus he wrote essays on money, religion, gender, capitalism and love to show how these reflected and influenced modern consciousness.

Action theory set up an alternative approach to that of functionalism and led to modifications of quantitative, positivist empiricism, shifting the emphasis towards various forms of qualitative research and analysis. Firstly, social scientists moved from the investigation of *social facts* to examining a socially meaningful world of intersubjective action and interaction. Secondly, social enquiry was shifted from observation of the structural determination of social life to an understanding of subjectivity. Finally, as the social world is treated as a world of meaning and value, the values of the analyst come into play. Values decide the problem which the analyst seeks to investigate, the way the phenomena relevant to the investigation are conceptualized and the explanations that are finally arrived at. Weber argues that all socio-cultural inquiry is value oriented in this way. Evidence, both experiential and factual, with which to test explanations, provides objectivity. Nor does a commitment to *verstehen* as a method preclude any interest in the causal explanation of action, though Weber rejects the positivist notion of general laws. For Weber explanations adequate at the levels of both cause and meaning are the ideal. The reconciliation between the two consists of showing how meanings are the motivational determinants of action.

SYMBOLIC INTERACTIONISM

Action theory established itself in Europe on the basis of Kantian idealism. A similar theory based in the philosophy of **pragmatism** arose in America called **symbolic interactionism**. Pragmatism, in the work of Dewey and Peirce, argues that all animal behaviour (which includes human beings) is based upon a problem-solving adaptation to the environment, but whereas in animals this behaviour is instinctive, in human beings it is a matter of mind. Unlike animals, human beings are conscious and sentient creatures and their environment is a symbolic universe with which they engage in terms of their understanding and not their senses.

Mead (1863–1931) brought the pragmatist perspective to bear on social behaviour, arguing that human social conduct has a symbolic character. What permits human beings to interact and form social relationships and society is their ability to understand one another's gestures and responses. This is because they share *symbols*, embodied in a common language. Language, then, is a system of symbols enabling communication. Social relations depend on people's use of language to 'take the role of the other', understanding others as being like oneself. The similarities with Weber's notion of intersubjective understanding are obvious. The social world is a world of inter-communicative *symbolic interaction*.

Mead's views led him to a theory of the *self*, which he saw as constructed through interaction in which the individual internalizes the other's definition of his or her behaviour. Within the individual, self-formation is generated in terms of a dialogue between two parts, the 'I' and the 'me'. The 'I' consists of the physiological and psychic impulses that produce gestural behaviour in the individual but the 'me' is the response of the other which is internalized by the individual. So the self becomes a society in miniature, replicating internally the symbolic interaction of society. This is what constitutes mind in human beings and provides for their consciousness and inner experiences. Human beings constantly consider, think and weigh up the possibilities of action. The self of human beings constantly changes through life as individuals learn to master new roles, incorporating new others, so acquiring new definitions and meanings and leading to new forms of action.

So, as in action theory, human behaviour is neither mechanical nor explicable in terms of laws. Symbolic interactionists believe that human action can be investigated only by gaining access to the meanings which guide it. This involves learning the culture or subculture of the people under study and means that the social world cannot be investigated under artificial conditions but only in naturally occurring situations. This is sometimes described as the position of **naturalism**. Note that this is different from the earlier use of the term 'naturalism', which in Chapter 2 was used to denote the position that the natural and social sciences should use the same methods, a view which symbolic interactionists would oppose. Symbolic interactionists are, in general, committed to field study based on participant observation and ethnographic analysis to describe what happens in social settings, how the people involved see their own actions, and the contexts in which action takes place (see Chapter 17 for a fuller description).

The Chicago school

The empirical programme of symbolic interactionism developed at the University of Chicago from the 1920s. Here, Park and Burgess created a large programme of research into urban life and culture focused mainly on Chicago itself. They applied anthropological methods to the study of various subcultures of the city. The prototype of all these studies in the Chicago school was Zorbaugh's *The Gold Coast and the Slum* (1929) which enquired into a district lying north of the business area. There were marked contrasts of social and living conditions there. For example, one part – the 'Gold Coast' – was a fashionable upper-class area, but behind that lay an area of 'hobohemia' that had become the final resort of the criminal and down-and-out. Zorbaugh's study described the varying ways of life of the inhabitants, to form a theory of city development and community.

The primary methods of the Chicago school were those of field research, interviews, life histories and ethnography based on participant observation. It established naturalism as the favoured approach to empirical research and produced a politics sympathetic to social and cultural relativism and to the underdog in society, allying itself with the disempowered in society. As Becker (1967) (who has been a leading inheritor of the symbolic interactionist tradition in Chicago) has put it, the question that the ethnographer must first ask is 'Whose side are we on?' before proceeding to engage in research.

PHENOMENOLOGY AND ETHNOMETHODOLOGY

Phenomenology is a philosophical method of enquiry, involving the systematic investigation of consciousness, brought to the study of the social world by Alfred Schutz. **Ethnomethodology** is a term coined by the American Harold Garfinkel. The two approaches share a concern with **microsocial interaction** – that is interaction on a small scale, between individuals or within small groups. Both focused intensively on language as the fundamental resource for microsocial interaction. There were clear reasons for these concerns. The overdeterminism of Parsons's version of functionalism, as well as its political conservatism, had become problematic. For example, he defined the individual as a collectivity member performing a social role by assuming 'obligations of performance in [a] concrete interaction system … normatively regulated in terms of common values and of norms sanctioned by these common values' (Parsons et al., 1961: 42). This 'over-socialized' concept of the individual (Wrong, 1961) as one who has internalized the social system's determinations of action is a marginalization of individual subjectivity. It reflects a concern only with the *typical* characteristics of the individual, avoiding the investigation of particular individuals making choices on the basis of their unique biographies and the specific features of the situations in which they do so.

Garfinkel regarded as unjustified the criticisms that Parsons's concept of the individual as a collectivity member was of an oversocialized individual. But he wanted to explore how social actors were actively engaged in playing their social roles. Additionally Garfinkel argued that people were actively engaged in producing social institutions and that the ordinary, everyday practices by which this was routinely accomplished showed the reality of society to be a **social construction**. Here, Garfinkel's views were comparable with those of Berger and Luckmann (1966) who had developed a related phenomenological perspective, expressed in their book *The Social Construction of Reality*. In this work they argued that from a stream of undifferentiated experiences people construct the phenomena of the world (objects, other people, social institutions). Such constructions will often then take on a hard **objectified** character, enabling them to 'act back' on consciousness. For example, in childhood we are taught the 'facts' of history, the 'truths' of ethical values and expected behaviour as if they are naturally handed down from some supra-human source.

Phenomenology

Schutz developed Weber's concept of *verstehen* to create his own theory of social action. Social actors, Schutz proposed, were governed by a principle of **reciprocity of perspectives**. This involves two working assumptions that social actors hold about each other as necessary conditions of their interaction. The first is the assumption that each person makes about the other that, if they change places, each will perceive their situation in the same way as the other. The second is that each takes for granted that the differences in perspective that result from their unique biographies and different experiences are irrelevant to their present interaction, and that both will define their current interaction in the same way. As Schutz pointed out, these assumptions are 'idealizations' rather than always being true of all interactions. This is revealed when communication difficulties arise, which people, on the whole, try to avoid. Schutz thus provided Garfinkel with an account of the means by which social actors construct and sustain the reality of their interactions. People transcend individual subjectivity to construct an *intersubjective* world. In effect, they *produce common sense*, and they do so quite ordinarily and routinely – and so are able to take it for granted.

Schutz, like other interpretivists, argued that, unlike the natural world, the social world is intrinsically meaningful. He disagreed with the positivist view that tended to treat consciousness as determined by the natural processes of human neurophysiology. Husserl (1859–1938), who had reintroduced phenomenology to modern philosophy, had argued that such a perception, which involves seeing the natural and the social worlds as factual, is a **naive attitude** because it does not attend to the more fundamental process of the *social production* of both worlds. Psychology is charged by

Husserl with a particular neglect in this respect because of its naive support of this assumption of the **facticity** of the world. Husserl further argued that, unlike the objects of the natural world, those of the social world depend upon human recognition for their existence: they are objects which have a constructed character. Yet social actors **naturalize** the 'facts' of the world in the common sense of their naive (or 'natural') attitude, treating what Durkheim called social facts as if they were really 'out there'. Husserl shows, in effect, how it was that Durkheim could recommend that social facts should be treated as 'things'.

Schutz refers to everyday language as the 'typifying medium *par excellence* … a treasure-house of ready made preconstituted types and characteristics, all socially derived, carrying along an open horizon of unexplored content' (1962: 14) These **first-order typifications**, as Schutz terms them, make inter-subjectivity possible and communicable by enabling individuals to formulate their own subjectivity in terms that are understandable by others who are able in turn to relate it to themselves. This, Schutz argues, is the appropriate way to understand the activity of social scientists who limit the open qualities of first-order typifications by defining and thus attempting to fix the meaning of particular terms, thus creating a new linguistic world of **second-order typifications**. Science can thus be differentiated from common sense, but the two share common materials, a feature which Garfinkel was to exploit.

Ethnomethodology

Ethnomethodology, as conceived by Garfinkel, involves investigation of the methods by which people make sense of their activities, both to themselves and to others. Drawing on the insights of phenomenology, social life is seen as a continual and routine accomplishment, particularly through the use of language. Thus ethnomethodologists speak of 'doing' things like walking, friendliness or sexual identity, to indicate the constructed nature of all human activity, including social science itself.

The concepts of **indexicality** and essential **reflexivity** summarize the ethnomethodological view of language, referring to the way in which the meaning of words depends on the context in which they are used, and their relationship to other words. Thus words 'index' meanings, rather than referring to fixed, permanent realities. Additionally, language is essentially *reflexive* on everyday actions, since in 'describing' those actions it makes them appear rational. Ethnomethodologists differ from Schutz in that they do not distinguish a world of scientific discourse from a world of everyday language. In Chapter 16 the work of Antaki and Rapley (1996) demonstrates this; they apply an ethnomethodological perspective to the social construction of facts in research interviews. They do so by using the method of *conversation analysis*, which is the most important research method to have emanated from ethnomethodology, and is described more fully in Chapter 20.

STRUCTURALISM

Structuralism shares with the interpretive theories reviewed so far a concern with the role of language in shaping social life, but is less interested in explaining social actions in natural settings. Instead, structuralist approaches can be seen as something of a return to the overdeterminism of functionalist theory, in that subjectivity is seen as being formed by deep 'structures' that lie beneath the surface of social reality. More positively, structuralist approaches offer valuable insights for researchers interested in analysing cultural forms (such as art, literature, images or film). This has been particularly evident in *semiotic* analysis, described in Chapter 18.

Something of the flavour of structuralism is provided in the following quotation from Lévi-Strauss, a leading French structuralist:

> The method we adopt, in this case as in others, consists in the following operations: (i) define the phenomenon under study as a relation between two or more terms, real or supposed; (ii) construct a table of possible permutations between these terms; (iii) take this table as the general object of analysis which, at this level only, can yield connections, the empirical phenomenon considered at the beginning being only one possible combination among others, the complete system of which must be constructed beforehand. (1969a: 84)

The idea here is that phenomena as diverse as myths, superstitions, kinship systems, restaurant menus and orchestral scores can be understood as surface phenomena of deeper **structures** that involve the systematic combination of elements. In Chapter 18 this is explained in detail in an analysis of Saussure's structuralist ideas about the elements that combine to create linguistic meanings.

Lévi-Strauss was interested in explaining human cognitive action which he saw as the product of universal structures. Whatever the variability of its surface, Lévi-Strauss asserted that the human mind has always worked in the same way. Social action itself is, for the purposes of structuralist analysis, a surface manifestation of a series of deep master patterns, internalized at the level of cognition. Particular cultures then, are seen as manifestations of an unconscious, universal rule system.

Lévi-Strauss in fact drew on Durkheim and his collaborator Mauss. Durkheim's 'social Kantianism' or 'soft idealism' was apparent in his later work (on religion, for example) where he appeared to contradict his early positivism and replaced his concern for social facts with an attention to symbolic formations that bind human relations. Mauss had suggested that such 'collective representations' were general psychological dispositions common to all humankind.

Structuralism essentially plays on the dichotomy between *essence* and *appearance*, suggesting a continuum between *depth* and *surface*. Lévi-Strauss (1969b) used a geological metaphor to develop this. He likens the formation of cultural phenomena to the layering, expanding, contracting and intruding of rock strata; each stratum appears unique but shares certain underlying elements with similar geological phenomena. Geologists understand such phenomena by the excavation of these strata to expose their patterns of interrelation. The structure derives from the pattern, so elements of a culture, as we experience them, are the surface appearances or manifestations of underlying patterns at a deeper level. Because culture is based on deep structures the rules may be only part of the unconscious of its members. Cultural symbols and representations are the surface structure and acquire the appearance of 'reality'.

POST-STRUCTURALISM AND POST-MODERNISM

Structuralism was the underlying orientation of much social and cultural research for an extended period until the late 1970s and early 1980s when the phenomenon of the 'post-' started to emerge. In the subsequent period post-modernism has developed from the status of an esoteric critique to that of a reality. It is difficult to discuss post-modernism separately from post-structuralism, as the two are intricately linked. Although post-structuralist ideas became prominent before the idea of the post-modern became widespread, the ideas are easier to understand if we treat the second event first. The appeal of **post-modernism** rests on three principles: firstly, that of the **decentred self**; secondly, an assault on all who claim that their arguments have authority; and thirdly, a commitment to instability in our practices of understanding. We shall consider each in turn.

The concept of the self, or of identity, as decentred involves a rejection of **essentialism** found, for example, in psychological theories of selfhood. **Anti-essentialism** consists of the claim that there are no human universals (such as 'instincts', 'needs' or 'drives') that determine identity. Instead, the self is a social construction. Foucault has been influential here, suggesting that a variety of **discourses** (systems of knowledge and their associated practices), including those embodied in psychological theories, construct the contemporary sense of self. Foucault's work involved analyses of the constitution of selfhood through discourses of penology (the prison system), sexuality, insanity and medical regimes. Society and culture, in Foucault's vision, are constituted through a symbolic system which must be viewed with the utmost suspicion. The system is a construction of meaning through the exercise of power. He invokes the concept of *governmentality*, which is 'the ensemble formed by the institutions, procedures, analyses and reflections, the calculations and tactics, that allow the exercise of this very specific albeit complex form of power, which has as its target population' (1979a: 20). Hacking (1990), for example, has presented an analysis, influenced by Foucault, on the role of quantification in governing social life. The 'avalanche of numbers' that began to be produced in eighteenth century European societies represented a new discursive construction of 'the population' and of the normal person (see Chapter 6 for further discussion of this). Hacking's

Foucauldian analysis can be seen as exposing and therefore undermining the power of such governmentality. Foucault's ideas have also helped to form *discourse analysis* (see Chapter 19).

The assault on authority in post-modernism is combined with a commitment to instability. In fact, the story behind post-modernism is about the conclusion of another, greater story, namely that of the Enlightenment. The Enlightenment established a view of human history and human purpose concerning 'achievement'; to put this another way it provided the **grand narrative** form for the history of modernity. Reason was to triumph over faith, humankind was to become the measure of all things, nature was to be quelled and put to the service of humankind, and time was to be measured in terms of a transition from darkness into the light, a transition and an implicit theory of moral evolution that came to be known as *progress*. The centrality of humankind linked to science was the methodology of this master plan. However, post-modernists believe that history has shown that the claims of the Enlightenment to objectivity and value neutrality have created a moral vacuum, in terms of war, terror and pollution. Post-modernists deliberately ignore or cast doubt upon gains in health, income, enlightenment, democratization and overall quality of life.

Post-modernism does not offer alternative ways of knowing the world which might help us appreciate the 'new', but instead enters critically into all discourse, while resting on the assertion of the unprivileged quality of all discourses. It belongs to no specific discipline, though its main protagonists are located within established and respectable traditions of thought. As an approach it constitutes an external attack on the methods and values of our time, or, simultaneously, is a symptom of our time which affects our conceptions and understandings of our society.

The roots of the idea of post-modernity are found in the work of the German philosopher Nietzsche (1844–1900). It was he who predicted and applauded an age of negativity. One of Nietzsche's central characters, Zarathustra, declares repeatedly that 'God is dead' by which Nietzsche intended to indicate the collapse of moral values. As opposed to metaphors employed in early social theory stressing 'integration', 'solidarity', 'community', 'structure', 'instrumentality' and 'culture', in sum, the language of *unification*, Nietzsche is recommending *dispersion*. The survival of the human spirit rests no longer in the hands of collectivities but in the affirmation of the new *Übermensch* (superman). Man must escape from the protective politics of order into an affirmation of life as 'the will to power'. This is a difficult vision to bring to bear on social research. What we seem to be hearing is that 'anything goes', as in Feyerabend (see Chapter 2). The darker side of Nietzsche's story is the interest displayed in his ideas by the Nazi movement.

Nietzsche's philosophical position is summarized in the title of one of his last works, *Beyond Good and Evil* (1886), an amoral and apolitical location from which to deconstruct the thought and practice of others. In the wake of Nietzsche's assault on ethics is that state of affairs that post-modernists call **polyvocality**, the many voices within a culture waiting to be heard, all with

an equivalence and a right, ranging from the oppressed to simply the previously unspoken.

Let us now investigate **post-structuralism**. The Nietzschean heritage was
influenced towards left-wing political thought by the French intellectual
avant-garde through such writers as Derrida, Foucault, Donzelot, Deleuze
and Guattari. Structuralism had established the premise that all cultural
phenomena are primarily linguistic in character. More than this the cultural
and linguistic system had come to be seen as an arbitrary but finite rule
system capable of generating any number of other rule systems. The potential built into such a cultural system lay in its power to realize an *infinite*
range of realities. This created a potential for instability which, through the
sustained method of **deconstruction,** post-structuralism pressed further.

Deconstruction, which is associated with the thinking of Derrida, includes
the demonstration that meaning is scattered or dispersed and cannot be easily
nailed down. When applied to texts or discourses, this undermines their
claim to authority. At its most extreme, the deconstruction of social research
texts produces apocalyptic thoughts about the impossibility of social science
and is a bleak vision indeed for practising researchers. More positively perhaps, deconstruction emphasizes awareness of the rhetorical strategies in
terms of which claims are made by authors (see Chapter 22). This can both
help in constructing better rhetoric, and be a useful aid to self-criticism and
the reformulation of better validated claims, though such strengthening of
textual authority would be anathema to the committed deconstructionist.

CONCLUSION

This chapter has summarized developments in social theory, from early
positivism, to functionalism, the interpretive tradition, and later structuralist
and post-modern views. In spite of the tendency towards nihilism in the
most recent developments in social theory, social and cultural research can
usefully draw upon a variety of theoretical perspectives. As an aid to making
links between the social theory reviewed here and the practice of research,
Chapter 9 demonstrates a variety of ways in which researchers can bring the
two together.

Further reading

Collins (1994) is an exceptionally clear guide to the earlier strands of
social theory reviewed in this chapter. May (1996) and Layder (1994)
provide helpful guides to social theory, and Smart (1993) provides a
guide to post-modernity which is very helpful. Game (1991) provides
a rationale for incorporating deconstructivism into the practice of
social research.

Feminist methodology

Heather Brunskell

CONTENTS

This chapter describes the way in which feminist social researchers enter into critical debate about research methodology and epistemology. It also shows how they practise research from a feminist standpoint and are politically committed to the identification of the social conditions of women and the transformation of gender relations. You will find, though, that it is difficult to identify a distinctly feminist method outside the range of social science methods described in this volume. This is because feminists, as researchers, use the range of methods available to all social researchers. If there is no distinctive feminist method, to what can the term 'feminist methodology' refer?

I will first define the term **methodology**, as it is generally understood in social science, drawing a distinction between method and methodology. Within social science research the choice of which aspects of the social world to research, the method for collecting the data, and then the ways to interpret those data is informed by the broad theoretically informed framework within which the research is carried out. It is these *combined* aspects which constitute methodology. However, when feminist researchers make choices about these things the broad theoretical framework which they use will also be informed by theories of gender relations. The most defining feature of a feminist theoretical perspective on social research is an understanding of the pervasive influence of gender divisions on social life.

This chapter argues that all social science methodologies are located within debates about **epistemology** (the concern with how we know what we know, and how we make claims that knowledge is true or not true). This is the case whether or not this is made explicit in any particular research project. Feminist researchers, in fact, often explicitly enter into epistemological debates, reflecting their concerns with how we can understand gendered relations and whether knowledge can be scientifically established. When feminist research is undertaken it is done so with a political commitment to the identification and *transformation* of gender relations. Because of this political commitment feminist knowledge is sometimes said to be biased. Hammersley (1995), for example, says that feminist social research lies outside mainstream social science. Its proponents argue, though, that feminist research is grounded in the very requirements of creative social science, refining and deepening our understanding of the criteria for judging the quality of social science and revealing how these have operated in the practice of science (Holmwood, 1995).

METHODOLOGY

As stated earlier, the term 'feminist methodology' does not indicate any particular choice of one method over another. Sandra Harding (1987: 2) argues that all methods, or evidence gathering techniques, within social science fall into one of three categories: listening to or interrogating informants, observing behaviour, or examining historical traces or records. Feminist researchers use any or all of these. They also draw on a variety of theoretical traditions through which the feminist perspective may then be expressed. I will show this by describing how feminist social researchers have used *symbolic interactionism* in their work. You will know from Chapter 3 that this is a broad theoretical framework which understands the social world in terms of the meanings which people attach to social action. The symbolic communication of actors is therefore the focus of research. The research methods favoured by symbolic interactionists include participant observation of actors in natural settings (see Chapter 17) and intensive interviews (see Chapter 16). The data collected by these methods are interpreted and analysed in terms of the overall theoretical framework which understands the social world as symbolic communication between actors in social interaction.

An illustration of a feminist researcher's use of symbolic interactionism is offered by Kathryn Pyne Addleson. Addleson (1993: 277) argues that symbolic interactionist theory can be useful in seeing how people in authority acting in a public arena help to shape the social meaning of public issues like abortion, poverty, racism, homelessness, drugs, teenage pregnancy, unemployment, working mothers, child sexual abuse, health care, gangs, AIDS, homosexuality, war and so on. But a feminist perspective provides an additional edge to this.

Addleson uses symbolic interactionist concepts to understand how gendered meanings are made, who gets to make them and for whose benefits. The topic of poverty in one-parent families illustrates this. When discussed by people in authority, such as policy makers and legislators, the existence of such parents is often attributed to the lack of moral values of the single mother and the system of welfare provision which supports her behaviour. The reduction of benefits could be the material consequence of such an explanation, which focuses on the *irresponsibility* of the single mother. A feminist social researcher, however, interested in describing the way in which single mothers *actually* organize their lives, reveals a picture of hardship and considerable *responsibility*, to oppose the perspective of the dominant discourse of policy makers. Symbolic interactionism, with its tradition of exposing the oppression of 'underdogs' (see Chapter 3), is ideally suited for such a research study.

What makes methodology feminist?

Feminist methodology within social science research was a response to a series of problems which emerged in the 1970s once a concern began with gender inequality and masculine dominance within the social world. One of the earliest definitions of feminist social research was formulated by Liz Stanley and Sue Wise who posited that feminist research is that which is 'on, by and for women' (1983:17). The topic of investigation thus focuses on the lives of women, but how to do this will depend on whatever seems to be the most appropriate methods or techniques for collecting and then analysing data. Essentially, though, data collection and analysis will be informed by feminist theory. Stanley and Wise (1983) also make a point addressed to *epistemology*. They argue that the subject position of the researcher, or the producer of knowledge, produces better knowledge if she is politically committed. A researcher is then not only a woman, she is a woman committed to working for the transformation of the condition of the lives of women.

Maynard describes an early driving force within feminism: 'to challenge the subordination, passivity and silencing of women by encouraging them to speak out about their own condition and in so doing to confront the experts and dominant males with the limitations of their own knowledge' (1994: 23). Feminist social research is therefore research which brings into focus areas of social life hitherto hidden from view or invisible, namely the social organization of women's experience. This involves a view that the production of knowledge prior to feminist intervention was not neutral since relations in which women were subordinate were invisible in non-feminist social science.

But feminist social research no longer remains strictly embedded in the recommendations for research practice summarized by Stanley and Wise. Not all feminists subscribe to a single theory of gender. Some feminists, for example, are influenced by Marxism. These theorists will understand social division in terms of class division within capitalism. But as feminist researchers they will also ask questions about why women's lives have been excluded from Marxist analysis, and what social class means when class analysis includes women. Other feminists are less interested in Marxist perspectives. Feminist social researchers locate themselves in diverse, broad social scientific theoretical frameworks. The choice of broad theoretical framework will influence the methodology and the research topic, as well as influence a variety of approaches to understanding gender relations and their place in social life.

The subjects of the research may also differ. Some researchers have a pre-eminent concern with women alone. Others focus on women's relationships with men from a woman's perspective, and again others may focus on men and masculinity. Different approaches lead to the posing of different questions and to the production of different knowledge. Although feminist work on gender is diverse, it is always framed by the search to identify power relations within a society characterized by male social dominance in which women are subordinated.

Epistemology

I have argued that the choice of methods of social science cannot be separated out from the theory informing their use. Nor can these theoretical frameworks be properly understood outside arguments which take place at the level of epistemology. Chapter 2 described debates within social science as to how we might gain knowledge of social life and what should count as knowledge. It also described the way in which the search for knowledge to adequately represent the reality of the social world is always informed by concern about the scientific status of social research. Thus, the fundamental question which has vexed and perplexed social science since its inception is how valid knowledge of the social world can be achieved when researchers are themselves embedded in the social world about which they seek objective understanding, and when the 'objects' of knowledge (people and their social relations) are not objects but people with agency who consciously interpret their own social behaviour. Feminist social research shares these concerns, which involve decisions about what to investigate, debates about the techniques for gathering research material, decisions about theory and analysis, and decisions (within epistemology) as to what might constitute the philosophical grounding for research. Initially, one can approach feminist epistemological concerns by learning more about the feminist critique of mainstream social research.

Social researchers have often disagreed about what society is, what knowledge of the social world is, and how that knowledge might be obtained. However, before the advent in the 1970s of a feminist perspective within social research (for example, in the work of Oakley, 1972; 1974), there had existed, across the range of approaches used by social researchers, what Rosalind Sydie (1987: 203) calls a *shared fixed principle* organizing that knowledge. This principle revolved around a particular meaning given to sex differences between men and women.

Knowledge of the social world, feminist scholars contend, was at that time constructed around a prior belief that biological differences between men and women constituted the *natural* basis upon which the different *social* relations between men and women were organized. Sydie argues that research traditions that otherwise were in competition were nevertheless united on this. Women were seen 'as biologically and therefore naturally different and constrained by that difference' (1987: 203). Generally speaking, women entered social research studies only as social problems or in discussions of the family. Women's social being was conceived as coextensive with their family function to nurture and socialize family members. In contrast, men's social being was located outside the family and was understood as coextensive with activity in the public realm. Men, unlike women, were conceived as actors on the public stage. The result was that social researchers found it impossible to understand fully women's experiences.

The assumption of a natural difference between the sexes was taken by social scientists to be a foundation for social organization. This rested on a way of thinking about sex and gender, involving male dominance and female submission, prevalent in the social and political life of early nineteenth century Europe, when the social sciences were conceived. Sydie argues that European societies and the sciences of society which they produced understood men to be unrestricted by their biological characteristics. In contrast, women's biology was understood to determine their social identities. Additionally, 'man' was understood to represent men, the 'norm', the generically human, against which norm women were measured as different. Sydie therefore argues that the knowledge produced by such social science is not objective (1987: 208). Marx, Durkheim and Weber, for example, can be seen as representing different epistemological positions on how research into the social world should proceed. Durkheim is usually taken to represent the *positivist* approach, Weber the *idealist* approach, and Marx the *realist* approach (see Chapter 3). Nevertheless none of them was able to explain why women were treated as inferior to men.

Research which assumes male social dominance to be natural not only produces a partial and limited perspective on the nature of social life but affects the framework of concepts within which the researcher works and then the explanation offered (1987: 203). Before feminist scholarship, social theory purported to speak for human beings when in fact it was 'grounded in, derived from, based on and reinforcing of the experience, perceptions and beliefs of men' (Du Bois, 1983: 106). Maria Mies (1983) describes the characteristics of social research which assumes men's natural superiority as **androcentric** (male centred).

Women's experiences

Common sense might suggest that the imbalance could be corrected. Women's social experiences, now understood as unrepresented in social research, could be understood and documented by any of the conventional methods social science offers for collecting data about the social world and then added to knowledge about men's experiences. For example, methods which ask social actors about their experiences could ask women how they understand their own lives. The result would be the sum total of the experience of both men and women and thus could be said to account for all of human social experience. But this solution is rejected by some feminists. Renate Duelli Klein (1983), for example, argues that this 'adding on approach' in itself merely substitutes women for men as 'objects' of research, doing nothing to alter a methodology which starts from an androcentric standpoint. Duelli Klein points out that research which is undertaken from this standpoint is *normative*. That is, its conceptual framework takes men as the norm against which data gathered on women are then measured and evaluated.

Caroline Ramazanoglu (1989) shows how such normative frameworks can operate in a research project. In the 1960s she carried out a survey of married women and mothers who were working full-time shifts as bus conductresses, canteen workers, or sugar packers. The research was conducted with an implicitly *positivist* methodology. She argues that, although it involved interviewing women, the research produced knowledge which was quite different from that which could have been produced from a feminist perspective. A survey from a feminist standpoint would have improved knowledge about women's social conditions.

Ramazanoglu says that, at the time, she took for granted that men were at the centre of the social world and defined women in relation to men. In the 1960s married women were primarily defined in terms of their responsibilities to husbands and children. Women working shifts were by definition 'abnormal', deviating from what was understood to be normal female behaviour. Additionally, Ramazanoglu argues, it was generally understood at this time within social research that objective knowledge could be produced from survey research. The positivist tradition in which the survey was undertaken involved a faith both in the possibility of controlling the subjectivity of the researcher and in the reliability and objectivity of numbers, but contained no theory of gender inequality. Ramazanoglu's research produced knowledge which did not identify and so could not question gender inequalities. This left the power relations between men and women unnoticed and so reproduced them. Ramazanoglu now argues that a feminist standpoint in the research on the shift-working women would have started by focusing on gender relations in the women's lives, not by assuming the abnormality of the women.

Ramazanoglu points out that feminism reopens the problem of how researchers can claim social scientific knowledge. This is not just a specific problem for feminists, but is a central problem for all social science. Researchers who ignore the differences between men's and women's lives could be said, from a feminist standpoint, to have invalid knowledge. Thus feminist theorists argue that non-feminist paradigms often fail to acknowledge the partiality of researchers' ideas about the social world.

Enlightenment and epistemology: where does our way of thinking come from?

The contention that social researchers are embedded in their social context is not new, but a feminist perspective adds the charge of androcentrism to this. Sandra Harding describes questions which arise when women are instead constituted as *subjects* rather than objects of social research: 'who can be a "knower" (can women?); what tests beliefs must pass in order to be legitimated as knowledge (only tests against men's experiences and observations?); what kinds of things be known (can "subjective truths" count as knowledge?)' (1987: 3). This extends far beyond a conception of 'bias' and leads us to epistemological debate about the nature of legitimate enquiry. Here, it is important to understand the legacy of the **Enlightenment**.

The Enlightenment (see also Chapter 3) was a complex period of debate in the eighteenth century. The dominant ideas which emerged valued *scientific* knowledge of reality and prioritized *reason* as the reliable way of producing truth. Feminists such as Mary Maynard (1994) argue that positivist epistemological approaches in social science are rooted in a series of dualisms derived from Enlightenment thought. Thus, a division was made between rational and irrational thought. Rational thought was believed to produce objective knowledge, eradicating subjectivity by the application of rules of method. Maynard argues that the scientist's rational, objective mastery over the self corresponded with the prevailing society's definition of masculinity, while emotion, subjectivity and being ruled by bodily nature were seen as defining femininity. Feminist methodology, at its inception in the 1970s, was therefore not just struggling with how to produce valid knowledge. In that feminist research researched the lives of women, and in that it argued that knowledge production is always a political act, it intruded into an Enlightenment conception of what constituted reason and 'neutrality'.

Feminists have engaged with the issue of validity and have developed theories to address the issue of what can count as true knowledge. Feminist researchers argue that all social research works within a conceptual framework which sets out the terms for what is to count as relevant information for a description and explanation of social reality. This framework dictates what is meant by scientific method, affecting how we can validate knowledge about the social world. Helen Longino, a philosopher of science, argues that, even within natural science, validating conceptual frameworks are chosen outside the dictates of data: 'how one determines evidential

relevance, why one takes some states of affairs as evidence for one hypothesis rather than another, depends on one's other beliefs, which we can call
background beliefs or assumptions' (1990: 43). Feminists argue that the
background assumptions of non-feminist social scientists have determined
their hypotheses about the nature of the gendered social world, and that
when the 'background assumptions are shared by all members of a community, they acquire an invisibility that renders them unavailable for criticism' (1990: 80). Thus social scientists had written about 'men' without
specifying what sort of people they meant. Kuhn's concept of the *paradigm,*
explained in Chapter 2, is helpful in understanding how this 'normal' social
science has worked in the past. The advent of feminist perspectives has
involved some serious challenges to the assumptions made by social scientists.

CHARACTERISTICS OF FEMINIST APPROACHES TO RESEARCH

Qualitative methods of social research have often been advocated by feminist researchers. In the early stages of feminist research an orthodoxy developed, which was at the time extremely useful, that feminist researchers
should employ qualitative rather than quantitative approaches, particularly
the in-depth face-to-face interview. As Duelli Klein insists, quantitative
methods, which are

> context stripping, unconscious of [androcentric] biases, and which rely on sexist ...
> gender stereotypes are not suited for research on how women (and men!) in
> today's society come into being, come into holding the views they hold ... such a
> process cannot be recognized, understood and worded by simply compiling data
> and analysing them. (1983: 93)

Informal interviews were seen as one way of accessing women's experiences
such as domestic violence, subordination at work and housework in ways
that had previously been ignored. (Chapter 16 contains an account of the use
of qualitative interviews by feminist social researchers.) Although the use of
qualitative methods almost became a new orthodoxy for feminist researchers, feminists have increasingly taken issue with this, putting forward a view
instead that the method adopted should be the one most appropriate to the
specific set of research questions and to the overall research context (Russell,
1975; 1986; Kelly et al., 1994). Some are critical of the polarization of quantitative and qualitative approaches, and advocate the use of *multiple* methods
(Kelly et al., 1994).

Jayaratne (1983), for example, points to the way in which quantitative
research can be an effective tool in influencing policy makers to adopt policies favourable to women. The political potential of such work is extremely
important. For example, the extent of violence in women's lives is underlined by studies which show its extent and severity. Quantitative research

which indicates the pervasiveness of wife battering has resulted in policies to combat the problem and encouraged many women who would have felt isolated and self-blaming to seek support. Discrimination against racial, sex or other groups can be indicated very powerfully by presenting statistics. Jayaratne argues that 'good' quantitative research as well as qualitative research is needed.

A survey of adult women done by Diana Russell (1986), to assess the prevalence and nature of sexual abuse of girls by adult family members, shows how both qualitative and quantitative approaches can be usefully combined. Russell used quantitative survey methods of gathering and analysing data on sexual assault, but also did in-depth interviews with respondents. The aim of the study, she claims, was to 'combine the most rigorous and scientifically sound methods of gathering and analysing data on incestuous abuse and other forms of sexual assault with a sophisticated and empathetic understanding of the experiences of sexual victimization' (1986: 37). Thus her social survey of households provided a sound basis for generalizing findings about incestuous abuse to the population of adult women in a major US city. She found that 16% of the 930 women had been sexually abused by a relative, usually male, before the age of 18, and that 4.5% reported having been abused by their fathers before this age. Another finding was that there was a strong relationship between abuse in childhood and later experiences of victimization. However, her in-depth interviews with 152 of the women were able to explore in a great deal more detail the variable meanings of the experience for the people involved. As a result of her research Russell argued that incestuous abuse could no longer be viewed as a problem that involves a few disturbed sex offenders. A full understanding of this problem requires seeing it within the context of severe gender and generational inequality.

The essential point, then, is to recognize that feminist social researchers can pursue their research agendas using a *variety* of methods. Ramazanoglu's research shows that work done using the survey method within the context of a positivist methodology can produce knowledge that disadvantages women. However, she argues that comparable survey research from a feminist theoretical perspective could produce improved knowledge of the social conditions of women's lives. Russell's work demonstrates the usefulness of a range of quantitative as well as qualitative methods within a feminist methodology.

Feminist research and political values

Claims by feminist researchers to being able to represent the realities of women's lives (or more recently of men's lives too) have been based on a moral and political commitment to opposing women's subordination (including the need to look at how some women subordinate others), as well as a commitment to produce valid knowledge. A feminist methodological approach must be consistent with the political aims of the women's movement for equality between men and women. As Duelli Klein puts it: 'a feminist approach to knowledge ... defines as an indispensable prerequisite women's right to a place among those who create and transmit knowledge on *our* terms' (1983: 101). Yet this raises the question of objectivity once again. Harding points to an epistemological paradox: 'How can such politicized research be increasing the objectivity of enquiry?' (1986: 24).

Critics of the feminist insistence that emancipation is a goal of research complain that such an idea 'conflates ... fact and value' (Silverman, 1993: 154). Silverman believes in both the possibility and the necessity of knowledge being produced outside the values of those who produce knowledge. If knowledge is not value free it leaves open the possibility, according to Silverman, that it will be tied to irrational forces. He argues that 'the first goal of scientific research is valid knowledge', and it is only how this knowledge is then used which is the political or value-laden question. To claim otherwise is to 'make an alliance with an awful dynasty that includes "Aryan science" under the Nazis, and "Socialist science" under Stalin' (1993: 154).

Feminist theorists, as we have seen, argue in contrast that *no* researcher practises research outside his or her system of values and that *no* social science method can ensure knowledge is produced independently of values. It is precisely those social scientists who claim that value neutrality is possible who reproduce the androcentric values of their culture, rendering the subjugated experiences of women invisible. Feminism argues that its values play a *positive* role in science. The feminist empirical enquiries that are offered as examples in this chapter pose, in their varying ways, a challenge to social science's existing approaches to achieving knowledge of the social world. They do this by identifying issues and problems of gender that are intrinsic to social research, but which are beyond solution through rules of method. From this feminist perspective the idea of a 'value-free science ... is not just empty but pernicious' (Longino, 1990: 191) since claims to have produced neutral knowledge conceal political interests. The background assumptions and values of scientists have remained invisible and thus unavailable for criticism or change.

Longino (1990) proposes that our conception of the methodologies of knowledge construction in the social sciences must be broadened to incorporate an understanding that social science's conceptual assumptions and reasoning are themselves social activities. The consequence of embracing the social character of knowledge, as feminists and other social theorists do, however, does not mean feminist social scientists have given up on producing valid knowledge. The production of feminist knowledge is a 'process of enlightenment', argues McLennan (1995), whose results subsequently become available for all to share. Social researchers from other traditions have responded, however reluctantly at times, to feminist insights, changing their own norms of acceptable social inquiry: 'feminism has literally revolutionised our sense of what today must count as adequate approximation to knowledge' (1995: 397)

CONCLUSION

This chapter has argued that feminist methodology, like all social science methodology, involves theory and analyses of how research should proceed, how research questions might be addressed, and the criteria against which research findings might be evaluated. Its specific areas of concern are the ways in which distinctively feminist research questions can be asked, and the political issues involved in the research process. It is undoubtedly the case that feminist social research, like other forms of social research, hopes to facilitate social change. It is also the case that feminist social research, like other forms of social research, has its particular methodological interpretations. However feminists argue that this does not make feminist social research uniquely political, but rather exposes *all* methods of social research as political.

This book describes the way in which the social sciences were partly constituted by methodological debates and disputes which have a history and a politics (Chapters 3 and 6). These disputes have not come to an end in our own time. We have not reached a resolution of debates about how to achieve knowledge outside the social conditions which make the knowledge possible. Feminist research into the social world is an extension and development of these debates in their state of current irresolution.

Further reading

Maynard and Purvis (1994) present a helpful collection of readings showing a variety of feminist perspectives on research. Harding (1986) addresses the relationship of feminist research to science, and Stanley and Wise (1983) give a classic early statement of feminist perspectives.

5

Gender, ethnicity and fieldwork: a case study

Anne-Marie Fortier

CONTENTS

This chapter is an account of my fieldwork experience in two London Italian social clubs, each run by a religious congregation. The study discussed here was conducted for the completion of my doctorate in sociology (Fortier, 1996). It is on the role of two Italian organizations in constructing an Italian group identity, at a time when the Italian population is fragmented and dispersed. To put it simply, it is on the construction of a cultural identity for an immigrant, multi-generational population, a linguistic and religious minority in Britain, which is absorbed within the white European majority.

I will use my research experience to provide examples of some of the more abstract issues introduced in the preceding chapters, namely the relationship between theory and empirical material, objectivity, and feminist methodology. **Fieldwork**, here, is used as a synonym of ethnography, which is conducted through participant observation and a combination of other methods (see Chapter 17). I use the phrase **participant observation** to designate the activities I observed personally and for an extended period. It suggests that I was 'involved' in the research settings – also called *the field* – and entails the establishment of personal relationships with individuals who are members of the social groups studied. Yet I would not wish to claim that my use of the method of observation led to some form of authentic, 'insider' knowledge, such as is sometimes claimed by the Chicago school ethnographers whose work was described in Chapter 3. A number of factors shaped the nature of my involvement in the field, including the contrasts between my personal politics, beliefs and lifestyle and those expressed by the different people with whom I interacted. My experience was in accord with James Clifford's depiction of ethnography as a series of 'partial truths' that emerge out of 'an open-ended series of contingent, power-laden encounters' (1986: 8) that reflect personal and ideological characteristics of both the researcher and the researched (see also Chapter 22 in this book).

This is not a step-by-step account of an ethnographic study (Chapter 17 outlines such steps in general, for readers who need this). Rather, this chapter centres on the **reflexive** character of doing research in general, and of fieldwork in particular: that is how, as a researcher, I was implicated in producing a particular account of a specific social group. In other words, I examine the implications of taking on board the feminist argument that no researcher practises research outside her or his system of values (see Chapter 4). To be sure, a number of factors affect the way an enquiry is conducted, including the researcher's *personal biography*. I use the phrase 'personal biography' loosely, to include features that researchers bring with them into the field, and that individuals from the social group they wish to enter will interpret in socially prescribed ways – such as gender or ethnicity. Personal biography also covers the individual's personal life experiences, which have some effect on the choice and study of a subject.

One of the factors that is most often said to affect the access, gathering and analysis of information is 'gender' (Warren and Rasmussen, 1977; Warren, 1988; Bell et al., 1993); another factor is 'ethnicity'. In sum, it is commonly held that the gender or ethnic identity of ethnographers limits their access to field situations that would otherwise be accessible to them. For example, male researchers might find it hard to gain access to events surrounding childbirth in some cultures, or female researchers may have difficulty in breaking into male 'enclaves'. In what follows, I want to take issue with this argument. Informed by current theoretical debates about identity formation, I was led, in the course of my study, to question the methodological and epistemological implications of simply assuming that gender and ethnicity can be understood as fixed things which may or may not affect the conduct of an enquiry. I will describe different moments of my enquiry in order to emphasize how gender and ethnicity are not fixed social categories, but rather are lived differently in different contexts. The essence of my argument is that rather than identifying how gender and ethnicity *affect* the research process, we need to examine how they are *negotiated*. In this respect my study shares some of the concerns of Moerman (1974) with 'ethnic identification devices', discussed in detail in Chapters 8 and 9.

The chapter is divided into four sections. Firstly, I present the key questions and theoretical concerns of the research proposal. Secondly, I briefly introduce the research settings and disclose the theoretical, practical and personal reasons for my choice of this area of enquiry. Thirdly, I present some fragments of my interactions in the field and how I used them as sources of knowledge, that is, as relevant 'data' for the final research account. These episodes are described in some detail in order to highlight how gender and ethnicity were negotiated, produced and interpreted by the researcher, and to emphasize how 'observation' and 'analysis' are not clearly separate stages in the research practice (Taraborrelli, 1993: 180; also Chapter 9 in this book). The concluding section pulls together the central issues raised by this case study and summarizes their methodological implications.

THE KEY RESEARCH QUESTIONS

Identity, in contemporary social theory, is widely conceptualized as having no fixed, essential or permanent character. The idea that we have a 'fully unified, completed, secure and coherent identity is a fantasy' (Hall, 1992: 277). It is now commonly accepted, within social sciences, that gender and ethnicity – to refer to the 'identities' discussed here – are socially constructed and historically specific, rather than being fixed essences. Yet too often, identity is conceived as resulting from the various social positions that any one person occupies: ethnic, 'racial', gender, generational, class and so on – for example, being French Canadian, white, woman, lesbian, academic, feminist. According to this view social positions are fixed, implying that we 'live our lives as general categories: as a lesbian I should do this; as a feminist I ought to do that' (Probyn, 1996: 22).

My research project aimed precisely at questioning such an **essentialist** view of identity in relation to ethnicity. It was born out of a deep dissatisfaction with studies which attempted to *define* ethnicity, as if it always already existed, to be 'found' and explained. Pushing the anti-essentialist critique to its limit, my suspicion for anything that might smack of essentialism led me to consider dismissing the concept of ethnicity altogether. Informed by the work of the 'Birmingham school' of cultural studies (see Centre for Contemporary Cultural Studies, 1982), I was weary of definitions of community and cultural continuity spelled out in terms of a primary ethnicity that grounds group identity formation.

My uneasiness was compounded by the political and social climate of 1990s Britain. Firstly, a new racist discourse that was systematized in the 1960s viewed culture as the basis of absolute and definite differences between groups; these differences were seen as deeply ingrained and inalterable, almost like biological properties of human relations. Secondly, the British 'identity crisis' was fuelled by animosity towards the European Community. This discourse sat uneasily with the promotion – by 'Europhiles' across Europe, including Britain – of a new European citizenship based on the idea of common European cultural heritage. I felt that Italians stood on the border between difference and sameness in their relation to British national culture; they occupied a double status of majority–minority in contemporary Britain. This carries important implications for our conceptions of so-called ethnic groups, which are consistently associated with minorities, that is people whose culture differs from the official definition of the 'national culture' of their country of residence. In addition, Italians were a highly dispersed population, thus questioning images of 'natural' community, based in part on geographical proximity conjured up by the idea of 'ethnic group'.

I therefore set out to explore the process of cultural identity formation of an immigrant population of London. I did not presume that Italians in London defined themselves only in ethnic terms. I investigated how particular definitions of gender, ethnicity, nation and generation were worked into representations of group identity. In sum, the main research questions were: how were Italian immigrants represented and constructed as a 'community' and how was an Italian group identity deployed?

CHOOSING THE RESEARCH SETTINGS

The choice of Italians in London was partly motivated by the fact that I had produced an earlier study on Italians in Montreal (Fortier, 1991), on the one hand, and by the scarcity of research on white immigrant populations in Britain, on the other. The selection of the research settings, for its part, resulted from a process of narrowing down the field of enquiry into something that could be manageable. From the outset I wanted to focus on institutional practices of identity formation, in contrast to individual forms of identity construction – the 'official discourse', as it were, rather than individual definitions and experiences of cultural identity. My aim was to look at the daily life of particular organizations, and to examine their role in the construction of a London Italian community. This entailed the use of a combination of methods, including *participant observation, semi-structured interviews* (see Chapter 16) and *textual analysis* of local Italian newspapers and monographs on Italians in Britain, written by Italians.

The decision to focus my attention on two socio-religious centres came after a series of preliminary interviews and a period of passive observation, which revealed the extent to which these organizations are pivotal in London Italian associative life. The first of the two centres is known as the *Italian Church* (this, as are all other names, is a pseudonym). Based in central London, it was founded in 1863 and stands at the heart of what used to be *il quartiere italiano*, or Little Italy. The second centre I shall identify as the *Mission*, befitting the nature of its congregation of missionaries catering to Italian emigrants world-wide. It is based in south-east London and was established in 1968.

The 'community' events I took part in were organized by one or both of the institutions. I spent 15 months doing fieldwork in order to cover all of the annual events. I attended Sunday lunches to celebrate Father's Day, Grandparent's Day, Valentine's Day, the annual picnic organized by the Mission, the annual remembrance ceremony in Brookwood military cemetery, the annual pilgrimage to the monastery of Our Lady of Mount Carmel in Aylesford (Kent), the annual procession in honour of Our Lady at the Italian

Church, and the annual dinner dance of the Federation of Italian Associations in England. Apart from these yearly ceremonials and festivities, I also observed the religious life of the Italian Church. I attended Sunday masses, first communions, confirmation celebrations and, towards the end of the fieldwork, I went to wedding ceremonies and funerals. My visits to the Mission, for their part, revolved around the weekly Women's Club meetings, and the weekly rehearsals of the Mission choir, of which I was a member and which was set up especially for the celebrations of the 25th anniversary of the Mission in December 1993.

Apart from the reasons stated above, elements of my personal biography influenced the choice of the research settings. Not only did a mixture of fascination and aversion for Catholicism fuel my strange desire to get closer to the two Italian churches, but I was also drawn by a sense of familiarity that, given my recent arrival in London, was of some comfort (though disturbing) in my own quest for a sense of belonging in this new city. Indeed, looking back at my first visits to the Italian Church, I remember how I felt oddly at home in this setting. Having recently moved to London from my native Quebec (Canada), this place constituted a small terrain of comfort in a largely non-Catholic country where I was constantly reminded of my Catholic upbringing, as if it were *the* explanation for my idiosyncrasies and 'quirks'. Indeed, I was never as 'Catholic' as I was over my five years of living in London. Thus my first visit to the Italian Church struck me because it was a place where my 'difference' seemed to dissolve, even though the ceremonies were not performed in the French vernacular I was brought up with. I found myself in a space where I recognized my self, in a way. It was a space of familiarity and identity, if only for the memories it conjured up, a space where I could actually witness part of my identity 'in action', in the making. It was a space, moreover, where I did not need to try to make sense of what was going on: all was familiar, intelligible, even if unpleasant and troubling given my renunciation of Catholicism years before.

This small experience gave me some insight into what it may mean, for some Italians, to return to the Italian Church, or the Mission's chapel; how these places may allow them to feel good about themselves. I understood how these churches may be places, outside the home, where people need not think about being Italian in a non-Italian, non-Catholic world; where cultural identity may be deeply felt. This, indeed, was the first of a series of moments where my personal odyssey so clearly spilled into my ethnographic work. Realizing this, I sought ways to proceed from this juxtaposition, to use this experience as a source of knowledge in my reflections on cultural identity formation.

TROUBLES IN THE FIELD: GENDER, ETHNICITY AND NEGOTIATING BELONGING

Establishing contacts with research subjects is usually a long process of patient negotiations, introductions and mutual familiarization. In my case I did not enter the field straight on. I first conducted a series of semi-structured interviews with a number of London Italian leaders and intellectuals, in order both to get a sense of the organizational structure of the 'community' and to hear their views on my research proposal. A short letter introducing myself and my project was either sent to potential interviewees, or handed to them on the day of our meeting. Throughout the fieldwork, I always presented myself as a researcher and briefly explained the nature of my study. I thought it was better to play it straight even if this entailed further negotiation. Most often, once access is established people tend to forget the intentions of the observer and let down their guard (Gans, 1968).

My first interviewee, a Scottish-Italian woman who has published some work on Italians in Britain, warned me that being a woman might hinder my access to the male-dominated Italian leadership, though I could 'pass' as an Italian. What concerned her was that being a non-Italian woman might be a liability. In her view, two entangled factors seemed central to facilitate the access to the 'truth' about the institutions: being of the 'right' ethnicity and of the 'right' gender.

As it turned out, being Italian did not really matter. Initially, it did come as a surprise to the people I met that I, a non-Italian French Canadian, was doing research on Italians in London. But this was not a basis of exclusion. Even when I apologized for my lack of fluency in the Italian language, this was usually shrugged off by comparing me to the English-born children of immigrants: 'Bah! Just like my daughter,' I was told, indicating that there is no uniform way of 'acting' that would display 'Italianness'. Some speak Italian fluently, some don't. My ethnic identity was part of negotiations between myself and the people with whom I interacted in order to 'locate' me in relation to them. The outcome was that we met on the terrain of our common status as foreigners in Britain. Being from Quebec, with a Catholic background, I was included within the folds of this 'minority'. What struck me was that my Italianness was not taken for granted (I was asked about my background and positioned as a foreigner) but my Catholicism was. The absence of overt attempts by club members to confirm my religious faith allowed me to presume it was not an issue. Indeed it was not, because it was *assumed* that I was a practising Catholic.

My inclusion as 'one of theirs' bears methodological implications for researchers studying ethnicity where studies on minority cultures are commonly conducted by presumed members of these groups. While it may be recognized that there are practical advantages to do with being brought up in the same 'ethnic' culture (familiarity with language, rituals, rules of behaviour, etiquette and so on), the view that such studies *ought* to be done in this way is indicative of a persisting assumption that ethnicity is the primary ground of cultural identity formation and the basis of human relations and solidarity. It obscures a number of social differences of class, sexuality, gender, even ethnicity, that exist within 'ethnic groups'. It also leads people to ignore the very particular context that is created from the relationship *between* the researcher and the individuals whose lives he or she is documenting. The same applies to gender: that is, it is not because I am a woman that I will have 'better knowledge' of Italian women in London. If my being a woman was an influential factor in the conduct of my research, it was as an object of negotiation, rather than as an attribute that would determine, once and for all, the kind of information to which I had access.

After months of numerous phone calls to the Mission in vain attempts to meet one of its leading priests, I finally expressed my anger at being put off to the woman who was acting as gatekeeper to the entire Mission. Apologetically, she explained that the priest was a very busy man, but immediately found a free slot for the following week. This led me to the interview which was crucial to the outcome of my research: not with the priest in question, but with the gatekeeper herself, who also happened to be the president of the Italian Women's Club (Club Donne Italiane, CDI). That day, I joined the organization and began attending their weekly meetings. Thanks to these women, I found out about the different 'community events' and more importantly, grew closer to some women who became my regular companions in these outings. Yet it soon became clear to me that my relations with these women were not straightforward. From the moment I entered the Women's Club, a gendered and sexualized identity was assigned to me and I walked into a world where specific injunctions of womanhood were spelled out. My gender, in other words, did not dissolve the distance between myself and these women: 'being a woman and being with women is not necessarily the same thing' (Probyn, 1993: 32). In the field, I was regarded as a young single heterosexual woman and perceived somewhat as an oddity because of my unmarried and 'unspoken for' status – and jobless to boot! In all social events I attended, most of the other thirtysomethings present were accompanied, most married and many with children. Within these settings, I was not yet an accomplished woman, and my single, student status became intelligible to many Italian women I related to only if they treated me like a child. Many of those to whom I revealed my age expressed great surprise, saying that they assumed I was much younger, the gap sometimes reaching 10 years! They also mothered me ('We worry about you, that's how mothers are'). With these men and women, I was a *ragazza* (a girl) or a *signorina* (a young or unmarried woman); the former is asexual, while the latter, though conceived as a heterosexual desiring being, cannot acceptably be heterosexually active according to the Catholic ethos. I was never, of course, a *signora* (an older or married woman). I was expected, however, to aspire to marriage and to look for a husband. I was never asked if I wanted to marry, let alone if I wanted to share my life with a man. It was assumed that this was the case.

My marital status was a point of curiosity, if not concern, for many of the women I was in regular contact with, as the following extract from my field notes testifies.

> Later on, while I was reading in the next room, Luisa came in to chat. She tells me about the 'young man who's been eyeing' me during choir rehearsals. 'I found out

about him,' she says. 'He's not married, not courting, not divorced. So . . . he's free, he's available . . . Now I have to know if Anna-Maria is courting, married or divorced.' 'None of the above,' I reply. Satisfied, Luisa starts enumerating the young man's good points. 'He's a nice man, studied at university . . . perhaps not to my liking, but. . . .' I grab the opportunity: 'I must admit he's not my type.' 'Well, we agree on that then!' She laughs: 'We'll just have to look out for another one.'

On another occasion, a Women's Club summer party, there was a draw for a weekend for two in a five-star hotel in Parma. As my thoughts wandered in a reverie about this luxury weekend with my girlfriend, I was abruptly brought back to earth by Monica, seated next to me: 'I want to know *everything* about the person you go with if you win!' Joking along, I grew increasingly uncomfortable at the thought of winning. I was desperately hoping not to win, because I wouldn't have known how to deal with my desire for discretion and my discomfort in the face of the prospect of lying about my self. I didn't win after all, but this did not stop Monica from insisting until she finally asked: 'Haven't you got yourself a boyfriend since you've been in London?', as if to seek confirmation of my 'normality', or so I felt. I answered Monica, giving details, prompted by her questions, about the men I had 'met' since arriving in London, and the discussion was brought to a close. Yet, despite my truthful answer, I was acutely aware of the discrepancy between the presentation of my ethnographic self and what I felt and believed in.

Participant observers and ethnographers are inevitably caught up in a web of demands that come from different directions at once: academia, personal interests (career oriented, the immediate requirements of the enquiry, family related, economic concerns), and the interests of the subjects (who may be sponsoring the study, or hoping for public visibility, or looking for an advocate of their 'cause' and so on). To put it crudely, deception and role-playing are part and parcel of participant observation and give the researcher a keen sense of what writers on the method have called **marginality**. The uniqueness of each setting and of each study, as well as the personal circumstances of the researcher, shape the types of relationships between the researcher and the individuals concerned by her or his inquiry. The disclosure of what we think, believe in, how we live, has to be negotiated and thought about on a daily basis (Gans, 1968; Mitchell, 1991; Shaffir, 1991; Ramsay, 1996). However, these very interactions can provide relevant information about the social dynamics that are at play in particular settings.

I did not slip painlessly into the Women's Club. My participation was fraught with feelings of self-doubt, apprehension and uncertainty as I negotiated the gap separating my lifestyle from those of the CDI members. There was a good deal of time and energy spent in learning to feel relaxed in their company. Processes of inclusion and (self) *erasure* were simul-taneously at play: I was both part of 'them', as an assumed Catholic or 'honorary' Italian, a young, heterosexual white woman, and on the margins, as a single, non-courting, student. I was somewhat of an ambiguous person, given my 'unspoken for' status at the age of thirtysomething. But my ambiguity was stabilized and mended through a combination of my own and other women's negotiations, performances and injunctions. *We* did this through performing heterosexuality, with repetitive exhortations casting me as a future wife-lover-mother. *I* managed it through coping and masquerading as well as by analysing the whole story in sociological terms!

In sum, disguise, secrecy and erasure seemed necessary strategies that allowed me to 'blend in' with these women. Troubling as they were, I eventually came to view these interactions as telling me something about the ways in which 'womanhood' is lived and negotiated amongst these people. They also revealed the centrality of gender and family relations in locating individuals' social status and in constructing cultural identity.

My project, most certainly, was modified in its own course. My experiences as a participant observer brought the complexities of gendered and ethnic identity disturbingly close to my own idea of selfhood. They helped me to understand even further the necessity of thinking identity as both deeply felt and socially constructed, and to reconsider the way ethnicity and gender are entangled in cultural identity formation. The main finding of this study was that we cannot fully separate ethnicity and gender as lying at the basis of distinct systems of power that criss-cross in group identity formation. Thinking about *gendered ethnicities*, for want of a better phrase, is not only a matter of relating ethnicity and gender, and honouring them as separate pieces that are brought together through an array of different practices within an imagined community. They are deeply embedded in one another because they are constructed along similar lines. To put it simply, what went on in these organizations was not only about ethnic (re)production; it was also about producing gendered systems of differentiation. The very simultaneity of these practices suggests that the lived experience of identity formation spills over the boundaries of the categories of gender and ethnicity.

CONCLUSION

By describing different moments of my field research, I have illustrated how gender and ethnicity were *negotiated* in my access and participation in the two Italian social clubs. Gender and ethnicity were both *assigned* to me by the Italians and were a *negotiable* dimension of the fieldwork process. Thus I have examined not only how gender and ethnicity *affect* the study, but also how my position as a particular kind of woman resulted from the very interactions between myself and the people I met in the field and was tied to the Italian emigrant project of identity formation. In other words, I used my relationships in the field as sources of knowledge in understanding cultural identity. As such, this case study is an example of how both theory and 'reality', observation and analysis, are entangled and that, if we accept that social research is informed by personal systems of values, beliefs, politics and histories (as, for example, is evident in discussions of feminist methodology), we need to find ways of making use of them. To paraphrase Elspeth Probyn (1993: 3), this is about conceiving ways of thinking the social through ourselves.

To be sure, the researcher's personal involvement with members of social groups generates a number of anxieties that he or she needs to mediate throughout the fieldwork and beyond. In this respect, ethnographers' anxieties do not 'vanish once the field is over' (Gans, 1968: 316). During and after my fieldwork, I worried about the expectations of those who generously let me into their milieu in the anticipation that I would write a book about them. Indeed I will, but I'm not sure whether my interpretation will please them, or, for that matter, whether its sociological jargon will be intelligible to them. This raises a number of issues about writing research accounts that are discussed in more detail in Chapter 22. I simply wish to stress that personal involvement does not end when the ethnographer leaves the research setting. Relationships with the members of the groups studied do carry on – either metaphorically or concretely – for a long time after the field study has been completed.

Further reading

Back (1996) is a rich and clear ethnographic study of black and white youths in south London in which he argues that cultural identities cannot be understood in terms of a primary ethnicity. In the Introduction and Chapter 1 the author addresses questions concerning the politics and partiality of British ethnic studies, and the status of researchers as natives or outsiders. Game and Metcalfe (1996) is a book on the practice of reflexive social science. Walkerdine and Lucey (1989) contains an introductory section in which these two authors, who are both of working-class background, discuss their position in response to transcripts of conversations between mothers and daughters in working-class and middle-class households.

6

The history of the social survey

Fran Tonkiss

CONTENTS

This chapter describes the historical development of quantitative methods for the investigation of social life. Focusing on developments in Britain in the nineteenth and early twentieth centuries, the discussion outlines the way that statistical and survey techniques were used to record, measure and compare a range of social factors such as poverty, disease, mortality and crime, thereby providing systematic information about the experiences and living conditions of a modern, urban population.

The discussion begins by looking at the emergence of a statistical science in the late eighteenth and early nineteenth century. Collection of social statistics was an important element in the Enlightenment project of a 'science' of society. The view of early statistical thinkers was that society was organized in terms of laws which could be quantified, predicted and mechanically adjusted through the use of rational and informed policy measures. This has sometimes been called *social engineering*. The discussion goes on to consider how survey methods have developed more recently in such fields as marketing, opinion polling, public policy and academic research.

In fact, from the outset, these methods of social investigation were closely tied to programmes of social reform. Different schemes linked the provision of information about the population with forms of legislation and intervention regarding its conditions, conduct and improvement. The central part of the chapter concerns the massive poverty surveys undertaken by Booth and Rowntree in the late Victorian period, examining how these sought both to develop more rigorous methods of social investigation, and to produce systematic knowledge about the causes of urban poverty.

Recent critical accounts of methods of social investigation have emphasized the manner in which social statistics and social surveys do not so much *reflect* as *constitute* what we have come to understand as 'society'. These **social constructionist** perspectives argue that the forms in which we gather, record and interpret knowledge about social life have important consequences for the way that we define and understand social structures, social groups and social problems. The chapter concludes by considering these critiques in relation to the early tradition of quantitative social research.

EARLY SURVEYS: POLITICAL ARITHMETIC AND SOCIAL ACCOUNTING

The social survey emerged in the nineteenth century as an important new method for gathering information about the population. This is not to say that the idea of counting and categorizing groups of people or recording information relating to their conditions of life was itself a new idea. A favourite example of historians is the 'survey' commenced in 1085 into the distribution of property and population in England, which formed the basis of the Domesday Book. Parish registers in England have long recorded demographic information in the form of returns of births, marriages and deaths, and these provided valuable data for the demographic studies – or *political arithmetic* – developed in the late seventeenth century by such figures as John Graunt, William Petty and Gregory King.

Throughout the eighteenth century, the political arithmetic of population and wealth was central to debates concerning social and economic conditions in Britain, as exemplified by Thomas Malthus's 1798 *Essays on Population*. Malthus's work suggested that the population was likely to increase at such a rate that the wealth of the nation would be insufficient to provide a subsistence to all. The alarm engendered by such speculations galvanized Parliament to legislate for the collection of the first population census in Britain in 1801. The population in this sense came to be thought about not just as a mass of people but also as a *datum* – a quantitative entity which might be measured and monitored in respect of its size, distribution and growth, and increasingly in terms of a plethora of local rates of disease, marriage, age, employment, wealth, birth, death and so on (see Hacking, 1990).

This pre-history of 'social accounting' indicates an enduring concern with the size, distribution and condition of people, property and wealth. However, the desire to enumerate was, up to the nineteenth century, not matched by effective or systematic counting and recording techniques. Early political arithmetic produced knowledge about the population in a largely speculative manner, and the 1801 census was itself rather patchy in terms of its methods of collection and the clarity of its questions. It was not until later in that century that more organized methods of information gathering and recording were developed, and it is at this point that we can begin to speak of **social statistics** and the social survey 'proper'.

There are two important things to note about the development of a statistical science in early nineteenth century Britain. Firstly, this new science was greatly influenced by models of *observation* and *induction* developed in the natural sciences. Early statisticians followed the example of natural scientists in their conviction that fact gathering on a large scale might lead to the development of rational and certain theories about the state of society. Indeed, it was widely held that the systematic collection of numerical facts might be used to establish certain causal 'laws' which governed social life and produced poverty, indolence and crime. (The discussion in Chapter 2 examines natural science models and their implications for the social sciences in more detail.)

Secondly, nineteenth century statistical science was tied to programmes of government. In their early development 'state-istics' were closely tied to other forms of statecraft, being used to produce knowledge about a population which might inform rational programmes of government. The population debate of the eighteenth century, initiated by Malthus, is one significant example of a set of social and economic problems which statistics appeared capable of settling. Was the population growing or declining? Were the poor outstripping other classes of society? Was the wealth of the nation increasing or decreasing? The 1801 census appeared to offer a rather crude but nevertheless *empirical* response to these questions, in that it was based on observation and data collection rather than on theory or speculation. Numerical facts provided a basis for members of the political elite to make rational and informed decisions about economic and, later, social policy.

The shortcomings of the 1801 census served only to galvanize a commitment to producing sound numerical information about the state of the nation. If the population question had been central to the development of statistics in the eighteenth century, this later gave precedence to debates over the 'condition of England' (see Polanyi, 1957; Kent, 1981). In a rapidly changing society marked by accelerating urbanization and industrialization, and by the growth of middle-class and working-class radicalism, it appeared increasingly important to members of the governing class to ascertain both the condition of different groups in society and any 'trends' towards social and economic decline and disintegration.

The main forums for providing these analyses were the statistical societies which emerged in the first half of the nineteenth century. Such societies were formed in a number of major urban centres throughout Britain, notably in London, Manchester, Bristol, Liverpool, Birmingham, Leeds, Belfast and Glasgow. A common set of concerns emerged in the statistical work different societies undertook. In particular, the state of the working classes in terms of their size, housing and employment, crime and destitution, sanitation, hygiene and disease, education (and truancy) preoccupied Victorian social researchers. These studies generally attempted both to produce factual knowledge about the extent and distribution of various social 'problems', and to establish causal patterns. Rawson's 1839 *An Inquiry into the Statistics of Crime in England and Wales*, for example, aimed to show regularities in patterns and rates of crime, concluding that criminal activity was most prevalent in large towns, and least prevalent in mining areas, in Wales, and in mountainous areas in northern England. This research was based on an analysis of census data together with statistics produced by the judicial system over a five-year period. William Guy's 1843 *An Attempt to Determine the Influence of the Seasons and Weather on Sickness and Mortality* was the first in a series of studies which he published establishing correlations between patterns of illness and a range of factors such as temperature, sex and sedentary occupations (Kent, 1981).

The Statistical Society of London had a particularly close relationship to government, providing information directly to parliamentary committees. At the same time government departments were setting up their own statistical sections, such as in the Home Office and the Board of Trade, and in 1836 the General Register Office was established to centrally collate information on births, deaths and marriages. The most comprehensive statistical work at this time was undertaken by government bodies such as the royal commissions into the Poor Laws and the condition of the Irish poor, and within the factory inspection system.

By the middle of the nineteenth century, then, a speculative and often haphazard desire to produce statistical information had become organized into systematic programmes to quantify the population and inform government policy, based on a belief that numerical facts provided the basis for rational and conclusive knowledge about social trends. It was a common conviction that statistical facts would 'speak for themselves' in ways which were not affected by the opinions or actions of the researcher. There are two objections to make here. The first is that the conclusions established by many early social surveys smack more of Victorian morality than of scientific fact. Kent cites the case of the Reverend John Clay's 1839 study of the *Criminal Statistics of Preston*, which sought to establish the causes of crime and to analyse annual variations in local crime rates. The causal factors identified by Clay included such categories as drunkenness, idleness, intellectual weakness, the keeping of bad company and temptation (Kent, 1981: 23). While such causal links may be arguable (a relationship between alcohol and crime, for example, is strongly supported by modern criminal statistics), the framing of these categories would appear to owe as much to a particular moral standpoint as to the self-evidence of numerical facts. The separation of facts from values in the collection and presentation of data was at best a rather shaky process, and is particularly questionable in light of the political uses which a great deal of social statistics served.

This point touches on the second objection to be made to the idea that statistical facts might 'speak for themselves'. Such a notion fails to address the wider social context in which statistics are produced, and the way in which statistical knowledge is taken up and used. The realm of facts which researchers elected (or were commissioned) to investigate was shaped by the broad political agenda of the day – especially in relation to concerns over the plight of the poorer classes and the unruliness of certain groups in society, with all the associated threat of social disorder – and these facts were intended to serve political ends. However, while the collection of statistical data sought to establish certain correlations and even causal linkages, it could not offer clear guides to policy. Nineteenth century social statistics were firmly wedded to reforming programmes of government, yet they could not in themselves suggest the most appropriate ways to initiate social and economic reforms.

For example, while a range of surveys produced a deal of knowledge about the extent and nature of poverty in Victorian society, their findings could not settle the question of whether public relief should be provided in order to ensure a subsistence for all, or whether the poorest segments of society should be forced to find their own subsistence in an unfettered market economy. If statistical facts could not *speak for themselves* independently of either the values of the researcher or the social context of their production, the extent to which they could *speak to* what were ultimately ethical and political problems was also rather limited. Information and quantification were not in themselves sufficient grounds for making decisions about the proper government of a modern population. Chapter 15 takes up these criticisms and assesses the extent to which they can be applied to modern official statistics.

EXPLORING BY NUMBERS: SURVEYS OF POVERTY

The explosion and rapid institutionalization of statistics in mid nineteenth century Britain was offset and to a significant extent surpassed by more qualitative accounts of life in a modern industrial society. While the range of statistical studies constitutes an extensive archive of data relating to the condition of Victorian Britain, the qualitative, journalistic and novelistic accounts of figures such as Engels, Mayhew, Disraeli and Dickens have tended to have more lasting influence in creating a picture of that society. Both Engels, in his *The Condition of the Working Class in England in 1844*, and Mayhew in his monumental 1851–52 study of *London Labour and the London Poor*, based their accounts partly on quantitative data concerning urban poverty. However the greater impact of their respective studies stems from their use of qualitative techniques of observation and 'interview' among the urban poor.

Booth

These different techniques of social investigation – the survey method, official statistics, participant observation and informants' accounts – were brought together in a systematic manner in Charles Booth's classic study of the *Labour and Life of the People of London*. Booth began his investigations in 1886 and published them in 17 volumes in 1902. Like Engels, Booth was a wealthy industrialist who was disturbed by the poor conditions of working-class life in late Victorian Britain. His extensive study into the labouring classes of London was framed by two concerns: the living conditions of working-class families; and the occupation and income of their 'breadwinners'. A house-to-house study of this vast population was made possible by enlisting the assistance of school board visitors who had intimate knowledge of their local district, while further information was obtained from local police, churchmen and district superintendents. Booth began his inquiries in the East End of London, which he took to represent the most destitute population in the city, and predicted that the rates of poverty throughout London would tend to be lower than in this especially deprived area.

On the basis of these investigations, Booth classified the population of London into eight different social classes, from the 'occasional labourers, loafers and semi-criminals' to the 'upper middle class'. While Booth's system of classification is rather imprecise – a category such as 'loafers', for example, is one which is difficult to specify with any sort of precision, and is distinctly value laden – his model is important in attempting to distinguish categories of 'the poor'. A **poverty line** was established, with the first four classes falling below it. Booth's poor endured lives characterized by economic hardship, lacking in domestic comforts, with low or irregular earnings; while at the bottom end of his scale, the 'very poor' existed in a state of chronic want.

The pilot study Booth and his assistants conducted in the East End had established relationships between occupation, income and living conditions for each family in the survey. This method produced an unwieldy mass of data and, in his larger-scale study of London, Booth took the street as the basic unit of analysis, classifying each unit in terms of the average condition of its residents. On this basis Booth produced a series of 'poverty maps' which sketched the geography of destitution and privilege across London, like a street map of poverty.

Booth's mammoth survey produced two major claims. The first of these was that the urban poor did not represent so great a threat to social order as was frequently imagined by the more feverish moralists of late Victorian times. Rather than constituting a danger to civilized life in the capital, London's poor – though struggling and often living in want – were for the most part respectable and orderly. By dividing up his poor into four classes, Booth was able to demonstrate that the 'undeserving', disreputable or criminal poor made up less than 1% of the urban population.

Booth's second claim concerned the causes of poverty. In order to establish **causal relationships**, Booth took a sample of 4,000 families from his larger study, and analysed the immediate causes of poverty in these cases. The majority showed that poverty might be traced to employment conditions such as irregular or inadequate earnings, rather than to moral or individual failings. However, Booth's scientific approach to social inquiry did not wholly escape the morality of his time, and his findings showed up correlations between patterns of poverty and 'questions of habit'. For example, in around 5% of cases, poverty was traced to the presence of a 'drunken or thriftless wife'.

Booth's findings contain a further important claim, one which has been backed up by more recent inquiries into patterns of poverty. An unexpected outcome of his comprehensive survey was that rates of poverty throughout London, averaging to around 31% for the whole city, were comparable to those Booth discovered in what he had assumed to be the extreme case of the East End. Across the capital, Booth found pockets of destitution and patterns of poverty, often alongside sites of relative privilege. While concentrated areas of material deprivation certainly existed in Victorian London – as they do in late twentieth century London – Booth's findings indicate that the distribution of poverty tends to be complex and is not reducible to certain poverty 'black spots'. This is in line with contemporary research which contests simplistic accounts of urban deprivation by demonstrating that not all residents of 'inner city' areas are poor, and that not all people living in poverty live in the 'inner city' (for example, Townsend et al., 1987). Booth's approach was distinctive and highly influential in showing the spatial distribution of poverty and wealth, alongside his concern with both structural and personal causal factors.

Rowntree

Booth's survey was to influence a further generation of empirical social research into the causes and extent of poverty. One of the most significant of these studies was Rowntree's survey undertaken in York and published in 1901 as *Poverty: A Study of Town Life*. Like Booth before him, Rowntree was a prosperous businessman who was concerned by Booth's 'problem of problems' – the persistence and severity of poverty in modern society. Rowntree set out to examine whether the patterns of poverty which Booth uncovered in London were matched by similar conditions in a provincial city such as York.

While Rowntree's study was deeply influenced by Booth's, it involved a number of significant methodological and analytic advances. Firstly, Rowntree undertook a comprehensive house-to-house survey of every working-class family in York. Booth's reliance on school board visitors as research assistants, conversely, meant that his study was limited to only those wage-earning families with children of school age. Secondly, Rowntree enlisted interviewers to derive data directly from the survey population themselves, rather than relying on the accounts of informants such as Booth's school board visitors, clergymen and police. Rowntree's third critical innovation was to establish a more systematic model for the analysis of poverty and social class. Rowntree distinguished between two basic forms of poverty:

primary and *secondary* poverty. Primary poverty was said to exist where a family's income was insufficient to provide for the basic physical necessities of life – or what Rowntree called 'physical efficiency'. Secondary poverty, on the other hand, existed where family income would provide for basic physical necessities, but did not allow for any further expenditure. Rowntree's definition of 'physical efficiency' was stringent, allowing for the barest dietary needs of the family, together with a modest provision for rent, clothing and fuel. Based on this calculation, Rowntree set a poverty line at 21s 8d weekly earnings for a family of two adults and three children. Rowntree established that average weekly earnings for unskilled labourers in York were 18s to 21s, insufficient to provide for the essential physical needs of a family.

In tracing the causes of primary poverty, Rowntree employed rather more rigorous categories than had Booth. He identified six major causal factors: the death of the wage-earner; illness or age of the chief wage-earner; unemployment; irregularity of work; largeness of family; and low wages. Of these six immediate causes of primary poverty, Rowntree concluded that the majority of families in York living below the poverty line had a chief wage-earner who was in regular work, but who earned wages which were too low to support the basic physical needs of their family. Low wages, that is, rather than individual or moral failings (Booth's 'questions of habit') or 'questions of circumstances' such as illness or family size, constituted the major cause of primary poverty.

While the York study represented a critical advance in quantitative techniques of inquiry into social problems, Rowntree's methodology was not watertight and aspects of his analysis reflected a particular moral standpoint. Informants, who were frequently the wage-earners' wives, could not always be relied upon to either know or accurately divulge their husbands' earnings. Moreover, the procedure for classifying 'secondary poverty' involved rather subjective assessments of families' spending habits and the appearance of want. While the causal factors established for primary poverty created a picture of the respectable poor, Rowntree tended to attribute secondary poverty to such factors as drink, gambling and improvidence. In spite of these drawbacks, the use of direct and comprehensive survey methods and of clear analytic categories marked off Rowntree's approach from earlier survey investigations.

Bowley

In common with Booth's work, Rowntree's investigations were both extremely time consuming and very costly. This is because they were **censuses** of the entire population covered, rather than **sample surveys** from which generalizations to the population are made on the basis of probabilities. A decade after the publication of these exhaustive urban surveys, an important innovation in social survey research was made in Bowley's study of the wage-earning class in Reading (Bowley and Burnett-Hurst, 1915). Bowley's distinction was to make use of **sampling** techniques, selecting every 20th building on the borough residential register, and excluding non-working-class households. This left Bowley with a sample of 743 wage-earning households, each of which was visited and surveyed. Additionally, Bowley developed methods for adjusting for non-response. Sampling techniques are explained in greater detail in Chapter 11.

Bowley took up Rowntree's definition of the poverty line, modifying it somewhat to reflect the changing dietary needs of children of different ages, and allowing rather more variation (and more meat!) in adult diets. This reliance on the earlier study – and Rowntree's own debt to Booth – indicates a move to greater **replication**, reference and comparison amongst surveys into social problems. Bowley himself undertook a second study in Reading a decade after his first (Bowley and Hogg, 1925), while a large-scale *New Survey of London Life and Labour* was published between 1930 and 1935 as a follow-up to Booth's pioneering work. Rowntree, meanwhile, administered two further surveys into working-class poverty in York (Rowntree, 1941; Rowntree and Lavers, 1951), which both modified his original poverty standard and rejected the measurement of secondary poverty.

LATER DEVELOPMENTS

The inter-war period saw the consolidation of the survey method, as the innovation of sampling allowed it to be used more widely, without the massive resources required by Booth or Rowntree. For a while, though, the topics investigated remained rather narrowly defined, so that in 1935 Wells was able to define a social survey as being a 'fact finding study dealing chiefly with working class poverty and with the nature and problems of the community' (1935: 1). The interests of people using social surveys became broader, though, as the growing discipline of town planning increasingly came to rely on surveys.

In the post-war period social surveys developed in four main institutional locations: market and audience research, opinion polling, government social surveys and academic social science. The first of these will be familiar to anyone who has ever been stopped in the street to be asked about shopping preferences and the like. Market researchers generally have to work quickly, generating results in a matter of a few days or weeks, and on limited budgets. Special sampling methods (see Chapter 11) have been developed to enable this. Opinion pollsters often work under similar constraints. Perhaps the most important contribution made by this type of survey work has been an appreciation of how question wording can affect response, leading to a reinforcement of the desire to standardize the wording of questions, and thus try to eliminate the influence of the interviewer whose rewordings might otherwise produce unreliable replies.

Most advanced industrial democracies have developed a government social survey department, reflecting the links between governmentality and quantification of the population outlined earlier. Britain is no exception. A department originally conceived in wartime to monitor the level of civilian morale later became the Government Social Survey. In 1970 this department merged with the General Register Office to become the Office of Population Censuses and Surveys (OPCS), recently renamed the Office for National Statistics (ONS). As well as the decennial census ONS monitors a number of continuous and regular sample surveys such as the General Household Survey, the Family Expenditure Survey and the Labour Force Survey, most of which are done at regular (annual or biannual intervals) on representative samples of the population. Additionally, a variety of *ad hoc* surveys are conducted according to the perceived needs of policy makers, on such diverse topics as retirement, training needs, women and employment, and the prevalence of disability. Together with the statistical series arising from the registration of birth, deaths, marriages and the like, the documents and reports produced by these activities comprise **official statistics**.

Government social surveys have characteristic strengths in the selection of large, representative samples, and in the training of interviewers to ask standardized, structured questions. Their weakness, for the purposes of social researchers, tends to be in somewhat unimaginative analyses of the data that emerge, and in a tendency to 'let the facts speak for themselves'. Thus they can be said to be **empiricist** in orientation (see Chapter 2), underplaying the role of theory in structuring the observations made through the survey instrument. Nevertheless, the availability of data sets generated by government social surveys in data archives offers an immensely valuable resource for researchers interested in the **secondary analysis** of such data for their own purposes (Dale et al., 1988). Secondary analysis is discussed in more detail in Chapter 15.

The use made of the social survey in the fourth institutional location, academic social science, is very diverse. Researchers working within the disciplines of social policy and social administration offer examples that are closest to governmental aims, and in area studies such as health or educational research the method has proved useful. Academic social science provides some of the most innovative and creative examples of the method, but also some of the poorest-quality social surveys that it is possible to find. In part these problems reflect the difficulties experienced in funding adequate surveys, for even a sample survey will be inadequate if it is too small, or time cannot be spent on piloting and developing high-quality questionnaires. However, perhaps the chief cause of these problems lies in the doubts that have been expressed – most powerfully by sociologists – about the value of quantitative methods. This has sometimes led to an unfortunate and self-confirming spiral, involving inadequate training, leading to poor-quality survey work, which in turn confirms critiques. The way out of this is to produce good-quality survey work, conducted by social researchers who are reflexively aware of both the limitations and the strengths of the method.

A helpful way to understand the range of social survey work in academic locations is to divide it into two types of survey: **descriptive** and **explanatory**. Descriptive social surveys are characteristic of an important strand of British sociology, represented in the work of the Institute of Community Studies (ICS) founded in the 1950s. Rather like the Chicago school ethnographers (see Chapters 3 and 17) who supplied descriptive accounts of urban social settings, researchers used the social survey to give accounts of such topics as family and kinship in east London (Young and Willmott, 1957), widowhood (Marris, 1958) and the experience of social mobility (Jackson and Marsden, 1962). An offshoot of the ICS, the Institute for Social Studies in Medical Care (ISSMC), applied the descriptive survey approach to a variety of topics in health care (for example Cartwright, 1964). This tradition is characterized by the use of both quantitative and qualitative data, so that the broad picture shown by the statistical tables is supported by the selection of quotations taken from interviews, so as to provide numbers with a 'human face'. The descriptive tradition, which is basically empiricist in its assumptions, continues to the present day, for example in studies of death and dying (Cartwright and Seale, 1990; Seale and Cartwright, 1994; Young and Cullen, 1996).

Explanatory social surveys attempt the more ambitious task of explaining why events occur, and they do this by looking for *causal relationships* (see earlier). Methods for doing this are explained in Chapter 14. They developed initially in the work of social scientists in the USA, shown most characteristically by Hyman (1955), Lazarsfeld and Rosenberg (1955) and Rosenberg (1968). The purpose of this type of analysis is to show how a variety of *phenomena* are determined by features of *social structure* (see Chapter 9). Classically, this was shown by Durkheim's analysis of the causes of suicide (see Chapter 2). An example from the American tradition is Hirschi and Selvin's (1967) attempt to discover the causes of 'juvenile delinquency', a phenomenon which they felt might be caused by a variety of social structural factors.

Explanatory data analysis of social survey data rests on the empiricist assumption that facts exist independently of theories. Theories exist to provide propositions and *hypotheses* (see Chapter 9) which are then confirmed or refuted by the facts. This is, of course, the language of natural science, and is associated with the positivist enterprise of discovering regularities and laws underlying the dynamics of society, and determining variation in social phenomena.

In Chapter 3 you encountered the interactionist critique of the over-deterministic model of human social action that this type of analysis involves. Researchers who prefer qualitative research in 'natural' settings, rather than the 'artificial' setting of the survey interview, prioritize the investigation of how people actively *constitute* phenomena (such as suicide, or delinquency) in their everyday interactions. On the other hand, it has proved possible to generate causal analyses from social survey data that have greater adequacy at the level of meaning, exemplified in the work of Brown and Harris (1978) on the social origins of depression. This work is discussed in Marsh (1982) and also in Chapter 12 of this book.

Finally, the feminist critique of positivism and the scientific method as *androcentric* developed in relation to the social survey from the early 1970s. This is seen most powerfully in the feminist critique of the structured interview (see Oakley, 1981 or Finch, 1984) which is discussed further in Chapter 16. But, as explained in Chapters 2 and 4, elements of the feminist critique of science have been more profound than this, pointing out the political implications of supposed 'value neutrality' and describing the stance of 'objectivity' as oppressive to women. More recently, though, feminist stances towards the quantitative social survey have been modified in the light of political expediencies, so that it is claimed that social statistics, and indeed the experimental method (albeit with appropriate ethical safeguards) in social research, can provide a powerful source of facts and figures in the pursuit of feminist political objectives (Jayaratne, 1983; Oakley, 1989).

CRITICAL PERSPECTIVES: THE POLITICS OF SOCIAL SURVEYS

Within contemporary social research, then, both the techniques and the value of quantitative approaches have been put into serious question. These criticisms have been directed on the one hand at the methodological claims of surveys and social statistics – in terms of their representativeness, their validity as a reflection of a complex social reality and the analytic usefulness of 'head counting'. On the other, the politics of quantitative social research have been challenged in relation to the latter's assumed neutrality, its treatment of people as 'just numbers', and its tendency to impose categories of meaning on aspects of social experience (for a discussion of these related problems of 'method' and 'epistemology' in relation to survey research, see Marsh, 1984). You will recall from Chapter 4 that this was Ramazanoglu's criticism of her own early social survey work.

An important strand of these critical challenges has involved a reappraisal of the historical tradition of survey research (Kent, 1981). A central argument here is that the kinds of investigation carried out by statistical societies, government inquiries and individual social explorers did much to 'make up' an image of society which reinforced the moral norms and political wisdom of their time, rather than to produce direct or value-free knowledge about the anatomy of modern society (see also Hacking, 1990).

These arguments are compelling, but are not entirely new. Accusing Victorian social surveyors of being involved in politics hardly constitutes a radical challenge; the various institutional bodies and individual researchers were self-consciously engaged in producing knowledge which would inform public debate and policy. The social survey developed throughout the nineteenth century from a research perspective which held that the application of scientific method to the study of society could provide a basis for rational social reform. What remains in question is how clearly survey findings can provide directives for political action. Research into poverty, for example, was undertaken and taken up by political conservatives, reformers and radicals alike. The accounts provided by a radical such as Engels, a conservative such as Booth and a reformer such as Rowntree suggest rather different solutions to the problem of poverty.

Booth's studies, for example, confirmed him in his belief in individualism and minimal government measures to ameliorate social conditions, although he also favoured the removal of the poorest classes of society – whose lives 'were in every way wasteful' (Kent, 1981: 59) – to industrial camps or, at worst, poorhouses. Rowntree, while inspired by Booth's methods, was a firm supporter of welfare measures and a public system of social security. These conclusions circulated within a larger set of social and political debates, which themselves shaped competing research agendas. Rowntree's 1951 study suggested that primary working-class poverty in post-war society had decreased to an almost insignificant level, and was in its turn challenged by the revival of the 'poverty debate' in the 1960s, galvanized by Abel-Smith and Townsend's (1965) research into *The Poor and the Poorest* in the 'affluent society' of late twentieth century Britain.

While survey research has clearly been linked to wider political debates, it might also be thought about in terms of the politics of social research itself. We have seen the way in which many Victorian surveys drew on and re-inforced aspects of a rather conservative social morality in using such explanatory categories as idleness or improvidence. It took some time for social investigators to accept the proposition that the practice of measure-ment itself tends to alter the thing that is being measured. Rowntree is a notable exception here in being profoundly aware of the static nature of statistical representation. A key argument within his original study was that there existed a 'life cycle' of poverty, such that those individuals and families he identified as living in primary poverty were not simply stuck in a mono-lithic underclass. Rather, Rowntree argued that there were certain life and work stages – what he called 'poverty periods' – which were more likely to produce conditions of primary poverty. Childhood and old age were the most severe periods of poverty in the life cycle of the labourer, while work-ing-class women frequently lived in primary poverty throughout the time that they were raising children. Such findings are strikingly in tune with established analyses of poverty current today.

The reappraisal of a historical tradition of survey research can provide valuable resources for thinking about the politics and methods of con-temporary social research. This is not simply a question of understanding where our research traditions have come from – although this is a critical issue – but is also one of examining the claims and the internal critiques made by earlier social researchers. While certain methods and moralities may seem rather unsophisticated to the contemporary reader, the enduring commitment of social researchers to producing useful knowledge about their society, as well as to processes of social and economic reform, suggest important guides for interrogating the aims and the certainties of current social research.

Further reading

Moser and Kalton (1971: Chapter 1) provide a clear introduction to the history of the social survey in Britain, and an overview of the various uses of survey methods. Abrams (1968) includes a useful introductory essay, together with primary extracts from social researchers including Rowntree and Bowley. Kent (1981) provides an extremely readable and comprehensive history of empirical social research (with a strong focus on quantitative methods), from the eighteenth century to the 1970s. Hacking (1990) is a fascinating critical account of the history of the social survey, using a range of examples from the fields of health, crime, and so on.

7

Historical and comparative research

Josep Llobera

CONTENTS

> The apparent strangeness and distance of the past enable one to discern features there that are camouflaged in the present by the very taken-for-grantedness of everyday experience. (Wright and Treacher, 1982: 2)

Exposing the processes that underlie the apparently fixed, objective structures and social relationships through which we lead our lives is one of the key tasks for contemporary social and cultural researchers. In this chapter it is argued that the **historical method**, whereby researchers examine the past in order to understand the present, and the **comparative method**, whereby researchers compare people's experiences of different types of society, are key methods for achieving this.

It is my view that these approaches involve bringing together academic disciplines that have suffered from a degree of separation in the recent past. C. Wright Mills wrote of sociology that 'All sociology worthy of the name is historical sociology' and added that 'the historical viewpoint leads to the comparative study of societies' (1959: 162, 167–8). In historical and comparative research, it is not only sociologists that benefit, but anthropologists and historians too, since the methods incorporate the perspectives, and can potentially solve some of the problems, that researchers from each of these disciplines have pursued.

I will show how this is done by, firstly, explaining in more detail the rationale for such an approach. The chapter will then review a number of historical and comparative studies which have exposed the processes that lie behind present-day social and psychological experience. Here, I will consider studies that work at both the **macro** and the **micro** levels. That is to say, I will consider large-scale phenomena, such as the role of revolutions and class struggle in explaining the rise of modern capitalism, as well as small-scale phenomena at the level of individual experience. At this latter, micro-level, I will focus in particular on the historical and comparative study of manners and decorum.

The chapter also shows how a variety of *conceptual frameworks* have been proposed and can be used by researchers working in this tradition, incidentally showing once again (see Chapter 2) tensions in the application of methods derived from natural science to social and cultural research. Finally, the issue of gaining *breadth* through the statistical study of large numbers of cases, versus *depth* through the intensive analysis of a few cases, is a tension of which you need to be aware in doing this type of research study.

RATIONALE

Let us now consider some of the reasons that justify comparative and historical research. Firstly, one can say that the past is in the present. Human cultures, whether modern or traditional, European or non-European, rely heavily on references to the past to justify the present. Thus, for example, the American constitution, the British monarchy, the parliamentary system, and so on are often explained by reference to a historical tradition. We are all the product of previous generations, not only biologically but also culturally.

Secondly, the use of history helps us to explain the origins and development of specific social phenomena, which otherwise would appear as universal and atemporal, and hence necessary. This is the point made by Wright and Treacher at the head of this chapter. Another way of saying this is that social research can help to **denaturalize** social phenomena: in this way they can cease to seem natural, inevitably fixed essences. Most social phenomena are in fact specific to a certain time and a certain place. For example, capitalism is a particular way of organizing society which appeared in Western Europe in the Middle Ages and developed between the sixteenth and eighteenth centuries, and later expanded, through the Industrial Revolution, all over the world. Historical and comparative research teaches us that capitalism, as a social system, does not derive from certain characteristics of human nature but stems from a historically specific combination of material, economic and social circumstances. This perspective frees us to imagine that it need not exist forever.

A third reason for doing historical and comparative research is that the academic disciplines within which social and cultural researchers often locate themselves, such as anthropology, history or sociology, emerged in a rather small corner of the world and at a particular stage of its development, although they often aspire to universalistic types of explanation. Many social theories are presented as if the generalizations that they embody are valid for all times and places, when in fact they were arrived at on the basis of limited contemporary Western experience. For example, grief, an emotion which is often regarded as driven by universal biological necessities in Western psychological theories, is revealed by comparative and historical research to be a far more variable and socially constructed phenomenon (Rosenblatt et al., 1976).

Fourthly, it can be argued that the only way of knowing where we are going is by knowing where we come from. Historical comparisons can tell us the likely effects of social action, the price we may have to pay to achieve certain social objectives. For example, it would be foolish for any radical social reformer to ignore the historical experiences of the Soviet Union or China or other such societies which have tried to construct socialism.

USING HISTORICAL AND COMPARATIVE METHODS

Social researchers taking these approaches vary in the extent to which they seek out original or primary data about the phenomena they seek to explain. Interviewing people directly, observing them, or analysing the documents they produce in going about their lives, perhaps in a historical *archive* of such documents, is sometimes known as the examination of **primary sources**. Thus, chronicles, diaries, official records, letters are often used by historians, who may find them in private collections, or lying unclassified in town, provincial, regional or state archives. Anthropologists, who commonly use ethnographic methods such as participant observation (see Chapter 17), engage in comparative, cross-cultural studies when they wish to generalize.

But there are also extensive possibilities in the use of **secondary sources** by researchers in this field. Most commonly this involves reviewing and synthesizing a range of research reports each describing a single but different society, whose authors had themselves built their descriptions on primary sources. In building theories on the descriptive, empirical research of others, the researcher is able to give any resultant explanatory theories a greater scope and relevance, while economizing on his or her own effort.

Additionally, in doing historical work researchers vary in the period over which their studies range, and this is to some extent determined by the topic. The time dimension required when dealing with individuals and primary groups such as nuclear families or work groups will be rather short, possibly the life-span of the individual or of the group. However, if researchers are concerned with more complex associations such as government bureaucracies, a medium-term perspective will be necessary. State institutions may require to consider an even longer period. Finally, some questions about national societies like England and France may find an appropriate reply only from a very long-term perspective (hundreds of years).

As well as using both primary and secondary sources, the approach can involve both quantitative, statistical data and qualitative material. A statistical approach to historical research was taken by Wrigley and Schofield (1989) in their study of demographic changes between 1541 and 1871. They used the records of English parish registers to present data showing fluctuations and an eventual rise in life expectancy over the years. They present data on average wage levels during the period to demonstrate that such economic conditions were not related to changes in life expectancy. However, their data are used to show that, as Malthus (see Chapter 6) predicted, until the 1750s the population size increased when wages were high and people felt more secure in having children, but then declined as wages dropped. From the 1750s, though, this Malthusian system of checks and balances closed, as the population increased without apparent influence by wage levels. This was due to increased efficiency in agricultural production, such that food became more easily available for the growing population.

A qualitative approach was taken by Norbert Elias (1978) who analysed extracts from European books on manners to show how social norms had changed over the years. Some of these extracts are shown below, with dates of authorship:

Thirteenth century	'When you blow your nose or cough, turn around so that nothing falls on the table'.
1558	'It does not befit a modest, honourable man to prepare to relieve nature in the presence of other people ... Similarly, he will not wash his hands on returning to decent society from private places, as the reason for his washing will arouse disagreeable thoughts in people.'
1560	'It is a far too dirty thing for a child to offer others something he has gnawed, or something he disdains to eat himself, unless it be to his servant ... he must not lift the meat to his mouth now with one hand and now with the other ... he should always do so with his right hand, taking the bread or meat decently with three fingers only.'
1672	'If everyone is eating from the same dish, you should take care not to put your hand in it before those of higher rank do so.'
1714	'Wherever you spit, you should put your foot on the saliva ... At the houses of the great, one spits into one's handkerchief.'
1859	'Spitting is at all times a disgusting habit, I need say nothing more than – never indulge in it. Beside being coarse and atrocious, it is very bad for the health.'

(from books on manners, quoted in Elias, 1978: 91, 92, 131, 143, 154, 156)

All except the first and last of these extracts describe behaviour that today would be considered abnormal, marking out a person as socially inferior, blameworthy and in need of correction. Yet they are presented as models of good behaviour. Elias describes how many aspects of 'manners' have changed, covering, in addition to the matters outlined above, attitudes to public nakedness, to sleeping in the same bed and towards defecating in the view of others, the use of forks and taboos on the use of knives at table. Changes in all of these, he argues, have been in the direction of increased propensity to feelings of shame and disgust. To explain this Elias uses the concept of *sociogenesis* to summarize his belief that these mass psychological changes are social in origin, rather than the product of some innate change in human nature. Thus he links the civilizing process to the growing complexity of modern society compared with feudal medieval societies.

In the past, for example, power was gained and defended by force of arms, and there were no very powerful sources of central authority. As these developed, however, social advancement came increasingly to depend on skills of diplomacy and the calculation of likely consequences of actions, involving intensive study of others' feelings and prediction of their likely reactions. Whereas in the past, other people could be simply divided into enemies and friends, now all people were, potentially, both. Interpersonal relationships thus became vastly more complex. Cults of refined sensibility, which arose at first in courtly society, spread gradually to other social groups in the towns, resulting today in a degree of social stratification of manners which now indicate class distinctions.

THE DEVELOPMENT OF HISTORICAL SOCIAL RESEARCH

The origins of contemporary social science lie in the work of eighteenth century Enlightenment thinkers, who believed that it was possible to discover the laws that governed social life, just as natural scientists were discovering those that determined natural and biological events (see also Chapter 3). Many such thinkers constructed their theories on the basis of historical comparisons. Thus Montesquieu's *Spirit of the Laws* (1748) was the first major text to claim that social life is subjected to laws. Many Enlightenment thinkers, influenced by Montesquieu, believed also that the development of different types of society could be best understood as **evolutionary** in their movement from one type to another over time.

The key concept which allowed the establishment of the social sciences on a solid foundation in the eighteenth century was that of **social totality**, that is, the idea that allows us to think of society as an interrelated whole consisting of different levels. This concept appeared in a framework which was *materialist* as well as evolutionary. Evolutionary theory claimed that history could best be explained by reference to a succession of stages. The scheme was also seen in terms of some kind of progress, say from rudeness to civilization. Materialist theories involved the idea that the economy and the environment play leading roles in determining (or conditioning) firstly the transition from one stage to another, and secondly the different levels of the social totality (in modern terminology these might be called the economic, political and ideological levels). Adam Smith (1723–90) presented a historical account along these lines, though in a sketchy form.

The views propounded by such thinkers, that is, the combination of the concept of social totality and the evolutionary and materialist theories, proved fruitful and accounted for the major developments in the social sciences in the nineteenth century. Thus the founders of nineteenth century social science – Comte and Spencer – made the idea of stages and laws of evolution central to their work. Comte proposed a 'law of three stages' in which he argued that societal evolution could be characterized as moving from an initial 'theological' stage, to a 'metaphysical' and then a 'positive' stage. Indeed, the name of this last stage signals Comte's involvement in founding **positivism** (see Chapter 3) as a philosophy of progress. Spencer, in an evolutionary theory that had strong parallels with Darwin's theory of the evolution of biological species, suggested that societies gradually moved, through a process of survival of the fittest, to the best possible form.

Evolutionism, however, gradually came to be discredited, and the enterprise of Comte and Spencer discussed as speculation. The metahistories propounded by the evolutionary schemes were thought to be insensitive to cultural differences, to be too Eurocentric, to encourage wild speculation and to fail to explain the transition from one stage to another. By the 1930s, with the influence of the functionalism of Malinowski and Radcliffe-Brown, and the emergence of Talcott Parsons's structural functionalism (see Chapter 3), evolutionism was pronounced dead and it became a term of abuse. In 1937, Parsons could start his book *The Structure of Social Action* with the famous rhetorical question: 'Who now reads Spencer?' In fact, evolutionism was not so much refuted, but merely abandoned.

At the institutional level the turn of the century coincided with the specialization of the social sciences, particularly with the constitution of sociology and anthropology as separate disciplines. This event, combined with the rejection of evolutionism, helped to shape a sociology uninterested in history and focused on modern or capitalist societies. Roughly speaking, while sociology concerned itself with Western societies, anthropology focused on non-Western ones, and history took as its object of study the chronology of past events. In any case, both sociology and anthropology dealt with timeless societies as their objects of study. Comparisons were also progressively abandoned.

This broad picture of decline, however, did not mean complete extinction. For example, Marxist scholars continued to pursue an interest in historical studies, and in the 1930s Norbert Elias pursued his own particular brand of historical sociology in his great study of *The Civilising Process* (originally published in German in 1939). Significantly, the study was not translated into English until 1978 (Volume 1) and 1982 (Volume 2), by which time there had been a revival of interest in historical and comparative methods.

It is difficult to pinpoint a single reason that accounts for the renaissance of historical sociology after 1960, but it is likely that concern to explain the reasons for the underdevelopment of the Third World were in part responsible, and led to more comparative and historical analyses. Evolutionary theory became fashionable again in anthropology and sociology. Even Parsons revived nineteenth century evolutionary approaches in the light of his own theoretical developments. In 1966 he published *Societies: Evolutionary and Comparative Perspectives*, in which he put forward three main stages of the evolution of society: primitive, intermediate and modern. Finally, the classical tradition (Durkheim, Marx and Weber) was once again read in the light of its contributions to the historical and comparative method.

CONCEPTUAL FRAMEWORKS

A number of conceptual frameworks have been proposed to guide historical and comparative research. To introduce these it is appropriate to take a little time explaining what is meant by the **experimental method** in social research, since one rationale for historical and comparative research is to understand it as the investigation of **natural experiments**.

The experimental method is commonly found in the natural science laboratory, where the experimenter attempts to determine the causal effects of a single factor upon some outcome. Thus, in evaluating the effects of a new drug in curing a disease, a biomedical experimenter may give one group of people (or laboratory animals) the new drug, and another group some dummy pill with an inactive substance. If the group receiving the experimental drug improves, the drug is said to be effective. The important point to note about laboratory experiments is that the researcher *controls* conditions, so that the only factor which varies between the groups is the presence of the proposed causal factor. Thus the dummy pill controls for the fact that people sometimes recover from disease because of the psychological effect of being treated, rather than the chemical effect of a drug. Both groups are therefore kept similar in this respect: all believe that they are receiving treatment. Psychological effects are therefore ruled out when explaining why those receiving the active substance recovered. (Chapter 14 contains a fuller discussion of experimental logic in social research.)

In social research, artificial manipulation of causal factors is usually impossible. Conceptual frameworks for historical and comparative research often draw on the idea that history and comparison often supply the researcher with a natural experiment. This can be seen in the application by researchers of the ideas of the nineteenth century philosopher John Stuart Mill (1806–73) who proposed five 'methods of experimental inquiry'. These are as follows:

Method of agreement	'If two or more instances of the phenomenon under investigation have only one circumstance

	in common, the circumstance in which alone all the instances agree is the cause (or effect) of the given phenomenon' (Mill, 1973: 390).
Method of difference	'If an instance in which the phenomenon under investigation occurs, and an instance in which it does not occur, have every circumstance in common save one, that one occurring only in the former; the circumstance in which alone the two instances differ is the effect, or the cause, or an indispensable part of the cause, of the phenomenon' (1973: 391).
Joint method of agreement and difference	'If two or more instances in which the phenomenon occurs have only one circumstance in common, while two or more instances in which it does not occur have nothing in common save the absence of that circumstance, the circumstance in which alone the two sets of instances differ is the effect, or the cause, or an indispensable part of the cause, of the phenomenon' (1973: 396).
Method of residues	'Subduct [subtract] from any phenomenon such part as is known by previous inductions to be the effect of certain antecedents, and the residue of the phenomenon is the effect of the remaining antecedents' (1973: 398).
Method of concomitant variations	'Whatever phenomenon varies in any manner whenever another phenomenon varies in some particular manner, is either a cause or an effect of that phenomenon, or is connected with it through some fact of causation' (1973: 401).

Although Mill himself felt that such approaches were likely to be inconclusive in the social sciences, later researchers have found them helpful, particularly the first two. In his seminal book *The Comparative Method*, Ragin states that 'most discussions of case-oriented methods begin (and often end) with John Stuart Mill's presentation of experimental inquiry in *A System of Logic*' (1987: 36).

The method of agreement is very popular in the social sciences. The task of the research is to eliminate possible causes of a phenomenon by showing instances in which, although the outcome is present, all the hypothesized antecedents but one are not. This cause would be considered the crucial one. Of course, there is always the danger that there might be a hidden cause which the comparison has missed. In the method of difference a contrast is established between two sets of cases: the first in which both cause and effect are present; the second in which both cause and effect are absent, although other circumstances would be similar. Both Mill and modern researchers agree that the latter method is more powerful and reliable than the former one.

Ragin (1987: 36–9) mentions the example of peasant revolts as a fertile area for the method of agreement. In the literature on this topic we can find a number of potential causes for peasant revolts: a powerful middle peasantry, a landless peasantry, quick agricultural commercialization, and traditionalism. Let us assume that all these four antecedents appear in a given case study. It is the task of the investigator to find other cases of peasant revolt in which one or more of the antecedents are absent. If the researcher is successful in finding cases in which peasant revolts are present, but say traditionalism, a powerful middle peasantry and a landless peasantry are absent, then the only cause left – rapid commercialization of agriculture – is the determining one. Following the same example, with the method of difference we would first establish a series of instances of peasant societies in which revolts had occurred and see that they did correlate with the antecedent of rapid commercialization of agriculture. In a second move we would look at peasant societies in which both the effect and the cause were absent, that is, neither peasant revolts nor rapid commercialization of agriculture existed. This double demonstration would strongly support the initial hypothesis that the cause of peasant revolts is the rapid commercialization of agriculture.

In all this, the degree of control over variables available to researchers is minimal, but diligent teasing out of explanatory factors, and threats to these explanations, followed by further work to evaluate these threats, are the hallmarks of good research of this type. You will find in Chapter 14 that there is a similar search for causal factors in statistical reasoning using survey data.

CONCLUSION

This chapter has reviewed the rationale for historical and comparative research, taking the view that such a perspective is often valuable in understanding what lies behind the everyday social experience, the social structures and cultural institutions that dominate modern life. Such work is useful in addressing problems at both the macro and micro levels. While some such work may involve going directly to primary sources, it is often more economical, and generates theory of potentially wider scope, to use secondary sources. Both qualitative and quantitative data can be usefully analysed.

In the section on conceptual frameworks the ideas of Mill were outlined, and their usefulness in later research was demonstrated. This by no means exhausts the range of conceptual frameworks available to researchers, some of which can be followed up in the suggestions for further reading that follow.

Further reading

Tilly (1984) attempts to systematize the different comparative and historical approaches used by social scientists. Abrams (1982) shows how the classical sociologists (Marx, Durkheim and Weber) used the historical and comparative method. Ragin (1987) is a very important book, outlining a variety of conceptual schemata available for researchers using this method.

Part II

BEGINNING RESEARCH

8

Research and social policy

David Silverman

CONTENTS

In my experience, researchers at the beginning of projects often make two basic errors. Firstly, they fail to distinguish sufficiently between research problems and problems that are discussed in the world around us. The latter kind of problems, which I shall call **social problems**, are at the heart of political debates and fill the more serious newspapers. They are often the focus of social policies and researchers may find themselves commissioned by policy makers to address such problems in their research. However, I will be arguing that although social problems, like unemployment, homelessness and racism, are important, by themselves they cannot provide a researchable topic.

The second error to which I have referred is sometimes related to the first. It arises where researchers take on an impossibly large research problem. For instance, it is important to find the causes of a social problem like homelessness, but such a problem is beyond the scope of a single researcher with limited time and resources. Moreover, by defining the problem so widely, one is usually unable to say anything at great depth about it. It is often helpful instead to aim to say a lot about a little problem. This means avoiding the temptation to say a little about a lot. Indeed, the latter path can be something of a 'cop-out'. Precisely because the topic is so wide-ranging, one can flit from one aspect to another without being forced to refine and test each piece of analysis.

In the first section of this chapter, I shall focus on the first of these errors – the tendency to choose social problems as research topics. However, in recommending solutions to this error, I shall imply how one can narrow down a research topic and thus deal with the second error. The second section of the chapter will consider a variety of roles that can be adopted by social researchers in relation to policy makers. Lastly, the chapter will illustrate some of these issues by describing my research in health care settings.

WHAT IS A PROBLEM?

One has only to open a newspaper or to watch the TV news to be confronted by a host of social problems. In the mid 1990s, the British news media were full of references to a 'wave' of crimes committed by children – from the theft of cars to the murder of old people and other children. There were also several stories about how doctors infected by HIV continued to work and, by implication, endangered their patients. The stories had this in common: they assumed some sort of moral decline in which families or schools failed to discipline children and in which physicians failed to take seriously their professional responsibilities. In turn, the way each story was told implied a solution: tightening up discipline in order to combat the presumed moral decline.

However, before we can consider such a cure, we need to consider carefully the diagnosis. Had juvenile crime increased or was the apparent increase a reflection of what counts as a good story? Alternatively, might the increase have been an artefact of what crimes get reported? Again, how many health care professionals actually infected their patients with HIV? I know of only one (disputed) case – a Florida dentist. Conversely, there is considerable evidence of patients infecting the medical staff who treat them. Moreover, why focus on HIV when other conditions like hepatitis B are far more infectious? Could it be that we hear so much about HIV because it is associated with stigmatized groups?

Apparent social problems are not the only topics that may clamour for the attention of the researcher. Administrators and managers point to 'problems' in their organizations and may turn to social scientists for solutions. It is tempting to allow such people to define a research problem – particularly as there is usually a fat research grant attached to it! However, we must first look at the terms which are being used to define the problem.

Let us imagine that a manager defines problems in their organization as problems of 'communication'. The role of the researcher is then to work out how people can communicate 'better'. Unfortunately, talking about communication problems raises many difficulties. For instance, it may assume that the solution to any problem is more careful listening, while ignoring power relations present inside and outside patterns of communication. Such relations may also make the characterization of 'organizational efficiency' very problematic. Thus administrative problems give no more secure basis for social research than do social problems. Of course, this is not to deny that there are real problems in society. However, even if we agree about what these problems are, it is not clear that they provide a researchable topic.

Take the case of the problems of people infected with HIV. Some of these problems are, quite rightly, brought to the attention of the public by the organized activities of groups of people who carry the infection. But social researchers should try to contribute the particular theoretical and methodological skills of their discipline, giving an initial research topic their own theoretical and methodological 'twist'. So economists can research how limited health care resources can be used most effectively in coping with the epidemic in the West and in the Third World. Among sociologists, survey researchers can investigate patterns of sexual behaviour in order to try to promote effective health education, while qualitative methods may be used to study what is involved in the 'negotiation' of safer sex or in counselling people about HIV and AIDS. For instance, in my research on HIV counselling (Silverman, 1996), I used tape recordings and detailed transcripts, as well as many technical concepts derived from my interest in conversation analysis (see Chapter 20).

It is therefore usually necessary to refuse to allow our research topics to be totally defined in terms of the conceptions of social problems as recognized by either professional or community groups. Ironically, by beginning from a clearly defined social science perspective, we can later address such social problems with, I believe, considerable force and persuasiveness. I shall seek to show this later in the chapter.

SENSITIVITY AND RESEARCHABLE PROBLEMS

I have been arguing that it is often unhelpful for researchers to begin their work on the basis of a social problem identified by either practitioners or managers. It is a commonplace that such definitions of problems often may serve vested interests. My point, however, is that if social science research has anything to offer, its theoretical imperatives drive it in a direction which can offer practitioners, managers and policy makers *new* perspectives on their problems. Paradoxically, by refusing to begin from a common conception of what is 'wrong' in a setting, we may be most able to contribute to the identification both of what is going on and, thereby, how it may be modified in the pursuit of desired ends. The various perspectives of social science provide a sensitivity to many issues neglected by those who define social or administrative problems. I will discuss three types of sensitivity in turn: historical, political and contextual.

Historical sensitivity

Wherever possible, one should establish **historical sensitivity** by examining the relevant historical evidence when we are setting up a topic to research. This is a point dealt with at greater length in Chapter 7, which outlined the uses of historical and comparative methods in social and cultural research. For instance, in the 1950s and 1960s it was assumed that the *nuclear family* (parents and children) had replaced the *extended family* (many generations living together in the same household) of pre-industrial societies. Research-ers simply seemed to have forgotten that lower life expectancy may have made the extended family pattern relatively rare in the past, and historical research has broadly confirmed that this was so (Laslett, 1979).

Again, historical sensitivity helps us to understand how we are governed. For instance, until the eighteenth century, the majority of the population were treated as a threatening mob to be controlled, where necessary, by the use of force. Today, we are seen as individuals with 'needs' and 'rights' which must be understood and protected by society (see Foucault, 1977). But, although oppressive force may be used only rarely, we may be con-trolled in more subtle ways. Think of the knowledge about each of us con-tained in computerized data banks and the pervasive video-cameras which record movements in many city streets. Historical sensitivity thus offers us multiple research topics which evade the trap of thinking that present-day versions of social problems are unproblematic.

Political sensitivity

Allowing the current media scares to determine our research topics is just as fallible as designing research in accordance with administrative or man-agerial interests. In neither case do we use **political sensitivity** to detect the vested interests behind this way of formulating a problem. The media, after all, need to attract an audience just as administrators need to be seen to be working efficiently.

So political sensitivity seeks to grasp the politics behind defining topics in particular ways. In turn, it helps in suggesting that we research how social problems arise. For instance, Barbara Nelson (1984) looked at how 'child abuse' became defined as a recognizable problem in the late 1960s. She shows how the findings of a doctor about the 'battered baby syndrome' were adopted by the conservative Nixon administration through linking social problems to parental 'maladjustment' rather than to the failures of social programmes. Political sensitivity does not mean that social scientists argue that there are no real problems in society. Instead, it suggests that social science can make an important contribution to society by querying how official definitions of problems arise. To be truthful, however, we should also recognize how social scientists often need to accept tacitly such definitions in order to attract research grants.

Contextual sensitivity

This is the least self-explanatory and most contentious category in the present list. By **contextual sensitivity**, I mean the recognition that apparently uniform institutions like 'the family', 'a tribe' or 'science' take on a variety of meanings in different contexts. This is linked to the idea of **anti-essentialism** discussed in Chapter 5, where you saw how Fortier, in her fieldwork with Italians in London, became interested in how gender and ethnic identities were negotiated in particular settings or contexts. Far from being fixed *essences*, determined perhaps by some unchangeable biological or cultural heritage, Fortier argued that these are in fact quite changeable, depending on the social context in which they are invoked. Thus gender and ethnicity can be understood as *social constructions.*

Contextual sensitivity is reflected most obviously in Moerman's (1974) study of the Lue tribe in Thailand. (This study will be discussed again in more depth in Chapter 9.) Moerman began with the anthropologist's conventional appetite to locate a people in a classificatory scheme. To satisfy this appetite, he started to ask tribespeople questions like 'How do you recognize a member of your tribe?' He reports that his respondents quickly became adept at providing a whole list of *traits* which constituted their tribe and distinguished them from their neighbours. For example, they claimed that the use of mattresses and blankets, the possession of a village 'spirit house', and the singing of particular types of folk song made them different from their neighbours, the Yuan. On the other hand they said they shared certain traits with the Yuan, such as the use of pillows. But Moerman began to feel that such a list was, in purely logical terms, endless. Perhaps if you wanted to understand this people, it was not particularly useful to elicit an abstract account of their characteristics, which Moerman called **ethnic identification devices.**

So Moerman stopped asking 'Who are the Lue?' He came to believe that ethnic identification devices were not used all the time by these people any more than we use them to refer to ourselves in a Western culture. Instead, Moerman started to examine what went on in everyday situations. Looked at this way, the issue was no longer who the Lue essentially were but when, among people living in these Thai villages, ethnic identification labels were used and the consequences of invoking them. For example, a common cause for their display was the presence of strange, Western anthropologists asking the people to identify themselves! Curiously enough, Moerman concluded that, when you looked at the matter this way, the apparent differences between the Lue and ourselves were considerably reduced. Only an ethnocentric Westerner might have assumed otherwise, behaving like a tourist craving for out-of-the-way sights.

But it is not only such large-scale collectivities as tribes that are looked at afresh when we use what I have called contextual sensitivity. Other apparently stable social institutions (like the family) and identities (gender, ethnicity and so on) may be insufficiently questioned from a social problem perspective. For instance, commentators says things like 'the family is under threat'. But where are we to find the unitary form of family assumed in such commentary? And doesn't 'the family' look different in contexts ranging from the household, to the law courts or even the supermarket? Rather than take such arguments at face value, the researcher must make use of contextual sensitivity to discover how things actually operate in a social world where, as Moerman shows us, people's practices are inevitably more complex than they might seem.

One final point: the three kinds of sensitivity we have been considering offer different, sometimes contradictory, ways of generating research topics. I am not suggesting that *all* should be used at the beginning of any research study. However, if we are not sensitive to *any* of these issues, then we run the danger of lapsing into a 'social problem' based way of defining our research topics.

WHAT IS THE SOCIAL SCIENTIST'S ROLE?

Even if we accept the argument above, we are still no clearer about the purpose of social science. To what ends are we attempting to be sensitive? The American sociologist Howard Becker puts this question very starkly: 'The question is not whether we should take sides, since we inevitably will, but rather whose side are we on?' (1967: 239). Not all social researchers would agree with Becker's call for moral or political partisanship. Perhaps responding to state apparatuses which are at best suspicious of the purposes of social science, many would go on the defensive. They might find it easier or more acceptable to argue that their concern is simply with the establishment of facts through the judicious testing of competing hypotheses and theories. Their only slogan, they would say, is the pursuit of knowledge. They would claim to reject political partisanship, at least in their academic work; they are only, they would say, partisans for truth.

I am not, for the moment, concerned to make a detailed assessment of either Becker's statement or the defensive response to it which I have just depicted. I believe both contain dangerous simplifications. As I shall later show, the partisans for truth are mistaken about the purity of knowledge, while Becker's rhetoric of 'sides' is often associated with a style of research which is unable to discover anything because of its prior commitment to a revealed truth (the plight of the underdog, the inevitable course of human history and so on). Curiously, both positions can be elitist, establishing themselves apart from and above the people they study.

For the moment, however, I want to stress a more positive feature of both arguments. Both recognize that no simply neutral or value-free position is possible in social research (or, indeed, elsewhere). The partisans for truth, just as much as the partisans of the 'underdog', are committed to an absolute value for which there can be no purely factual foundation. As Weber (1946; 1949) pointed out in the early years of this century, all research is contaminated to some extent by the values of the researcher. Only through those values do certain problems get identified and studied in particular ways. Even the commitment to scientific (or rigorous) method is itself, as Weber emphasizes, a value. Finally, the conclusions and implications to be drawn from a study are, Weber stresses, largely grounded in the moral and political beliefs of the researcher.

Using Weber's ideas, I develop below the position of the partisans for truth. To simplify, I refer to this as the position of the *scholar*. I retain the term *partisan* for those who claim their primary allegiance is to purely moral or political positions.

The scholar

In his two famous lectures, 'Science as a vocation' and 'Politics as a vocation' (Weber, 1946), Weber enunciated basic liberal principles to a student audience in 1917. Despite the patriotic fervour of the First World War, he insisted on the primacy of the individual's own conscience as a basis for action. Taking the classic Kantian position (see Chapter 3), he argued that values could not be derived from facts. However, this was not because values were less important than facts. Rather, precisely because 'ultimate evaluations' (or value choices) were so important, they were not to be reduced to purely factual judgements. The facts could tell you only about the likely consequences of given actions but they could not tell you which action to choose. For Weber, the very commitment to science was an example of an ultimate evaluation, exemplifying a personal belief in standards of logic and rationality and in the value of factual knowledge. Ironically echoing certain aspects of the 'Protestant ethic' whose historical emergence he himself had traced (see Chapter 3), Weber appealed to the scholar's conscience as the sole basis for conferring meaning and significance upon events.

Weber's appeal to Protestantism's and liberalism's 'free individual' is fully shared, 50 years on, by Norman Denzin. Denzin (1970) rejects any fixed moral standards as the basis for research. For example, it is sometimes argued that it is wrong for social researchers to observe people secretly. Denzin does not agree. Nor is he prepared to recognize that research must necessarily contribute to society's own self-understanding. Both standards are, for him, examples of 'ethical absolutism' which fail to respect the scholar's appeal to his own conscience in the varying contexts of research. Denzin's stand is distinctively liberal and individualist: 'One mandate governs sociological activity – the absolute freedom to pursue one's activities as one sees fit' (1970: 332). What 'one sees fit' will take into account that no method of sociological research is intrinsically any more unethical than any other. Citing Goffman, Denzin argues that, since the researcher always wears some mask, covert observation is merely one mask among others.

Denzin does suggest that the pursuit of research in terms of one's own standards should have certain safeguards. For instance, subjects should, wherever possible, be told of the researcher's own value judgements and biases, and should be warned about the kinds of interpretation the research may generate within the community. But he is insistent that the ultimate arbiter of proper conduct remains the conscience of the individual researcher.

Weber and Denzin's liberal position seems rather unrealistic. Curiously, as social scientists they fail to see the power of social organization as it shapes the practice of research. For while Denzin acknowledges the role of pressure groups, he remains silent about the privileged authority of the 'scientist' in society and about the deployment of scientific theories by agents of social control as mobilizing forms of power/knowledge.

The partisan

Unlike scholars, partisans do not shy away from their accountability to the world. Instead, the partisan seeks to provide the theoretical and factual resources for a political struggle aimed at transforming the assumptions through which both political and administrative games are played. In Silverman (1985), I used Howard Waitzkin's study of American medical consultations as an example of partisanship. Waitzkin has the laudable aim of relating 'the everyday micro-level interaction of individuals' to 'macro-level structures of domination' (1979: 601). For instance, when a doctor says 'good' after a patient has said he is now able to go back to work, Waitzkin argues that the doctor's comment reinforces a capitalist work ethic. Again, when a doctor's diagnosis appears to emphasize the mechanical workings of the body rather than the patient's personal experiences, Waitzkin once more interprets this in terms of the hidden hand of capitalism treating people simply as machines.

As Rayner and Stimson (1979) point out, Waitzkin's interpretation of such data depends upon a mechanistic version of Marxism which reduces the doctor–patient relationship simply to an ideological state apparatus of the capitalist state. Knowing what he is going to find, Waitzkin treats his data largely as illustrative of a preconceived theory. Two things never seem to strike him. Firstly, it is possible that what he finds is true but not necessarily caused by the factors in his theory. For instance, Strong (1979) suggests that doctors' use of the machine analogy in describing the body may be a feature of medical consultations in all industrialized social systems and not, as Waitzkin suggests, specific to capitalism. Secondly, he seems unaware that contrary evidence should be hunted down and followed up. For instance, Waitzkin notes – but makes nothing of – his own apparently contrary findings that women patients receive more information, while 'doctors from working-class backgrounds tend to communicate less information than doctors from upper-class backgrounds' (1979: 604).

Just as the partisan does not seek to be surprised by their data, he or she tends to be elitist in regard to political change. Not surprisingly, Waitzkin (1979: 608) seeks to encourage 'patient education' to invite the questioning of professional advice. At the same time, he makes nothing of patients' self-generated attempts to challenge professional dominance. Waitzkin illustrates some of the more unfortunate consequences of the researcher adopting the role of the partisan. In the same way as the Bible advises 'look and ye shall find', so partisans (Marxists, feminists, conservatives) often look and then find examples which can be used to support their theories.

We have seen, then, that neither the position of the partisan nor that of the scholar provides a satisfactory basis for social science. The partisan is often condemned to ignore features of the world which do not fit his or her preconceived moral or political position. The scholar goes too far in the other direction, wrongly denying that research has any kind of involvement with existing forms of social organization. Both positions are too extreme and thus fail to cope with the exigencies of the actual relationship between social researchers and society. The rest of this chapter is, therefore, devoted to describing a more pragmatic position which seeks to outline what social science can contribute to society.

SOCIAL SCIENCE'S CONTRIBUTION: A QUALITATIVE SOCIOLOGIST'S EXPERIENCE

For the past 20 years, I have conducted qualitative research in a range of health care settings from outpatient clinics to AIDS counselling sessions (see Silverman, 1987; 1996). In this section, I will explain two practical contributions of my research in hospital clinics, namely, the revelation of surprising facts and the possibilities for influencing health care practice.

Revealing surprising facts

Sometimes, in my own research, without any intellectual intent, I have revealed things opposed to what we might readily assume about how people behave. In work I was doing in a children's heart unit, in the early 1980s, we interviewed parents of children. Parents told us that one of the things that made their first outpatient consultations so difficult was that there were so many people in the room. This was a very serious occasion which, to many parents, would give their child a sentence of life or death. And it was confusing and intimidating, they said, because of the many doctors, nurses and sociologists present.

We found this quite convincing but used a problematic kind of measure to look at this further. We looked through our tape-recorded consultations where there were different numbers of people in the room and then we counted the number of questions asked by parents. Table 8.1 presents our findings. As you can see, our findings went against the common-sense expectation that the more people in the room, the fewer questions would be

Table 8.1 *Questions asked by parents by number of medical staff present*

	Number of consultations	Total questions	Average questions
1–4 medical staff	17	48	2.8
5+ medical staff	23	99	4.3

$p < 0.05$.

asked since the parents would have been, as they claimed, more intimidated. Based on its crude measures, Table 8.1 shows that, in our sample, parents asked more questions when there were five or more people in the room. I won't go into detail about what we made of this. But let me reassure you that we did not say that this meant that parents were wrong. On the contrary, there was evidence that parents were trying to behave responsibly and were appealing to the number of people present at the consultation as one way of depicting the pressures which they were under. The numbers present thus worked not as a *causal* factor in determining parents' behaviour but as something which could subsequently be used to rationalize their guilt at not asking as many questions as they would have liked.

We started to develop policy interventions in relationship to what the parents were telling us. For instance, how could a context be created where parents could display their responsibility to medical staff who, unlike researchers, could not visit them in their own homes? In due course, at our suggestion, the hospital created an additional clinic which was held some weeks after the first hospital interview. Here children were not examined and parents were free to interview doctors. The intervention was liked by both parents and doctors. Doctors liked it because it provided a good opportunity to get to know families before they were admitted to the ward. Parents said that they felt under less time pressure because their child did not need to be examined and because, in the weeks that had passed since their first hospital visit, they had had time to work out what they wanted to know. Moreover, many mothers commented that they felt that their children had benefited as well because, while their parents spoke to the doctor, they could spend time in the hospital children's play-room. Consequently, the hospital now seemed a less frightening place to these children. So this is an example of a situation in which sociological research, by discovering new facts, has come up with a practical solution to an everyday problem.

Another example of discovering new facts arose from my research on three cancer clinics (Silverman, 1984). In this research, I looked at the practice of a doctor in the British National Health Service and compared it with his private practice. This study was relevant to a lively debate about the British National Health Service and whether there should be more private medicine. I showed that the private clinic encouraged a more 'personalized' service and allowed patients to orchestrate their care, control the agenda, and obtain some 'territorial' control of the setting. However, despite these 'ceremonial' gains, in the 1980s the NHS provided cancer patients with quicker and more specialized treatment. So the cancer study serves as a example of how researchers can participate in debates about public policy.

Debating public policy

Returning to the two positions I outlined earlier, the scholar argues that research need never have any relation to public debates about social policy. By contrast, the partisan, while very interested in such debates, is likely to bring too many preconceptions to them. How have I tried to enter into such debates without limiting myself to the assumptions of either position? Let me take an example from the same heart unit which we have already discussed. At one point, we were looking at how doctors talked to parents about the decision to have a small diagnostic test on their children. In most cases, the doctor would say something like: 'What we propose to do, if you agree, is a small test.' No parent disagreed with an offer which appeared to be purely formal, like the formal right (never exercised) of the Queen not to sign legislation passed by the British Parliament. For a subsample of children, however, the parents' right to choose was far from formal. The doctor would say things to them like the following: 'I think what we would do now depends a little bit on parents' feelings'; 'Now it depends a little bit on what you think'; 'It depends very much on your own personal views as to whether we should proceed.' Moreover, these consultations were longer and apparently more democratic than elsewhere. A view of the patient in a family context was encouraged and parents were given every opportunity to voice their concerns and to participate in decision-making. In this subsample, unlike the larger sample, when given a real choice, parents almost always refused the test.

It turns out that this smaller sample was composed of Down's syndrome children, who had mental and physical disabilities in addition to their suspected heart disease. Moreover, the policy of the consultant at this unit was to discourage surgery, all things being equal, on such children. So the democratic form coexisted with (and was indeed sustained by) the maintenance of an autocratic policy.

The research thus discovered the mechanics whereby a particular medical policy was enacted. The availability of tape recordings of large numbers of consultations, together with a research method that sought to develop hypotheses *inductively* (see Chapter 2), meant that we were able to discover a phenomenon for which we had not originally been looking. More importantly, from the point of view of our present concerns, the research underlined how power can work just as much by encouraging people to speak as by silencing them (see Foucault, 1977; 1979b).

'Democratic' decision-making and 'whole-patient medicine' are thus revealed as discourses with no intrinsic meaning. Instead, their consequences depend upon their deployment and articulation in particular contexts. So even democracy is not something that we must appeal to in all circumstances. In contexts like this, democratic forms can be part of a power play. As in the previous illustration, we had discovered a surprising fact. In this case, this fact was relevant to an important public debate about the care of disabled children.

Two practical consequences arose from the study of Down's syndrome consultations. First, we asked the doctor concerned to rethink his policy or at least reveal his hidden agenda to parents. We did not dispute that there are many grounds to treat such children differently from others in relation to surgery. For instance, they have a poorer post-surgical survival rate and most parents are reluctant to contemplate surgery. However, there is a danger of stereotyping the needs of such children and their parents. By 'coming clean' about his policy, the doctor would enable parents to make a more informed choice.

The second practical point, revealed by this research, relates to my earlier remark about the limits of reducing social problems to issues of 'poor communication'. In some respects, this doctor's 'democratic' style seems to fit the requirements of 'good communication'. However, as good practitioners realize, no style of communication is intrinsically superior to another.

CONCLUSION

In these examples, we see how social research can contribute to the community precisely by insisting on the relevance of its own social science perspectives and refusing to limit its vision to commonsensically defined 'social problems'. By pursuing rigorous, analytically based research guided by its own sensitivities, we can contribute most to society.

Further reading

Silverman (1993) presents a more detailed introduction to issues in research methodology, focused on qualitative methods. Hammersley (1995) contains several relevant essays dealing with the relation between politics and social research. Silverman (1997) is a collection of essays on qualitative research methods with a chapter by Bloor on 'Addressing social problems through social research'.

Research and social theory

David Silverman

CONTENTS

Until recently, the different social sciences seemed to vary in the importance that they attached to theory. To take just two examples, psychologists and anthropologists, for all their differences, seemed to downplay theory. In psychology, the benchmark was the laboratory study. For psychologists, the motto seemed to be: 'demonstrate the facts through a controlled experiment and the theories will take care of themselves'. Anthropologists were just as interested in 'the facts'. However, their most important facts were revealed in observational case studies of groups or tribes usually found in faraway lands. Nonetheless, until recently, most English-speaking anthropologists followed psychologists in elevating facts above theories. This can be described as an **empiricist** approach in that facts are assumed to exist prior to the theories that explain them. In Chapter 2 there is a discussion of this empiricist vision which elucidates these points.

More recently, theory has become more important in both anthropology and psychology. Psychologists, for example, have become interested in discourse analysis (see Chapter 19). Anthropology has been particularly influenced by post-structuralist and post-modern theories (see Chapter 3) and theories of gender (see Chapter 4). By contrast, generations of British sociology students have long been made very aware of the primary importance attached to theory in their discipline. For instance, although undergraduate sociology courses tend to be split into three main areas (the 'holy trinity' of social theory, social structure and research methods), it is the course in social theory which is usually given the most prestige. Using the example of sociology, it is worth examining how far this elevation of theory is appropriate or fruitful.

DO WE NEED THEORY?

The main complaint about courses in social theory heard from students relates to the complex and confusing philosophical issues which are raised and the use of impenetrable jargon. It may seem that students have to learn a new language before they can begin to ask properly accredited questions and, moreover, that this new language seems to be of doubtful relevance to the social or political issues which may have brought them to the subject in the first place.

Even if they can penetrate the jargon, students may be puzzled by discovering that, just as they have learned the ideas of one social theorist, the rug appears to be pulled out from under their feet by an apparently devastating critique of those ideas. So Durkheim, they learn, is a positivist (obviously disreputable) and mistakes society for a biological organism. And Marx's social theories are largely inappropriate to the age in which we live. As each succeeding theorist is built up, only to be torn down, people become understandably concerned about the point of the whole exercise.

The situation would not be so bad if theoretical ideas could be applied to research studies. But even brilliant contemporary syntheses of social theory (like those in the works of Anthony Giddens) seem to have an uncertain relationship to actual research. Moreover, when you open a typical research study, although you may see a passing reference to the kind of social theories you have learned about elsewhere, you will very likely find that theory is rarely used or developed in the study itself, except as some kind of ritual reference to add legitimacy to an otherwise 'factual' piece of research.

Does that mean that we do not need theory to understand social research? To answer that question let us take a concrete example from Eric Livingston (1987). Livingston asks us to imagine that we have been told to carry out some social research on city streets. Where should we begin? He sets out four 'data possibilities' for such a study: official statistics (traffic flow, accidents); interviews (how people cope with rush hours); observation from a tower (viewing geometrical-shapes); observation or video at street level (how people queue or otherwise organize their movements).

As Livingston points out, each of these different ways of looking involves basic *theoretical* as well as methodological decisions. Very crudely, if we are attached to social theories which see the world in terms of correlations between *social facts* (see the discussion of Durkheim in Chapter 2), we are most likely to consider gathering official statistics. By contrast, if we think, like Weber, that social *meanings* are important, we may be tempted by the interview study. Or if we have read about contemporary American theories like interactionism or ethnomethodology, we are likely to want to observe or record what people actually do *in situ* and elect the third or fourth options. But note the very different views of people's behaviour we get from looking from on high (the third option), where people look like ants forming geometrical shapes like wedges, or from street level (the fourth option), where behaviour seems much more complex.

The point is that none of these views of data is more real or more true than the others. For instance, people are not really more like ants or complex actors. It all depends on our research question. And research questions are inevitably theoretically informed. So we *do* need social theories to help us to address even quite basic issues in social research. Let me underline this point through an extended example.

THEORY IN THE FIELD: WHO ARE THE LUE?

In this section, I will look in greater detail at Moerman's (1974) study, first introduced in Chapter 8, of a tribe living in Thailand. You will recall that as an anthropologist, Michael Moerman was interested in learning how a people categorized their world. Like most anthropologists and Chicago school ethnographers (see Chapter 17), he used native informants who, when asked questions like 'How do you recognize a member of your tribe?', produced a list of traits which Moerman called **ethnic identification devices**.

You will recall that Moerman was troubled about what sense to read into the Lue's own accounts. His questions often related to issues which were either obvious or irrelevant to the respondents. As he puts it: 'To the extent that answering an ethnographer's question is an unusual situation for natives, one cannot reason from a native's answer to his *normal* categories or ascriptions' (1974: 66, my emphasis). So Moerman started to see that ethnic identification devices were not used all the time by these people any more than we use them to refer to ourselves in a Western culture. This meant that, if you wanted to understand this people, it was not particularly useful to elicit from them what would necessarily be an abstract account of their tribe's characteristics. So instead, Moerman started to examine what went on in everyday situations through observation.

However, it was not so straightforward to switch to observational methods. Even when ethnographers are silent and merely observe, their presence indicates to people that matters relevant to 'identity' should be highlighted. This was also Fortier's experience in the London Italian social clubs which she studied (Chapter 5). Consequently, people may pay particular attention to what both the observer and they themselves take to be relevant categorization schemes – like ethnic or kinship labels. In this way, the ethnographer may have 'altered the local priorities among the native category sets which it is his task to describe' (1974: 67). What, then, was to be done? A clue is given by the initially opaque subheadings of Moerman's article: 'Who are the Lue?', 'Why are the Lue?', 'When are the Lue?'

Moerman argues that there are three reasons why we should *not* ask 'Who are the Lue?' First, it would generate an inventory of traits. Like all such inventories it could be endless because we could always be accused of having left something out. Second, lists are retrospective. Once we have decided that the Lue *are* a tribe, then we have no difficulty in 'discovering' a list of traits to support our case. Third, the identification of the Lue as a tribe depends, in part, on their successful presentation of themselves as a tribe. As Moerman puts it: 'The question is not "Who are the Lue?" but rather when how and why the identification "Lue" is preferred' (1974: 62). He adds that this does *not* mean that the Lue are not really a tribe or that they fooled him into thinking they were one. Rather their ethnic identity arises in the fact that people in the area use ethnic identification devices some of the time when they are talking about each other.

Of course, some of the time is not all the time. Hence the task of the ethnographer should be to observe when and *if* ethnic identification devices are used by the participants being studied. Moerman neatly summarizes his argument as follows:

> Anthropology [has an] apparent inability to distinguish between warm ... human bodies and one kind of identification device which some of those bodies sometimes use. Ethnic identification devices – with their important potential of making each ethnic set of living persons a joint enterprise with countless generations of un-examined history – seem to be universal. Social scientists should therefore de-scribe and analyse the ways in which they are used, and not merely – as natives do – use them as explanations. (1974: 67–8)

You will see, in the introduction to Chapter 14, that it is possible to conduct causal inquiries into social phenomena such as the use of ethnic identifica-tion devices. In that chapter a statistical approach to investigating causation is outlined. Moerman preferred a qualitative approach to explaining 'Why are the Lue?', drawing on his observations of when the devices were used and what his informants said about them. He suggests that they are used in order to provide the Lue with a sense of distinction and self-esteem in distinguishing themselves from 'hill' or 'jungle' people, whom they consider to be barely human, and 'officials' or 'townsfolk' who would otherwise be understood as insufferably superior. The Lue occupy a somewhat ambig-uous position in a nation experiencing tensions between movement from a 'tribal' to a 'civilized' society and this gives added motivation for the display of characteristic labels of 'identity'.

Moerman's study can be understood as relating to broader theories of *anti-essentialism* and *social constructionism* now prevalent in contemporary social theory (see Chapter 3). It reveals that any empiricist attempt to describe things 'as they are' is doomed to failure. Without *some* perspective or, at the very least, a set of animating questions, there is nothing to report. Contrary to crude empiricists, who would deny the relevance of theory to research, the facts *never* speak for themselves.

IMPLICATIONS: THEORY AND RESEARCH

Moerman's research points to the way in which idealized conceptions of phenomena like 'tribes' can, on closer examination, become like a will-o'-the-wisp, dissolving into sets of practices embedded in particular settings. Nowhere is this clearer than in the field of studies of the 'family'. As Gubrium and Holstein (1987) note, researchers have unnecessarily worried about getting 'authentic' reports of family life given the privacy of the household. Thus researchers may be satisfied that they have got at the 'truth' of family life only when they have uncovered some hidden secret (for example, marital disharmony, child abuse), regarding public presentations as a 'false front'. This, classically, is the perspective of Chicago school ethnography which often involved a sense of triumph in revealing matters hidden from view by official smokescreens. But this implies an idealized reality – as if there were some authentic site of family life which could be isolated and put under the researcher's microscope. Instead, discourses of family life are to be found largely in people's talk, in a range of contexts. Many of these, like courts of law, clinics and radio call-in programmes where people often reveal what they mean by the term 'family', are public and readily available for research investigation.

If 'the family', like a 'tribe', is present wherever it is invoked, then the worry of some researchers about observing 'real' or 'authentic' family life looks to be misplaced. Their assumption that the family has an essential reality looks more like a highly specific way of approaching the phenomenon, most frequently used by welfare professionals and by politicians.

As it turns out, finding the family is no problem at all for ordinary people. In our everyday life, we can always locate and understand 'real' families. In this regard, think of how social workers or lawyers in juvenile or divorce courts 'discover' the essential features of a particular family. Because we cannot assume, as these practitioners must, that families are 'available' for study in some kind of straightforward way, *how* we invoke the family, *when* we invoke the family and *where* we invoke the family must be central theoretical concerns for social researchers.

But, faced with a topic to study, like 'families' or 'tribes', how do we actually make the move towards a theoretically informed understanding? One way to develop theoretical understanding of observational data is to begin with a set of very general questions. Good examples of such questions are provided by Wolcott: 'What is going on here? What do people in this setting have to know (individually and collectively) in order to do what they are doing? How are skills and attitudes transmitted and acquired, particularly in the absence of intentional efforts at instruction' (1990: 32). Already here, we can see that Wolcott's questions are guided by a particular theoretical focus on people's knowledge and skills. This emerges out of a set of assumptions common to qualitative researchers informed by *interactionism* and *ethnomethodology* (see Chapter 3).

These assumptions are as follows. Firstly, common sense is held to be complex and sophisticated rather than naive and misguided. Secondly, social practices rather than perceptions are the site where common sense operates. Thus the focus is on what people are doing rather than upon what they are thinking. For example, researchers should study people talking to one another, having meetings, writing documents and so on. Thirdly, 'phenomena' are viewed within such inverted commas. This means that, like Moerman and Gubrium, we should seek to understand how phenomena (such as ethnic identification devices or families) are produced through the activities of particular people in particular settings.

Of course, these are not the only kind of assumptions that may properly inform social research. Depending on our preferred theoretical framework, we might take a completely different position. For instance, researchers interested in the effects of social structure (as Durkheim was in his study of suicide) or feminists would argue that **social structures** (which Durkheim called *social facts*, as was shown in Chapter 2), such as social class, ethnic identity or family type, exist beyond face-to-face interaction. Many feminists would focus as much on what people were thinking (and feeling) as on what they were doing (see also Chapter 4). The issue, for the moment, is not which theoretical framework is 'best' or even most useful. Instead, I have been suggesting that *some* theory of human or social action necessarily informs any piece of social research. Given this, we always need to try to specify our theoretical assumptions rather than to use them unconsciously or uncritically. In this way the practice of research becomes more fully **reflexive**.

THEORIES, MODELS AND HYPOTHESES

I have so far concentrated on showing how theories are used in social research through the use of concrete examples. But what precisely is a 'theory'? And how does it differ from a 'hypothesis'? Table 9.1 defines these and other basic terms in research.

As we see from the table, **models** provide an overall framework for how we look at reality. In short, they tell us what reality is like and the basic elements it contains. In social research, examples of such models are *functionalism* (which looks at the functions of social institutions), *behaviourism* (which defines all behaviour in terms of 'stimulus' and 'response'), *symbolic interactionism* (which focuses on how we attach symbolic meanings to interpersonal relations) and *ethnomethodology* (which encourages us to look at people's everyday ways of producing orderly social interaction).

Concepts are clearly specified ideas deriving from a particular model. Examples of concepts are 'social function' (deriving from functionalism), 'stimulus/response' (behaviourism), 'definition of the situation'

Table 9.1   *Basic terms in research*

Term	Meaning	Examples
Model	An overall framework for looking at reality	Ethnomethodology, feminism
Concept	An idea deriving from a given model	Social practices, oppression
Theory	A set of concepts used to define and/or explain some phenomenon	Ethnic identification devices, social construction
Hypothesis	A testable proposition	'Tribes invoke ethnic identification devices more frequently when threatened by external enemies'
Methodology	A general approach to studying research topics	Quantitative, qualitative
Method	A specific research technique	Social survey, conversation analysis

Source: adapted from Silverman, 1993: 1

(interactionism) and 'the documentary method of interpretation' (ethno-methodology). Concepts offer ways of looking at the world which are essential in defining a research problem.

Theories arrange sets of concepts to define and explain some phenomenon, for example the nature of 'tribes' and 'families'. As we have already seen, without a theory these phenomena cannot be understood. In this sense, without a theory there is nothing to research. So theories provide the impetus for research. As living entities, they are also developed and modified by good research. However, as used here, models, concepts and theories are self-confirming in the sense that they instruct us to look at phenomena in particular ways. This means that they can never be disproved but only found to be more or less useful.

This last feature distinguishes theories from **hypotheses**. Unlike theories, hypotheses are tested in research. Examples of hypotheses, discussed in Silverman (1993), are: 'how we receive advice is linked to how advice is given'; 'responses to an illegal drug depend upon what one learns from others'; 'voting in union elections is related to non-work links between union members'. As we shall see, a feature of many qualitative research studies is that there is no specific hypothesis at the outset but that hypotheses are produced (or induced) during the early stages of research. In any event, unlike theories, hypotheses can, and should be, tested. Therefore, we assess a hypothesis by its validity or truth.

A **methodology** is a general approach to studying a research topic. It establishes how one will go about studying any phenomenon. In social research, examples of methodologies are **quantitative** methodology, which uses numbers to test hypotheses and, of course, **qualitative** methodology, which tries to use first-hand familiarity with different settings to induce hypotheses. Like theories, methodologies cannot be true or false, only more or less useful.

Finally, **methods** are specific research techniques. These include quantitative techniques, like statistical correlations, as well as techniques like observation, interviewing and audio recording. Once again, in themselves, techniques are not true or false. They are more or less useful, depending on their fit with the theories and methodologies being used and the hypothesis being tested or the research topic that is selected. So, for instance, behaviourists may favour quantitative methods and interactionists often prefer to gather their data by observation. But, depending upon the hypothesis being tested, behaviourists may sometimes use qualitative methods – for instance in the exploratory stage of research. Equally, interactionists may sometimes use simple quantitative methods, particularly when they want to find an overall pattern in their data.

The relation between models, concepts, theories, hypotheses, methodology and methods is set out schematically in Figure 9.1. Reading the figure anti-clockwise, each concept reflects a lower level of generality and abstraction. The arrow from 'findings' to 'hypotheses' indicates a feedback mechanism through which hypotheses are modified in the light of findings.

Let me now try to put flesh on the skeleton set out in Figure 9.1 through the use of some concrete examples. Imagine that we have a general interest in the gloomy topic of death in society. How are we to research this topic? Before we can even define a research problem, let alone develop a hypothesis, we need to think through some very basic issues. Assume that we are the kind of social scientist who prefers to see the world in terms of how social structures determine behaviour, following Durkheim's injunction to treat social facts as real things (see Chapter 2). Such a *model* of social

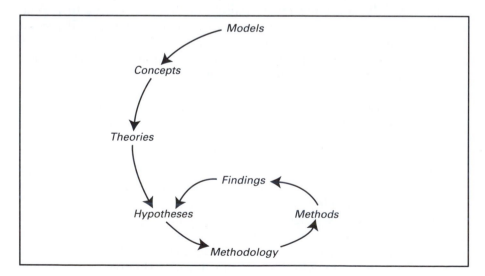

Figure 9.1   *Levels of analysis*

life will suggest concepts that we can use in our research on death. Using such a model, we will tend to see death in terms of statistics relating to rates of death (or 'mortality'). And we will want to explain such statistics in terms of other social facts such as age or social class.

Armed with our concepts, we might then construct a *theory* about one or other aspect of our topic. For instance, working with our assumption that death is a social fact, determined by other social facts, we might develop a theory that the rate of early death among children, or 'infant mortality', is related to some social fact about their parents, say their social class. From this theory, it is a quick step to the *hypothesis* that the higher the social class of its parents, the lower the likelihood of a child dying within the first year of its life. This hypothesis is sometimes expressed as saying that there is an *inverse* relationship between social class and infant mortality.

As already implied, a model concerned with social facts will tend to favour a quantitative methodology, using methods such as the analysis of official statistics or the use of large-scale social surveys based on apparently reliable fixed-choice questionnaires. In interpreting the findings of such research, one will need to ensure that due account is taken of factors that may be concealed in simple correlations. For instance, social class may be associated with quality of housing and the latter factor (here called an *intervening* variable) may be the real cause of variations in the rates of infant mortality. Multivariate analysis of this sort is discussed in Chapter 14.

This overall approach to death is set out schematically in Figure 9.2. Figure 9.3 sets out a very different way of conceiving death. For interactionist social researchers, social institutions are created and stabilized by the actions of participants. A central idea of this model is that our labelling of phenomena defines their character. This, in turn, is associated with the concept of

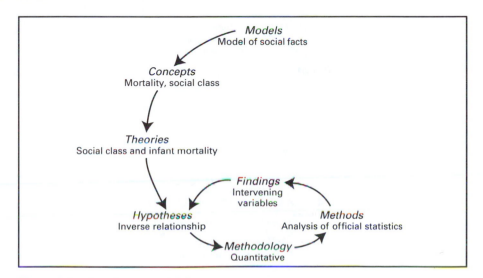

Figure 9.2   *Death as a social fact*

definitions of the situation which tells us to look for social phenomena in the ways in which meaning gets defined by people in different contexts. The overall message of the interactionist approach is that 'death' should be put in inverted commas and hence leads to a theory in which 'death' is treated as a *social construct*.

Of course, this is very different from the social fact model and, therefore, nicely illustrates the importance of theories in defining research problems. Its immediate drawback, however, may be that it appears to be counter-intuitive. After all, you may feel, death is surely an obvious fact. We are either dead or not dead and, if so, where does this leave social constructionism?

Let me cite two cases which put the counter-argument. First, in 1963, after President Kennedy was shot, he was taken to a Dallas hospital with, according to contemporary accounts, half of his head shot away. My hunch is that if you or I were to arrive in a casualty department in this state, we would be given a cursory examination and then recorded as 'dead on arrival' (DOA). Precisely because they were dealing with a President, the staff had to do more than this. So they worked on Kennedy for almost an hour, demonstrating thereby that they had done their best for such an important patient.

Now think of contemporary debates about whether or when severely injured people should have life-support systems turned off. Once again, acts of definition constitute whether somebody is alive or dead. And note that such definitions have real effects. Of course, such a constructionist version of death is just one way of theorizing this phenomenon, not intrinsically better or worse than the social fact approach. But, once we adopt one or another model, it starts to have a big influence upon how our research proceeds. For instance, as we have seen, if 'dead on arrival' can be a label applied in

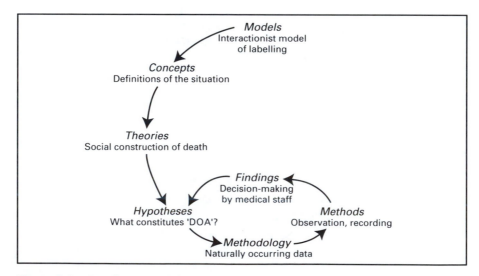

Figure 9.3 *Death as a social construction*

different ways to different people, we might develop a hypothesis about how the label 'dead on arrival' is applied to different hospital patients.

Because of our model, we would then probably try to collect research data that arose in such **naturally occurring** (or non-research-generated) settings as actual hospitals, using methods like observation or audio or video recording. Note, however, that this would not rule out the collection of quantitative data (say from hospital records). Rather, it would mean that our main body of data would probably be qualitative. Following earlier research (for example, Jeffery, 1979; Dingwall and Murray, 1983) our findings might show how age and presumed moral status are relevant to such medical decision-making as well as social class. In turn, as shown in Figure 9.3, these findings would help us to refine our initial hypothesis.

GENERALIZATIONS AND THEORY BUILDING

Theorizing about data does not stop with the refinement of hypotheses. In this section, I will show how we can develop generalizations out of success-fully tested hypotheses and, thereby, contribute to **theory building**. (This topic is also discussed in Chapters 12 and 17.) Firstly, we need to recognize that **case studies**, limited to a particular set of interactions, still allow one to examine how particular sayings and doings are embedded in particular patterns of social organization. We first caught sight of this earlier in this chapter when I mentioned how Moerman (1974) used his research in Thai-land to suggest generalizations which included English-speaking societies.

A classic case of an anthropologist using a case study to make broader generalizations is found in Mary Douglas's (1975) work on a central African tribe, the Lele. Douglas noticed that an ant-eater that Western zoologists call a 'pangolin' was very important to the Lele's ritual life. For the Lele, the pangolin was both a cult animal and an anomaly. It was perceived to have both animal and human characteristics. For instance, it tended to have only one offspring at a time, unlike most other animals. It also did not readily fit into the Lele's classification of land and water creatures, spending some of its time on land and some time in the water. Curiously, among animals that were hunted, the pangolin seemed to the Lele to be unique in not trying to escape but almost offering itself up to its hunter. Fortunately, Douglas resisted what might be called a 'tourist' response, moving beyond curiosity to systematic analysis. She noted that many groups who perceive anomalous entities in their environment reject them out of hand. To take an anomalous entity seriously might cast doubt on the **naturalized** status of your group's system of classification.

The classic example of the rejection of anomaly is found in the Old Testa-ment. Douglas points out that the reason why the pig is unclean, according to the Old Testament, is that it is anomalous. It has a cloven hoof which, following the Old Testament, makes it clean, but it does not chew the cud – which makes it dirty. So it turns out that the pig is particularly unclean precisely because it is anomalous. Similarly, the Old Testament teachings on intermarriage work in relation to anomaly. Although you are not expected to marry somebody of another tribe, to marry the offspring of a marriage between a member of your tribe and an outsider is even more frowned upon. In both examples, anomaly is shunned.

However, the Lele are an exception: they celebrate the anomalous pangolin. What this suggests to Douglas is that there may be no *universal* propensity to frown upon anomaly. If there is variability from community to community, then this must say something about their social organization. Sure enough, there is something special about the Lele's social life. Their experience of relations with other tribes has been very successful. They exchange goods with them and have little experience of war. What is involved in relating well with other tribes? It means successfully crossing a frontier or boundary. But what do anomalous entities do? They cut across boundaries. Here is the answer to the puzzle about why the Lele are different.

Douglas is suggesting that the Lele's response to anomaly derives from experiences grounded in their social organization. They perceive the pangolin favourably because it cuts across boundaries just as they themselves do. Conversely, the ancient Israelites regarded anomalies unfavourably because their own experience of crossing boundaries was profoundly unfavourable. Indeed, the Old Testament reads as a series of disastrous exchanges between the Israelites and other tribes.

Douglas is, of course, applying the historical and comparative method outlined in Chapter 7. She moves from a single-case explanation to a far more general theory of the relation between social exchange and response to anomaly. Glaser and Strauss (1967) have described this movement towards greater generality as a move from **substantive** to **formal** theory. In their own research on hospital wards caring for terminally ill patients, they show how, by using the comparative method, we can develop accounts of people's own awareness of their impending death (a substantive theory) into accounts of a whole range of 'awareness contexts' (formal theory). (See also Figure 12.6.)

Douglas's account of the relation between responses to anomaly and experiences of boundary crossing can also be applied elsewhere. Perhaps bad experiences of exchanges with other groups explains why some Israeli Jews and Palestinian Muslims are so concerned to mark their own identity on the 'holy places' in Jerusalem and reject (as a hateful anomaly) multiple use of the same holy sites?

In any event, Douglas's study of the Lele exemplifies the need to locate how individual elements are embedded in forms of social organization. In her case, this is done in an explicitly Durkheimian manner which sees behaviour as the expression of a 'society' which works as a 'hidden hand' constraining and forming human action. Alternatively, Moerman's work indicates how, using a constructionist framework, one can look at the fine detail of people's activities without treating social organization as a purely external force. In the latter case, people cease to be 'cultural dopes' (Garfinkel, 1967) and skilfully reproduce the moral order.

HOW TO THEORIZE ABOUT DATA

Unlike Moerman or Douglas, most readers will not bring to their research any very well-defined set of theoretical ideas. If you are in this position, your problem will be how you can use data to think in theoretical terms. The list below is intended merely as a set of suggestions. Although it cannot be exhaustive, it should serve as an initial guide to theorizing about data. It can also be read in conjunction with the discussion of the three kinds of research sensitivity in Chapter 8.

In carrying out your research, I suggest that you think about the following five issues. Firstly, consider *chronology*: can you gather data over time in order to look at processes of change? If not, it is worth searching out historical evidence which may at least suggest how your research problem came into being. Secondly, and reiterating Chapter 8, consider *context*: how are your data contextualized in particular organizational settings, social processes or sets of experiences? For instance, as Moerman shows, answering an interviewer's question may be different from engaging in the activity which is the topic of the interview. Therefore, think about how there may be many versions of your phenomenon.

Thirdly, make use of *comparison*: like Mary Douglas, who generated her theory by comparing how different groups treated anomalies, always try to compare your data with other relevant data. Even if you cannot find a comparative case, try to find ways of dividing your data into different sets and compare each. Remember that the comparative method is the basic scientific method. Fourthly, consider the *implications* of your research. When you are reporting your research, think about how your discoveries may relate to broader issues than your original research topic. In this way, a very narrow topic (for example, how the Lele perceive the pangolin) may be related to much broader social processes (for example, how societies respond to anomalous entities). Lastly, be like the Lele and engage in *lateral thinking* if you can. Don't erect strong boundaries between concepts but explore the relations between apparently diverse models, theories and methodologies. Celebrate anomaly!

CONCLUSION

The philosopher of science Thomas Kuhn (1970) has described social science as lacking a single, agreed set of concepts (see Chapter 2). In Kuhn's terms, this makes social research pre-paradigmatic or at least in a state of competing paradigms. As I have already implied, the problem is that this has generated a whole series of social science courses which pose different approaches to research in terms of either/or questions. Classically, for example, qualitative methodology is thought to be opposed to quantitative.

Such courses are much appreciated by some students. They learn about the paradigmatic oppositions in question, choose A rather than B and report back, parrot fashion, all the advantages of A and the drawbacks of B. It is hardly surprising that such courses produce very little evidence of independent thought. This may, in part, explain why so many undergraduate social science courses actually provide a learned incapacity to go out and do research.

Learning about rival 'armed camps' in no way allows you to confront research data. In the field, material is much more messy than the different camps would suggest. Perhaps there is something to be learned from both sides, or, more constructively, perhaps we start to ask interesting questions when we reject the polarities that such a course markets? Even when we decide to use qualitative or quantitative methods, we involve ourselves in theoretical as well as methodological decisions. These decisions relate not only to how we conceptualize the world but also to our theory of how our research subjects think about things. Theory, then, should be neither a status symbol nor an optional extra in a research study. Without theory, research is impossibly narrow. Without research, theory is mere armchair contemplation.

Further reading

Chapter 1 in Silverman (1993) discusses some basic issues in starting to theorize about research data. Gubrium (1988) is a very useful short introductory text on theorizing about qualitative data. Sudnow (1968) is an important, clearly written example of a constructionist treatment of death in an American hospital.

Writing a research proposal

Moira Kelly

CONTENTS

This chapter will emphasize and demonstrate the value of writing a clearly thought-out research proposal, providing guidelines as to what it should contain, and why. Bearing in mind that social science graduates will have to apply their knowledge and earn a living in an increasingly competitive marketplace, the development of practical skills such as writing research proposals is important. But the main reason for writing a research proposal is to think through ideas for a project so that they can be presented for critical appraisal. Additionally many funding bodies ask people or institutions to put in applications or tenders in the form of a project proposal based on a brief. Thus developing the ability to effectively plan and to apply the theories and methodologies described in this text is often demanded in the world outside the academy. Here is the policy of one such organization, the Economic and Social Research Council (ESRC) in the UK:

> Any lingering public perception of social science as a source of irrelevant, introverted and incoherent output is set for radical alteration ... In future, research which makes a difference to the health and wealth of the population rather than merely supports 'ivory tower' academic excellence will be the ESRC's priority. (Economic and Social Research Council, 1996)

Of course, a key issue in research design is the way in which the research problem is defined and, as was argued in Chapter 8, social and cultural researchers need to resist the temptation to accept the definitions of social problems offered them by policy makers. Chapter 8 shows how one such social problem, communication between staff and patients in a health care setting, can be developed into a researchable topic. It is important that we as social scientists use our skills and knowledge to define the research problem. Although we can use common-sense concepts up to a point, we cannot expect such concepts to do the analytical work of theoretical concepts. The research proposal stage is often the point at which such issues are decided and this will exert a profound influence over the conduct of the research.

At a more practical level it can be valuable to receive comments from others at various stages when writing a proposal. These can be from a supervisor or tutor, fellow student, colleague, or experts in the field. Presenting ideas to someone for comment at an early stage helps to develop them. Comments may highlight areas not presented clearly, or which need more work, or aspects which are untenable in some way. Collaborating with others and submitting joint proposals for funding are common, which is another reason for getting used to sharing research ideas with supportive peers. Feedback can be on theoretical or practical issues which are both important. For example, there is a need to know that the research question has been well constructed, but also that it is possible to gain access to the data needed to answer it.

QUANTITATIVE AND QUALITATIVE RESEARCH

> Whether the research is qualitative or quantitative, cross-sectional or longitudinal, exploratory or confirmatory, the same criteria are used to judge its contribution – and it is only through the creative and insightful use of methods which address these criteria that we can expect to improve the quality of our contribution to knowledge. (Najman et al., 1992: 155)

The basic principles covered in this chapter are essentially the same for any type of social research. A proposal should contain a clearly conceived question, problem or hypothesis; the methods proposed should be likely to produce robust data which will provide an answer to the question, and the proposal should show that ethical behaviour will be followed. However, there does need to be some flexibility in the way this is set out, often influenced by whether a quantitative or a qualitative approach is to be taken.

Quantitative research designs have often been based on the methods of natural science, so proposals have tended to follow those lines. A set format is often appropriate. Proposals for quantitative research could be said therefore to be more straightforward, with information fitting into certain categories. Standards used in quantitative research have to some extent influenced expectations for qualitative research proposals. This can present a challenge for those proposing to carry out exploratory qualitative studies in which it may be counter-productive to pre-specify everything at the proposal stage. When using qualitative methods there is therefore the need to be creative and flexible in putting ideas across, especially if the audience is used to receiving proposals for quantitative work. The most important thing is to be clear about what you are doing and why.

For quantitative research, perhaps involving a social survey, a well-thought-out design, specified in the proposal, is crucial. Certain criteria must be addressed at the planning stage. The *validity* and *reliability* of the data must be considered, such as specifying a sample size sufficient to perform the statistical analysis necessary to answer the research question. For example, if I want to test for significant differences between males and females in my survey, I need to ensure a large enough sample of both sexes in order to perform the appropriate statistical tests. When undertaking quantitative research it is common to get advice from someone with statistical expertise at an early stage. (These topics are explained further in Chapters 11, 12 and 13.)

Proposal formats which are more sensitive to qualitative research are, however, beginning to develop. This has been stimulated by researchers in certain academic disciplines, which were traditionally dominated by quantitative methods, having become more convinced of the need for a range of research methodologies to address social problems. The perceived value of qualitative research has consequently been increased. From another perspective, though, qualitative researchers may increasingly be expected to demonstrate rigour in terms of the reliability and validity of their findings. The way in which rigour will be achieved needs to be described in the research proposal, whatever the methodology.

A PAPER EXERCISE?

Having to set down ideas formally at the beginning of a project may seem like a time-consuming activity when you have developed an interesting idea and have limited time available. However, if it is already viable, it will not take too long to put into the form of a proposal. This will provide the plan for the whole project which can then be referred to at different stages. Social research can throw up the unexpected as it progresses, especially if it is exploratory.

It is likely that at the start of writing the proposal gaps or difficulties will arise. Various options may need to be considered before the project seems workable. This is a normal part of the research process. It is important that any grey areas or loose thinking are addressed at the beginning, such as the reasons for choosing one method over another. It may be difficult to rectify early mistakes in the late stages of a research project. Writing a proposal is a key way of minimizing such problems.

The proposal will also form the basis of, or at least inform (if it is exploratory qualitative research), the final research report. It will constitute a framework which can be altered, amended, expanded, or reduced in the process of becoming a feasible research study. Once the written proposal is finalized, it does not have to stand in stone; there is a need for flexibility to cope with problems or issues which were not expected.

WHERE TO START?

You may already have an idea which you wish to investigate, or may need to think of one that is feasible. The beginning is not usually a blank page: researchers have normally already done some work in developing their ideas, having probably done some reading, with notes on this that can be used. Think about what you know about your idea, and what you would like to know. A researcher might want to see if findings from a study in one area can be replicated in another. For example, one could apply a research design used to investigate people in another country to the UK context. Bell (1993) suggests drawing up a list of questions you are interested in at this stage. For example, let us imagine that the topic concerns students' experience of paid employment. Some questions related to this topic could be:

1 What is the proportion of students working to supplement their grants and is it increasing?
2 How many hours do students work on average in paid employment?
3 What factors influence them working, for example class, age, sex, geographical region, ethnic group?
4 How does having to work affect their studies?
5 Does working while a student increase their chance of getting future work?
6 What sort of jobs do they do?
7 How do they feel about having to work?
8 How does working affect the social aspect of student life?

Writing down such questions is the first part of drafting a proposal. To develop the project requires moving beyond the stage of jotting down questions, and structuring the project so that what you are planning to do, why you are planning it, and how you intend to do it are clear. Krathwohl (1988) suggests that 'signposts' in the way a proposal is presented are helpful.

These may be subheadings indicating main areas to be included. I will use one such sequence of subheadings now, to explain what can usefully be placed under each.

Title

This should describe briefly what the project is about: for example, 'Employment patterns in full-time undergraduates: a proposed survey of students in London'. Information is provided on the subject area, target audience, and where it will be carried out. Your name and those of any others involved if it is a collaboration should also be stated with the title.

Background or introduction

It is then important to introduce the subject and supply some background information. Social science covers all aspects of social life, and uses a wide range of theoretical perspectives and methodologies. Potential readers may need to be able to understand your proposal without necessarily having a thorough knowledge of the particular field. Similarly they may not be an expert in the methodological approach chosen. The main aim of a reader may be to appreciate the nature and feasibility of the study, rather than to gain in-depth knowledge of the subject and methodology.

Continuing the example of a hypothetical study of students and paid employment, I would now write that one reason for choosing this is the continuing debate about funding for higher education in the UK. State funding has been cut and there is a lot of media coverage on the hardship faced by students, suggesting that an increasing number of students have to work part time in order to support themselves. I would like to explore this phenomenon, to see if this is really the case, to what extent it is happening, and what effects it is having on students who have to work to help support themselves. For example, it may affect the time that students have to study, thus producing poorer examination results, or it may affect their social lives in adverse ways. An introductory statement would point out all of this, but do so quite briefly, in order to give the reader a quick preview of the problems addressed by the research project. Following this, it would be important to undertake a brief review of the relevant literature (which would be expanded in the main research report).

Literature review

One of the first things a reader will want to know is whether this research has been done before. Any major research in the field needs to be described. It can then be shown how the project will add to current knowledge. Librarians can advise on a range of resources which may be helpful. A major source of relatively up-to-date information can be accessed through computer databases which contain abstracts of recently published research.

The literature review will reflect whether the study is aiming to influence social policy or social theory. For example, one way of taking forward my proposed study of students is to include reference to current and previous higher education policy in the literature review. This emphasizes the policy relevance of my research. Alternatively, I could discuss literature with a strong social theory perspective, such as interactionist studies of the meanings students attach to paid employment while studying full time. Thus the type of literature explored here will have a bearing on the eventual use of the findings of your study. It is possible for studies to have implications for both social policy and social theory, but the literature reviewed will then need to include reference to both of these.

The extent of the literature review at the proposal stage will depend on the nature of the study, the time available, and to whom it will be submitted. Funding bodies will send a proposal out for peer review, so you need to ensure you have included research by any key people in the field. On the other hand, it is important to be selective in your reading, and stick to the things which are directly relevant to your research. This is a skill in itself. Finding and exploring the literature can be very time consuming. If you have time, you may wish to contact people who are currently working in the field who can give you an idea of any work in progress.

A qualitative research proposal may involve a less comprehensive literature review at this stage, as data analysis may inform which literature is relevant. For example, if you are undertaking an exploratory study of students and paid work, you could assume that working is found to be stressful and undertake an extensive review of the literature on student stress. However, it may be that your data analysis indicates that students find working a positive experience which enables them to make friends outside college and gives them money to go out. In this case it would be better to review some of the relevant literature at the proposal stage, but allow the data analysis to inform a more extensive literature review. However, you will need to ensure that you build in time at the data analysis stage of the project to do this.

Aims and objectives

Now that the relevance of the area to be investigated has been highlighted, the research problem needs to be defined more precisely. How specific the research problem is made at this stage will depend on what is to be discovered. It is common in the natural sciences to set up a *hypothesis*. As was shown in Chapter 9, this is a statement specifying the relationship between two or more variables. Studies using quantitative designs can be used to test hypotheses (as discussed in Chapter 11). For example, one could try to see if the following statement is true: 'Full-time undergraduate students who are in paid employment are more likely to experience psychological stress than those who do not work.' On the other hand a research problem for a quantitative or qualitative study could be: 'To describe the effects of paid employment on the lives of undergraduate students'. This type of research problem allows greater flexibility in terms of what findings will be.

A number of objectives may be drawn up which describe what you need to do to achieve your aim, and thus address your research problem. For example, in relation to the second research problem stated above, an objective could be to undertake a survey of full-time undergraduate students to describe the patterns of undergraduate employment in London. This would include the number of students who work, their income, the number of hours worked per week, factors influencing the decision to take up or not take up work, their perceptions of the effects of the work upon their studies, and their examination results.

Objectives should be clear and it should be easy to decide whether they have been achieved or not. Definitions of the research problem or hypothesis and objectives are, as previously stated, an important part of a proposal. It is therefore important to spend some time working these out. In exploratory research the objectives may need to be quite broad. It is not uncommon for inexperienced researchers to get carried away with the methodology or idea and lose sight of whether the method will achieve the objectives. It is advisable to check them against each other regularly when developing your proposal. Pragmatic factors such as the time available may influence your research problem and objectives. It is tempting to set an impossible research task. However, as suggested in Chapter 8, it is advisable to set out to say 'a lot about a little' .

Methods

The way in which aims and objectives will be achieved will be set out in this section. An explanation of the *methods* to be used (for example, a survey based on random probability sampling, or discourse analysis of interview transcripts) and an explanation of why these methods are the most appropriate will be needed. For example, I could say that in order to ascertain patterns of part-time employment in students a survey of a random sample of 100 undergraduates in one university will be undertaken. Alternatively I could propose that unstructured interviews with five working and five non-working students will be carried out. I might then say that a comparative analysis of interview transcripts will be carried out, using discourse analysis, to explore how the students construct the meaning of employment and studying in their lives.

The methods section should also include other information about how the research will be carried out, including the sampling, recruitment of respondents, establishing access to the field, and in quantitative studies, what variables you intend to include in the analysis. The emphasis here will be influenced by the method. For example, a survey of students could be through face-to-face interview, a postal questionnaire, or telephone interview. Therefore I need to specify how I will carry out the survey. In a study using discourse analysis of interview transcripts, I need to set out what form the interviews with students will take, such as how I introduce the topic, and what areas will be covered.

Data analysis

A short summary of how you intend to analyse the data should be included. This is relevant to both quantitative and qualitative research. For example, you need to include the key variables you will use for subgroup analysis such as age, sex, ethnic group. Any statistical data analysis packages you plan to use should be stated. Methods of qualitative analysis should also be included where possible, and any qualitative data analysis computer programs specified. How you will ensure the *reliability* and *validity* of your findings should be clarified here and in the methods section. (These terms are defined in Chapter 11.)

For example, in a postal survey of students, one way of producing reliable and valid data is to pilot the questionnaire with a small group of students before sending it out to the main sample. I can then check to see whether any of the questions are ambiguous and interpreted differently by different people. Statistical methods which will be used to ensure that findings from the survey are valid and reliable can be stated. Statistical methods can be used to assess the likelihood of findings coming about through chance. In order to do this you need to ensure that you have included enough people to carry out appropriate statistical analysis. Statistical methods are explored further in Chapters 13 and 14.

Reliability and validity are also important in qualitative research. The principle is basically the same, ensuring consistency and accuracy in the way the data are collected and analysed. In a study involving open-ended interviews with students I might plan to use a short topic guide with all the interviewees, but also to use open-ended questions which will allow any new topics which I had not initially incorporated to be added to the topics included. I would state that in order to maximize the reliability of the findings all interviews will be transcribed and a number of categories produced based on an initial reading of the transcripts. Each interview will then be systematically analysed using these categories. Written analysis will be supported through extracts from the data.

Ethical issues

The ethical aspects of research have at times been given minimal formal consideration. Milgram's (1963) psychological study of conformity, which required people to give what they thought was an electric shock to someone if they did not answer a question in the right way, demonstrates this. Humphreys's (1970) sociological study of clandestine homosexual behaviour, where he secretly observed men in public toilets without their consent, has also been criticized on ethical grounds. It has increasingly come to be the case, though, that social researchers are expected to take ethical issues into account when developing a proposal. The amount of attention to ethical issues required depends on the sensitivity of your proposed study. For example, ethical issues surrounding interviews about sexual health will be much more sensitive than interviews about work patterns. It is important that no harm, physical or psychological, will come to anyone taking part in your research. In health services research, researchers are often required to submit proposals to an ethical committee for review in order to gain access to the field because ethical issues are particularly pertinent to research in health-related areas. Universities usually have ethical committees also, to which students and staff may be required to submit project proposals before a study can be carried out.

Ethical issues in social research are not always clear cut, but a key one is the preservation of confidentiality and the privacy of people involved. For example, in my proposed study I need to consider how I will ensure that individual students will not be identifiable when I present my findings. I also need to consider how I will gain consent from the students I want to interview. One possibility is to give all potential interviewees a letter with information about the study and its purpose, and ask them to sign a consent form. I can also state that I will ensure that the interviews will be identifiable only by myself through a coding system.

Dissemination and policy relevance

Dissemination is an issue which is receiving increasing emphasis, especially from bodies which fund research. Social research findings are used in two main ways: application to social policy, and building social theory. Social scientists have been criticized in the past for not sharing their research findings with those who may use them. Some funding bodies now require that applications for funding include plans for communication and details of how findings will be shared with users.

Continuing my hypothetical example, I might say that it will contribute to knowledge about the effects of employment on academic standards and student welfare. I could argue that it has policy relevance in that, depending on the results, it can provide direction for the development of support services for students, or contribute to policy debates about student grant levels. The study will also contribute to the development of social theory. For example, discourse analysis of interview transcripts will contribute to new understandings of how people construct narratives of self-identity in relation to work and studying. Additionally, I might say that a report will be written and submitted to the National Union of Students and the university Student Welfare Department, and that it is planned to submit a paper to the next Sociology Association conference.

References and appendices

Any references to other studies made in the text should be listed at the end of the proposal. Referencing should be done according to a standard system such as the Harvard system, which requires standard information about books and articles to be presented in a particular order (for example, author, date, title, publisher). Place any appendices before the references, in the order in which they have been mentioned. Appendices will include any relevant papers you intend to use, such as questionnaires and consent forms.

Resources

Formal applications for funding will usually require detailed budget break-downs. A proposal should show that plans have been tailored so that they are feasible within budgetary limits. Resources can be anything you need for the successful completion of your study, including money, personnel, equipment or time. Let us imagine that in my study I had planned to send a postal questionnaire to all the 2,000 full time undergraduate students at my university. I have managed to gain a small grant from an interested organiz-ation for postage and printing of questionnaires. However, taking into account all the postage and printing costs, I can survey only 500 students. Similarly, in the study involving unstructured interviews I need to visit interviewees in their homes, which means that I need a budget for travel. This, together with other factors such as the time involved in travelling, has prompted my decision to limit the number of interviews I will undertake.

Schedule or timetable

It is valuable to have some form of structured timetable for a project. We often set ourselves unrealistic time-scales for projects, for example by underestimating how long it will take to gain access to the people we need to interview, or by not foreseeing that we may need to send out a second questionnaire to increase our response rate. In considering my hypothetical project I realize that I need to allow time to negotiate access to student names and addresses through the university. The time available is 32 weeks from start to finish. I have been advised that it will probably be easiest to contact students during term time, so I need to take this into account in my plan. Below is a plan for the qualitative interview study:

Proposal to be submitted to university ethical committee	Week 2
Contact university for names and addresses of students	Week 6
Begin interviews	Week 8
End interviews	Week 15
Complete data analysis	Week 23
First draft sent to others for comments	Week 26
Submission of final report	Week 32

And here is the survey proposal timetable. It can be seen that a longer time has been allowed for data analysis in the qualitative study. This will include time to explore relevant literature. The plan for the survey study follows similar lines, but has more structure:

Proposal to be submitted to university ethical committee	Week 2
Contact university for names and addresses of students	Week 6
First draft of literature review completed	Week 8
Questionnaire ready for piloting	Week 10
Complete pilot questionnaire	Week 12
Send out questionnaire	Week 14
Inputting of data completed	Week 22
Data analysis completed	Week 25
First draft sent to others for comments	Week 26
Submission of final report	Week 32

REVISING THE PROPOSAL

A proposal will start off as an outline and usually require several revisions. Each section mentioned here affects the others. For example, your time schedule will influence the method you have chosen, which has been influenced by your research problem. You need to make sure that all aspects of the proposal look as if they will work in relation to each other. It is useful to think in terms of how the human body functions. If we undertake strenuous physical exercise like running a marathon, we will need to drink a lot more fluid than usual in order not to become dehydrated and to last the course. We thus need to plan ahead and to make sure we have access to fluid along the way. The main thing to check is that the method will enable you to achieve your objectives. Researchers tend to be over ambitious in the amount they set out to do. This is where it is helpful to get advice from others. Alternatively, new lines of inquiry may be suggested by others, whose practical implications need to be thought through.

It is also important to present work in a way that is accessible to other people. Strunk and White (1979) provide a useful guide, based on examples, on how to develop a good writing style. They suggest that 'the approach to style is by way of plainness, simplicity, orderliness, sincerity' (1979: 69). We all develop our own personal writing styles over time. It is valuable to ask others for their comments. For example, did they understand the reason for carrying out the research from the proposal? It is easy to get very wrapped up in the subject and think that, because we are convinced of the particular value of our research, others will be too. The way in which the proposal is presented can enable the reader to appreciate what you are planning to do.

Ideally, a research proposal should be concise. This may seem impossible considering the amount of detail given here about what to put into a proposal. This is where revision and writing style is important. The reader will want to easily see what you are proposing, whilst at the same time have their attention held by the content. Krathwohl (1988) suggests that the proposal should be easy for the reader to skim. Dividing the proposal up using some of the headings discussed here will help with this. Effective use of language is important. For example, where possible use short, simple sentences.

CONCLUSION

The amount of detail to be included in a research proposal will depend on what it is for. A proposal for a small-scale study will usually be quite short, with maybe only a couple of sentences on some sections discussed here. All the areas covered should be at least given some thought. A proposal should be as short as possible, whilst at the same time containing all the necessary information the reader will need to appreciate what you plan to do and why.

Further reading

Homan (1991) provides a useful review of the role of ethics in social research, including the questions which may be raised at various stages of the research project. Bell (1993) is a good basic guide to carrying out a research project from start to finish. Strunk and White (1979), first published in 1919, is an interesting and helpful little book on how to write well, containing lots of useful examples of good and not so good writing style.

Part III

DOING RESEARCH

Doing social surveys

Clive Seale and Paul Filmer

CONTENTS

Historically, as was shown in Chapter 6, social surveys have been associated with quantification and the production of social statistics. In this chapter, therefore, we will explain the basic techniques of the quantitative social survey, focusing in particular on the design of interviews and questionnaires and on sampling. A case study of a social survey of craftspeople in the United Kingdom will be used to illustrate the survey method. Although we will focus largely on the production of quantitative data and representative sampling, we will also touch on the role of social surveys in producing qualitative data and the use of more exploratory sampling methods. These methods are discussed in more detail in later chapters.

NEGOTIATING AIMS

In the classical social survey the questions that a researcher asks are determined by the aims of the study. It is therefore important to be as clear as
possible about aims *before* beginning questionnaire design. In this respect
classical social surveys differ from the approach of ethnographers (Chapter
17) or some who use qualitative interviewing (Chapter 16) who may start out
with only loosely specified aims, finding that these become clearer as the
study progresses.

The aims of a study may be fairly broad, such as: 'I will try to find out as
much as I can about the way higher education determines career destina-
tions.' Alternatively, they may be quite precisely specified, in which case
they are called *hypotheses* (see Chapter 9). An example might be an attempt to
discover whether the following statement is true or false: 'People with university degrees are more likely to be in professional or managerial jobs
10 years after the end of full-time education, compared with people of the
same age without degrees.'

The aims of a social survey may be derived from the theoretical concerns
of an academic discipline, from the social policy concerns of people trying
to remedy some social problem, or from the personal interests of the
researcher. Chapter 8 discussed the difference between theoretical and
policy concerns, revealing that the social researcher is sometimes placed in
the position of questioning the assumptions made by policy makers who
commission research studies. In particular it was pointed out that at the
beginning of a project researchers should be particularly careful not to
accept uncritically the fixed definitions of phenomena (for example, of 'a
tribe' or 'a family') often contained in descriptions of 'social problems'
offered by policy makers. The final list of aims constructed for a social
survey will reflect a process of negotiation between the various people concerned with the study, who may each have rather different concerns.
A final list might look like this:

1 To discover whether possession of a university degree enhances the job
   prospects of black people as much as those of white people.
2 To discover whether people without degrees are more likely to have jobs
   in which they experience alienation.
3 To compare the experiences of women and men graduates in balancing
   the demands of home and work.

Note that the statements contain a list of *phenomena* (for example 'university
degree', 'black people', 'alienation', 'home') *all* of which in an interactionist
or constructionist perspective would be seen as variably constituted across
different social settings. For the social survey researcher the means by which
phenomena are constituted are not *primary* concerns, but they should be
secondary ones, in that an awareness of this will feed into the design of
questionnaires and interviews that are sensitive to variations in social

context. Such sensitivity can help the researcher to avoid imposing categories that do not reflect the realities of people's lives, as was done in Booth's imposition of moralistic 'questions of habit' to explain poverty (see Chapter 6).

The first aim is fairly precise, and could be of concern to social policy makers. A researcher might question the validity of categorizing people as 'black' or 'white' and prefer a more detailed and sensitive set of categories. The second aim is also fairly precise and would be of interest to sociologists testing an academic theory of the relationship between class position and the Marxist concept of alienation. The third is more broadly defined and might have arisen from the personal concerns of the researcher planning the survey, although policy makers could be equally interested (for example, those concerned to promote equality of opportunity between the sexes).

GATHERING INFORMATION

It is often assumed that people are questioned when a social survey is carried out. The classic image of the survey interviewer, clipboard in hand, interrogating a respondent, springs to mind. Surveys of entities other than persons, however, can and have been done. Thus one can survey countries to compare them on some feature (for example, rate of economic growth), or one can survey institutions (for example, to discover how schools vary in their exam results), or households (for example, to find out the total income of the family). These are known as variations in the **unit of analysis**. Sometimes it is appropriate to question people directly in order to find the required information (for example, to discover a household's income), but information (or **data** as we will now call it) is also available in official records. Thus, schools keep records of their exam results, and governments may survey schools for this information.

More usually, though, the social survey researcher will be concerned to ask questions of people. A number of choices in how to do this are available. Choosing between an **interview** and a self-completed **questionnaire** on which the respondent writes their answers is the first decision that faces the researcher. Within these there are also choices to be made, each with advantages or disadvantages. Thus, interviews can be done face to face or by telephone. A questionnaire can be sent and returned by post, or handed directly to the respondent who completes it on the spot and hands it back. Additionally, some interviews contain pauses for respondents to complete questionnaire sections. This can be particularly advantageous if a topic is felt to be socially embarrassing to discuss face to face and has been used, for example, in surveys of sexual behaviour.

Interviews have certain advantages over questionnaires. The interviewer can explain questions that the respondent has not understood and can ask for further elaboration of replies (for example, 'Why do you say that?'). In general, being asked questions by a sympathetic listener is experienced as more rewarding by respondents than the chore of filling in a form for some anonymous researcher, so it is generally found that fewer people refuse to take part and more questions can be asked of each person. However, interviews are more time consuming for the researcher and it may be the case that **interviewer bias**, where the interviewer influences the replies by revealing their own opinions, can be avoided by postal questionnaires. (You will know, however, from Chapter 2, that the idea that 'bias' is a problem to be avoided is itself questioned by some researchers.)

Questionnaires have the advantage of being cheap, but are more suited to issues where there are only a few questions which are relatively clear and simple in their meaning, and the choice of replies can be limited to fixed categories. They are especially useful in surveying people who are dispersed over a wide geographical area, where the travelling demands on an interviewer would be excessive.

Types of interview

The interview is a more flexible form than the questionnaire and, if intelligently used, can generally be used to gather information of greater depth and more sensitive to contextual variations in meaning. The classical survey research tradition, geared to producing quantitative data, is generally associated with interviews where the wording and order of questions are exactly the same for every respondent. Variation in responses can thus be attributed to respondents and not to variability in the interviewing technique. Wording the questions in the same way for each respondent is sometimes called **standardizing**. Asking the questions in the same order is called **scheduling**.

Interviews, however, can be non-scheduled, though still partly standardized. Here, the interviewer works from a list of topics that need to be covered with each respondent, but the order and exact wording of questions are not important. Generally, such interviews gather qualitative data, which need to be coded into categories if they are to be made amenable to statistical analysis. Chapter 16 discusses qualitative interviewing in more depth, where you will learn more about interviews which are neither scheduled nor standardized. Here, the interviewer elicits each respondent's unique personal story, following up leads where they seem interesting and not worrying about whether each person has discussed the same topics as every other person in the survey. Such interviewing is mentioned here because it is important to dispel the notion that social surveys always involve rigidly fixed questioning devices, where people are treated like machines and the end purpose is solely to categorize and count. On the one hand, qualitative material can be of great interest in a social survey. On the other hand, as will become evident in Chapter 12 on coding, qualitative material of all types can be usefully quantified if this furthers the aims of a research project.

DESIGNING QUESTIONS

The aims of a survey should determine the questions that go into an interview schedule or a questionnaire. If the survey aims to produce quantitative
data, the questions asked will also closely parallel the **variables** that will later
be used in statistical analysis. A variable is something on which a unit of
analysis (for example, a person) *varies*. For example, people may vary
according to whether they are male or female, or whether they answer 'Yes'
or 'No' to a question asking whether they have a degree qualification. Sex
and the possession of a degree are therefore both questions and variables.

Concepts and indicators

If you examine the three aims of the survey discussed in the first section of
this chapter you will see that they contain a number of **concepts**. These are
possession of a degree qualification, being black or white, having a job,
alienation, gender and the demands of home and work. A concept describes
a *phenomenon* like ethnic identity, tribe or family type. In designing questions, a researcher should ensure that the concepts contained within the aims
of the study are *comprehensively* covered. If one forgot to ask a question about
whether people had a degree qualification, for example, it would not be
possible to fulfil the aims of the study.

The questions chosen can be understood as **indicating** the concepts contained in the aims. Ensuring good links between concepts and their indicators lies at the heart of good question design. Some concepts are easier to
indicate than others. The concept of *sex* or *gender*, for example, is in most
cases not controversial and might, in an interview, be indicated by the
interviewer recording their impression rather than asking a question about
it. The concept of having a degree qualification might also be indicated fairly
easily, by asking a person to list their educational qualifications. Whether a
person has a job, however, might pose more problems. What does one do
about part-time workers, for example? Do we count housework as a 'job'?
How do we decide whether someone is 'black' or 'white'? What if the
respondent feels they are one thing, but we feel they are another?

Additionally, many of the more interesting concepts in social research are
multidimensional, which is to say that they are made up from several different things. Alienation is an example. Finding questions to indicate the
extent of a person's alienation requires some further conceptual work, and
perhaps some reading to see how different authors have used the term. The
sociologist Gerry Rose (1982) has suggested that a researcher interested in
finding indicators for this concept would need to subdivide it into several
components. Alienation involves, amongst other things, a sense of power-
lessness, of normlessness (being outside normal society), isolation and self-
estrangement (seeing a part of oneself as if it were a stranger). It is easy, for
example, to see how one could be powerless without being isolated, so in
order to count as 'truly' alienated a person would need to indicate that they

experienced all of its components, requiring questions indicating each of the dimensions of alienation.

Types of question

Figure 11.1 gives examples of three types of question: open, closed, and pre-coded. **Open questions** gather qualitative data, often written down verbatim or tape recorded. These may be reported by the researcher as interesting comments, or may be coded into categories which are then amenable to quantitative analysis (shown in Chapter 12). Their advantage is that they allow a respondent to answer on their own terms, enabling the researcher to discover unexpected things about the way people see a topic.

Closed questions, on the other hand, specify more closely the terms of reference for the respondent to use in formulating their reply. This may be because the aims of the study are quite specific about this. Such questions tend to invite one-word answers rather than the lengthier replies that open questions often produce. If more detail is required it is often useful to add a **probe** such as 'Why do you say that?' in order to learn more about the person. The researcher interested in counting replies will still need to construct categories into which replies can be placed.

Open

1 What happens at work when things go wrong?
2 How do people in this union feel about attending meetings?
3 How would you say you and your family are getting along financially now, compared with a year ago?

Closed

1 When things go wrong at work, do the people blame each other or don't they?
2 Do most people in this union feel they should attend meetings?
3 Would you say you and your family are better off financially than you were a year ago?

Pre-coded

1 When things go wrong at work, do the people blame each other

always	1
some of the time	2
or never?	3

2 What proportion of people in this union feel they should attend meetings:

most	1
some	2
or none?	3

3 Compared to a year ago, would you say you and your family are financially

better off	1
about the same	2
or worse off?	3

Figure 11.1   *Open, closed and pre-coded questions*

Pre-coded questions (sometimes called *fixed-choice* questions) do not require this as the responses allowed are pre-specified. This can be convenient for the researcher wishing to conduct a quick analysis of replies, but can be frustrating for respondents if their true feelings do not fit into the categories offered. The over-use of pre-coded questions is common in social surveys and has been the basis of much criticism of the survey method, which is then accused of imposing the researcher's meanings on people, rather than allowing people to speak for themselves.

Postal and self-completed questionnaires are, then, normally both standardized and scheduled, often using fixed-choice questions to inquire into fairly simple topics. They are rarely suitable for gathering qualitative data. This is not to say that they *cannot* be used in this way if people are sufficiently motivated to spend the time writing about themselves. However, this usage is rare. Interviews are a more flexible method, and can be used to gather richer data.

Some common problems of question design

The best way to find out whether a question 'works' is to try it out on a number of people. One of the more common problems that such **piloting** of a question can then reveal is that it is not answerable, or that its meaning is ambiguous. The respondent may say that he or she doesn't really understand what the question is getting at, or may give a reply that reveals they have interpreted it in a very different way from what was intended. Practice in designing questions, trying them out and revising them will improve your skills in making good questions in much the same way as practising a musical instrument will improve your musical performance. Eventually you will learn the art of imagining the range of possible reactions there could be to a question, so that your first attempts at design will become progressively more successful, just as the musician learns to 'sight read' new music.

Figure 11.2 contains a number of questions illustrating common problems of question design. Question 1, for example, was taken from an actual social survey done in the 1950s. The logic is too complex for the respondent to know what she is being asked, and a solution might involve asking a series of questions about frequency and timing of sexual intercourse, contraception

---

1 Has it happened to you that over a long period of time, when you neither practised abstinence, nor used birth control, you did not conceive? (yes/no)
2 Do you have a television set?
3 What kind of house do you have?
4 Shouldn't families these days do more to care for their elderly relatives?
5 How much alcohol do you drink each week?

Figure 11.2 *Questions exhibiting common problems*

and conception which the researcher would need to analyse in order to answer the original question.

The second question seems to be quite answerable, but contains a hidden ambiguity which centres on the use of the word 'have', which could refer to the concept of legal ownership, or to viewing rights. This may be an important distinction on a research project concerned to use this, say, as an indicator of a person's material wealth. On another project, perhaps concerned with television viewing habits, this will be a less important distinction. Thus the aims of the project will influence the evaluation of question wording.

The third question also contains this ambiguity in the word 'have', but has additional ambiguity in the word 'kind', which could be understood in a variety of ways by respondents (for example, detached or semi-detached, rented or privately owned). If this is important to the aims of the project, one should specify the frame of reference that the researcher wishes the respondent to use when answering the question (for example, 'Is your house detached or semi-detached?'). On the other hand, if the researcher is interested in exploring the way people think about their houses (in other words, how they 'constitute' the word 'house' in a research interview setting), the question may be good as it stands. It is, however, a question that presumes that all respondents live in houses rather than flats, mobile homes or other forms of dwelling, so should be preceded by a question that filters out people in those circumstances.

The fourth question would, in many textbooks on methods, be criticized as an example of a leading question, one where it is difficult for the respondent to disagree without going against the implied values of the person asking the question. Replacing the question with a more neutral item (for example, 'What is your view of the care elderly people receive from their relatives these days?') might be recommended. Leading questions, however, can be useful in identifying people who hold particularly strong or socially unacceptable views. Someone who feels that families these days do too much for their older members might be of particular interest to the researcher, who might select them for a particularly detailed analysis. Additionally, one could argue that both question 4 and the suggested 'neutral' alternative are hypothetical questions, and that more realistic replies would be gained by asking about specific cases (for example, 'So how do you feel about the amount of help given by Mr X to his mother?').

All interviews are, of course, 'hypothetical' situations, in which the respondent is temporarily taken out of his or her normal environment to answer a series of questions which may be of little importance in guiding actions in everyday life. This is a general problem of interviews (discussed in Chapter 16), and it should be remembered that questioning people in this way is but one way of producing data for a social survey. There is no reason why a survey should not also involve observation of people in their everyday lives. Asking about alcohol consumption in an interview (as in the fifth question in Figure 11.2) is notoriously prone to eliciting underestimates.

Other socially charged topics also demonstrate this: men tend to over-estimate their number of sexual partners in interviews; women tend to underestimate. People are reluctant to confess to crimes in an interview setting. It is sometimes hard to deal with this source of invalidity, but a start can be made by combining interviews with observation. For example, one researcher estimated alcohol consumption by counting empty containers in people's rubbish bins.

In classical social survey work language is treated as a **resource** to find out about people's lives outside the interview or questionnaire setting. This view of language is different from the view taken by those doing discourse ana-lysis (Chapter 19) and conversation analysis (Chapter 20). Using language to find out about people's lives requires that both the researcher and the respondent agree on shared meanings for words. Eliminating ambiguity is therefore very important, and there are sometimes strenuous efforts made to enter the linguistic world of the respondent, which may contain words with meanings that are not shared by the wider population. This is illustrated by the questions in Figure 11.3, taken from two social surveys into sexual behaviour. The first was designed for use with a sample of people from the general population; the second from a survey of gay men in London. The wordings reflect extensive pilot work to establish the terms used to describe various sexual acts that would be understood unambiguously by the even-tual respondents.

From a self-completed questionnaire designed for use with women in the general UK population
When, if ever, was the last occasion you had sex with a man?
Was a condom (sheath) used on any occasions in the last 4 weeks?
When, if ever, was the last occasion you had vaginal sexual intercourse with a man?
When, if ever, was the last occasion you had oral sex with a man by you to a partner?
When, if ever, was the last occasion you had oral sex with a man by a partner to you?
When, if ever, was the last occasion you had anal sex with a man?
When was the last occasion you had genital contact with a man not involving intercourse?

Source: from a survey reported by Wellings et al., 1994

From a face-to-face interview schedule designed for use with gay men
How many times in the last month have you: wanked / been wanked; sucked / been sucked; fucked / been fucked; rimmed / been rimmed; fingered / been fingered; fisted / been fisted; performed water sports / had water sports done on/to you; done scat to/on / had scat done on/to you; given an enema to / been given an enema; body rubbed / been body rubbed; thigh fucked / been thigh fucked; performed corporal punishment on / had corporal punishment done to you; massaged / been given a massage; tied up / been tied up?

Source: Project Sigma questionnaire, reported by Davies et al., 1993 and Coxon, 1996

Figure 11.3   *Adapting language to reflect usage by respondents: two surveys of sexual behaviour*

VALIDITY AND RELIABILITY

At its broadest, **validity** concerns the degree to which the findings of a research study are true. It is helpful, however, to understand validity as made up from various components. These are indicated in Figure 11.4.

Internal validity will be discussed in Chapter 14, where causal reasoning from quantitative data will be introduced. **External validity** will be discussed later in this chapter, when it will be seen to be an aspect of sampling. So far, in this chapter, we have discussed **measurement validity** in considering the best way of designing questions so that they accurately indicate the concepts and phenomena of interest in a research study.

The measurement validity of questions can be improved by various methods. The first and perhaps most common method is known as **face validity**, whereby the researcher thinks hard about whether the questions indicate the intended concept. The assessment of face validity may be helped by asking people with practical or professional knowledge of the area to assess how well questions indicate the concept. Thus a sequence of questions designed to indicate a person's health status might be assessed by a group of nurses or doctors. **Criterion validity** involves comparing the results of questions with established indicators of the same concept. Thus, one might compare the results of an interview survey of people's health status with the results of a doctor's examination of the same people. **Construct validity** evaluates a measure according to how well it conforms to expectations derived from theory. Thus, if we have reason to believe that health status is related to social class, we would expect our measure of health status to give different results for people from different social classes. The construct validity of certain questions may only be established after a series of studies and analyses in which researchers build up a greater understanding of how the questions relate to other constructs.

None of these methods of improving measurement validity is perfect. Argument about the face validity of indicators often reveals disagreement about the meaning of concepts. For example, what do we mean by 'health'? Although our indicator may agree with some external criterion, who is to say that the external criterion is valid? Thus a doctor's judgement about health status is not infallible. Construct validity depends both on a theory being correct, and on other measures of other concepts in the theory being valid. If social class is not related to health, or if our measure of social class is itself

---

1 *Measurement validity* The degree to which measures (for example, questions on a questionnaire) successfully indicate concepts.
2 *Internal validity* The extent to which causal statements are supported by the study.
3 *External validity* The extent to which findings can be generalized to populations or to other settings

---

Figure 11.4   *The components of validity*

not valid, then associations between health and social class cannot show the validity of our measure of health.

This lack of finality about judgements of validity, though, is a characteristic of all empirical research and is not just confined to quantitative social survey work. Any study can be improved if the researcher has a keen awareness of validity issues, and uses the methods available to improve it.

If a question obtains a different answer from a person each time it is asked, then it is said to lack **reliability**. This may be because it is ambiguously worded, thus meaning different things to the person answering on each occasion, or because it is asking about something that the person considers unimportant, about which it is unnecessary to be consistent. Alternatively, the person asking the question may influence the person differently on different occasions, perhaps by rewording the question, or by some non-verbal cue. Asking clear and relevant questions, either worded in the same way for each respondent or which are asked by a researcher who has a good understanding of their purpose, are likely to increase reliability.

A question can be reliable without being valid. Thus, it is fairly easy to design a reliable question asking a person's gender that, each time it is asked, will get the same reply from a person. It is not valid, though, to use this as an indicator of social class. A question cannot be valid without being reliable; if people give different answers every time they answer a question it can have no stable meaning, and therefore cannot consistently indicate an underlying concept.

SAMPLING

Random sampling

In the early days of the social survey this type of research required immense resources as it was felt that in order to discover the conditions of the population it was necessary to conduct a complete **census** of all its members. This is characteristic of the work of Booth and Rowntree, described in Chapter 6, who surveyed the entire populations of London and York in order to discover the extent and causes of poverty.

The application of **sampling theory** to the social survey by Bowley (Bowley and Burnett-Hurst, 1915) made the **sample survey** possible, a cheaper method involving the random selection of a **sample** from a defined **population**. Generalizing the results found in the sample to the population from which it was drawn became a matter of assessing the likelihood of results having occurred by chance, a topic which will be covered in greater detail in Chapter 13. Here, methods of random sampling will first be outlined, followed by some other non-random techniques which often prove useful in doing social surveys.

The first step in drawing up a **simple random sample** is to define the population of interest. It is quite common for researchers to embark on a social survey without thinking about this, possessing only vaguely

Doing research

thought-out ideas about the social group to which they wish to generalize their results. If a population has been defined, however, the next step is to seek out a list of all the units of analysis (sometimes called *sampling elements*). Such a list is known as a **sampling frame**. Figure 11.5 lists a number of sampling frames, together with populations they may be understood to cover. Lists of people and organizations are very common in the bureaucratic society in which we live, and provide the survey researcher with many opportunities. However, the first thing to note about the sampling frames in Figure 11.5 is that they all have limitations in their coverage of the populations concerned. The electoral register, for example, may under-represent people who frequently move house, or who are alienated from the formal political process. Not everyone owns a telephone, and even amongst telephone subscribers there are those who do not wish their number to be placed in the directory. For these sorts of reasons, social surveys requiring general population coverage in the United Kingdom now often use the 'postcode address file' used by the postal service, which is a complete listing of all postal addresses in the country.

Once a sampling frame has been obtained, all of its elements should be numbered, and the sample size decided upon. To obtain a simple random sample, one can use a table of random numbers, of the type commonly printed in statistics textbooks, from which to pick the numbers of the sampling elements to be surveyed. Alternatively, if one is certain that the sampling frame lists all of the elements in a random way, it is possible to use a **sampling interval** to select elements by **systematic sampling**. For example, if a population contains 100,000 people, and we wish to select 1,000 of these, our sampling interval is calculated by dividing 100,000 by 1,000 to give a figure of 100. Starting at a randomly selected person with a number below 100, one then selects every hundredth person in the list.

The essential point about both of the above methods of sampling is that every member of the population has a chance of being selected. The

---

Covering the general population
Register of electors; telephone directory; birth certificates; death certificates

Covering institutions
Directory of universities, schools or colleges; health services directory; directory of penal institutions

Covering professional groups
Medical directory; registers of psychologists, nurses, osteopaths; register of chartered surveyors

Some other groups
A university department's list of students attending a course; hospital admissions daily log book; a school register of pupils; an employer's record of employees; a solicitor's records of clients

Figure 11.5   *Examples of sampling frames*

statistical procedures used to calculate the likelihood of sample results having occurred because an unrepresentative sample has been chosen (discussed in Chapter 13) can only be applied if this condition is met.

It is possible to select random samples in a variety of other ways. Two will be explained here, stratified random sampling and cluster sampling. The first of these increases the likelihood of selecting a representative sample; the second reduces this, but may be the most practical option in certain circumstances.

Random sampling relies on chance to get a group of people (or elements) whose characteristics mirror those in the population concerned. Thus, we might hope in a random sample taken, say, from the population of people aged between 20 and 25 in a country to see roughly equal numbers of men and women. The larger the sample, the more likely it is that this will occur (thus sample size influences representativeness). However, in any such randomly selected sample it is always possible that, by some chance, we will select only one sex. **Stratified sampling** allows us to guard against this possibility. In the case of sex, for example, we might first list all of the women in the sampling frame, and then all of the men. If the sampling interval is still 100, every 100th woman is then selected, and then every 100th man, as in systematic sampling.

Here, sex is the **stratifying factor**, and in order to use this we need to know the sex of every member of the population listed on the sampling frame, so that it can be arranged accordingly. In fact, it is wise to use any information available on a sampling frame as a stratifying factor as this will almost always improve representativeness. One might, for example, stratify by age as well as sex, in which case one would arrange the sampling frame so that it listed 20-year old women, then 20-year-old men, then 21-year-old women, then 21-year-old men and so on. All of this depends on this information being recorded against each person listed on the frame.

As an extra consideration, researchers sometimes select samples using **disproportionate stratification**. This can be useful if there is a minority group within a population of particular interest for the study. Thus, a sample of 100 from the general population of a country would be unlikely to contain many millionaires. If one were particularly interested in comparing the lives of such people with those of people less well off, and if one knew the incomes of every person listed in the sampling frame (quite a demanding requirement!), one could list the millionaires separately and choose every second one, as opposed to every 100th person in the list of poorer people.

Cluster sampling may be useful if the population is very widely dispersed, and the resources for travelling are limited. Thus, in a survey of students in universities, one might choose five universities at random from a list of all universities. From lists of all the students in those five universities, an interviewer could then choose a random sample of students (thus 'clustered' in those institutions). This also has the advantage that only five universities need to be approached for listings of all their students. However, it introduces the possibility of choosing five universities unrepresentative of all universities which would be avoided if students were randomly selected from all institutions in the country.

Whatever random sampling method is chosen, a survey is still likely to involve a certain amount of **non-response** as not everyone wishes to take part in social surveys. This also reduces the representativeness of a sample survey, and it is important to do everything possible to ensure a high **response rate**. Normally, one might expect a response rate of 70–80% in an interview survey, and a little less in a postal questionnaire survey, as people find it more rewarding to talk face to face than to fill in forms. However, these expectations are likely to vary across different topics, with some subjects (for example, the death of relatives, or personal sexual behaviour) being more difficult than others to get people to agree to discuss. In a random sample survey, the response rate should always be reported and, if possible, information given about the characteristics of non-responders, so that likely bias can be assessed.

Non-random sampling

It is not always practical to randomly sample from a population. In some circumstances it might not be desirable either. The primary concern addressed by random sampling is that of *external validity*, the capacity to generalize from a sample to a population. In some survey designs, this is not a high priority. Firstly, the topic may be such that charges of unrepresentativeness are unlikely to 'stick'. Thus, the sociologist Geoffrey Baruch (1981) analysed the stories about medical consultations told by eight parents of children attending two medical clinics. If he had been trying to use these interviews to generalize about all parents' satisfaction with the quality of medical care in the country as a whole, we would feel this to be a hopelessly inadequate sample. However, his purpose was to analyse the language used during the interview to present parents' actions in a moral light, suggesting that 'atrocity stories' about poor behaviour by doctors were often told in order to achieve this effect. It is plausible to argue that such a phenomenon would have been found in almost any sample of eight parents that he might have picked for interview.

Mary Douglas's work, discussed in Chapter 9, demonstrates a different rationale for generalizing findings which has been called **theoretical generalization** (Mitchell, 1983). You will recall that Douglas concluded from her case study of the Lele, when compared with the ancient Israelites, that groups faced with enemies and unused to crossing boundaries were less likely to celebrate anomaly in their classificatory thinking. The logic here is that the processes (or 'structures') described are so universal that when identified in just one case they are likely to hold true of all cases. Of course, this is a structuralist logic (see Chapter 3) that is questioned in some areas of social theory, but it demonstrates that non-random sampling methods may have a rationale rather different from statistical representativeness.

This is also exhibited by a method called **theoretical sampling**, first developed by Glaser and Strauss (1967) in order to generate theories about the process of dying. Applied to the social survey, this involves the selection of people for interview (or settings for study) according to whether they have characteristics that are likely to help in developing an emerging theory. An example taken from a research project current at the time of writing (being done by Marion Garnett) concerns the topic of the use of alternative medical therapies by nurses. An initial three interviews showed that all of the nurses described therapies involving different types of massage as contributing to a new form of nursing expertise that involves the expression of care by touch. A fourth interview will now be conducted with a nurse chosen explicitly on the grounds that she practises an alternative therapy that does *not* involve massage or touch, to allow other, theoretically interesting meanings that nurses claim for their use of these therapies to emerge. (Theoretical sampling is discussed further in Chapter 12.)

More commonly, however, non-random methods are used as a 'second best' when a sampling frame is unavailable. A variety of methods exist. One can ask for a **volunteer sample**, as where a magazine prints a questionnaire for interested readers to return, or where an advertisement is posted on a notice board. Sometimes a **snowball sample** is drawn up, with an interviewer asking each person they interview who else they know who might be willing to be interviewed about a topic. This can be a very helpful way of gaining access to people who, without such a personal contact, might otherwise refuse to be interviewed. It has, for example, proved useful in interviewing people involved in illegal drug use and prostitution, where the stigmatized nature of these activities means that potential interviewees are more likely to talk to someone who has found them through a mutual contact.

Market researchers often use a method called **quota sampling** because it is relatively cheap and quick to carry out. Here, interviewers must find people to interview who fulfil specified criteria (often in terms of their age, sex and social class). This can quickly build up a sample that contains people who mirror the distribution of these characteristics in the population as a whole. Typically, people are stopped in the street and asked their age and occupation. If the potential respondent fits the requirements of the 'quota' (for example, for a certain number of middle-class, middle-aged men), the interview then proceeds.

When a survey is small scale, it is often not practical to attempt to be representative or to use random sampling from a sampling frame. It may be a better use of resources to select people for interview who vary on a particular characteristic, such as age or gender, that might throw up interesting differences between people that could later be confirmed in a larger study. Thus 10 men and 10 women might be chosen on the basis of snowball or volunteer recruitment, and results analysed in terms of the gender differences in replies. It is important then to exercise caution about representativeness when presenting the results.

CASE STUDY: WORKING IN CRAFTS

We will now show how the general principles of the social survey method were applied to a particular research question, investigating the socio-economic conditions of people working in an area of cultural production in the UK, that of crafts. (One of the workshop exercises at the end of this book involves examination of parts of the questionnaire used in this survey.) The study was conducted in the early 1980s by Bruce and Filmer (1983) and set the parameters for a later updating study by Knott (1994). Both were commissioned by the UK-based Crafts Council and involved negotiation of the aims of the study with the officers directly responsible for the commission.

The Council had been in operation since 1970, initially as the Crafts Advisory Committee of the Design Council, funded by an annual government grant. It had gathered considerable information about the crafts and their practitioners during this time – but mainly of an *ad hoc* character. A new government had been elected in 1979 and, in pursuing a policy of cutting expenditure, it had already cut the very much larger grant to the Arts Council. The Crafts Council considered, not without reason, that it could be next and that it could defend its need for continued funding only on the basis of specific and accurate information about its constituency. Yet there was no detailed general picture of the numbers and social and economic conditions of craftspeople in England and Wales, or of the types of craft that they practised. It was the need for this information that dictated the aims of the study.

The aims of the study

The primary objectives were:

1 To establish as precisely as possible the number and occupational distribution of practising craftspeople in England and Wales.
2 To assess the socio-economic conditions of craftspeople, their personal circumstances, work situation, fulfilment and difficulties.
3 To obtain information about the character, extent and adequacy of financial and organizational assistance available to them.
4 To provide information about the character and adequacy of training and education in crafts.

The third and fourth of these aims related more directly than the first two to the activities of the Council, since it operated a number of schemes to provide grants for equipment, training and other forms of assistance to craftspeople, not all of whom agreed with or approved of the Council's activities. This meant that, as an important feature of seeking to ensure validity for the study, the researchers had to reassure craftspeople that they were working independently of any direction from the Council at every stage which involved gathering information from them.

Gathering information

The *units of analysis* of the study were the craftspeople of England and Wales, but since the first aim of the study was to establish how many of them there were, and what kinds of craftwork they were doing, deciding how to gather information raised some interesting questions. Firstly, the researchers had to decide how craftspeople were to be defined for the purposes of the study. That is to say, the *phenomenon* to be investigated required clarification so that they could use a definition that came reasonably close to the ways in which people constituted themselves as craftspeople across a range of settings. This was a far from straightforward matter.

The charter which established the Crafts Council charged it with responsibility for the promotion of 'fine crafts', echoing, perhaps, the already chartered Arts Council's responsibility for fine art. But 'fine crafts' was a term without any previous history, and one which contradicted quite directly the more recent pre-industrial and early industrial traditions of craft production – of training through apprenticeship in highly skilled manual production of functional objects. Many contemporary craftspeople sought to continue and adapt these traditions, despite the difficulties in doing so in a mass-production industrial economy. Others, however, had begun to redefine their role in terms of a new concept of the artist craftsperson, and it was to these that the Crafts Council had seemed mainly to be directing its provision. In part, artist craftworkers were redefining themselves as closer in occupational identity to fine artists. The labour-intensive character of their skilled manual work in a machine-industrial economy meant that the comparatively small numbers of goods they produced were often expensive and, for that reason, not likely to be treated as functional for everyday use by those who purchased them. The process of redefinition of the occupational role of craftspeople had also been affected by some far-reaching changes in the structures of fine art higher education in Britain at the end of the 1960s, which had brought crafts (as applied arts) to the centre of art school curricula over the following decade.

A study of craftspeople in Australia (Committee of Enquiry into the Crafts in Australia, 1975) had used a helpful definition of 'a person who applies skill in a largely manual operation and is significantly responsible for the finished product or products which result'. They bore in mind also an evaluative goal for craft as 'the best workmanship allied to the best design'. They worked finally with a loose formulation of craft as the application of skills to realize a prepared design, to reproduce the items made, to select the raw material and to take advantage of it as it is being worked. Such skills were seen to require considerable training and experience to reach a high level of performance and enable the maker to produce work of a distinctive individual style.

Since the budget for the research was relatively small and the numbers of potential respondents to be sampled had yet to be established, the researchers decided that the primary means of gathering information would be by self-completed postal questionnaire. It would also be *standardized* and *scheduled* because of the basic character of information required. Other sources of information, particularly in relation to the third and the fourth aims, were available from the Council's own records and from further and higher educational institutions. These became important when constructing the *sampling frame* (see below).

The questionnaire would be *piloted* on a small sample, once the scale of the population had been established, and the researchers decided that, once the final questionnaire had been distributed and preliminary results obtained for analysis, they would undertake *non-scheduled* field interviews with craftspeople selected from different crafts and regions. The content of these would be based on the comments which respondents would be invited to add to their completed questionnaires, and would provide another way of trying to ensure the validity of the research, by finding out whether the information produced by questionnaires and other sources made sense to craftspeople themselves.

Design of questions

As a result of piloting, the researchers designed a questionnaire consisting of *pre-coded* (or *fixed-choice*) questions. Three areas of questioning were particularly interesting *indicators* of *concepts* included in the aims of the research. The questions associated with these are shown in Figure 11.6.

The first group of questions asks respondents about their level of involvement in crafts. One might normally expect to ask respondents in a conventional occupational group simply whether they worked full time or part time. The researchers had learnt from the pilot, however, that for a variety of clear reasons many craftspeople considered themselves to be at some times permanently and at others temporarily parttime and at still others full time. Moreover, crafts can be a precarious occupation because it yields relatively low levels of income to most of its practitioners, who may decide to move into other kinds of work either temporarily or permanently, and these variations had to be catered for in the answers from which respondents could choose.

The second group of questions asks about income. Questions on this topic, like those on alcohol consumption, are notoriously likely to yield misleadingly low figures. Whatever assurances of anonymity and confidentiality may be given by researchers to respondents, the latter appear to work on the assumption that the tax authorities may be informed of their declarations of income. The researchers on this study found the most effective way of eliciting reasonably accurate answers was by asking them to indicate their net income from craftwork in one year – that is, their craft income after the deduction of all related costs.

The third group asks respondents to detail their education and crafts training, and to state whether they had found these useful in their subsequent work in crafts. More than half had undergone further or higher education in crafts, but more than four-fifths stated that their courses had been of no value in explaining the difficulties of running a business in crafts. Many craftspeople also claimed that they were self-taught.

Sampling

Since one of the aims of the 1983 study was to ascertain the size of the population of craftspeople in England and Wales, the task of establishing a

---

1 Questions indicating level of involvement in craftwork
Your present crafts involvement (please tick the categories that apply to you):

full time / temporarily part-time / regularly part time / work occasionally for sale / still a student or trainee / craftwork mainly a hobby / retired / no longer doing craftwork / not in crafts at all

Hours spent on craftwork: about how many hours per week, on average, do you spend on your own craftwork (including all related work such as selling and maintenance)?

up to 20 hours / 21 to 30 hours / 31 to 40 hours / 41 to 50 hours / 51 to 60 hours / over 60 hours

2 Questions indicating income from craftwork
How much of your own personal income comes from your own craft production?

all or nearly all / 60 to 80% / 40 to 60% / 20 to 40% / under 20%

What did you make from your own craft production last year (namely 'profits' – what was left from all sales/fees and so on after meeting all related expenses)?

£10,000 or more / £8,001 to £10,000 / £6,001 to £8,000 / £4,001 to £6,000 / £2,001 to £4,000 / £1,001 to £2,000 / £501 to £1,000 / £201 to £500 / less than £200 / made a loss / no sales

3 Questions indicating level and usefulness of training in craftwork
Please tick all the ways in which you got training and early crafts experience:

mostly self-taught / evening classes or part-time courses / apprenticeship / art or design course at a college (full time) / working with experienced craftspeople / other training (please describe)

Further and higher education: have you any of the following qualifications? Please mark the ones you have:

a degree or diploma in art or design / an academic or professional degree or diploma (not related to art or design) / a trade certificate or diploma / a teaching qualification / other further education (please say what it was)

Was your school work up to 16 a useful preparation for your craft training or studies?

yes / in part / no

If you took a course at college, was your course good for

giving technical skill?	yes / in part / no / can't say
understanding design?	yes / in part / no / can't say
explaining how to run a business in crafts?	yes / in part / no / can't say

---

Figure 11.6   *Questions asked in a survey of craftspeople*

sampling frame took on especial significance. In effect, it became the means by which as accurate as possible an estimate of the numbers of craftspeople could be accomplished.

Six lists of craftspeople were already in existence when the research began, each compiled according to different criteria, for different purposes and with varying degrees of accuracy or completeness. Three were held by the Crafts Council: its register of craftspeople, which was non-selective; its selective 'index' of artist craftspeople, whose work it endorsed (an aid to craftspeople in securing commissions); and its records of applicants for the grants it awarded for setting up workshops, acquiring specialist equipment, and training in new skills. A fourth list came from the national membership of the British Crafts Centre. To these were added lists of craftspeople kept by the Regional Arts Associations in England and the Welsh Arts Council, and the lists of members kept by various craft guilds and societies. Further additions were made to these lists by construction of a *volunteer sample* from contacts offered by craftspeople on existing lists, by those teaching crafts in further and higher education and through other self-referrals of crafts-people. These were facilitated by announcing the research in the crafts press generally, inserting a pre-paid self-referral card in an issue of the bimonthly *Crafts* magazine published by the Council, and distributing cards to craft shops and centres and to suppliers of raw materials to craftspeople. After amalgamation and correction of duplications of names, these lists were used as a basis for an estimate of some 20,000 active craftspeople in England and Wales.

However, a simple random sample of this population was not possible. The development of the sampling frame had identified 10 types of craft, differentiated mainly in terms of the materials used. But the numbers of craftspeople were not evenly distributed between them. More than half were engaged in two types of craftwork (either textiles or pottery/ceramics) and a further quarter in another two (either precious metals/jewellery or wood). This necessitated the construction of a *stratified sample* to ensure that it included representative proportions of respondents from the other six minority groups of crafts, which together accounted for only 20% of the population.

The final sample numbered almost 4,000, of whom 1,800 (45%) responded. There was a considerable range of additional comments from respondents to a final *open* question which asked: 'Please write here to expand on any issues mentioned earlier, or to raise any other matters.' These amplified their experiences of working in crafts, and the comments were used to illustrate the tables of data and the discussion of results in the final report. Combined with respondents' answers to fixed-choice questions on their attitudes to their work, the thoughtful and articulate nature of these comments enabled a social survey that was designed for the most part to elicit *quantitative* data to yield a great deal of *qualitative* information also, and hence to deepen the texture of its analysis of contemporary craftspeople.

CONCLUSION

This chapter has reviewed the basic techniques involved in doing social surveys, from the negotiation of aims, and the design of questions, questionnaires and interviews, to issues of validity and reliability and sampling techniques. The application of many aspects of these techniques has been shown in an extended example of a survey of craftspeople. Throughout, the emphasis has been on the provision of practical advice in a context which remains sensitive to both the strengths and the limitations of the method.

Further reading

De Vaus (1991) is a popular and well-written guide to doing social surveys, taking the reader through all of the stages described in this chapter and including quantitative data analysis. Moser and Kalton (1971), although old, is still the most comprehensive and in-depth guide to all aspects of doing social surveys, with a strong quantitative emphasis.

12

Coding and analysing data

Clive Seale and Moira Kelly

Social and cultural research involves taking a particular view of the world, choosing a way of seeing a topic that is different from other possible ways. The selection of certain things rather than others to be called 'data' is an important part of this, but once a researcher is faced with a pile of questionnaires, interview transcripts, field notes or tape transcripts, a further selection occurs. Certain parts of the data will be considered more relevant than others. Additionally, the researcher will usually be interested in detecting *patterns* in the data. A pattern demands that things that are similar are identified. **Coding** involves placing like with like, so that patterns can be found.

Coding is therefore the first step towards data analysis. Decisions taken at this stage in a research project have important consequences. The quality of a coding scheme influences the eventual quality of data analysis, for it is in coding schemes that a researcher becomes committed to particular ways of categorizing the world. Coding schemes can be narrow, artificial devices that hinder thought, or they can contain the seeds of creative new insights.

In this chapter we will first describe the coding of data to prepare it for the statistical procedures described in Chapters 13 and 14. This sort of work is largely associated with the social survey (Chapter 11), but can also be applied to methods normally called 'qualitative'. The chapter will then consider the coding of qualitative data of the sort often produced in ethnographic work or the other methods described in Chapters 17–21. We end with a case study of coding on a particular research project. The use of computers in analysing both quantitative and qualitative data will also be illustrated.

CODING FOR QUANTITATIVE ANALYSIS

The data matrix

At the heart of the statistical analysis of social survey data lies the **data matrix**, as is suggested by Catherine Marsh in her definition of the social survey:

> a survey refers to an investigation where ... systematic measurements are made over a series of cases yielding a rectangle of data ... [and] the variables in the matrix are analysed to see if they show any patterns ... [and] the subject matter is social. (1982: 8)

Table 12.1 shows a small data matrix, derived from a hypothetical social survey in which five people were asked four questions: their sex, their age, whether they were working full-time, part-time or not at all, and the extent of their satisfaction with their work. This last question gave people five options, ranging from 'very satisfied' (1) to 'very dissatisfied' (5). These questions become the **variables** in the matrix. In other words, they are qualities on which the cases (in this case, people) vary.

It will be seen that there is a simple pattern in the matrix, with people beyond conventional retirement age (cases 1 and 5) being out of work. Additionally, the people in work are all females; the people out of work are all male. People out of work were not asked an irrelevant question about job satisfaction, so the *Jobsat* variable for these cases shows data to be missing.

Table 12.1   *A data matrix*

| People | Sex | Variables or questions | | |
		Age	Working	Jobsat
Case 1	Male	66	No	Missing
Case 2	Female	34	Full time	1
Case 3	Female	25	Part time	2
Case 4	Female	44	Full time	5
Case 5	Male	78	No	Missing

The variable called *Sex* is a **nominal** variable (sometimes also called *categorical*). This means that it applies a *name* to the quality, but that there is no sense of magnitude between the different categories of that quality. In this respect it is different from the *Jobsat* variable, where there *is* a sense in which the categories of the variable have magnitude. Someone who says they are 'very satisfied' can be understood as having 'more' satisfaction than someone who says they are 'very dissatisfied'. Variables like this, with a sense of rank order or magnitude, are known as **ordinal** variables. *Age* clearly has a sense of magnitude as well, but this is known as an **interval** variable. This is because there is a fixed and equal distance between the points on the scale. Thus the 'distance' between a person who is 25 and another who is 20 years old is the same as that between a 15-year-old and a 20-year-old. The mathematical operations of addition and subtraction 'make sense' with an interval scale, whereas they do not with an ordinal scale, where the 'distances' between the points of a scale are unknown quantities. The distinction between nominal, ordinal and interval variables becomes important when data analysis begins (see Chapters 13 and 14).

Another feature of the variables in Table 12.1 is that they are expressed in either **string** or **numeric** form. String variables use letters to indicate values; numeric variables use numbers. *Age* and *Jobsat* are numeric; the rest are string. When entering data like these into a computer it is generally advisable to give string variables numeric values. Although most computer packages accept string variables, some place restrictions on the analyses that can be performed with them. The variable *Sex* could be transformed into a numeric variable by giving 'male' the value of 0, and 'female' the value of 1. The variable *Working* could be transformed by the following: 'none' = 0; 'part time' = 1; 'full time' = 2. Finally, some variables are **dichotomous** (consisting of only two values). *Sex* is an example of a dichotomous variable. It is not difficult to imagine how the information in Table 12.1 might have been recorded originally on a form or questionnaire for each of the cases, and then transferred from such forms into the data matrix.

Different question formats

Figure 12.1 shows some examples of questions in different formats. For each format there are different ways of transferring information into a data matrix. Note that the first three questions in Figure 12.1 are *closed* and largely *pre-coded* (see Chapter 11), which is to say that they allow answers from a range of pre-specified choices. The fourth question is an *open* one.

Question 1 can easily be transferred to a data matrix as a *numeric* variable. What would one do, though, if someone did not know their age in years, or refused to answer, or forgot to answer that question? A *missing value* would then be entered at that point in the matrix. If 0 or 99 were chosen to represent a missing value, we would have to be sure that there were no newborn babies or 99-year-olds in the sample, otherwise we would have used up a value needed for these people. One solution is to incorporate negative

1 What is your age in years?
2 Would you say that your health, for your age, is:

excellent	1
good	2
fair	3
or poor?	4
Other (please specify)	....

3 Please indicate which of the following you have experienced in the past year by underlining the conditions that apply:

   (a) persistent cough
   (b) cold or flu
   (c) measles
   (d) mumps
   (e) rubella.

4 At times people are healthier than at other times. What is it like when you are healthy?

Figure 12.1   *Different question formats*

numbers as missing values (for example, 'missing' = –1). Another would be to treat *Age* as a variable with three digits, so that a 99-year-old would be recorded as 099, and the missing value could then safely be allocated a number such as 999.

Question 2 is a bit like the 'job satisfaction' question represented in the data matrix shown in Table 12.1. People, or cases, can be given a value between 1 and 4 in the matrix to indicate the judgement they made about their state of health. However, as is common on this sort of item, a space was allowed for respondents who wanted to describe their health in terms different from those offered by the question. Managing this at the data entry stage depends on how many people chose this option, and whether the detail of their replies is important in achieving the aims of the research study. If replies are rare and the issue is of low importance, one could simply categorize these people as a 5. Alternatively, one could go through all of the questionnaires where people had chosen this option, and devise a category system to place replies into categories with common elements, each of which would be given a separate number: 5, 6, 7, 8 and so on. This procedure is in fact the same as that which will be described for question 4, the open question, below.

Question 3 is an example of a **multiple response item**. Here, respondents can underline (or tick) as many or as few items as they wish. It is best to treat this as a question containing five *dichotomous* variables. If an item is ticked, for example, one could record the person as saying 'yes' to that question; if an item is not ticked, the person has said 'no'. These could be given *numeric* values ('yes' = 1; 'no' = 2, for example), so that the answer of a person indicating they had a cough and a cold but none of the other conditions might be a row of the following numbers: 1 1 2 2 2 . The first number is the person's answer to question 3(a), the second to question 3(b) and so on.

The fourth question is an open one, asked on an actual interview survey of 9,000 people's health and lifestyles (Blaxter, 1990). Such a question gathers qualitative rather than quantitative data, but it is possible to categorize replies so that quantitative analysis can proceed. In one sense, this is done in *all* quantitative data analysis. The world is essentially a qualitative experience; the quantitative researcher imposes categories upon the world and counts them (see Chapter 6). In *pre-coded* items, such as question 2, the categorizing occurs as the respondent answers the question. In question 4, the information can be **post-coded**, that is, coded after the answer has been recorded. This means that respondents are less constrained by the question wording to respond in the researcher's fixed terms, and the researcher has more knowledge about the variety of *meanings* that have contributed to answers and to the development of coding categories. This is likely to improve the *measurement validity* (Chapter 11) of a question though, as with most of the good things in life, better-quality work demands more time and effort. There is always a temptation to opt for a badly designed pre-coded question in order to save the effort required to analyse qualitative data.

Mildred Blaxter devised a coding scheme for replies to the question about health based on a close reading of 200 of the 9,000 interviews in the survey. The categories devised, together with illustrative examples, are shown in Figure 12.2, which shows that a five-category variable was derived.

---

1 Unable to answer

'I don't know when I'm healthy, I only know if I'm ill'; 'I'm never healthy so I don't know'.

2 Never ill, no disease

'You don't have to think about pain – to be free of aches and pains'; 'Health is when you don't have a cold'.

3 Physical fitness, energy

'There's a tone to my body, I feel fit'; 'I can do something strenuous and don't feel that tired after I've done it'.

4 Functionally able to do a lot

'Being healthy is when I walk to my work on a night, and I walk to school to collect the grandchildren'; 'Health is being able to walk around better, and doing more work in the house when my knees let me'.

5 Psychologically fit

'Emotionally you are stable, energetic, happier, more contented and things don't bother you so. Generally it's being carefree, you look better, you get on better with other people'; 'Well I think health is when you feel happy. Because I know when I'm happy I feel quite well'.

Source: Blaxter, 1990: 20–30

Figure 12.2 *Categorizing qualitative answers to an open question: 'At times people are healthier than at other times. What is it like when you are healthy?'*

Cleaning data

Although it is possible to analyse questionnaire data manually it is usually the case that computers will save time. Familiarity with the use of statistical programs increases the possibilities for generating new ways of searching for patterns in data at the touch of a button, even with quite small data sets. We assume, then, that data entry into a computer is an important goal of the initial preparation of data. Once entered, the data should be **cleaned**.

Data entry often involves errors. This may, for example, be due to pressing the wrong key. Some computer programs have ways of guarding against certain types of key stroke error. Thus, if the researcher 'tells' the computer that a variable can have only the values of 1 or 2, but a 3 is erroneously entered, the computer will not accept that value. Alternatively, some programs allow the researcher to 'tell' the computer that the values of one variable depend on the values of another, so that if a person answers 'no' to a question about whether they work or not, the value of a later variable (such as 'satisfaction with job') *must* be a missing value.

However, even with such tricks, errors creep in. With modern spreadsheets it is often quite a simple matter to run one's eye down a column of figures to check that no 'out of range' values occur. Alternatively, a variety of data cleaning procedures can be helpful in the early stages of analysis. (Chapter 13 contains explanations and examples of the following procedures.) A **frequency count** for a variable will detect out of range values. A **cross-tabulation** can be used to see if people have answered a question which, according to the values of another variable, they should not have done. Additionally, cross-tabulations can show illogical combinations: if someone is aged 25 it is likely to be an error if they are recorded as having a child aged 20.

Coding meaning

Categorizing the qualitative replies to open-ended questions in a structured interview is one way of turning quality into quantity so that patterns can be detected in data analysis. It is, however, possible to go a step further than this and code material derived from unstructured interviews, where different respondents are asked different questions, or simply encouraged to tell the story of their lives. This coding method was used by George Brown and Tirril Harris (1978) in their study of the role of *life events* in causing depression.

Brown and Harris rejected what they called the 'dictionary approach to meaning' evident in other researchers' methods for measuring the importance of life events in disrupting people's lives. In such an approach, which relies on people simply reporting whether particular things happened to them in a certain period, different events are given different 'weightings' according to how disruptive the researchers feel the event would be. Thus in one such device (Holmes and Rahe, 1967), researchers gave a weighting of 100 to 'death of a spouse', 73 to 'divorce', 47 to 'dismissal from work' and 11 to 'minor violations of the law' to indicate the severity of each event. The problem with this approach is that an event like 'dismissal from a job' will not have the same meaning in everyone's life. An actor, well accustomed to moving in and out of different jobs, will find this less distressing than a 50-year-old miner, made redundant after a lifetime of work in an area with no alternative sources of employment. Another way of putting this is that Holmes and Rahe's approach demonstrates a low level of *contextual sensitivity* (Chapter 8) to the variable way in which people constitute the meaning of life events.

Brown and Harris therefore proposed that in order to measure the impact of life events on people it was necessary to gather a great deal of qualitative information about the person's life. This was done in lengthy qualitative interviews (see Chapter 16), in which women were encouraged to talk freely about their circumstances. A group of researchers then read the transcripts of these interviews and rated different aspects of the impact of the various life events reported. Examples of how events were rated according to the long-term threat they posed for people's lives are given in Figure 12.3.

Brown and Harris were then able to incorporate the measures into a sophisticated analysis of the social causes of depression. In doing this they were following Durkheim in his study of the effect of social structure on rates of suicide (see Chapter 2). Unlike Durkheim, though, who simply guessed at the meaning of events to people (such as religious affiliation), Brown and Harris had specifically investigated meanings. Coding at this level involves more than just transferring information from a form into a computer, and is linked with complex issues of measurement validity. This example also shows that simplistic notions of a quantitative–qualitative divide are inappropriate.

CODING FOR QUALITATIVE ANALYSIS

You have seen how the replies to open questions in structured interviews can be coded, and how Brown and Harris coded whole interviews to assess

---

(a) Severe
Woman's father died aged 81. She was married and he had lived with her for seven years.
Woman's husband was sent to prison for two years; woman was pregnant.

(b) Non-severe
Woman had to tell her husband that his sister had died.
Woman was in a car accident. In a rainstorm a woman 'walked into the car'; her husband was driving. The woman left hospital the same evening as the accident. There were no police charges.

Source: adapted from Brown and Harris, 1978

Figure 12.3   *Severity of life events in terms of long-term threat*

the severity of life events. Qualitative data, however, do not emerge only from interviews. Field notes of observations during ethnographic work (Chapter 17), visual images (Chapter 18), published texts (Chapters 19, 21), transcripts of conversations (Chapter 20) and historical documents (Chapter 7) all commonly provide qualitative material for analysis. Sometimes the amount of such material collected during a research project is mountainous, and one purpose of data analysis is to *reduce* this, by excluding irrelevant material, and grouping together things that are similar. Another reason for coding such material, however, is to develop and test out theories. It is often the case that the coding of qualitative data begins *before* data collection has finished. Indeed, the development of a coding scheme may determine the sort of data which are collected next in a project. Coding schemes are the creative beginnings of the eventual insights which the researcher hopes to gain by investigating the social world.

Additionally, systematic coding can help in improving the validity of reports of qualitative data. This is done chiefly by presenting *counts* of how many times, and in which circumstances, a thing happens, and by using coding categories to search for **negative instances** that may contradict, or help to develop, an emerging theory. These will be described in the sections that follow, together with examples of the use of computer programs for qualitative data analysis that can aid the process of counting and theory development.

Coding, computers and counting

The initial stage when faced with an interview transcript, or with a set of notes describing observations, or some other qualitative material, is to develop a set of codes that both reflect the initial aims of the research project, and take into account any unexpected issues that have emerged during data collection. Unlike the classical quantitative social survey, where the aims of the research project stay relatively fixed from beginning to end, qualitative research can often be more exploratory, and can end up addressing issues that were not imagined before the project began.

An example of this is given by a research project currently being done by Marion Garnett into nurses' use of alternative therapies. Here, the initial aims of the project included discovering whether nurses use these therapies to get patients to engage in intimate, self-revelatory talk. Additionally, the researcher wished to find out whether nurses' use of these therapies was a part of a more generalized commitment to 'green' issues. Accordingly, qualitative interviews with nurses involved questioning about these issues. The coding of interview transcripts has initially involved the application of codes called *confessional talk* and *green issues* to segments of text where these topics are discussed. However, and unexpectedly, the researcher found that nurses involved in certain sorts of alternative therapy discussed the role of touch in expressing a caring relationship, and in helping patients with stigmatized conditions (for example, AIDS or breast removal) to feel better about their bodies and more accepted by other people. Accordingly, two new codes have been identified to indicate segments of talk that refer to the topics of *touch* and *stigma*. Thus, a nurse talking about a patient with AIDS said:

> I have done [massage] with somebody who's got really bad psoriasis and I've been able to massage . . . and that's been good for that person psychologically because he had quite a bad body image and he felt like he hadn't been touched and he felt quite repulsed by his skin, so to actually have someone else touch him was quite, it was probably the best thing.

On this project, then, we have described four emerging codes: confessional talk, green issues, touch and stigma. They relate to the initial aims of the research, to unexpected features that emerged during data collection, and potentially to areas of social theory (for example, Goffman's 1968 theory of stigma). Initial coding consists, then, of reading through material and identifying where themes of particular interest are illustrated by data.

Coding schemes like this develop as a research project proceeds. Firstly, the meaning of particular code words can develop as new segments of data prove hard to fit into existing coding categories. It is, therefore, important to record definitions of code words, and any changes to these. Secondly, codes can subdivide, so that a category begins to develop branches. Thus, for example, we might expect the category *green issues* to contain a variety of subtopics as more data are collected. It might, for example, involve strong commitment versus strong rejection of these issues; it might involve commitment to a green diet (vegetarianism), to green politics, or to personal usage of alternative medical therapies. Some people will exhibit particular combinations of codes that others do not.

Although not as widespread as the use of statistical packages, the use of computers to analyse qualitative data has been growing in popularity amongst social researchers who find it a convenient way to file and retrieve, as well as generate theory from, large amounts of qualitative data. Figure 12.4 shows a transcript of a conversation between a doctor (MD) and some physiotherapists about their management of a particular patient, Earl Michaels. It is taken from the manual of a computer program for the analysis of qualitative data called ETHNOGRAPH, one of several such programs now available. Another popular program is NUD•IST, the use of which is shown later in this chapter (see also Miles and Weitzman, 1995 for a review of available programs).

Note that every line of the transcript is *numbered*. The numbered transcript has been printed out with a large space on the right-hand side of the paper, enabling the researcher to write in code words that identify particular groups of lines as being 'about' a particular topic. Thus, lines 12 to 16 and 30 to 33 are about *pain*. You will see that a particular segment of text can be 'about' a number of different things: lines 12 to 16 are about *motive, eval, pain, progress* and *evidence*. One of the features of ETHNOGRAPH, as well as many other such programs, is that they enable the data analyst to search for segments of text according to whether code words overlap. Thus, one might wish to look for every instance across a series of such transcripts where talk about *pain* overlaps with talk about *motive* in order to see how health care staff talk about patients' motivation to overcome painful conditions.

Additionally, use of a computer program allows other sorts of searches to be carried out. ETHNOGRAPH identifies speakers in a conversation by means of *speaker identifiers*. In Figure 12.4 these are indicated by MD, PT-1 or PT-3, before the colon at the beginning of each speaker's turn. It is possible, for example, to search for what physiotherapists (PT) say about pain, and to compare this with a search for what doctors (MD) say about pain. If one knows anything about speakers, such as their gender or their age, one can

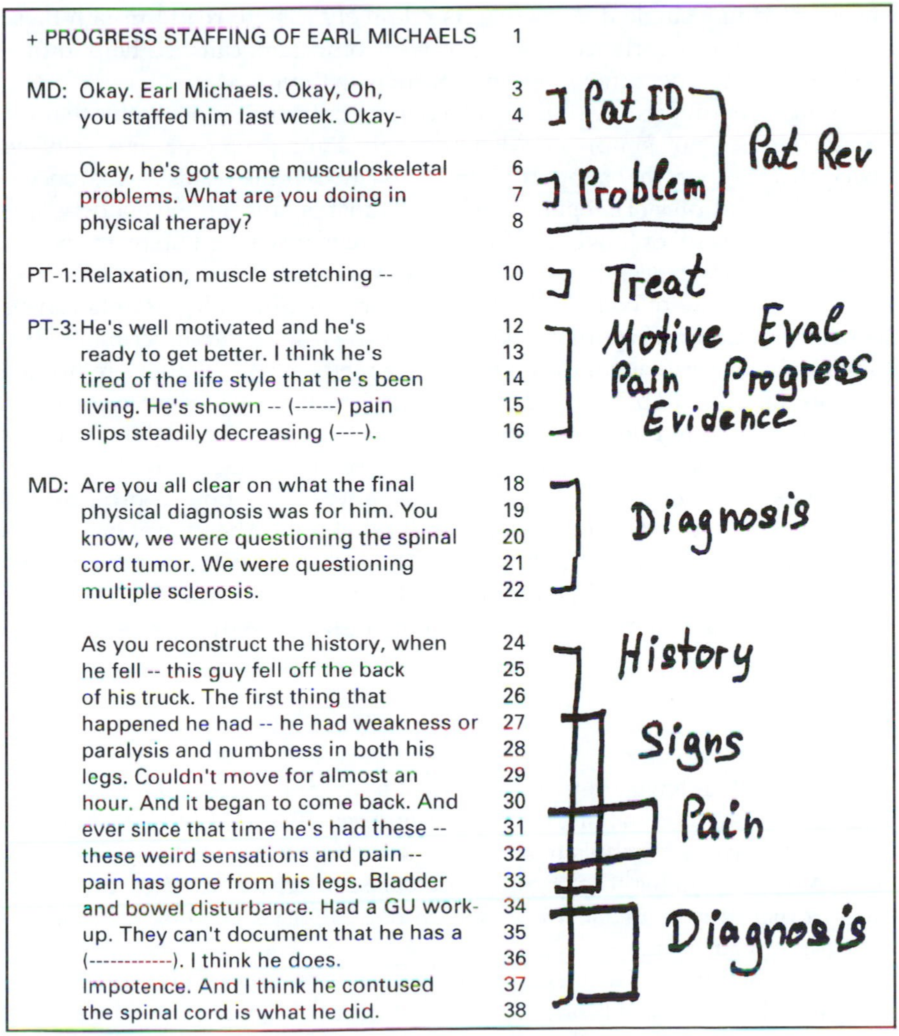

Figure 12.4 *Coding example*

'attach' this to each speaker identifier. Additionally, one can attach information to whole data files. For example, if Figure 12.4 were a part of a larger project, involving transcripts of a number of 'case meetings' between health care staff, one could categorize transcripts according to characteristics of the patients being discussed. Combining all this information one might conduct searches to discover what male doctors say about the pain experience of male patients, compared with what they say about the experience of female patients, and so on.

The use of computers, then, enables the rapid retrieval of information from a mass of otherwise unwieldy transcripts, and is a superior method to manually cutting out segments from the transcript and sorting these into piles. Additionally, computers can help to develop more refined coding schemes. Once a researcher has all the examples of a particular coding category listed in a single document, it is relatively easy to read through these and detect subcategories of existing codes. Computers can also help in producing *counts* of the number of times particular things occur.

Counting in qualitative research can help in reassuring the reader that the researcher has not simply trawled through a mass of data and selected anecdotes to report that support his or her particular bias. This is an aspect of *validity* (see Chapter 11). If phrases such as 'most people felt', 'usually people I interviewed said' or 'it was rarely observed' can be backed up by the actual number of times events occurred in field notes or interview transcripts, then the reader has more confidence in the report. Additionally, counts can be helpful in making comparisons between settings, as David Silverman (1984) found in his observational study comparing medical consultations in private clinics with those in public health service clinics. Out of 42 private consultations, subsequent appointments with the doctor were fixed at the patient's convenience in 36% of cases; in 60% of cases the consultation involved polite 'small talk' about either the doctor's or the patient's personal or professional lives. The corresponding percentages in the 104 public health service clinics observed were significantly smaller (10% and 30%). This supported the researcher's impression that a more personal service was given in private clinics. (Table 8.1 contains details of another study he did which involved such counting.)

Careers and typologies

Two devices that have often proved useful in organizing qualitative data for analysis are the notions of **career** and **typology**. The first of these helps to explain the progress people make through social settings or experiences; the second of these helps to categorize the sorts of experience they can have. Each of these represents a way in which new theories can be developed to account for observations.

Perhaps the best-known usage of the concept of *career* occurs in Howard Becker's (1963) study of how people come to use marijuana. Here, he argued that individuals passed through three stages in careers that ended in becoming a user. These are described below, together with code words (not reported by Becker) to describe them:

1 Learning the technique of smoking to produce effects.	*technique*
2 Learning to perceive the effects.	*perceive*
3 Learning to enjoy the effects.	*enjoy*

A variety of instances in his data illustrate these themes. A numbered version of one extract is produced below.

I didn't get high the first time . . .	1
The second time I wasn't sure,	2
and he [smoking companion] told me,	3
like I asked him for some of the	4
symptoms or something . . .	5
So he told me to sit on a stool.	6
I sat on – I think I sat on a bar	7
stool – and he said 'let your	8
feet hang' and then when I got	9
down my feet were real cold you	10
know . . . and I started feeling it,	11
you know. That was the first time.	12
And then about a week after that,	13
sometime pretty close to it, I	14
really got on. That was the first	15
time I got on a big laughing kick,	16
you know. Then I really knew I	17
was on.	18

Lines 1–12 concern *technique*, lines 10–18 concern *perceive* and lines 15–18 concern *enjoy*.

Other research workers using the concept of career to organize their data include Sally MacIntyre (1977) who interviewed unmarried women who had become pregnant. She mapped their subsequent careers through various events and decision points (whether to have an abortion, whether to marry, whether to offer their baby for adoption and so on) to produce a variety of 'career outcomes' (for example, single motherhood, marriage). Patricia Taraborrelli (1993) describes how she used the idea of career to understand people's experience of caring for spouses who had developed Alzheimer's disease. Figure 12.5 shows her flowchart describing three 'career paths'. People who had had previous experience of caring for chronically sick individuals followed pattern B, whereby at diagnosis they quickly adopted what the researcher termed the 'carer's perspective', involving a practical approach to the problem. Such carers successfully distinguished caring *for* their spouse from caring *about* their spouse. Thus they were willing to seek practical help with care from formal services without feeling that this meant

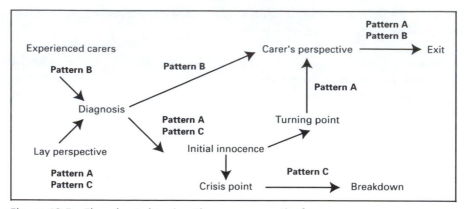

Figure 12.5 *Flowchart showing three career paths for carers*
Source: Gilbert 1993:183

they did not care about the person enough to do the work themselves. Others, however, had to learn this hard lesson, and after a period of 'initial innocence' would follow one of two paths: a 'crisis point' leading to break-down (pattern C), or a 'turning point' where they successfully adopted the carer's perspective and learned to seek the help they needed (pattern A).

While MacIntyre and Taraborrelli used the device to explain a variety of *different* career outcomes, others have found it useful in explaining single outcomes. Cressey (1953), for example, did this in his study of people con-victed for financial embezzlement. He found that four career steps were needed for individuals to commit this crime. They had firstly to be in a position of financial trust, secondly to have a financial problem that could not be shared or discussed with others, thirdly to recognize embezzlement as a solution and fourthly to develop a way of rationalizing the crime to persuade themselves that it was a justifiable thing to do (for example, by calling it a 'loan').

In each of these cases, the researchers will have developed coding cat-egories to identify segments of data illustrating the phenomena they describe (such as the moment a person recognized embezzlement as a solu-tion, the 'crisis point' accounts given by Taraborrelli's carers, the decision points described by the women MacIntyre interviewed).

Typologies, on the other hand, are a means of categorizing events or people without necessarily involving a sense of progression from one event to another. Glaser and Strauss (1966) in their study of dying people devel-oped a typology of *awareness contexts*, shown in Figure 12.6. It will be seen that by incorporating the idea of 'determinants' of particular awareness contexts, the researchers are proposing a causal theory. In fact, Becker and Cressey, in the studies described earlier, do the same thing, claiming that *all* the steps in the career path are needed before the relevant career outcome can be achieved.

We have now moved some way from the relatively simple procedure of coding segments of text into categories in order to show how this can quickly

Typology
1 *Open awareness*   Everyone knows the person is dying.
2 *Closed awareness*   The dying person does not know, but other people do.
3 *Suspicion awareness* The dying person suspects.
4 *Pretence awareness* Everyone, including the dying person, pretends that they
                        do not know.

Determinants of closed awareness
1 Patients are inexperienced at recognizing signs of impending death.
2 Medical staff are skilled at hiding the truth.
3 Staff have a professional rationale that says that it is best to withhold the truth.
4 The patient has no family allies.

Figure 12.6   *Awareness contexts: a typology and its determinants*

develop into a complex process of **theory building** from data. This is discussed in Chapter 9 and also in Chapter 17, where it is called the *discovery of
grounded theory*. It is relevant here to note that, in qualitative research, coding
and analysis of data are activities that can begin in the early stages of data
collection. The ideas that emerge will frequently determine where the
researcher next looks for data. Thus, the researcher may be interested in
using *theoretical sampling* (Chapter 11) to develop a strategy for data collection. This might involve searching for **negative instances** that contradict an
emerging theory, so that a better theory can be developed. Theoretical sampling to search for such variation is described in the following account from
Glaser and Strauss, concerning the way in which their typology of awareness
contexts was developed:

> Visits to the various medical services were scheduled as follows: I wished first to
> look at services that minimized patient awareness (and so first looked at a premature
> baby service and then a neurosurgical service where patients were frequently
> comatose). I wished next to look at dying in a situation where expectancy of staff and
> often of patients was great and where dying tended to be slow. So I looked next at a
> cancer service. I wished then to look at conditions where death was unexpected and
> rapid, and so looked at an emergency service . . . So our scheduling of types of service
> was directed by a *general conceptual scheme* – which included hypotheses about
> awareness, expectedness and rate of dying – as well as by a *developing conceptual
> structure including matters not at first envisaged.* (1967: 59, my emphasis)

We can now turn to a case study, illustrating the coding of both quantitative
and qualitative data on a particular research project.

CASE STUDY: A COMPARISON OF TWO CARE SETTINGS

The main aim of this research project (Seale and Kelly, 1997a; 1997b) was to
compare inpatient care for dying people with cancer and their spouses in

hospice and hospital. Seventy bereaved spouses were interviewed retro-
spectively using a semi-structured interview format. They were questioned
about the nature, timing, source and purpose of medical treatments, nursing
interventions and inpatient experiences since the illness was first diagnosed.
The interview also covered sources of information about the illness, the
events leading to the last admission and satisfaction with care. Some questions on the interview schedule were pre-coded and some were open-ended;
therefore both quantitative and qualitative data analyses were required. The
data analyses was assisted by the use of two computer software programs,
SPSS for statistical analysis and NUD•IST for qualitative data.

Quantitative coding

SPSS performs a range of data analysis functions once data have been
entered into the program in the form it can understand. The first stage was to
devise a coding scheme. This was partly done when the interview schedule
was drawn up. However, responses to some questions had to be worked out
and added after the data had been collected. For example, for the question:
'Was anyone with him/her when he died?' the responses 'yes' = 1, 'no' = 2
were recorded, so a 1 or a 2 could be entered directly into the computer.
However, if the respondent answered 'yes', the interviewer then asked an
additional (or probe) question 'Who?' and wrote down the answer verbatim.
This verbatim material had to be coded once all the interviews were done,
into categories such as 'hospital doctor', 'hospital nurse', 'GP' and so on.

   Surveys often involve questionnaires which have coding boxes down the
right-hand side, which allow responses to be easily coded or the answers to
be recorded in coded form during the interview. As this would have taken
up too much space on our questionnaire (owing to the need for space for
responses to the open-ended questions), a separate *coding sheet* was drawn
up after the interviews were done. To make this, we looked at all the questions in which the responses could be recorded quantitatively, drew up a list
of the possible responses to each question and gave each one a numbered
code. For example, the question 'Who helped with care at home?' had four
possible responses: 1 = 'nurse'; 2 = 'doctor'; 3 = 'friend'; 4 = 'family member'.

   The coding sheet had a list of the question numbers on the left-hand side,
and a grid in which we could then record the coded answer on the right. For
example, one of the questions was 'What was the time from the first sign (of
cancer) to diagnosis?' As people could not usually work this out accurately
from memory, the approximate date of the first sign of the cancer was
recorded, and then the approximate date of the diagnosis. Later, when
completing the coding sheet, the number of days between the two could be
worked out and recorded. This would have taken up too much time during
the interview.

   Once a coding sheet for each interview had been completed, we needed to
set up the SPSS program for data entry. This involved 'telling' the computer
the names of the variables, and what was to count as a 'missing value' for

each variable. We also needed to tell SPSS the labels to give each value of a variable (for example, that for the variable *Sex* a 1 meant 'male' and a 2 meant 'female'). Each completed interview, known as a *case*, was given a serial number, and formed a *row* in the data matrix. Each question, or variable, formed a *column* in the data matrix. Once entered, the data entry file was saved on to the hard and floppy disk drives.

Entering the data into the program, or inputting, is relatively straight-forward if the coding is prepared. Data were put into the data entry file one case at a time; thus once all the information on the first case had been entered, we started on the second case and so on until all 70 cases had been entered. The next stage was to analyse the data, which by then included several hundred variables.

Quantitative data analysis

The first task was to undertake *descriptive statistics* (see Chapter 13) in order to gain an impression of the sample characteristics such as the age and sex breakdown of the respondents. We could then 'map out' the data, and see what areas it might be interesting to explore further. So, for example, we ascertained the numbers of male and female respondents, types of cancer diagnoses, treatments that patients had received, and spouses who had been present at the death. As well as *frequency counts* for these variables, we checked the average age of the people who died and their length of final admission.

The next stage was to explore the relationships between different variables. For example we wanted to see whether patients who died in hospital were more likely to be receiving active treatment for their cancer at the time of death than patients who died in hospice. We found that people who died in hospital were more likely to be still under active treatment at the time of death in that 9 out of 33 hospital patients, but only 2 out of 33 hospice patients, had active medical treatment until death. This process of cross-tabulation of variables was carried out with many combinations, furthering our aim to see how people's experiences and the quality of their care varied between the two settings.

Qualitative data analysis

One of the main aims of this study was to assess the quality of care for people who died and their spouses. This could be only partly addressed through analysing the quantitative data. The information collected through open-ended questions enabled us to explore the issue in more depth, through recording the respondents' perceptions and experiences in their own words and analysing their responses. One area we wished to find out about was the circumstances surrounding the final admission, as this information would potentially provide useful information for hospice and hospital staff on planning patient admissions. We decided to use NUD•IST to help with the qualitative data analysis.

NUD•IST, like ETHNOGRAPH, is primarily an instrument which files information systematically, enabling you to retrieve and manipulate it without sifting through lots of paper. We had information which had been given in response to open-ended questions, and field note data from all the interviews. The interviews had been tape recorded (with the permission of the respondent), and responses to open-ended questions were also recorded verbatim during the interview. These responses were typed up using a word processing program. Each case was then put into the format required by NUD•IST and printed out.

Interview transcripts of several cases were searched manually for key themes, and a coding sheet was drawn up with *text codes* rather than numerical ones. For example, whenever anyone mentioned the activities of a hospital doctor, this segment of text was coded as *Hospdoc*. If they mentioned a general practitioner, such a mention was coded as *GP*. Parts of the text where people described the experience of pain were marked as *Painsev*. The code words could be added to if more themes appeared later. NUD•IST was then 'told' the codes that applied to particular segments of text. In addition, NUD•IST was told, for each interview, whether it was with a man or a woman, whether the person had or had not received hospice care, as well as various other bits of information about key variables.

Coding thus broke the material down into manageable chunks ready for analysis. We searched using a code *Lastad* to retrieve all the segments which related to the reasons prompting the patient's last admission to the hospice or hospital. We could now focus in on this issue, since printing all the segments out together (divided by whether patients were in a hospital or a hospice) enabled us to look through all the relevant segments at the same time. We read and reread the segments, recording any themes which seemed to be coming from the data, checking to see if any particular categories seemed to arise. Once key categories had been found, we counted the number of times they came up. This helped us to interpret the findings, as

Table 12.2   *Content analysis of segments referring to causes of the last admission to hospice or hospital*

	Hospice	Hospital
GP called (urgent)	0	10
GP called (not urgent)	9	11
Ambulance called	1	12
Planned admission	0	6
To give the carer a rest	5	0
Symptom control	8	0
Admission was from hospital	6	0
Patient asked	3	0
Spouse asked	2	0
Nurse was involved	14	3
Hospice doctor involved	5	0

shown in Table 12.2. It can be seen from the table that urgent admissions involving ambulances were more characteristic of hospital admissions, whereas hospice admissions were more planned. We were able to use this pattern to select representative quotes from the interviews, which we presented in our final written report. We concluded that the circumstances surrounding the final admission to hospital sometimes did not allow for constructive planning by hospital staff. The next stage was to relate the findings to other research on emergency admissions to hospital for people with terminal illness.

CONCLUSION

This chapter has reviewed methods for coding data in order to prepare them for analysis. Both statistical and qualitative analyses have been covered since an important theme of this book is to encourage the use of both forms of data in research projects. The work of Brown and Harris is interesting in spanning the quantitative/qualitative distinction and one can say that this is an example of the 'celebration of anomaly' recommended in Chapter 9 as an appropriate guiding principle for researchers. Additionally we have shown that an interaction between data collection, analysis and theory building is appropriate; the creative construction of coding schemes lies at the core of such activity.

Further reading

De Vaus (1991) contains a helpful discussion of coding for quantitative analysis. An appendix to the ETHNOGRAPH manual (Seidel et al., 1995) provides an excellent general model for coding and analysing qualitative data. Coffey and Atkinson (1996) explain and illustrate a variety of approaches to qualitative data analysis, including those based on the sort of coding explained in the chapter, as well as some others.

Statistical reasoning: from one to two variables

Clive Seale

CONTENTS

The use of statistics in social research has a long history, described in Chapter 6. There, you saw that the production of social statistics has been closely tied to programmes of legislation and social reform. Official statistics (see Chapter 15) demonstrate the linkage between numbers and modern techniques of government. Critiques of the use of statistics by both the government and social researchers have often involved pointing out how these come to structure the way in which people think of their social worlds (in terms of deviations from the norm or the average, for example). In this sense, social statistics can be seen as not simply describing a pre-existing reality, but representing it in a selective way, and indeed shaping it.

Sometimes attempts to shape social realities with numbers are very overt. People faced with complex statistical presentations often say that you can 'prove anything with statistics', or reference is made to 'lies, damn lies and statistics'. This thought is often to the fore when a politician presents numbers to support a point. We always expect another politician to use the same source to prove an opposing point. It seems as if no final truth can be reached by such means. This can lead people to reject learning about numbers, perhaps supported by school experience of mathematics, where the subject appears arid and difficult, having no obvious purpose beyond passing exams. Humanities or social science subjects seem to offer much more immediate emotional and practical engagement, experienced especially when encountering impassioned critiques of the impersonal world of science, technology and numbers.

Yet where does this rejection leave us? Although the dismissal of statistical ways of understanding the social world may be accompanied by a fine sense of moral justification, making us feel initially quite powerful, it is in the last analysis a defeatist approach. Engagement with the modern world must involve an understanding of the language through which power is exercised and negotiated. We must understand what underlies the arguments of politicians in order to present opposing views. The conclusions which social researchers reach on the basis of statistical analyses cannot be evaluated unless we know how to use the technology that led to them.

Research reports in the quantitative tradition often present statistical tables, with the author's interpretation of them in the surrounding text. It may be tempting to concentrate on the text rather than 'read' the table and draw one's own conclusions. The purpose of this and the following chapter is to help you to read research reports so that you can understand and then assess whether a researcher's conclusions are supported by the numerical data they present. The chapters will also help you to construct statistical arguments of your own. This first chapter on statistical reasoning will begin by outlining some key ideas about **univariate** statistics, before going on to **bivariate** statistics. That is to say, it will discuss the presentation of single *variables* (see Chapter 12) before discussing ways in which two variables can interact. This will lead, in the chapter that follows, into a discussion of how statistical reasoning can be used to construct arguments about **causality**, the idea that one variable has caused another variable to vary.

UNIVARIATE STATISTICS

In Table 12.1 a data matrix was shown, consisting of five cases and four variables. Let us now imagine that we have surveyed a further 15 people and have asked them the same questions, resulting in the data matrix shown in Table 13.1.

If this raw data matrix were presented in a research report it would be difficult, in its present form, to see the main patterns that exist in the data (for example, the number of females). A variety of ways of re-presenting the data are possible, one of which is called the **frequency distribution**. This shows, for a single variable, such as *Age*, the number of times each value of the variable occurs. It may be accompanied by percentages that help to summarize the distribution in various ways. Table 13.2 shows frequency distributions for two of the variables in Table 13.1, produced as output from SPSS. The first variable is *Sex*, and the frequency distribution indicates that there were 10 males and 10 females in the survey (males were coded as

Table 13.1   *A data matrix*

| People | Sex | Variables or questions | | |
		Age	Working	Jobsat
Case 1	Male	66	No	Missing
Case 2	Female	34	Full time	1
Case 3	Female	25	Part time	2
Case 4	Female	44	Full time	5
Case 5	Male	78	No	Missing
Case 6	Male	40	Full time	2
Case 7	Male	33	Full time	1
Case 8	Male	16	No	Missing
Case 9	Female	35	Full time	1
Case 10	Female	45	Full time	2
Case 11	Male	30	No	Missing
Case 12	Female	56	Part time	4
Case 13	Male	79	No	Missing
Case 14	Male	60	Part time	4
Case 15	Female	55	Part time	4
Case 16	Female	54	Part time	5
Case 17	Male	55	Full time	1
Case 18	Male	17	No	Missing
Case 19	Female	23	Full time	3
Case 20	Female	20	No	Missing

1; females as 2). Another way of putting this is that 50% were males and 50% were females, indicated in the column marked '%'. If you look at the distribution for *Jobsat* you will see a slightly more complex picture. There were 4 people who said they were 'very satisfied'. These were 20% of the total of 20 people, as is indicated in the first value in the '%' column. However, 7 people did not answer this question, so they are counted as 'missing' and it is inappropriate to include them in the percentage. Therefore the 'Valid %' column presents percentages which exclude these 7 cases. Thus 4 is 30.8% of the number answering the question (13 people). The final column is 'Cumulative %'. This shows that if we add the 3 people who were 'fairly satisfied' to the 4 people who were 'very satisfied' (making 7 in all), we have 53.8% of the 13 valid cases. The next value in the last column (61.5%) includes the next level of the variable (the one person who was 'neither' satisfied nor dissatisfied) and so on, until 100% is reached.

It would make little sense to present a frequency distribution like this for the variable *Age*. There are two 55-year-olds, but apart from that there is only one person for each category of age in the matrix. If we wish to summarize the distribution of an *interval* variable like this (see Chapter 12) some other types of statistic are useful. Firstly, it is helpful to know the **mean** age, which is the statistic we commonly know as the 'average'. In this case, the value is 43.25, calculated by adding together all the ages (the *sum*) and dividing by 20 (the number of cases). In the language of statisticians, this is known as a **measure of central tendency**, one of three statistics that help to indicate the

Table 13.2   *Frequency distributions of two variables produced by SPSS*

Sex

Value label	Value	Frequency	%	Valid %	Cumulative %
Male	1	10	50.0	50.0	50.0
Female	2	10	50.0	50.0	100.0
Total		20	100.0	100.0	

Valid cases 20. Missing cases 0.

Jobsat: are you satisfied with your job?

Value label	Value	Frequency	%	Valid %	Cumulative %
Very satisfied	1	4	20.0	30.8	30.8
Fairly satisfied	2	3	15.0	23.1	53.8
Neither	3	1	5.0	7.7	61.5
Fairly dissatisfied	4	3	15.0	23.1	84.6
Very dissatisfied	5	2	10.0	15.4	100.0
Missing	9	7	35.0		
Total		20	100.0	100.0	

Valid cases 13. Missing cases 7.

central point of a particular distribution. There are two other, less commonly known measures of central tendency which you may occasionally see referred to. One of these is the **median**, which is the number positioned in the middle of a distribution, below which half the values fall. In the case of *Jobsat*, for example, the median is 2. In fact, the median is more suited to variables measured at ordinal level. The third measure of central tendency is the **mode**, normally used for nominal variables. This is the most frequently occurring value in a distribution.

In addition to these measures of central tendency, you will sometimes find social researchers referring to the **standard deviation** in research reports. This is a statistic which indicates how widely dispersed are cases around the mean. If many of the values of cases are far away from the mean, the standard deviation will be high. If most of the values are close to the mean it will be low. In the case of *Age* the standard deviation (sometimes written as SD) is 19.197, indicating quite a wide dispersion (a lot of the values are quite far away from 43.25). If all of the 20 people had been aged, say, between 40 and 47 the standard deviation would have been smaller. If a researcher reports the mean and standard deviation of interval variables this tells us a great deal about the variable, even without seeing the raw data that led to them.

Another way of presenting information about frequency distributions is by the use of graphs. These can be helpful in making a more immediate impact on readers than do tables. Figure 13.1 shows some graphical representations of two of the variables in Table 13.1. Both *Jobsat* and *Age* are represented as **bar charts** and as **pie charts**. However, you should note that the values of *Age* have been **recoded** or collapsed into larger categories of 20 years each. Recoding interval variables loses a certain amount of fine detail, but can be helpful in highlighting the main features of a distribution, or in preparing a variable with many categories for inclusion in a bivariate table.

BIVARIATE ANALYSIS

Univariate analysis can show us how a single group of people vary on some characteristic, such as sex, age or job satisfaction. It can be very useful to know, for example, whether one social class is larger than another in a given population, or the proportion of people who are likely to vote for a particular political party in a general election. Once such questions are answered, though, almost inevitably further questions spring to mind. Are men more satisfied with their jobs than women? Is full-time work more or less fulfilling than part-time work? Do some social classes experience better health than others? How is social class related to voting intention? All these are

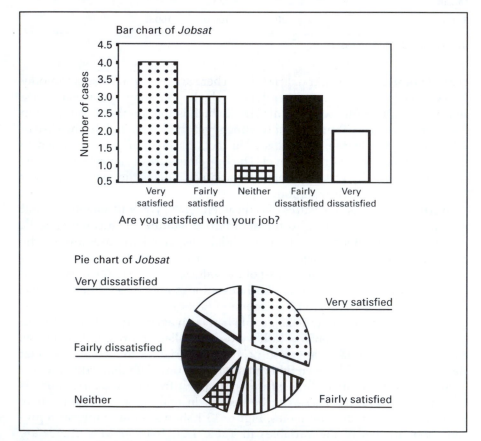

Figure 13.1   *Graphical representations of frequency distributions*

examples of questions about the relationships between *two* variables and are thus answerable by **bivariate** analysis. **Multivariate** statistics deal with relationships between three or more variables. For example, we might wish to know whether the relationship between social class and voting is stronger for one sex than another. Multivariate analysis will be touched on in the next chapter.

The best way to approach bivariate analysis is through the analysis of **contingency tables**. These are devices which show the relationships between two variables each of which has only a few categories. Bivariate analysis for *interval* variables which, if not recoded, generally have too many values for inclusion in tables, is described later in the chapter.

Contingency tables

Table 13.3 shows output from SPSS from the data matrix produced for the research project comparing hospice and hospital care whose coding was

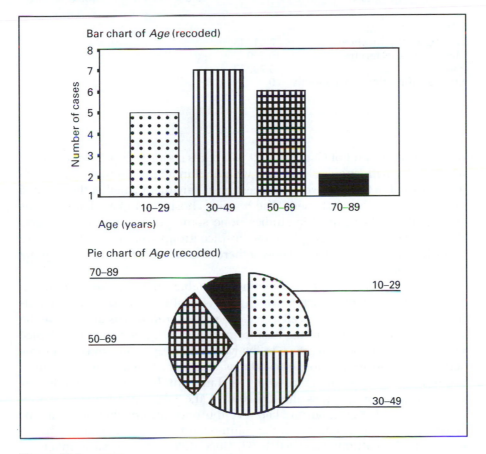

Figure 13.1   *cont.*

Table 13.3   *Example of a contingency table produced by SPSS*

Q11H 'The hospice/hospital is like a family' by Q3F 'Type of institution where died'

Count Row % Column %		Q3F Hospice 1	Hospital 2	Row totals
Q11H	Yes 1	15 71.4 45.5	6 28.6 18.2	21 31.8
	No 2	18 40.0 54.5	27 60.0 81.8	45 68.2
	Column totals	33 50.0	33 50.0	66 100.0

Chi-square significance	0.01738
Minimum expected frequency	10.500
Phi	0.29277
Number of missing observations	0

described at the end of Chapter 12. It compares spouses of people who died in a hospice with spouses of people who died in a hospital to see how each group varied in their answers to a question asking them whether they agreed or disagreed with a statement 'The hospital/hospice is like a family.' This statement had been used in studies done some years before (Parkes and Parkes, 1984) in which people in the hospice group were found to be more likely to agree. We wanted to know if there was still a difference between the two types of institution.

Table 13.3 is an example of a contingency table, showing the relationship between two variables, each of which has two values. The 15 in the top left-hand group of numbers, or **cell** as it can be called, represents in this case the number of respondents in the hospice group who agreed that the hospice was like a family. Adding the 6 in the hospital group who agreed with this statement when applied to the hospital, we see that a total of 21 people out of the 66 who answered it agreed with the statement. In adding 15 to 6 in this way, we are going across the top row of the table to calculate the **row marginal** of 21. Marginal numbers are the ones around the 'margins' or edges of the table. Going down the columns of the table, we can see that in each case the **column marginal** is 33, since there were equal numbers of people in the hospice and hospital groups. Conveniently, SPSS prints out the percentage of the total represented by each marginal figure. Thus 21 is 31.8% of the total, which is 66 (or 100%).

Inside each of the cells, SPSS has placed three numbers: first the count, as described above, and then two percentage figures. As the guide at the very top left of the table tells us, these are, respectively, the **row percentage** and the **column percentage**. The first of these enables us to see the proportion of those who answered in a particular way to the question who were in each group. Thus, we can say that 71.4% of those who answered 'yes' were in the hospice group, compared with 40% of those who answered 'no'. This is not particularly helpful, as we want a more direct comparison of the hospice and hospital groups. Therefore, we should look at the column percentages, which show that 45.5% (15/33) of the hospice group said 'yes', compared with only 18.2% (6/33) of the hospital group. If we were using this output to write up results, we would not in this case report the row percentages. Deciding whether row or column percentages are appropriate is sometimes difficult, but it is often helpful to try to put one's conclusion into words, and speak it out loud to see which way of 'seeing' or 'saying' the result seems to make most sense. Another 'rule of thumb' that can be helpful is to place the *independent* variable (see Chapter 14) across the top of the table, and then use a column percentage.

As with univariate statistics, bivariate statistics can be presented in graphical form, often giving them greater impact. Figure 13.2 shows how the two groups differed in their answers to the question by means of a bar chart. The vertical axis (*y* axis) shows the percentage agreeing or disagreeing with the statement; the horizontal axis (*x* axis) distinguishes between the hospice and hospital groups, with the hospice group shaded darker.

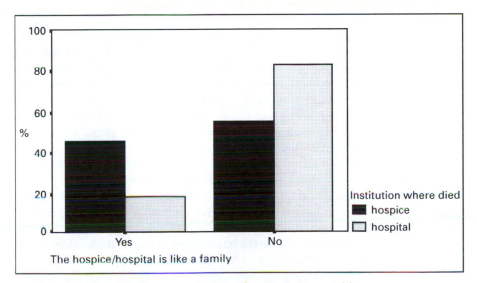

Figure 13.2   *Graphical representation of a contingency table*

Statistical significance

We might stop at this point in our analysis of Table 13.3, and conclude that the hospice is more likely to be judged to be 'like a family'. However, this would be a mistake. How can we know whether this result is not simply caused by chance? Perhaps we have, at random, happened to pick unrepresentative samples of people who are more inclined to feel this way about hospices. In other words, how likely is it that we can generalize from the sample of 66 to the population from which it is drawn, which in this case is all spouses of people dying in these settings? Estimation of the likelihood that a sample result is true of the population involves **statistical inference**. A variety of statistics that help to do this are available, but the one most commonly used for contingency tables is known as the **chi-square test**.

In Table 13.3 the significance of the chi-square value is given below the table as 0.01738. This is sometimes known as the *p*-**value**, with *p* standing for *probability*. If multiplied by 100, it can be expressed as a percentage, in this case 1.738%. In ordinary language it is then possible to say that in fewer than 2 out of 100 possible samples of 66 that we might have selected at random for this study would this difference between the hospital and hospice groups have occurred by chance. We might therefore wish to conclude that this is probably not a chance result, and that if we had been able to study the entire population of people experiencing care in these settings, we would find this sort of difference. Using the jargon of statistics, we can say that we will accept the hypothesis that the two variables are related. Sometimes this can be expressed as its negative: we *reject* what is known as the **null hypothesis** that the two variables are *unrelated*.

Probability values are sometimes given in reports of quantitative research, either at the bottom of contingency tables, or in the text after a result has been reported. Thus, if we were to report the result shown in Table 13.3, it might be phrased as follows: '45.5% of the hospice group agreed with the statement, compared with 18.2% of the hospital group ($p < 0.02$).' The part in brackets means 'probability is less than 2 in 100.' Many social researchers accept as significant any *p*-value of less than 5 in 100 ($p < 0.05$), inferring that the result is likely to hold true in the population if this level is reached. Sometimes, however, a level of 1 in 100 ($p < 0.01$) is taken, if the researcher wishes to be particularly cautious in drawing conclusions about the population concerned. This is a matter of judgement, and readers of research reports can decide for themselves whether a researcher is justified in emphasizing a finding as long as the relevant *p*-value is reported.

The value of chi-square is affected by sample size. Intuitively this makes sense: we are bound to have more faith that a random sample of 1,000 is representative of the population, compared with a random sample of 10, in which we are more likely by chance to have selected atypical individuals. A statistically significant result (in other words, a low *p*-value) is more likely with large samples. Additionally, the principles underlying chi-square require that the **expected values** in at least 20% of the cells in a contingency table are more than 5. Thus, SPSS has produced a 'minimum expected frequency' of 10.5 for the data in Table 13.3, indicating that is valid to use the results of chi-square. Expected values for particular cells are those which we would expect by chance given the distribution of the marginal figures in a table. Thus the expected value for the top left-hand cell is calculated by multiplying the left-hand column marginal (33) by the top row marginal (21) and dividing by the total sample size (66) to get 10.5. You will see that the *actual* value (usually called the **observed value**) in that cell is 15. The calculation of chi-square involves comparing the observed values with the expected values in cells.

The mathematical calculations that underlie the chi-square statistic are not particularly complex. It is unnecessary to learn them in order to analyse data, although your intuitive understanding of the meaning of *p*-values will be enhanced if you have done the calculation by hand a couple of times. The suggestions for further reading at the end of this chapter contain books where these calculations are shown if you wish to take this further. In general, however, computer packages such as SPSS now make this superfluous knowledge for the data analyst. The important thing to grasp is the meaning of statistics such as the chi-square, rather than the underlying mathematics. Very few people who drive a car, or use a word processor, see the need to know how an engine works, or to understand the programming language used by software manufacturers. On the whole the social researcher concerned with data analysis does not need a full understanding of mathematical and statistical principles in order to produce good work.

Finally, the chi-square is not the only test of significance. Others exist for data that are not arranged in contingency tables. However, all have the same underlying purpose of allowing estimates to be made about the likelihood of a sample having produced a chance result. Whatever the underlying statistic, this likelihood is usually expressed as a *p*-value.

Interval variables

When variables have many values, as is often the case with interval variables such as *Age* in Table 13.1, they can be recoded into a few categories (as is shown in Figure 13.1 for *Age*) so that they can be presented in bar charts or tables. However, this represents a loss of information. In its raw form, the variable *Age* distinguishes between a 41-year-old and a 59-year-old; in its recoded form these people are placed in the same category. Wherever possible it is best to keep interval variables as they are. This involves different statistics to indicate significance, and allows us to introduce the topic of association.

Figure 13.3 shows four graphical representations of possible relationships between *Age* and *Income*. These are called **scattergrams** and have been produced by SPSS. The first of these, described as showing a **positive** relationship, shows a scatter of points rising from the bottom left corner to the top right. Each of the points represents a person about whom two facts are

Doing research

recorded: their age and their annual income. Look at age 20 on the horizontal
x-axis. Move directly upwards until you reach the point just above the

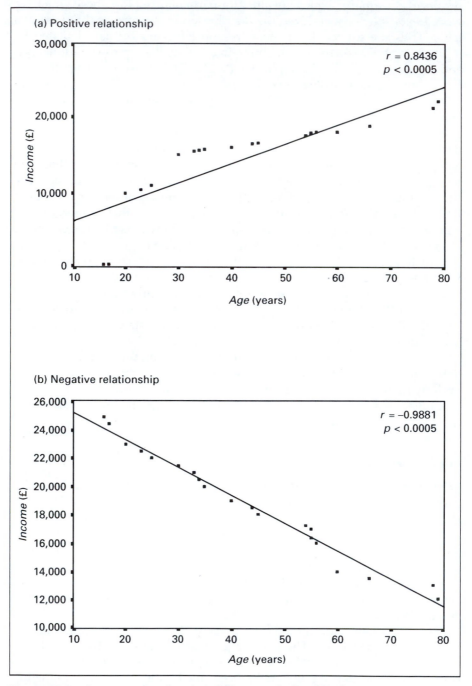

Figure 13.3 *Scattergrams showing different relationships between
age and income*

sloping line. If you then go directly left you will meet the *y*-axis at 10,000. This is a 20-year-old person who is earning £10,000 per annum. You will see on this first scattergram that, roughly speaking, the younger the people are the less they earn; the older the people are the more they earn. In other

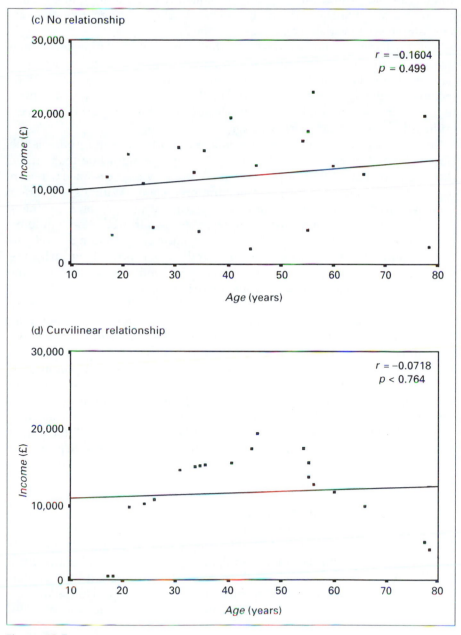

Figure 13.3　*cont.*

words, as one variable increases, the other variable increases too. This is the defining characteristic of a positive relationship.

The next scattergram demonstrates a **negative** relationship, which means that the older people get the less they earn. Thus, the youngest person on the plot, represented by the point at the top left of the scattergram, is 16 years old and has an income of £25,000 a year. The oldest, at the bottom right, is 79 and has an income of £12,000. The defining characteristic of a negative relationship is that as one variable increases, the other one *decreases*.

The third scattergram demonstrates the absence of a relationship, while the fourth one shows a **curvilinear** relationship. Here, middle-aged people have the highest income, while very young and very old people have lower incomes. You may feel that this represents the true picture of most people's lifetime earnings, with income rising steadily in the early part of a career, tailing off again around retirement age.

The line that runs through the points in each of these scattergrams is the **line of best fit** or **regression line**. It is the single straight line that can be drawn through the cluster of points that involves the least distance between it and all the points. It is useful in making predictions. With a scattergram such as that in Figure 13.3a, we can try to predict what a person's income is likely to be at a certain age. For example, at age 50 our prediction would be that a person should be earning £16,407. This figure can be found by going to the 50-year mark on the *x*-axis, moving directly upwards until you strike the regression line, and then moving horizontally left until you strike the *y*-axis. You will see that making a guess where there is no relationship (Figure 13.3c) or where there is a curvilinear relationship (Figure 13.3d) would be misleading as, in practice, the points are very far away from the regression line. Making predictions only really makes sense if there is a positive or negative linear relationship when most of the points are reasonably close to the line.

This brings us to the topic of **association**. You will see that within each scattergram is a value for *r*. This indicates how close the points are to the line and measures how *strong* the relationship is. If most of the points are close to the line, this statistic will be close to +1, indicating a strong positive association, or −1, indicating a strong negative relationship. In fact, if all the points fall on the line, *r* is either +1 or −1 exactly. If there is broad scatter of points, as in the third scattergram, *r* will be close to zero, indicating no association. The statistic *r* is the **Pearson's correlation coefficient**. This is an indicator of association suitable for use with two interval variables. You will also notice that a *p*-value is given. In the first two scattergrams this is well below 0.01, indicating that the relationship is very likely to hold true in the population, if this is a random sample drawn from that population. In both of the first two cases, then, we would say that the relationship is strong and statistically significant. In the last two we could not say this. You should notice that Pearson's *r* is not suited to indicate curvilinear relationships. Unless we saw the fourth scattergram, we would not be aware that this relationship actually existed.

In contingency tables too we can indicate the strength and direction of associations. Below Table 13.3 there is a value of 0.29277 for a statistic called *phi*. This is one of a number of tests of association that can be applied to tables. They all have slightly different characteristics, and the choice of which one to use is governed by the level of measurement of the variables in the table (for example, whether nominal or ordinal), and by how many cells there are in the table. SPSS gives on-screen help in selecting the test most appropriate for each type of table. All of them are designed, as far as possible, to conform to the same characteristics as Pearson's *r*. That is, a perfect negative association is indicated by –1, a perfect positive association by +1, and the absence of association by zero. For example, a value of 0.29277 indicates a fairly weak relationship between the two variables. It makes little sense to speak of direction in the case of tables such as Table 13.3, since the variables are both nominal, with no sense of magnitude to them.

Although it is good practice to report both a test of significance and one of association when writing up the results of a research project, tests of association are often omitted when considering data in tables. This is because a judgement of strength and direction can be made simply by examining the percentages in the table. Additionally, the various tests of association for tables do not always 'behave themselves'. For a variety of reasons, some do not indicate the direction of associations, or may indicate stronger or weaker associations than really exist. For these reasons they are rather rough-and-ready tools, compared with the more consistent chi-square test.

Comparing the means of two groups

So far, we have considered relationships between two variables measured at the same level. Quite frequently, however, the social researcher is concerned with comparing the average values between two or more groups of people. Thus, we might be interested in how men and women differ, on average, in their incomes, or in how different social classes differ in the hours spent watching television a week. This type of relationship can be understood as one between a nominal variable and an interval variable. One way of approaching this is to establish whether there is a statistically significant difference between the *means* of the two groups. We can return here to differences in income, and try to establish whether men have a higher income than women.

Table 13.4 shows SPSS output from a data set containing 10 men and 10 women who have been asked to indicate their annual income. The value for the means shows that men (*Gender 2*) earn considerably more, on average, than women (*Gender 1*): £18,380 compared with £11,035. The standard deviations for each are given, indicating a greater spread of incomes for women. The statistical significance is based on the significance of the *t-value* (this procedure is known as a *t-test*) and two of these are shown: one for equal variance ($p=0.002$) and another for unequal variance ($p = 0.004$). (The **variance** is the square of the standard deviation.) Whether the variances are equal is shown by the significance of Levene's *F*-test, which stands at

Table 13.4   *SPSS output comparing levels of income of men and women*

t-tests for independent samples of *Gender*

Variable	Number of cases	Mean	Income (£) SD	SE of mean
Gender 1 (women)	10	11,035.0000	6,011.011	1,900.848
Gender 2 (men)	10	18,380.0000	1,788.730	565.646

Mean difference = –7,345.0000.
Levene's test for equality of variances: $F = 6.978$, $p = 0.017$.
t-test for equality of means: 95%.

Variances	t-value	d.f.	Sig.	SE of diff.
Equal	–3.70	18	0.002	1,983.225
Unequal	–3.70	10.58	0.004	1,983.225

$p = 0.017$, indicating that the variances are unequal, so the second t-value ($p = 0.004$) is taken. This indicates that it is likely that this difference holds true in the population from which this sample was drawn.

Sometimes in social research it is important to compare the means of more than two groups. Thus, for example, social class might be measured as upper, middle and lower. If we wished to compare the mean income of groups defined in this way, the t-test would be inappropriate, and a related procedure known as the *analysis of variance* would be used. Details of this are beyond the scope of this chapter, but can be explored in further reading.

CONCLUSION

In this chapter, we have moved from the analysis of single variables to a consideration of two-variable analysis. You should by now be familiar with the idea of a frequency distribution, and of statistics such as the mean that measure the central tendency of such distributions. You were introduced to the use of the standard deviation to indicate the dispersal of cases around the mean. Further on in the chapter, the anatomy of contingency tables was discussed, followed by a discussion of statistical significance and the way this is indicated for tables by the p-value derived from chi-square. It is important to distinguish the idea of statistical significance from the idea of association. The former enables us to judge whether we can infer from a sample to the population from which it is drawn. The latter describes the strength and direction of relationships between variables, regardless of sample size. With large samples even quite weak associations will be significant; with small samples it will be hard to attain significance whatever the strength of association.

The discussion of association moved us away from tabular analysis to consideration of scattergrams and relationships between interval variables.

Different strengths and directions of association were illustrated. The use of regression to predict values of one variable from another was briefly touched upon, before the application of tests of association to data in tables was explored. Finally, we considered the use of the *t*-test to indicate the significance of differences between the means of two groups.

Throughout the chapter there has been an emphasis on the perspective of the social researcher doing data analysis, rather than the mathematician or statistician. Arguments about society and culture can be as readily constructed with numbers as they are with words, and often with considerably greater persuasiveness. It may be important to present results in an attractive and immediate way in reports of social research; this is why the chapter has shown you ways in which numbers can be converted into graphical displays. Additionally, the use of computer packages such as SPSS has transformed the experience of data analysis for social researchers. No longer does this need to be preceded by lengthy courses in underlying formulas. User-friendly help screens that guide the analyst in choosing appropriate tests, as well as integrated graphics packages, mean that quantitative data analysis is no longer the exclusive preserve of the mathematically inclined.

Further reading

De Vaus (1991) gives a brief but clearly explained guide to the main principles of quantitative data analysis. Rose and Sullivan (1993) give an excellent book-length introduction to the topic, together with a data disk so that readers can carry out the procedures using statistical software. Bryman and Cramer (1994) relate their explanations of statistical methods to output from SPSS. A good way to begin analysing quantitative data is to start using SPSS for Windows, which has a helpful tutorial, a demonstration data set, and plentiful on-line help.

Statistical reasoning: causal arguments and multivariate analysis

Clive Seale

CONTENTS

It was argued in Chapter 3 that the search for causal explanations has often been a part of a *positivist* enterprise, reflecting a desire to generate law-like statements about the workings of society, so that social life is thought of as analogous to a physical structure, or at best a biological organism. Additionally, in Chapter 9, concerning the uses of theory in social research, it was argued, using the example of Moerman's (1974) study of the Lue, that qualitative research is particularly suited to showing *how* people generate meaningful social life. For example, the Lue achieve their ethnic identity by using 'ethnic identification devices' strategically in interactions with, say, visiting anthropologists. (Thus, they claim to like certain foods above others, or to possess certain beliefs, which they say are 'characteristic' of their particular ethnic identity.)

The sociologist Max Weber is often associated with the *interpretive* approach to social research aspired to by many qualitative researchers. It is therefore of importance to note that Weber's criteria for adequate explanations of social life involved explanations adequate at the levels of both cause and meaning (Marsh, 1982). Put in another way, we could argue that as well as asking *how* people achieve various effects (or meanings) in their social lives, we should also be concerned with *why* certain effects are achieved rather than others. Thus I might be concerned, if I were an anthropologist studying ethnic identification devices, to discover which devices were preferred in different settings, or whether the Lue differed in the intensity of their usage of these devices from other social groups. A hypothesis derived from some general theory might drive such an inquiry. For example, could it be that social groups that are under intense threat of extinction are more concerned to preserve 'ethnic identity' than others? This might be reflected in the more frequent usage of ethnic identification devices in social settings where previously they were rarely used. Or, following Mary Douglas's theory (see Chapter 9) we could hypothesize that more threatened social groups are less likely to tolerate anomalies, this being reflected in the frequencies with which certain foods were eaten. These are examples of *causal* hypotheses. Quantitative methods can help to establish whether such hypotheses can be supported. I hope that it will be clear that crude beliefs in the unity of science (for example, that people and molecules are similar classes of being), or a lack of interest in how people actively construct meaningful worlds, are not necessarily involved when pursuing an interest in causal explanations. This chapter will show you how to construct causal arguments with statistics. It depends on a thorough understanding of the concepts introduced in Chapter 13.

CONDITIONS NEEDED TO ESTABLISH CAUSALITY

In deciding whether one thing (A) has caused another (B), three basic conditions must be met. Firstly, A must precede B in time (the problem of **time order**); secondly, A must be *associated* with B; and thirdly, the association must not be caused by some third factor C (the problem of **spurious causation**).

Thus, in examining the hypothesis that people with a higher educational level (A) therefore subsequently achieve higher income levels (B), it is no good if a person's income is assessed before their education is complete (a *time order* problem). Additionally, there is unlikely to be a causal relationship if people with a high educational achievement do not differ from those with a low educational achievement in their incomes (in which case we would say that there is no association between the variables). Most difficult to establish in social research, however, is the issue of whether some third variable – such as parental social class (C) – is associated with both educational achievement (for example, rich parents send their children to private schools) and income (for example, a private income from family wealth). In this case, an apparent relationship between education and income may be spurious since both educational achievement and income have been affected by the third variable.

Experimental and quasi-experimental design

In natural science, the *experiment* is used to establish causality (these ideas are also discussed in Chapter 7). For example, let us say that as biomedical researchers we wish to establish whether a new drug is effective. Here, an experimental research design known as the **randomized controlled trial** is very effective in establishing causality. A group of experimental subjects (say 100 people with a given disease) is allocated *at random* to one of two groups: the *treatment* group, who receive the new drug, and a *control* group who do not receive the drug. If the disease is relieved in the treatment group, the drug is judged to be effective. The essential point here is that the people are allocated *at random* to either group. This means that the two groups are unlikely to differ from each other in any systematic way. That is to say, the only variable that is allowed to vary is the issue of whether a person in the experiment receives the new drug or not. Any subsequent difference can then be attributed to the effect of the drug with some confidence. (In fact, other procedures are also usually built into such trials to ensure more complete control of all variables.)

In social research, it is very hard to conduct experimental trials like this, though experiments are not unknown in social science – particularly in social psychology. For the most part, though, it is difficult to manipulate people's social worlds to the extent required in a full experiment. To test the hypothesis that social groups threatened with extinction use ethnic identification devices more intensely, one would have to randomly allocate people to ethnic groups. To test the hypothesis that higher education causes income levels to vary, one would have to randomly allocate people to different types of lifetime educational experience. Clearly this is ridiculous. While it is sometimes possible in social research to use experimental designs, the intervention often changes people's social realities so much that the setting involved becomes artificial (for example, the psychology laboratory), so that generalizing results from the experimental setting to the real world becomes difficult.

In dealing with data derived from social surveys, therefore, one is usually faced with the necessity to adopt a **quasi-experimental** approach. This involves the manipulation of data so that a causal *argument* is gradually built up from the data, in which associations between variables are demonstrated, arguments for and against the view that these are causal associations are considered, and then further data analysis is done to test out these arguments. There are a variety of ways in which this can be done, but the most accessible of these is to conduct analysis via *contingency tables*. The **elaboration paradigm** is a term used to describe this type of analysis of tables, which was developed by quantitative social researchers in America in the 1940s and 1950s (see Chapter 6 for a historical account of this). Rosenberg's *The Logic of Survey Analysis* (1968) provides a classic account of the approach. The present chapter will focus on explaining the techniques of the elaboration paradigm, though at the end other techniques of multivariate analysis will be briefly illustrated.

THE ELABORATION PARADIGM

Dependent and independent variables

Before beginning this section, it is worth pausing for a moment to define what is meant by the division of variables into those called **independent** and those called **dependent**. Crudely, one can understand an independent variable as being a *cause*, and a dependent one as being an *effect*. The effect variables 'depend upon' variation in the cause variables. In the examples discussed so far in this chapter, independent variables have been the degree to which social groups face the threat of extinction, and the variation in educational achievement people experience. Dependent variables are the intensity with which people use ethnic identification devices, and people's income.

Establishing whether a variable can be considered dependent or independent is sometimes not straightforward, it may, for example, depend on issues of time order. Take the example of education and income. Clearly it is reasonable to assume that in a sample of middle-aged adults, their income might be determined to some extent by whether they were university graduates or not. But let us imagine that by 'income' we mean the overall wealth of people's family of origin. In this case, many people's 'income' will have been established long before they entered the education system. Indeed, it may have been established before they were born! Here, 'income' precedes education and, one could argue, could be considered to be the independent variable (the cause), with education being the dependent variable (the effect). Establishing the point in time at which variables are measured is important in constructing an argument about which can be considered dependent on the other. For this, one needs an understanding of the way in which the data being analysed were originally produced.

Relationships between three variables

Table 14.1 shows a series of tables in which different sorts of relationships between three variables are shown, below an initial or **zero-order** contingency table. Look first at this top table ((a)(i)), which shows the relationship between educational achievement and income. For simplicity, all the variables in the table are *dichotomous*, that is, they have two values. Thus educational achievement and income are divided into 'high' and 'low'. This is a rather crude measurement of these variables; the ideas of the elaboration paradigm can be applied to more sophisticated measures too.

Within each cell is a *count* and a *column percentage*. In the zero-order table, this indicates that 60% of the 200 people with 'high' levels of educational achievement have achieved a 'high' income, compared with 40% of the 200 people with a 'low' level of education. This is a moderate association, but is a statistically significant result. Phi, a measure of association, has a value of 0.20; gamma, another measure of association, and perhaps the one best suited to this type of table, as it is designed for ordinal variables, gives a value of 0.38. You will recall from the previous chapter that tests of association generally conform to the rule that a value of 0 indicates the absence of association, and a value of +1 or −1 indicates either perfect positive or perfect negative association. The p-value, based on chi-square, is 0.00006, way below

Table 14.1 *Demonstration of the elaboration paradigm: the relationship between education and income, as affected by gender*

(a) (i) *Zero-order table showing an association*

Income	Educational achievement	
	High	Low
High	120 (60%)	80 (40%)
Low	80 (40%)	120 (60%)
Total	200 (100%)	200 (100%)

p = 0.00006; phi = 0.20; gamma = 0.38.

(a) (ii) *Replication*

Men

Income	Educational achievement	
	High	Low
High	40 (61%)	26 (39%)
Low	26 (39%)	40 (61%)
Total	66 (100%)	66 (100%)

p = 0.01481; phi = 0.21; gamma = 0.41.

Women

Income	Educational achievement	
	High	Low
High	80 (60%)	54 (40%)
Low	54 (40%)	80 (60%)
Total	134 (100%)	134 (100%)

p = 0.00149; phi = 0.19; gamma = 0.37.

(a) (iii) *Spurious or intervening*

Men

Income	Educational achievement	
	High	Low
High	112 (78%)	64 (76%)
Low	32 (22%)	20 (24%)
Total	144 (100%)	84 (100%)

p = 0.78290; phi = 0.02; gamma = 0.04.

Women

Income	Educational achievement	
	High	Low
High	8 (14%)	16 (14%)
Low	48 (86%)	100 (86%)
Total	56 (100%)	116 (100%)

p = 0.93038; phi = 0.01; gamma = 0.02.

(a) (iv) *Specification*

Men

Income	Educational achievement	
	High	Low
High	90 (60%)	50 (33%)
Low	60 (40%)	100 (67%)
Total	150 (100%)	150 (100%)

p < 0.00000; phi = 0.27; gamma = 0.50.

Women

Income	Educational achievement	
	High	Low
High	30 (60%)	30 (60%)
Low	20 (40%)	20 (40%)
Total	50 (100%)	50 (100%)

p = 1.00000; phi =0.00; gamma = 0.00.

(b) (i) *Zero-order table showing no association*

Income	Educational achievement	
	High	Low
High	120 (60%)	120 (60%)
Low	80 (40%)	80 (40%)
Total	200 (100%)	200 (100%)

$p = 1.00000$; phi = 0.00; gamma = 0.00.

(b) (ii) *Suppressor*

Men

Income	Educational achievement	
	High	Low
High	20 (67%)	20 (20%)
Low	10 (33%)	80 (80%)
Total	30 (100%)	100 (100%)

$p < 0.00000$; phi = 0.43; gamma = 0.78.

Women

Income	Educational achievement	
	High	Low
High	100 (59%)	100 (100%)
Low	70 (41%)	0 (0%)
Total	170 (100%)	100 (100%)

$p < 0.00000$; phi = –0.45; gamma = –1.00.

the level of 0.05 where one normally accepts that two variables are likely to be related in the population from which a sample is drawn.

One can imagine that a researcher might have generated this first table in order to present an argument that gaining educational qualifications tends to cause people to get more highly paid jobs. Initially, it seems, the zero-order table supports this view. But a counter-argument might be that in fact this is a *spurious* result. In other words, the argument would be that although there is a statistical association between these variables, it is in fact caused by some other factor. Gender, for example, may explain the association. Perhaps it is the case that, in the population from which this sample is drawn, boys are encouraged by their parents to do well at school and to think of themselves as high achievers in the job market. This factor of gender-biased parental encouragement may have produced the initial association, suggesting that it is caused by gender (or rather the things associated with gender) rather than representing any real causal relationship between what one learns in the education system and the jobs one can do as a consequence.

In order to *test* this counter-argument the research can break down the initial zero-order table into two tables, first examining the relationship for men, and then that for women. This generates **conditional** or **first-order** tables, showing how the relationship between the variables in the zero-order table looks when considered separately for different values (in other words, male and female) of the third or **test variable**. **Replication** is said to occur if the original relationship remains, as is the case in the first pair of conditional tables ((a)(ii)). Here, the researcher can conclude that gender does not affect the relationship between educational achievement and income. This is reflected both in the percentages and in the two tests of association, which

Doing research

show little change when compared with the zero-order statistics (although note that the *p*-values are no longer so low as the sample size has reduced in each of the two tables compared with the size of sample in the zero-order table).

In the next pair of conditional tables ((a)(iii)) you will see that the tests of association are both close to zero in both tables. Additionally, the *p*-value indicates that neither table shows a statistically significant result. If you examine the percentages you can confirm that there is no association between the variables. Educational achievement appears to make no difference to income, once gender is taken into account (or 'controlled for'). If the original relationship disappears once a test variable is entered, as it does here, we may conclude either that the relationship was **spurious**, which is to say that gender has caused the association between educational achievement and income, or that the test variable is an **intervening** one. For a variable to be considered intervening, it must be caused to vary by the independent variable in the zero-order relationship, and in turn must cause variation in the dependent variable. An example of this might be the fact, as most people believe, that educational achievement intervenes in the relationship between people's social class of origin and their eventual social class in adult life. Here, the argument goes, people who are well off provide the type of education that allows their offspring to enter occupations of similarly high status to their parents. In Table 14.1, though, it is not reasonable to argue that gender intervenes between educational achievement and income. This is because one's level of educational achievement does not cause one's gender to vary! Clearly, gender is largely established by the time one enters the educational system. In fact, the zero-order association is caused by the fact that boys tend to be both high achievers and high income earners, while girls are the opposite. That is to say, gender is independently associated with both educational achievement and income. An argument about *time order*, then, must be generated in order to distinguish between spurious and intervening variables. The tables alone will not solve this problem for you.

A further possible outcome when a test variable is entered is that one of the conditional tables will demonstrate an association, whereas another will not. This is known as **specification** because the test variable has specified the conditions under which the original relationship holds true (this is also sometimes called *interaction*). Thus, in the third pair of conditional tables ((a)(iv)) the relationship between education and income is present for men but not for women. Try reading the percentages in the table, and the tests of significance and association, to see how this can be supported. Such a finding may lead the researcher into further theorizing and data analysis. Could it be that men take more vocationally oriented courses than women, for example? Clearly, further data collection and analysis would be needed to explore such a relationship.

Finally, we can consider the idea that a test variable may hide or **suppress** the existence of a relationship in a zero-order table. It is often the case that social researchers faced with a table that suggests the absence of association between two variables give up on their hypotheses at that point, concluding that further reasoning along these lines is inappropriate. It is sometimes said that the presence of association is not enough, on its own, to demonstrate causation. However, it is not often appreciated that *absence* of association is not enough to prove *absence* of causation. Table 14.1 shows how this can occur. The second zero-order table ((b)(i)) suggests that 60% of people have a high income, regardless of their educational achievement. The conditional tables ((b)(ii)), though, suggest that for men there is a strong positive relationship between educational achievement and income, while for women educational achievement appears to militate against achieving a high income (a negative relationship). Clearly, if such a finding occurred it would be of particular interest, and would justify further argument and data analysis to establish what had led to this pattern.

Notice, too, what has happened to the tests of association (phi and gamma) in tables (b)(ii). In the left-hand table, these are positive values, reflecting the positive nature of the relationship. In the right-hand table, they are negative values. Note too that in the right-hand table gamma gives a value of -1.00, which in theory is supposed to indicate a perfect pure relationship. A glance at the table reveals this to be misleading; it is in fact an artefact of the way in which gamma is calculated that has distorted the value in a table where one of the cells has no cases in it. It is for this sort of reason that it was stated in the last chapter that tests of association are somewhat crude devices, and that examination of percentages is recommended as well when interpreting tabulated results.

To summarize, the elaboration paradigm is a way in which tabular analysis can be used to assess the adequacy of causal arguments in social research. Through elaborating the relationships found in bivariate analysis by entering third variables as tests of causal propositions, one can gradually build up plausible arguments about what might be going on in an area of social life. One can never, eventually, prove beyond reasonable doubt that one event has caused another. In fact, this method of analysis follows closely the ideas of Popper, who proposed that science proceeded by sustained attempts at *falsifying* theories (see Chapter 2). When all plausible counter-arguments to a proposition have been tested, progress has been made. On the way, deeper understanding will have been achieved through the fruitful interaction between data and argument that is the characteristic of good data analysis.

OTHER METHODS FOR MULTIVARIATE ANALYSIS

It is a good idea to begin to learn about multivariate analysis by using tables and the elaboration paradigm, since one can see in the cells in the tables, and in the percentages, exactly what happens to each case in the data matrix as variables are entered into the analysis. This helps in retaining a firm grounding in the data; one does not then become detached from it in a self-sustaining technical world of statistical procedures whose meaning and interpretation may be somewhat unclear. However, multivariate analysis with tables has some disadvantages. Firstly, in order to use interval variables one must recode them into manageable categories, thus losing information. Secondly, as more variables are entered (and one can go on elaborating first-order conditional tables by entering fourth or fifth variables to produce second-order and third-order tables and so on), retaining a sense of the question one is testing becomes increasingly difficult. Problems also arise with low numbers in each cell, as subtables require the sample to be split up into ever smaller groups. This makes significance testing difficult.

A popular method of multivariate analysis that preserves interval variables as they are, and which enables the researcher to understand the interactions between quite large numbers of variables simultaneously, is **multiple regression**. This technique preserves the idea that in social statistics one must often recognize that events have multiple causes, rather than single ones. If one wishes, for example, to understand what causes people's income to vary, one must recognize that this is down to a number of factors, perhaps including parental income and social class, educational achievement and gender. Discovering the relative *strength* of different variables thought to be causal factors then becomes the task of data analysis. Multiple regression provides the researcher with statistics that enable an estimate of this.

A related technique is that of **logistic regression**. While multiple regression is suited to estimating the impact of variables upon an interval-dependent variable (for example, income measured in units of currency), logistic regression is suitable for assessing the influence of independent variables on a dichotomous dependent variable. It has the advantage of producing a statistic whose meaning is intuitively easy to grasp: the **odds ratio**. Here, I will demonstrate the use of this technique in a particular piece of data analysis in order to show the potential of the method. To learn how to use the technique yourself, you will need to consult more advanced texts. You should note, however, that the concepts learned in the elaboration paradigm underlie other techniques of multivariate causal analysis.

Table 14.2 presents results from an interview survey of the bereaved relatives, friends and others who knew a sample of people who had died (Seale and Addington-Hall, 1994; 1995a; 1995b). The respondents were asked whether, in their opinion, the person had died at the best time, or whether it would have been better if the person had died earlier than they did. They were also asked whether the person who died had ever expressed a wish to die earlier, or asked for euthanasia. It is commonly said by those who oppose the legalization of voluntary euthanasia that if people are looked after well enough, particularly if they are looked after in hospices devoted to the care of dying people, this will remove people's desire for euthanasia, as they will learn to accept the benefits of a natural death. The data analysis set out to test this proposition.

Table 14.2(a) shows the proportion of people who said an earlier death would have been better, or who asked for euthanasia, according to whether

Table 14.2   *Hospice care, euthanasia and the wish to die earlier: bivariate and multivariate analysis*

(a) Bivariate analysis

| | Hospice care | | No hospice care | |
	Domiciliary only	Inpatient		
Proportion of respondents saying better earlier	28% (of 327)	36% (of 312)	26% (of 1179)	$p < 0.01$
Deceased said wanted sooner	26% (of 362)	22% (of 338)	22% (of 1277)	$p > 0.01$ (not sig.)
Deceased wanted euthanasia	7.9% (of 356)	8.8% (of 329)	3.6% (of 1264)	$p < 0.01$

(b) Multivariate analysis (logistic regression)

| | Hospice care | | Number of people |
	Domiciliary only	Inpatient	
Respondent: better earlier	1.4	1.7*	856
Deceased: wanted earlier	1.4	1.0	921
Deceased: wanted euthanasia	2.0	2.1	912

* $p < 0.05$.
Odds ratios have 'no hospice care' as reference category.
Source: adapted from Seale and Addington-Hall, 1995a

they had received hospice care. It shows, for example, that of people who received no hospice care, 3.6% were said to have wanted euthanasia. By comparison, 7.9% of the 356 people who received domiciliary hospice care (for example, visits at home by a specialist nurse), and 8.8% of the 329 people who had inpatient hospice care (in other words, who were admitted to a bed in a hospice), were said to have asked for euthanasia. If you look at the percentages given for the 'better earlier' and 'wanted sooner' questions, a somewhat similar pattern is evident. In two cases, the difference between the groups is statistically significant (shown by the p-value). Note that we are analysing three separate dependent variables here, represented by the three questions.

One might conclude from this that people who argue that hospice care reduces the desire for euthanasia have got it wrong. It appears to be the case that the opposite is true: hospice care actually seems to *increase* the incidence of requests. This, however, would be a superficial conclusion. Firstly, there is a potential *time order* problem. The interview did not establish whether requests for euthanasia, or the expression of wishes to die sooner, occurred before, during or after episodes of hospice care. It is possible that some people became so distressed that they made this request, and subsequently entered a hospice where they changed their minds owing to the good care they received. However, this time order problem does not apply to respondents' own views about the desirability of an earlier death, since hospice care had occurred many months before the interviews were done.

Another objection is that a variety of other things are likely to cause people to want to die sooner, or relatives to feel that an earlier death would have been better. People who receive hospice care might be different from people who do not. We cannot conduct a randomized controlled trial here (McWhinney et al., 1994). Perhaps people who enter hospices have more distressing symptoms, or greater levels of dependency. Other analyses of the data (Seale and Addington-Hall, 1994; 1995b) had shown that older people were more likely to want to die sooner, and that respondents who were spouses rather than other types of relative or friend of the person who died were less likely to feel that an earlier death would have been better. Maybe these factors differed systematically between people who received hospice care and people who did not. In other words, a series of plausible reasons as to why the three *zero-order* associations reported in the top half of the table might be *spurious* were considered.

Logistic regression allows the data analyst artificially to hold certain variables 'constant' in order to assess the independent impact of key variables of interest. This impact is represented in terms of *odds ratios*. The odds ratios shown in Table 14.2(b) can be understood by giving a verbal interpretation of one of them: respondents for people receiving inpatient hospice care were 1.7 times more likely than respondents for people not receiving such care (the 'reference category') to say that it would have been better if the person had died earlier. The asterisk indicates that this is a statistically significant result. The odds ratios ensure that like is being compared with like; symptom distress, dependency, age and whether the respondent was a spouse or not, were all held constant in order to make this comparison.

Of course, other potential spurious variables could have caused the association. By thinking through plausible objections to a causal proposition (for example, the rather surprising idea that something about hospice care caused respondents to feel that an earlier death would have been better), measuring the variables involved in these objections, and then including them in multivariate data analysis, a variety of arguments can be investigated.

CONCLUSION

The ideas of the elaboration paradigm are a useful start in multivariate analysis. The detailed explanation of more advanced techniques such as multiple or logistic regression are beyond the scope of this book. However, I hope that this chapter, and the previous one, will have given you an introduction to quantitative data analysis that is sufficient to demystify the procedures involved. Good data analysis proceeds by being constantly aware of the main issues that are being investigated. Statistics are a tool for taking forward an argument. It is unfortunate that technical complexity has sometimes been elevated to an end in itself, so that the researcher loses sight of the basic issues at stake in a piece of data analysis. The tendency towards complexity for the sake of it is also evident in other areas of social research, notably in some of the more theoretically driven forms of qualitative research, such as semiotics (Chapter 18), discourse analysis (Chapter 19) and conversation analysis (Chapter 20). It is the aim of this volume to show you that these methods are within your grasp, and these two chapters have attempted to apply that general principle to quantitative work.

Further reading

De Vaus (1991) gives a brief but clearly explained guide to the main principles of quantitative data analysis. Rose and Sullivan (1993) give an excellent book-length introduction to the topic, together with a data disk so that readers can carry out the procedures using statistical software. Bryman and Cramer (1994) relate their explanations of statistical methods to output from SPSS. A good way to begin analysing quantitative data is to start using SPSS for Windows, which has a helpful tutorial, a demonstration data set, and plentiful on-line help.

15

Using official statistics

Don Slater

CONTENTS

We live in a society in which most important social phenomena – at least those which fit the agenda of the state, media and public opinion – are turned into numbers. As you saw in Chapter 6 these are produced by large-scale institutions, state and private, and the research agencies which service them. Such organizations require numerical information in order to plan and monitor their activities, to calculate their costs, efficiency, impact, options and so on. The numbers are intrinsic to rationalized organization and are often a by-product of the day-to-day operations of large organizations and their information-gathering activities. For example, in addition to various regular surveys of employment such as the Labour Force Survey, the UK Office for National Statistics (ONS) also collects, as a product of filling in forms registering people for various benefits, detailed statistics on unemployment.

These officially produced statistical representations of social phenomena offer researchers an extraordinary resource. Their first, but also most contentious, advantage is the appearance of objectivity that accompanies the use of numbers in modern times. Another attraction of official statistics is their large-scale nature, offering a basis for generalizing findings, for claiming representativeness and for investigating relationships between social variables that cannot be identified at a local level. They are useful, therefore, in placing smaller-scale (perhaps qualitative) studies in broader context.

Thirdly, most official statistics are published in the form of a **statistical series**. That is, they are collected at intervals, often over considerable periods. The UK census, for example, has been collected once a decade since 1801; UK deaths have been officially registered since 1837. Thus, in addition to allowing generalization across social space, official statistics often allow comparison over time. In using statistical series for this, though, the researcher should try to be aware of changes in assumptions and definitions, practices of data collection, summary categories and so on that might affect the trends displayed. For example, official UK definitions and measures of employment changed, owing to government policy shifts, over 20 times during the 1980s alone. Nonetheless, researchers can attend to these changes, take them into account and still find unrivalled resources for longitudinal analysis.

In this chapter I shall firstly consider a variety of critiques made of official statistics. This will involve gaining a better understanding of how they are produced, during which time they are implicated in a variety of distortions. In the second half of the chapter I shall show how researchers, if duly informed by a critical awareness of their limitations, can nevertheless use official statistics to considerable effect. I shall demonstrate this by focusing on the *secondary analysis* by social researchers of officially produced data sets.

CRITICAL PERSPECTIVES ON OFFICIAL STATISTICS

Official statistics attract both huge credibility ('numbers don't lie') and utter disbelief ('there are lies, damned lies and statistics'). As shown in Chapter 6, numbers have often appeared to offer a neutral way of representing society and social relations. This idea was promoted in nineteenth century social science and derives partly from the attachment to a positivist agenda. Quantification appeared to offer the best approximation to that theory-free description of the world which (it was believed) characterized natural sciences (see Chapters 2 and 3). The idea that numbers never lie arises from the view that truthful descriptions emerge when human intervention is eliminated from the process of representing human societies. But critiques of the validity of official statistics, as of statistics in general, assert that numbers are human and social products, indeed by-products of highly self-interested and even politicized actions and institutions.

Initially most criticisms focused on technical matters affecting validity and reliability and resulted in both altered practices (for example, refinement of questionnaire design and data processing methods) and organizational changes (for example, major reorganization of the UK government statistical office under Sir Claus Moser from the late 1960s onwards). From the 1960s onwards critiques became more radical, as part of anti-positivist trends in social science. Some critical assaults specifically targeted official statistics (for example, Marxist critiques of the ideological assumptions and state institutional interests through which statistics are produced, such as

Hindess, 1973). Others saw official statistics as providing glaring examples of the problems involved in the generation of *any* numerical representations of social relations (for example, ethnomethodologists such as Atkinson, 1978). The view was that statistics, including official ones, could not provide objective representations of social phenomena. The task these critics set themselves was to undermine the prestige and credibility of numbers.

In this radical perspective statistics, and hence the representations of reality they conjure up, are not so much *collected* as *constructed* or *produced*. The argument goes that statistics tell us very little about the social phenomena they purport to describe but actually reflect the social agencies and practices through which they are generated. Hence, for example, we might use official statistics 'describing' the crime rate to investigate the changing policies of the police or to chart public attitudes to, say, violent crime or sexual assaults, but we could not rely on them for an accurate quantification of these crimes themselves. The figures reflect the social processes through which they were produced rather than the 'reality' they seek to enumerate.

Levels of critique

These kinds of conclusions have been arrived at by strategies that can be divided into three levels of critique: issues of *interpretation*, of *institutional practices*, and of *general considerations* of government and ideology. I will consider each in turn.

Firstly, the act of counting social things involves complex acts of interpretation. *Social facts* are produced through such acts of interpretation. The difference between calling a dead body a case of suicide, accidental death, manslaughter, death by natural causes or death by misadventure presumes a social system of classification produced through custom, legislation, medical practice and so on. Acts of social interpretation are required in order to assign a particular dead body to one of these categories. Most famously Douglas (1967) showed that Durkheim's assumption in *Suicide* that coroners' verdicts could be taken as a valid statistical basis for social research into suicide was false. Through looking at what coroners actually did Douglas was able to show variability in how they interpreted the presence or absence of a suicide note, evidence about the individual's circumstances and state of mind prior to death and so on. They did this within cultural contexts influencing their perception of events. For example, in different communities there is more or less shame or religious prohibition attached to suicide.

Against this it is important to note that while all social facts are constituted through acts of interpretation, this is not always an important issue. Some statistics are more valid and reliable for practical purposes than others. For example, although statistics on suicide may depend on inconsistent interpretations, birth and death statistics are less likely to be unreliable. Failure to register is rare and there is little interpretive ambiguity as to whether a particular body has just been born or just died (though the assignment of *cause* of death may be inconsistent). Additionally it can be argued that *all* social research involves interpreting social events in relation to a system of social categories.

Nevertheless, the generation of official statistics results from long chains of interpretation. A form to be filled in at an employment office is designed by officers to whom words like 'work', 'cohabitation', 'part-time' seem uncontroversial. The many individuals filling out the form, though, have to interpret these terms in order to answer the question, and do so in the context of needing to obtain benefits ('When my neighbour fixed my drains in exchange for the work I did on her car, was that part-time work?'). The upshot of these acts of interpretation, duly coded, are then raw material for more interpretation in the process of data analysis and presentation.

The second level of critique relates to institutional practices. This is a matter of both institutional culture and policy, ways of doing things as well as the interests and aims of organizations. For example, crime statistics are heavily influenced by practices such as plea bargaining, whereby the definition of an act as a particular kind of crime may involve a calculation of the likelihood of various outcomes in court. Whether a killing is a 'murder' or 'manslaughter' is not then intrinsic to the act, or solely judged by a judge or jury. It also entails institutional ways of processing crime that involve criminals, victims and lawyers. Yet it is these processes that produce the statistics on violent crime. Additionally, changes of policy can produce huge variations in the statistics, unrelated to changes in the social reality they purport to describe. Thus a rise in rates of rape or ethnic violence may reflect not an increase in the number of actual acts but rather an increased willingness on the part of the public, police and courts to take these events seriously, register them and pursue them to convictions.

The third level of critique concerns general considerations of government and ideology, setting the production of official statistics within a broader social and ideological context. The assumptions they embody are seen as centrally related to issues of power, interest and control. For example, Oakley and Oakley (1979) note that sexism may be built into official statistics in various ways. Most official statistics have assumed the household norm of a nuclear family with male 'head of household', making women invisible. Similarly, 'work' is generally defined as paid work outside the home, thus ignoring women's work within the home. Another example concerns measurements of class and socio-economic status. Official statistics often define these categories in terms of the income and occupation of a male 'head of household'.

Although the assumptions underlying statistics may be drawn from generalized ideologies such as sexism, they also involve institutional policies. Hence, for example, debates over unemployment statistics in the 1980s involved political differences about what constituted unemployment and who was expected to be employed in the first place. For example, conservatives treated any form of work as full employment (even when seasonal, temporary, casual or part-time) and did not tend to expect more than one member of a household to work; left-of-centre analysts identified work with full-time employment and considered women without paid work as unemployed. The employment statistics became an explicit battle zone for these issues with often more than one major revision per year. Another celebrated example is that of 'mugging', which became the centre of a moral panic in Britain over the 1970s (Hall et al., 1978). Hall et al. trace the notion of 'mugging' to political strategies for managing economic and social crises, focusing fears on racist stereotypes of black youths as symbols of threat to social order. However, there was no legally defined crime of mugging and no statistical category existed to measure it. Existing statistics from the figures for robbery, assault, and so on were manipulated, so that one could observe pressures in the media, criminal justice system and government to make the figures fit the political agenda.

The crime rate

In many ways the official statistic that most clearly fits these critiques has been the crime rate. Official crime rates, as they appear in the press, generally represent the end point of a long process by which certain acts are defined as criminal, incidents of those acts are observed and notified to the police, and the police regard them as serious enough to record and investigate them (and may then be able to bring them to court and obtain a conviction). But about 80% of the crimes registered by the police are reported by members of the public, as opposed to being uncovered by the police themselves. The crime rate therefore depends substantially on the public's view both of crime and of the role of the police in relation to different kinds of crimes. For example, it depends on the kinds of criminal acts visible to the public: burglary is visible, but white-collar crimes, like computer fraud, generally are not. The public's view of what constitutes a crime, or a crime that demands police intervention, also varies and changes: domestic violence was until recently considered a private matter by many communities but it is now understood to be a criminal matter in which the police are expected to intervene.

The crime rate also reflects the state of police–community relations. For example, it has been argued that much of the increase in violent crime over the last 20 years can be attributed to declining public tolerance of violence and a changing role of the police in relation to it. A classic contrast might be between a bobby on the beat, 30 years ago, coming across a regular Saturday night closing-time brawl and sending the lads off home; and police being called to the scene today, arresting the offenders and adding to the crime rate. Thus different police roles produce different crime rates.

In producing the crime rate, then, the incidents reported to the police must also actually be registered by them. They must believe the report of the member of the public, and agree that the observed event actually constitutes a crime, that it is serious enough to investigate, and that it makes sense to investigate in terms of both police resources and priorities. As part of this process, the police have also to apply various legal definitions, rules of thumb and calculations about legal procedure in order to interpret and classify the reported event as one kind of crime rather than another, as murder rather than manslaughter, or aggravated assault as opposed to grievous bodily harm. In all of these things there is room for variable inter-pretations.

Official crime rates can be contrasted with other measures, the most vivid being *victim studies* such as the British Crime Survey (Home Office, 1983). Such studies are based on asking a representative sample of the population what crimes they have themselves experienced, regardless of whether they were reported to the police. Victim surveys consistently show massive undercounting of crime in the official statistics and other dis-crepancies between the two statistical sources. Much of this discrepancy is due to the features we have discussed above: relations between commu-nities, police and courts which lead to different rates of reporting crimes. At the same time, it would be a mistake to declare victim studies unpro-blematically true, without applying to them the same kinds of questions about interpretive, institutional and ideological factors. For example, respondents may be employing common-sense as opposed to legal defini-tions of what constitutes a serious criminal act or wrongdoing, so that the figures may not be comparable; they may have different views as to what constitutes a serious crime and what counts as good evidence that a crime has actually occurred at all. A victim survey should be assessed as critically as official statistics.

USING OFFICIAL STATISTICS

All of this, however, does not make official statistics in principle unusable by social researchers. All forms of social research involve encounters with social worlds, and the data they produce bear the mark of these encounters. The issue is not 'statistics versus no statistics', but rather 'how can we under-stand the social production of statistics so that we can use them appro-priately and critically?' The very fact that official statistics emerge from identifiable social institutions and processes helps us to bring methodologi-cal issues more clearly to the fore. In this second half of the chapter I will show how official statistics can be used by social researchers, focusing par-ticularly on **secondary analysis**.

To some extent, statistics have been criticized partly because they have allowed state organizations to monopolize their advantages and use them in their own interests. This is especially the case if social researchers cannot analyse the data for themselves, which is what is involved in the secondary analysis of official statistics. This situation has improved, owing to wide-spread access to very powerful desktop statistical software and the increas-ing availability of official statistics in digital form. However, greater opportunities for secondary analysis have not extended to greater control by academics or the public over the kinds of questions originally asked, or the coding categories used.

Before showing how such analysis can proceed it is worth noting that fresh analysis of original data is often unnecessary to make good use of official statistics. Existing statistical series and the reports of *ad hoc* government social surveys commonly contain a wealth of information in large tabulations, much of which lies unexamined by the government officials who originally produced them. I will illustrate this with an anecdote, supplied by Seale (personal communication).

In late 1996 Seale visited the Caribbean island of Trinidad, in order to help the Department of Community Medicine in the medical school develop a course for family doctors. In particular, he was to help in designing the part of the course involving the care of elderly patients. To prepare for this, he interviewed local doctors and social workers. Doctors told him that in Trinidad families looked after their own; elderly people were surrounded by extended families who cared for them when sick, meaning that the doctors could concentrate on biomedical aspects of care alone. Social workers, though, told a different story. They complained of the failure of doctors to refer patients to them, and pointed to changes affecting Caribbean family structure. Economic dislocation meant that the children of many elderly people lived far away, or had to work all day. More of the elderly lived alone, without someone to call on for help at times of need. The caring extended family, argued social workers, was a cosy myth.

Social research is not big business in Trinidad, and the production of official statistics is somewhat patchy, but Seale found in the local library an official report entitled *Health Profile of the Elderly in Trinidad and Tobago* (Pan American Health Organization, 1989). Based on a survey of the elderly population, the report was a wealth of official statistics, and included the fact that 13.6% of people aged 60 or more lived alone, and 24.1% of people aged 80 or more. The position of elderly women who lived alone was found to be particularly difficult, with a high proportion recording that their health needs were not met, and that they felt they had no one to call on to help them when sick.

Clearly, it would have been an advantage to have in-depth qualitative studies of selected families in order to understand more about people's situations. Perhaps the variable meanings of 'living alone' and 'help' could have been explored by such studies. But these bare official statistics were sufficient in reinforcing the course planners' belief that general practitioners needed to address the social needs of their elderly patients to a greater extent, because the rosy picture of support from extended families now seemed overstated.

SECONDARY ANALYSIS OF OFFICIAL STATISTICS

While the potential of published statistical tabulations is sometimes not fully exploited by social researchers, for some purposes these are insufficient. The officials generating tabulations cannot be expected to predict all of the uses data will have, so secondary analysis is often appropriate. Data archives in the USA, the UK and many other countries contain raw data from government censuses and surveys in order to encourage such use. The broad principles of secondary analysis are similar to those of any researcher engaged in statistical reasoning (Chapters 13 and 14): be aware of the conditions under which data have been produced, and ensure that any generalizations (particularly those that involve causal statements) have been fully exposed to possible counter-arguments.

Unlike the researcher who has designed a tailor-made survey, the researcher using officially produced data has little control over the variables

Table 15.1   *Construction of a disability index*

Coded from answers to six questions: 'Do you usually manage to. . . ?'

> get up and down stairs and steps
> get around the house
> get in and out of bed
> cut your toenails yourself
> bath, shower or wash all over
> go out and walk down the road.

The answers are scored:

> 0 on your own without difficulty
> 1 on your own, but with difficulty
> 2 only with help from someone else, or not at all.

Degree of disability	Scale values	Scale items
None (49%)	0	None
Slight (25%)	1	Has difficulty cutting toenails
	2	Needs help/cannot manage to cut toenails
Moderate (14%)	3	Has difficulty in going up and down stairs
	4	Has difficulty managing to go out and walk down the road
	5	Has difficulty having a bath/shower or wash all over
Severe (7%)	6	Needs help/cannot manage to go out and walk down the road
	7	Needs help/cannot manage to go up and down stairs
	8	Needs help/cannot manage to have a bath/shower or wash all over
Very severe (4%)	9	Has difficulty in getting around the house
	10	Has difficulty in getting in and out of bed
	11	Needs help/cannot manage to get in and out of bed
	12	Needs help/cannot manage to get around the house

Total 100% (*N* = 3,691)

Source: Arber and Ginn, 1991: 202

Table 15.2 *Caring contexts for elderly men and women, by level of disability (column %)*

	All elderly people		Elderly person has:			
			severe disability (score 6–8)		very severe disability (score 9–12)	
	Men	Women	Men	Women	Men	Women
All care is extra-resident						
Elderly person lives alone	19.8	47.5	26.1	51.9	14.3	29.2
Co-resident care in elderly person's own household						
Lives with spouse	70.1	36.4	58.5	31.2	69.0	27.4
Lives with others	5.9	8.4	9.2	9.0	7.1	17.7
Co-resident care: elderly person is not householder						
Lives with adult children	2.1	4.6	6.1	6.3	4.8	21.2
Lives with others	2.2	3.1	–	1.6	4.8	4.4
Total	100	100	100	100	100	100
(*N*)	(1,477)	(2,155)	(65)	(189)	(42)	(113)

Source: Arber and Ginn, 1991: 145, Table 8.4

measured. Sometimes little can be done about this, but at times creative solutions can be found in the transformation of existing variables into **derived variables**. An example of this is found in the work of Arber and Ginn (1991) who draw upon secondary analysis of the 1985 British General Household Survey (GHS) to present a series of compelling arguments about the disadvantages faced by elderly women. Their work also demonstrates the feminist use of quantitative methods (see Chapter 4), reinforcing the view that feminists need not confine themselves to qualitative methodology.

The derived variable generated by Arber and Ginn is shown in Table 15.1. The 'disability index' was created by combining answers from six questions (each of which had three possible answers) to form a scale ranging from 0 to 12, where people with no disability scored 0 and people with 'very severe' disability scored 9 or more. The percentages are the proportion of people aged 65+ in the survey who fell within each broad category of disability. The production of this variable was not the original intention of the people who designed the GHS, but Arber and Ginn found it to have considerable *construct validity* (see Chapter 11). That is to say, as one might expect, scores on the index increased with age and it correlated well with high use of health and welfare services.

Table 15.2 shows how this index of disability was then used to show differences between elderly men and women. It shows, for example, that half (51.9%) of severely disabled elderly women lived alone compared with only a quarter (26.1%) of the men. This meant that more women needed to rely on people from outside their homes for help. Men, on the other hand, were much more likely to be able to rely on their spouse. As well as gender-specific cultural expectations about who should give care, demographic factors lay behind this: on average women live longer than men, and tend to have married men older than them, so are more likely to be widowed. As you saw, the picture for the elderly in Trinidad, though not painted in such detail, seems to be moving towards a state of affairs that is somewhat similar; however, without qualitative research to show how the broad statistical pictures relate to the finer details of family life, this convergence should not be overstated.

CONCLUSION

The analysis of official statistics, then, places a method of great potential in the hands of researchers who have the skills to use them appropriately. It is always necessary to take account of the conditions of their production, and unwise to assume that the meaning of data is precisely as government officials intend. New variables may have to be created from old, and there will be times when the ingenuity of researchers in doing this will face the limits of the original data forms. Yet this is another reason for social researchers to get involved in using official statistics, as only by doing this can they be improved.

Further reading

Irvine et al. (1979) is a classic text reviewing a range of criticisms of official statistics. A more recent book, edited by Levitas and Guy (1996), updates this, documenting the political manipulation of official statistics in Britain, but also showing readers what can be retained that is of value. Dale et al. (1988) supply an excellent account of the procedures involved in secondary analysis, together with a guide to sources of data.

16

Qualitative interviewing

Clive Seale

CONTENTS

The interview is probably the most commonly used method in social research. It is more economical than observational methods (see Chapter 17) since the interviewee can report on a wide range of situations that he or she has observed, so acting as the eyes and ears of the researcher. The researcher can also use an interview to find out about things that cannot be seen or heard, such as the interviewee's inner state – the reasoning behind their actions, and their feelings.

You saw in Chapter 11 that the interview has been an important method for researchers doing social surveys, producing both qualitative and quantitative data. However, in the *classical* tradition of social survey work, represented by the sort of interviews done by Booth and Rowntree, as well as later social survey organizations such as the UK Office for National Statistics, the interview is used for rather narrowly defined purposes. In fact, one can say that a particular *epistemological* position is taken in the classical survey research tradition (see Chapter 2 for a definition of this term). The social world is assumed to have an existence that is independent of the language used to describe it. The accounts given by interviewees are assessed according to how accurately they reflect this real social world. Therefore, in the classical tradition, interview data are assessed for *bias* in the extent to which they represent a distortion of the truth.

At the opposite end of the spectrum from this *realist* approach is an *idealist* one (see Chapter 3), in which interview data – or indeed any account of the social world – are seen as presenting but one of many possible worlds. Since humans can know and describe the world only via language, it is ultimately not possible to judge whether one account corresponds more closely to the 'true' state of the world than another. Faced with an interviewee's account, researchers can only investigate the 'version' which the account seeks to display, examining, for example, how the speaker uses various rhetorical strategies in order to achieve particular effects. The anthropologist Evans-Pritchard (1940), in his fieldwork with the Nuer in southern Sudan, wanted to demonstrate how difficult it had been to gain information by direct questioning amongst this group as, unlike their neighbours, the Zande, they were skilled in deflecting questions. Here is an example of an interview he conducted:

I: Who are you?
Cuol: A man.
I: What is your name?
Cuol: Do you want to know my *name*?
I: Yes.
Cuol: You want to know *my* name?
I: Yes, you have come to visit me in my tent and I would like to know who you are.
Cuol: All right. I am Cuol. What is your name?
I: My name is Pritchard.
Cuol: What is your father's name?
I: My father's name is also Pritchard.
Cuol: No, that cannot be true. You cannot have the same name as your father.
I: It is the name of my lineage. What is the name of your lineage?
Cuol: Do you want to know the name of my lineage?
I: Yes.
Cuol: What will you do with it if I tell you? Will you take it to your country?
I: I don't want to do anything with it. I just want to know it since I am living at your camp.
Cuol: Oh well, we are Lou.
I: I did not ask you the name of your tribe. I know that. I am asking you the name of your lineage.
Cuol: Why do you want to know the name of my lineage?
I: I don't want to know it.
Cuol: Then why do you ask me for it? Give me some tobacco. (1940: 12–13)

In presenting this extract Evans-Pritchard is showing readers that in this cultural setting it is very hard to use interviews as a **resource** for discovering things about people's lives. Instead, he uses the extract for a different and very telling purpose: what happens during the interview itself is of interest. Analysed as a social event in its own right, as a **topic** rather than a resource, the interview is used as an opportunity to conduct direct observation. Evans-Pritchard is therefore able to draw conclusions about how the Nuer typically behave when faced with strangers (such as visiting anthropologists).

This, then, indicates that the *analytic status* of interview data can be treated in different ways by social researchers. On the whole, researchers in the classical, quantitative survey tradition treat interview data as a resource to discover 'real' facts about the social world interviewees experience. Treating interview data as a topic is generally only feasible when data are *qualitative*, as such an approach demands that researchers look closely at the way in which interviewees choose and use particular words or phrases to generate 'ideas' or representations of their social worlds. This chapter will show you some ways in which this sort of analysis can be done. However, it is also the case that many qualitative researchers wish to treat interview data as a resource rather than just a topic, as they remain committed to elements of a realist epistemology.

THE SEARCH FOR AUTHENTICITY

Criticisms of the classical approach

The interpretivist reaction against quantitative methodology in the 1960s and 1970s (see Chapter 3) involved three main criticisms of the classical approach to interviews. Firstly, it was argued that what people said in interviews (and questionnaires) was not necessarily what they did in practice. This was an argument favoured by those seeking to develop anthropological methods (ethnography) in social research (for example, Becker and Geer, 1957). Hughes presents an anecdote to show how this can occur:

> As early as 1934 La Piere travelled with a Chinese couple in the United States, reporting the treatment they received in hotels, camping sites, motels and restaurants. Of the 251 establishments visited, only one refused to accommodate the couple. Six months later, La Piere sent a questionnaire to each ... [asking] 'Would you accept members of the Chinese race as guests in your establishment?' ... Only one 'yes' response was received. (1976: 164)

In fact, of course, this is an argument that could be levelled at all interviews, whether in the quantitative or qualitative traditions, but it was felt to apply particularly to *scheduled, standardized* formats. Here, researchers typically meet the interviewee only once, trust therefore not being well established, and the interviewee is unable to talk about topics not on the interview schedule, or to answer in ways that deviate from pre-coded options. This was seen as generating a degree of alienation in interviewees from the aims of the research, and increasing the propensity to give misleading replies.

More specifically directed at quantitative methodologists was the point that variability of meaning was so great that attempts to standardize meaning in the form of, for example, fixed-choice attitudinal questions were doomed to failure. This was expressed most powerfully by the ethnomethodologist Cicourel:

> Standardized questions with fixed-choice answers provide a solution to the problem of meaning by simply avoiding it ... The meaning of questions with fixed-choice answers ... is dependent on interpretive rules ... The correspondence between the hypothetical world inferred from questionnaire items and actual behaviour of the actor remains an open empirical problem ... Questionnaire items (that measure attitudes) become 'frozen', clock-time slices of hypothetically defined situations. (1964: 108, 113–14)

Thirdly, and this was raised most commonly by feminist social researchers, the standardized, scheduled interview format, where the interviewer steadfastly refused to reveal his or her views to avoid the introduction of 'bias', was seen as exploitative. An unequal, unbalanced relationship was thereby set up, where the researcher possessed all the power to define what was relevant and what was irrelevant. Interviewees were constrained to answer only on certain topics that the researcher had deemed to be important, leaving the respondent little opportunity to determine the agenda.

DOING QUALITATIVE INTERVIEWS

On the one hand, and particularly from Cicourel's work, there developed an interest in interview data as a topic (of which more later). On the other hand, many qualitative researchers advocated the pursuit of truth by different means. They felt that certain types of interview format were more likely to gain authentic accounts than others, as well as being less exploitative. Variously termed 'depth', 'unstructured' or 'life history' interviews, this type of interaction involved researchers themselves doing interviews, rather than the 'hired hand' approach of large-scale survey research, where teams of interviewers were trained to ask the same questions in the same way of everyone they interviewed. Because the interviewer was also the person deciding on the purposes of the research, this enabled much greater flexibility during the interview itself. Interviewers could invent questions on the spot in order to follow up interesting leads, and the freedom from the need to construct a data matrix (where all respondents have to give information on the same variables) meant that different respondents could discuss different topics. Sue Jones gives something of the flavour of the approach:

> In qualitative research the notion of some kind of impersonal, machine-like investigator is recognised as a chimera. An interview is a complicated, shifting social *process* occurring between two individual human beings, which can never be

exactly replicated ... There cannot be definitive rules about the use of open-ended questions, leading and loaded questions, disagreements with respondents and so on. Such choices must depend on the understanding researchers have of the person they are with and the kind of relationship they have developed in the encounter. Some relationships may allow, without destroying trust or comfort, much more of the to-and-fro of debate and between two human beings than others. What is crucial is that researchers choose their actions with a self-conscious awareness of why they are making them. (1985: 48–9)

Commonly, an interview of this sort is done with the use of a **topic guide**. This acts as an aid to the interviewer, a sort of check-list that she or he can refer to when deciding what to turn to next as the interview proceeds. A loose notion that each interviewee should be encouraged to talk about similar topics informs such guides. Figure 16.1 is an extract from a relatively structured topic guide, taken from a study of people who had ceased using marijuana.

On the other hand, the interviewer may dispense with such guides altogether, inviting the interviewee to talk about whatever they feel is relevant. The interviewer's task then becomes one of monitoring what is emerging, perhaps gently guiding the speaker on to certain topics that seem promising,

---

1 First trying marijuana.
2 Circumstances surrounding first contact.
3 State of being following first contact.
4 Conditions for continual use.
5 Conditions for curtailment or stoppage.
6 Present situation.
7 Current attitudes towards usage.

Expansion of section 5
5 Conditions for curtailment or stoppage:
  A Why did you decide to stop or cut down?
  B What was happening to you at this time? (e.g. were you still in school, working, etc.?)
  C Was the drug still relatively accessible to you?
  D Did your decision to stop have anything to do with what was taking place in your life career? (This is, was the usage of marijuana on a regular basis becoming too great a risk in moral, social, or legal terms?)
  E Did any particular person or persons influence your decision to stop or cut down? Who, and how did they influence you?
  F (To be asked of those who have *stopped completely*) Since having given up marijuana, have you felt any strong yearning to try it again or resume your use of it? Tell me about it (times, occasions, places, etc. in which yearning is experienced). How do you handle these feelings when you get them – what do you tell yourself or do in order to resist the desire?

                          you

Source: quoted in Lofland, 1971: 78–9

Figure 16.1   Example of an interview topic guide

or asking for clarification when points made by the speaker seem unclear. This can involve drawing a person into telling a story in their own words by using interventions such as 'tell me more' or semi-verbal cues like 'uh-huh' which encourage an interviewee to continue speaking. The emphasis is on allowing the speaker to say how they see things, in their own words, rather than making them follow the researcher's agenda. Thus the interviewer's role is explicitly *non-directive*.

Such interviews are generally tape recorded, and the transcription of taped interviews in order to prepare them for analysis constitutes one of the major chores of qualitative interviewing. Though laborious, the experience of transcribing can bring a much closer appreciation of the meanings in the data, and this is often the time at which ideas for coding (see Chapter 12) arise, as well as ideas for topics to pursue in subsequent interviews, perhaps as a part of a *theoretical sampling* strategy (see Chapter 11).

Interviews like this may be done as part of a wider involvement in the field, perhaps as a part of a participant observation, or as a series of interviews with the same person, so that both parties know each other better than in the one-off interview situation typical of survey research in the classical tradition. The trust that this generates may then be a way of getting respondents to speak about more intimate matters than they would otherwise, and indeed to 'tell the truth' rather than distort their account in order to please (or mislead) the researcher. This view is evident in Janet Finch's account of her interviews with clergymen's wives:

> I arrived at one interviewee's home ... only to find she was being interviewed by someone else. This seemed like the ultimate researcher's nightmare, but in the end proved very much to my advantage. The other interviewer was ... ploughing her way through a formal questionnaire in a rather unconfident manner, using a format which required the respondent to read some questions from a card ('Do you receive any of the benefits listed on card G?', and so on) ... I recorded in my fieldnotes that the stilted and rather grudging answers which she received were in complete contrast with the relaxed discussion of some very private material which the same interviewee offered in her interview with me. My methodological preferences were certainly confirmed by this experience. (1984: 73)

Feminist perspectives

The development of trusting relationships between researcher and researched, and the goal of using social research to further the interests of the people who participate in research studies, has been the avowed aim of many feminist social researchers. Classical survey research interviewing, in which the interviewer adopts a supposedly 'objective' stance by pretending to have neutral views on all of the topics enquired about, is rejected. The implied goal of an objective social science is seen as a sham, brought about to hoodwink respondents into exploitative social relationships (see Chapter 4 for a more extended discussion of this view).

One of the most influential accounts of feminist commitment to qualitative interviewing has come from Ann Oakley, who drew on her experiences of interviewing women about childbirth for a research study. As well as rejecting the use of standardized, structured interviews, she also expresses criticism of the non-directive approach used in some unstructured qualitative interviews, as this too can be seen as potentially exploitative. If non-directive elicitation is the only strategy used by an interviewer, then this mirrors the strategy of the structured interviewer, taught to avoid biasing replies by using neutral probes. In fact, Oakley argues, social researchers should come clean about their agendas, should tell interviewees as much as possible about the purposes of their research and the possible uses of their research findings, and should also answer interviewees' questions, telling the interviewee about their own lives and opinions. Thus, she argues that

> when a feminist interviews women ... use of prescribed interviewing practice is morally indefensible ... in most cases, the goal of finding out about people through interviewing is best achieved when the relationship of interviewer and interviewee is non-hierarchical and when the interviewer is prepared to invest his or her own personal identity in the relationship ... Personal involvement is more than just dangerous bias – it is the condition under which people come to know each other and to admit others into their lives. (1981: 41, 58)

Oakley describes how the women she interviewed had many questions for her about the experience of childbirth. She saw no reason why she should not discuss her own experiences of motherhood with them, and her involvement in some cases became one of friendship, maintained after the research project finished. As an example of the sort of material that emerges in these circumstances of mutual support and trust, she gives the following extract:

> *A.O.:* Did you have any questions you wanted to ask but didn't when you last went to the hospital?
> *M.C.:* Er, I don't know how to put this really. After sexual intercourse I had some bleeding, three times, only a few drops and I didn't tell the hospital because I don't know how to put it to them. It worried me first off, as soon as I saw it I cried. I don't know if I'd be able to tell them. You see, I've also got a sore down there and a discharge and you know I wash there lots of times a day. You think I should tell the hospital; I could never speak to my own doctor about it. You see I feel like this but I can talk to you about it and I can talk to my sister about it. (1981: 49–50)

Oakley's views about interviewing have not been without their critics. Cornwell (1981), for instance, an anthropologist who did depth interviews over repeated meetings with people in the East End of London, has observed that the implication that some have drawn from Oakley – that only women researchers should interview women respondents if they are to gain authentic accounts – is in fact no guarantee of this. Social class and ethnic differences between interviewer and interviewees can put up barriers at least as high as gender differences. Additionally, Malseed (1987) has argued that Oakley underestimates the extent to which researchers in the classical survey research tradition have shown awareness of issues of trust and the influence of gender during interviews.

Lastly, the commitment of feminist social researchers to qualitative methods is not universal. Jayaratne (1983) has observed that feminist political aims might just as well be furthered by quantitative methodology, and the work of Arber (Arber and Ginn, 1991; also described in Chapter 15) shows classical survey research being used to good effect in demonstrating the disadvantages suffered by elderly women compared with elderly men in a patriarchal society. Indeed, Oakley herself has demonstrated flexibility in using classical, quantitative survey methods to investigate ways of providing support to vulnerable women (Oakley et al., 1994).

Limitations of treating the interview as a resource

Such criticisms developed by interpretivist and feminist social researchers are based on the view that there is an authentic or true account of social situations. In this respect they can be understood as holding to a *realist* epistemological position, which views some accounts as more true than others, in that they correspond more closely to the real nature of the social world. Many valuable studies have been done on this basis and it remains a key commitment of most qualitative social researchers.

At the same time, these approaches can be seen to be somewhat romantic, believing that authentic accounts of what 'things are really like' will be given in moments of emotional intimacy where souls are bared and pretence is stripped away. Getting past defences, or falsity, through developing trusting and honest relationships can sometimes become almost an end in itself, as is suggested in this quotation from a methods textbook:

> Humanistic approaches favour 'depth interviews' in which interviewee and interviewer become 'peers' or even 'companions' ... [supporting] meaningful understanding of the person ... and wholeness in human enquiry. (Reason and Rowan, 1981, quoted in Silverman, 1993: 95)

There is a danger here of imagining that a particular interaction format (the unstructured interview) is an automatic guarantee of the analytic status of the data that emerge. It is of course important to hold on to the idea of trust in interview situations, and to understand the effects of lack of trust on the accounts that then emerge from interviews. However, other approaches to the analytic status of interview data are possible and I shall now turn to these. In the section that follows there are a number of examples taken from research studies, whereas few were discussed in relation to interpretive and feminist perspectives earlier. This is because the approach now described is somewhat counter-intuitive and is best demonstrated by actual examples. It does not imply any devaluing of approaches previously described in the chapter.

THE INTERVIEW AS A TOPIC

Evans-Pritchard jokes that his interviews with the Nuer people were so frustrating that they gave him 'Nuerosis'; the extract at the start of this chapter shows that seemingly uncontroversial inquiries about, for example, a person's name might be blocked. Yet his interview is very revealing at another level, showing for example what a precious thing a name can be, and how dangerous it can be to 'give' one's name to a stranger. One might also use the extract to demonstrate the bargaining skills of the interviewee, or as evidence about the desirability of tobacco amongst the Nuer.

An interest in the way people use language as a form of social action, a resource with which certain 'realities' can be created or ends achieved, is a feature of conversation analysis and discourse analysis, both of which are discussed in detail later in the book (Chapters 19 and 20). Chapter 3 provides the theoretical context of these methods. In fact, Cicourel, whose influential critique of fixed-choice questionnaire items was mentioned earlier in this chapter, was an important figure in the development of *ethnomethodology* (the theoretical framework underlying conversation analysis).

I will focus here on describing several studies which, although they analyse interview material at different levels, share a common thread of treating the interview event itself as an opportunity for direct observation, a 'local accomplishment' of interviewer and interviewee.

Accomplishing measurement

Antaki and Rapley (1996) present an analysis of tape recordings of psychologists using a structured interview schedule to measure 'quality of life' in people with learning disabilities. This is an example of a 'qualitative' analytic approach (conversation analysis) being applied to a 'quantitative' interview situation. The analysis reveals a great deal about power differentials between psychologists and their clients.

Antaki and Rapley point out that the task from the interviewer's point of view is fraught with potential conflict, since the measurement of quality of life can have profound consequences for the people whose lives are being measured. The results of tests like these are used to decide, for example, what sort of institutional setting a person with learning disabilities should live in. The measurement instrument applied during the interview aims to be objective and neutral; yet the interviewer is also a representative of 'officialdom' so the questions have a far from neutral underlying agenda. Here is the beginning of one interview:

Int.: Do you know what I'm here for?
Resp.: What?
Int.: Well, you remember oh about two years ago I think it was that
Resp.: Yeh
Int.: About two years ago I came round and spent some time chatting didn't we and just watching what was going on
Resp.: Aye
Int.: Well I just wanted to come back and see how you were getting on now and just run through some
Resp.: Yeh
Int.: some questions with you about how you feel about things and living here and what you do and all that sort of thing yeh? Is that all right? (1996: 301, adapted)

Here, a rationale for the talk has been spelt out. This immediately 'marks' the event as different from 'normal' conversation, where people do not do such things. A 'cover identity' to mask the official nature of the assessment has been set up, one which tries to portray the event as just an informal chat about 'how you feel about things'. Occasionally, however, the interviewees would 'break' this cover, revealing that they too knew that this was an official event, with potentially serious consequences for them. For example:

Int.: But how much fun do you have? Do you have lots
Resp.: Sometimes I have the
Int.: or not much
Resp.: Not a lot
Int.: Not a lot, not a lot of fun?
Resp.: I don't be bad – no
Int.: OK. (1996: 303, adapted)

Here, the respondent has interpreted a question about 'fun' as also enquiring about being 'bad'. Anxieties about the hidden purpose of the interview are thus breaking through. The interviewer managed such disruptions in a variety of ways. One persistent problem for the interviewer occurred when respondents 'mistook' the friendly, conversational style of the questions, which enquired into quite intimate areas, as a general invitation to engage in 'troubles talk' – accounts of the respondents' personal life problems. Here is one such example:

Int.: Right, OK then, the things that you do during the day Arthur, do you think that they help other people or they help people a little bit
Resp.: They help me a little bit
Int.: Right, or they don't really help
Resp.: See, I'm badly sighted you know a bit
Int.: Right
Resp.: I'm blind a bit you know

Int.:   Yes, right, OK then. [Pause] So at Fresh Fields when you're doing
          your job. [Pause] Do you think you're good at your job? (1996: 309,
          adapted)

The 'troubles talk' occurs when the respondent decides that it is the right
moment to explain the problems caused by his poor sight. In order to circle
the appropriate pre-coded answer on the interview schedule, the interviewer does not 'need' this material, so discourages lengthy exploration of
the topic by not responding to the information with any elaborated expressions of concern, and by moving on to the next question on the schedule.
This reveals the interview, once again, to be an official testing event, rather
than just an informal chat.

This study, through a detailed analysis of the language used in an interview setting, therefore reveals a great deal about the micro-politics of this
setting, as well as showing the role of psychometric testing as a management
device. This does *not* mean, however, that the psychometric measurement of
quality of life is invalid (in other words, that the treatment of the interview as
a *resource* must be ruled out). The numbers that result from such interviews
may indeed reflect something about the relative quality of life of the
interviewees outside the interview situation. Conventional notions of
criterion validity (see Chapter 11), for example, could still be applied to the
measurements.

Linguistic repertoires

One of the most productive concepts in analysing interviews as topics is that
of the **linguistic repertoire**, describing the resources upon which people
draw in constructing accounts. Certain words, phrases and ideas, which are
characteristic of certain popular *discourses* (see Chapter 19), are used to
achieve various effects. I shall use an example from Potter and Mulkay
(1985). They draw on an earlier study (Gilbert and Mulkay, 1984) which
examined the way biochemists, when interviewed, justified their ideas about
the truth or falsity of scientific theories.

Potter and Mulkay are firmly committed to the analysis of interview
material as a topic. In taking this position they completely rule out the
possibility that it might be used as a resource:

> For the most part interviews are used as a technique for obtaining information that
> will enable the analyst to describe, explain and/or predict social actions that occur
> outside the interview ... this approach to interviews makes the analyst's con-
> clusions heavily dependent on the interpretations of social action carried out by
> participants ... a radical revision is therefore required in our use of interview
> material ... interview data should be used to reveal the interpretative practices
> through which participants come to construct versions of their social world ...
> accounts cannot be read as a literal depiction of social action ... there are no
> unproblematic means for separating those accounts that are literal descriptions

from those that are not ... accounts can only be properly understood in relation to the specific interactional and discursive occasion ... we cannot treat [accounts] as unproblematic windows onto the social or natural world. (1985: 247–8, 265–6)

Potter and Mulkay noticed that their interviewees were often self-contradictory in explaining why they preferred particular scientific theories rather than others. They rejected the idea of trying to establish which explanation was the 'true' one, preferring instead to look at the way in which interviewees strategically presented different explanations at different moments. Scientists drew on two interpretive repertoires at different moments in the interviews, which the researchers called the *empiricist* and the *contingent* accounts. The empiricist account was rather like the justification of scientific theories that is presented to pupils in school: that the decision about whether to adopt a theory as true depends upon whether experimental results support the theory. In this account, the scientists suggested that experimental findings *required* them to adopt particular theories. Here is an example: 'I was impressed by the data that indicated that the original version of the Spencer hypothesis could not be correct ... There were a few *key* experiments that convinced me' (1985: 260).

The contingent account, on the other hand, was less close to the 'official' version of science. It treated experiments as less certain criteria, and the interpretation of experimental results was seen as influenced by 'non-cognitive factors' such as the persuasiveness with which they were presented, or the prestige of the journal in which they were published. In fact, the contingent account is more reminiscent of Feyerabend's description of how science progresses (see Chapter 2), suggesting that expediency is a motive in adopting theories. Here is an example: '[whether other people accept your theory] depends on where something is published, how convincing your arguments are, the reputation of the individual who makes the hypothesis, and so on ... I don't know what the factors are that predict when things will really click and when they won't' (1985: 260).

The empiricist account, the researchers found, was predominantly used to explain the speaker's own beliefs, since it gave these greater legitimacy. The contingent account was used to make sense of persistent disagreements between scientists, to explain people's failure to adopt a theory now considered to be true, in spite of experimental evidence which supported it, and to throw doubt upon other scientists' reluctance to accept the speaker's own favourite theories. Together, these two accounting systems constituted resources, or *linguistic repertoires*, upon which speakers could draw when required.

Moral reputations and self-identity

Interviews are also moral arenas, in which the speaker's own reputation is displayed, sometimes by contrasting this with the incompetence or poor behaviour of other people. Baruch (1981; 1982), interviewing mothers about

what had happened in their medical consultations, found that his interviewees sometimes told 'atrocity stories' about doctors who had questioned
their reputations as good mothers. For example, one mother said:

> I went to the baby clinic every week. She would gain one pound one week and lose
> it the next. They said I was fussing unnecessarily. They said there were skinny and
> fat babies and I was fussing too much. I went to a doctor and he gave me some stuff
> and he said 'You're a young mother. Are you sure you won't put it in her ear
> instead of her mouth?' It made me feel a fool. (1982: Appendix 2, 1)

For Baruch the issue of how doctors actually behaved in consultations is not
an issue; the fact that these stories are told, whether true or not, is the topic of
interest, revealing how people feel about doctors, and how they attempt to
deal with power imbalances in the relationship.

Another way of analysing the interview as a topic is to understand the talk
as generating various versions of preferred self-identity, containing moral
elements. This can often be seen when speakers are describing how they
reacted to fateful moments that threatened the coherence of a secure personal narrative of self-identity. Catherine Riessman (1990) has presented an
analysis of the narrative structure of an interview she did with a man who
suffered from multiple sclerosis along these lines, indicating that this man
attempted to portray himself as a devoted husband and a responsible
worker, in spite of the fact that his marriage had broken down and he had
lost his job, for reasons ultimately connected with his illness. Thus, he
describes events with his wife:

> OK, when she left in February we tried to get back together in May ... That night
> about twelve o'clock there was a call and it was her, and Susan [their daughter]
> picked the phone up and she had been drinking and she had wanted to come home
> so Susan went down to the motel and picked her up ... brought her down here. She
> slept here that night. She came into my room, gave me a big hug and a big kiss, said
> 'I'm glad to be back.' I said 'I'm glad you're back,' I says 'We have all missed you.'
> The following day she seemed like she had a split personality, seemed like she
> changed into a different person. She got up in the morning. I came out and sat in
> the chair here an' she went back to the same routine that she had done before she
> decided to move out. She's telling me that I'm gonna be put in a nursing home ...
> she's going to sell the house. And I said 'hey, look, no, nothin' is gonna change, it's
> not gonna be any different than before we were married. Now if you want to stay
> here you can, you know, you gonna be – act the same way you were before you
> left.' So she just packed up and left. (1990: 1196–7, adapted)

Telling vivid stories like this one, which dramatizes and re-enacts a particular interaction, Riessman says, has the effect of drawing the listener into
the speaker's subjective experience. The speaker here displays evidence of
magnanimous character, being willing to forgive, and contrasts this with the
poor behaviour of his wife (her drinking, her 'split personality'). Riessman
observes that he does not present other possible versions that might reflect

badly upon his self-identity of competent masculinity by, for example, dwelling on sexual problems he may have experienced in his relations with his wife as a result of the illness.

CONCLUSION: THE INTERVIEW AS BOTH TOPIC AND RESOURCE

This chapter has reviewed different analytic stances towards interview data, focusing largely on the analysis of qualitative material arising from relatively unstructured forms of interaction between interviewer and interviewee. I have argued that an important contrast exists between approaches that treat interview data as a *resource* to discover things about events outside the interview situation, and other approaches which treat the interview as a *topic*, where the accomplishments of participants are investigated through a detailed examination of the language people deploy. To pursue the first of these approaches, some interpretive researchers advocate that trust be generated through non-directive questioning formats, which allow people to account for themselves in their own terms. Some feminist researchers advocate this too, although here there is a greater concern about the power imbalances that may arise if a purely non-directive (and therefore non-committal) approach is adopted.

Pursuing the second agenda are conversation and discourse analysts, who are concerned with the local effects achieved during interviews, whereby speakers may select from a variety of resources, or linguistic repertoires, particular versions of events. Speakers can be understood as displaying and defending narratives of competent or moral self-identity. The interviewer's role in the production of meanings generated in interviews becomes a topic of interest.

These stances towards the analytic status of interview data are *not* mutually exclusive, in spite of the occasional extremist statement by researchers concerned to develop particular approaches (for example, the statement made by Potter and Mulkay above). In my view, it is perfectly acceptable to adopt a policy whereby interviews are treated as potentially both topic *and* resource. Philosophical discussions of realism recognize that some things are more easily identifiable as 'real' (that is to say, having an existence independent from language) than others. Thus, for example, trying to find out the gender of a respondent's children may be seen as a fairly uncontroversial factual matter on which it may be appropriate to rely on interview data as a resource (and even one where a pre-coded question item is the best way of getting the information). Trust may play a role here in gathering data that are factually true. Trying to find out about a respondent's 'attitudes' about some topic of concern, though, may encounter more serious problems of validity. An appreciation of the complexities of language in use can help to guard against simplistic notions that the interview is an unproblematic window on the social world. At the same time, interviewees are usually constrained to make their accounts relate to reality. Examining how different versions of reality are deployed by interviewees should not blind us to the fact that only certain versions are likely to be plausible.

Further reading

Cain and Finch (1981) present a general argument seeking to reconcile readings of research data as both topic and resource, alongside feminist and other perspectives. Denzin (1989) gives an overview of a variety of approaches to interviewing. Silverman (1993: Chapter 3) presents a sophisticated discussion of different ways of approaching the analysis of qualitative interview data. Scott (1984) gives a feminist account of interviewing. West (1990) argues against the view that interviews are solely opportunities for people to construct versions of reality, suggesting instead that they can be used as a resource, and their truth status checked by observational methods.

Doing ethnography

David Walsh

CONTENTS

[Ethnography is] a particular method or set of methods which in its most characteristic form ... involves the ethnographer participating overtly or covertly in
people's daily lives for an extended period of time, watching what happens, listening to what is said, asking questions – in fact, collecting whatever data are
available to throw light on the issues that are the focus of research. (Hammersley
and Atkinson, 1995: 1)

This describes the essence of ethnography, showing it to be based in what is
known as **participant observation**. This makes the researcher, as participant
observer, the primary research instrument. Ethnography, then, contrasts
with 'scientific' methods of social science research that, based upon a universalistic model of science, emphasize its neutrality and objectivity,
attempting to generate data untouched by human hands. Ethnography
belongs to the theoretical tradition which argues that the 'facts' of society

and culture belong to a different order from those of nature (see Chapters 2 and 3).

THEORETICAL FOUNDATIONS

Anthropologists developed ethnography to become their primary and almost exclusive method. Faced with non-Western societies which largely possessed an oral culture, anthropologists were encouraged by a perception of their diversity to take an attitude of **cultural relativism**, whereby the values and institutions of any given society were seen to have an internal logic of their own. Any attempt to judge other societies as inferior or superior, in this view, is condemned as **ethnocentric**. Eventually this attitude was to lead to the view, amongst some, that rationality itself was simply a value position promoted by Western societies. Anthropologists took the view that society and culture could only be studied from inside by the immersion of the researcher in the society under study.

Later, sociologists pursuing *action theory* and *symbolic interactionism* came to use the method, as you saw in Chapter 3. It is, however, in *phenomenology* that we can see the most evocative conception of the ethnographer's role. Phenomenology, as was explained in Chapter 3, focuses on the inter-subjective constitution of the social world and everyday social life. Schutz (1964) in a seminal essay on *The Stranger*, shows how a social group has its own cultural pattern of life – folkways, mores, laws, habits, customs, etiquette, fashions and so on – that, as far as its members are concerned, are taken for granted, habitual and almost automatic. Members living inside the culture of their group treat it as simply how the world *is* and do not reflect upon the presuppositions on which it is based or the knowledge which it entails. But the stranger entering such a group does not have this insider's sense of the world, and instead finds it strange, incoherent, problematic and questionable. Yet the stranger can become a member of the group through *participation,* becoming transformed into an insider, inhabiting it in the same taken-for-granted way as existing members. At the same time, being a stranger creates an attitude of objectivity because the stranger must carefully examine what seems self-explanatory to the members of the group. The stranger knows that other ways of life are possible.

Schutz's stranger provides a model for the ethnographer using participant observation. The ethnographer tries to treat the familiar world of 'members' as **anthropologically strange**, to expose its social and cultural construction. This is particularly demanding when a researcher is studying a group with which he or she is familiar, but represents an ideal attitude of mind for the researcher to pursue nevertheless.

Constructionism is the view that society is to be seen as socially constructed on the basis of how its members make sense of it and not as an object-like reality (see also Chapter 3). It is latent in *symbolic interactionism* but more apparent in *phenomenology*. It has now become the primary theoretical foundation of contemporary ethnography. Indeed, one can see *ethnometh-odology* as forming a part of this constructionist approach. Ethnomethodologists, though, are less interested in how people *see* things than more conventional ethnographers, and are more interested in how people *do* things, particularly in their uses of language. Chapter 20 shows how the method of *conversation analysis* has arisen from these concerns. Although such approaches share a view that the subject matter of social and cultural research is different from that of the natural sciences, they are nevertheless characteristically committed to a *realist* and scientific view of the world.

However, an altogether different version of ethnography has also emerged out of constructionism which urges a radical break with all ideas of objective scientific inquiry. This position involves not simply seeing ethnography as a revelation of social construction but seeing ethnographic research as *itself* participating in the construction of the social world. Bauman (1987) has summarized this by distinguishing a traditional form of social research which is 'legislative', in that the ethnographer rules some accounts of the world true and others false, and a newer form that is more genuinely interpretive. This view involves seeing social research as one possible interpretation amongst many. The American anthropologist Clifford Geertz (1973) has played an important part in forming this different sense of ethnography. Geertz argues that:

> man [*sic*] is an animal suspended in webs of significance he himself has spun and I take culture to be those webs, and the analysis to be therefore not an experimental science in search of law but an interpretive one in search of meaning. It is explication I am after, construing social expressions on their surface enigmatical. (1973: 5)

This leads Geertz to the view that the task of ethnography is to produce its own distinctive form of knowledge which he calls **thick description**. Although the ethnographer continues to use the same techniques of data collection as conventional ethnographers, the focus of analysis turns much more to seeing culture as a system of *signs*. Here, the ethnographer comes close to doing a *semiotic* analysis (see Chapter 18). The easiest way to understand this is to imagine the ethnographer as being like a literary critic attempting to understand the organization, construction and meaning of a literary text. The ethnographer then finds a whole web of cultural structures, knowledge and meanings which are knotted and superimposed on to one another and which constitute a densely layered **cultural script**.

Famously, Geertz analyses the many layers of meaning involved in Balinese cockfights in a demonstration of this approach. He sees the event of a cockfight as an example of a cultural script being written, or enacted. Through an intensive and dense description of a cockfight, Geertz makes broader cultural interpretations and generalizations. Yet Geertz understands his own analysis of the various meanings of the event as a reflexive interpretation of it, rather than an objective description. This, of course, raises the issue of *validity*. If ethnographers are simply in the business of introducing new texts into a society and culture that is little more than an interplay of 'texts', we must give up any notions of science or truthfulness. As was shown in Chapter 3, this is Foucault's position, suggesting that the 'human sciences' are 'regimes of truth'. Post-modern thinkers usually then abandon the enterprise of social research, preferring to take refuge in deconstructive activity.

There have been some very interesting deconstructions of ethnographic writing (reviewed in detail in Chapter 22). These emphasize that ethnographers are story-tellers and, like all such, create narratives of tragedy, irony and humour which make their writing a literary activity. They use the same fundamental resources of literature and the same sorts of recipes and material in conveying arguments and persuading readers that their accounts are plausible reconstructions of social actors and social scenes.

But it seems wrong for social researchers wholly to accept this post-modern discourse, to abandon all forms of realism as the basis for doing ethnography, and to accept that all is textuality and construction. It could be argued that this takes reflexivity too far and shuns the empirical too much. The rhetorical strategies of ethnographic writing should be acknowledged, but this cannot be the end of the story. The social and cultural world must be the ground and reference for ethnographic writing, and reflexive ethnography should involve a keen awareness of the interpenetration of reality and representation.

DOING ETHNOGRAPHY

Quantitative research committed to a *positivist* vision of the unity of science (and as you have seen in previous chapters, this is something of a stereotype) attempts to establish correlations between objectively defined variables as a basis for explanation. This proceeds through a research design which is organized as a logically sequential and separate series of stages, beginning from theory and going through hypothesis generation and data gathering to hypothesis testing. Frequently, one-off interviews or questionnaires are used. Ethnography departs from this. Firstly, ethnographers study people in their natural settings, seeking to document that world in terms of the meanings and behaviour of the people in it. It places in doubt the variables which quantitative research analyses, examining instead their socio-cultural construction. Secondly, it does not follow the sequence of deductive theory testing because it is in the process of research itself that research problems come to be formulated and studied. Often these prove to be different from the problems that the ethnographer had initially intended to study. Theory is often *generated* rather than solely tested. Indeed the 'discovery of grounded theory' during fieldwork has been the subject of much debate in the literature on ethnography (Glaser and Strauss, 1967) and will be discussed later in this chapter in more detail. (Theory building from data is also discussed in Chapters 9 and 12.)

Ethnography is distinctive in three ways. Firstly, as stated above, there are no distinct stages of theorizing, hypothesis construction, data gathering and hypothesis testing. Instead the research process is one of a constant interaction between problem formulation, data collection and data analysis. The analysis of data feeds into research design; data collection and theory come to be developed out of data analysis and all subsequent data collection is guided strategically by the emergent theory. Secondly, ethnography brings a variety of techniques of inquiry into play involving attempts to observe things that happen, listen to what people say and question people in the setting under investigation. So it involves, as McCall and Simmons put it:

> genuinely social interaction in the field with the subject of study ... direct observation of relevant events, some formal and great deal of informal interviewing, some ... counting, [the] collection of documents and artifacts, and open-endedness in the directions the study takes. (1969: 1)

Thirdly, the observer is the primary research instrument, accessing the field, establishing field relations, conducting and structuring observation and interviews, writing field notes, using audio and visual recordings, reading documents, recording and transcribing and finally writing up the research. So ethnography has a large constructional and reflexive character. It is essentially the observer who stands at the heart of ethnography and of its open-ended nature.

The observer position

Observation, inquiry and data collection depend upon the observer gaining access to the appropriate field and establishing good working relations with the people in it. They need to be relationships that are able to generate the data the research requires. The identity that the observer assumes determines the success of this.

A first issue is whether to take an **overt** or **covert** role in the setting. This, in turn, very much depends on the situation and on the **gatekeepers** who control access to it. Gatekeepers are the sponsors, officials and significant others who have the power to grant or block access to and within a setting. Sometimes, the ethnographer is faced with situations in which relevant gatekeepers are unlikely to permit access, so that covert or secret research is the only way of studying them. This has been done, for example, in studies of the police (Holdaway, 1982), religious sects (Shaffir, 1985), organized crime (Chambliss, 1975) and right-wing political movements (Fielding, 1981). Here, the observer seeks to present himself or herself as an ordinary, legitimate member of the group. This may solve the problem of access and observation as long as the covert role can be maintained, but successful maintenance produces major problems of an ethical and practical kind and a massive problem if the cover is 'blown'. Normally, then, totally covert research is rare in ethnography. More commonly the researcher lets some

people know about the research and keeps others in the dark or only partially informed about the purposes of the research. Some ethnographers
argue on ethical grounds that the researcher should always adopt a completely overt role in which the purposes of the research and its procedures
are explained to the subjects under study. But Hammersley and Atkinson
(1995) argue that, whereas deception should be avoided if possible, telling
the whole truth about research may not be wise or feasible. Since research
problems will change over the course of fieldwork, what the researcher can
say about aims is often little more than speculation. Additionally, to produce
too much information ahead of time may influence the behaviour of the
people under study in such a way as to invalidate the findings.

Generally, then, a series of potential observer roles are open to the ethnographer. Junker (1960) identifies four. Firstly, there is the *complete participant*.
This entails complete covert research. Although it seems to carry the attraction of generating a complete knowledge of the situation, apart from the
problems outlined above it produces others too. It can place a severe
restriction on the character of the data collected because the observer, as a
completely participating member of it, becomes hedged in by the expectations of the role he or she has adopted. So many lines of inquiry will be
missed and optimal conditions for data collection may not be available.
Finally it carries the risk of 'going native', where the observer abandons the
position of analyst for identification with the people under study.

Secondly, Junker describes the role of the *complete observer*. Here the
researcher simply observes people in ways that avoid social interaction with
the observed, as Corsaro (1981) did in a study of nursery school children in
the classroom which involved observing them through a one-way mirror.
This reduces the possibilities of people reacting to being observed (known as
reactivity) or of 'going native', but introduces the potential problem of *ethnocentrism* instead, in which the observer, by not interacting with the people
under study, cannot get at their meanings and so imposes an alien framework of understanding on the situation. Moreover it places severe limits on
what can be observed, although it can be a valuable supplement to other
forms of ethnographic research.

The third role is that of the *participant as observer*. Here, the observer and
the people being studied are aware that theirs is a field relationship which
minimizes the problems of pretence. It involves an emphasis on participation and social interaction over observing in order to produce a relationship
of rapport and trust. The problem is that it carries the danger of reactivity
and of going native through identification with the subjects of study, unless
the intimacy created in social interaction is restrained by attempts to maintain the role of the stranger on the part of the observer. The fourth role is that
of the *observer as participant*. Here the balance is in favour of observation over
participation. This prevents the researcher from going native but restricts
understanding because limited participation in social activities heightens the
possibilities of superficiality, so that important lines of inquiry may be
missed or not pursued, things go unobserved and the activities of

participants are not properly understood. Typically most overt ethnography takes up a position somewhere between the third and fourth roles. Overt observer roles can never be entirely fixed and can and do change (the opposite is true if research is covert). Indeed changes in the observer's role in the field over the course of fieldwork may be vital in producing new information, generating new data and creating new and fruitful problems and lines of inquiry that extend the scope of the research. In the end, however, the best observational position for the ethnographer is that of the *marginal native,* which will be described later in the chapter.

Beginning an ethnographic study

Although ethnography does not work with a logically sequential research design that compartmentalizes it into distinct stages it does have phases and activities that give it a **funnel structure** in which the research is progressively focused over its course. At the start of this funnel the researcher will be involved in formulating ideas about the sort of problem to be investigated. In ethnography, however, what the researcher initially sets out to investigate may change over the course of fieldwork, as problems are transformed or emerge in the field. The process of observation itself establishes problems and the possibilities of inquiry into them. Yet all ethnography begins with some problem or set of issues, which some call **foreshadowed problems**, that are not specifically formulated hypotheses and which can have many sources. As was shown in Chapter 10, the requirement to write a research proposal may be the opportunity to lay out the nature of such foreshadowed problems. At the same time it is important not to let such an exercise close down avenues of inquiry that deviate from the proposal. One of the strengths of ethnography is its open-ended nature.

To begin with, the ethnographer needs to consult relevant *secondary sources* on the problems and issues under consideration, which can range from allied research monographs and articles through to other sources like journalistic material, autobiographies and diaries and even novels. But the focusing of research problems cannot really be started until initial data have been collected. As Geer says, one begins with early working hypotheses but ultimately goes on to generate 'hypotheses ... based on an accumulation of data ... [that] ... undergo a prolonged period of testing and retesting ... over the period of [research]. There is no finality to them. They must be refined, expanded and developed' (1964: 152). Even at the early stage theory enters into the selection of research problems, as was shown in Chapter 9. Moreover, the initial consideration of foreshadowed problems has to begin a process that moves between the immediate empirical situation and an analytical framework.

However, the research problem is very much shaped by the nature of the setting chosen for study. Choice of setting may have arisen on an opportunistic basis. For example, a natural disaster may have occurred, or the researcher may come across the reconstruction of an organization, or the replanning of a city, or may find an entry opened through personal contacts. In choosing a setting the researcher may then need to 'case' it, with a view to assessing its suitability and feasibility for research purposes. This will involve assessing the possibilities for access to it, collecting preliminary data on it, interviewing relevant participants and finding potential gatekeepers. Finally, the practical issues of the time and money needed to do research will need to be considered.

It is important that the setting is a *naturally occurring* one, although it need not be geographically self-contained. It can be one which is constituted and maintained by cultural definitions and social strategies that establish it as a 'community'. For example, a study of green political movements would be like this. It may be necessary to go outside the setting to understand the significance of things that go on within it.

If the setting is a single case, this can pose problems of representativeness. This, though, can be circumvented by selecting on the basis of intrinsic interest and theoretical usefulness (see the discussion of *theoretical general- ization* in Chapter 11). Sampling within settings also occurs so it is important to make decisions about what to observe and when, who to talk to, and what to record and how. Here three dimensions of sampling are relevant. The first is *time:* attitudes and activities may vary over time so a study may have to represent this. The second is *people:* people vary so a range of types should be investigated. Finally, people do different things in different *contexts* so a variety of these will have to be studied. *Contextual sensitivity* (see Chapter 8) is vital to ethnographic study.

Access

Initial access to the field is essential but is also an issue to be resolved throughout the whole of the data collecting process. There are numerous aspects to the problem. At a first level, gaining access to a situation is an entirely practical matter which entails using the ordinary interpersonal resources, skills, and strategies that all of us develop in dealing with the conduct of everyday life. But access is also a theoretical matter in ethno- graphy because, as Hammersley and Atkinson (1995) argue, the discovery of obstacles to access can help one to understand the social organization of a setting, showing, for example, how people respond to strangers.

'Public' settings (for example, the street, a beach) although seeming to offer no difficulties of access are, in fact, difficult for research. This is because deliberate and protracted observation can place the observer in a potentially deviant position, perhaps appearing as someone loitering with the intent to commit a crime. More typically, access to 'private' settings is governed by gatekeepers who are not always easy to identify, though common sense and social knowledge can provide the vehicles for doing so. In formal organiza- tions the gatekeepers will be key personnel in the organization, but in other settings the gatekeepers may be different. Whyte's (1943) classic study of slum ghetto life and its gang structure depended on finding and being befriended by 'Doc', a leading gang leader, who provided the **sponsorship** through which the ghetto was studied. But whoever the gatekeepers are, they will be concerned with the picture of their community, subculture, group or organization and may want it and themselves painted in a favourable light. This, in turn, means they are likely to keep sensitive things hidden. They may also prevent the study of mundane matters because they take them for granted and see them as uninteresting.

Access affects the accuracy of ethnographic study because it determines how and where fieldwork can be organized. Relations with gatekeepers can either be facilitative, because friendly and co-operative, or the reverse and so obstructive. But even facilitative relations with gatekeepers will structure the research since the observer is likely to get directed to the gatekeeper's existing networks of friendship, enmity and territory. It may not be possible for the observer to become independent of the sponsor so the observer can be caught in a variety of webs of client–patron relationships in which all kinds of unsuspected influences operate. The observer must find a way of using this to get relevant information. For example, Hansen's (1977) study of a Catalonian village in Spain became possible only when he accepted aristocratic sponsorship and worked with the aristocrat–peasant hierarchy since the assumptions and interactions of village life were based on this.

Gatekeepers will have expectations about the ethnographer's identity and intentions, as will other people in the field. Hammersley and Atkinson (1995) argue that it is particularly important as to whether the host community sees the researcher as an expert (and thus a person to be welcomed because he or she is helping to sort things out) or a critic and very unwelcome. On the other hand, if the researcher is defined as an expert this may conflict with the cultivated naivety involved in being a stranger. Moreover, even with a friendly gatekeeper, the researcher will be faced with the fact that not everything is equally available to observation. People will not or cannot divulge everything, or may even be unwilling to talk at all. So access to data is a recurrent problem that only subtle negotiations with gatekeepers and careful manoeuvring of the researcher into a position to get data can resolve. This requires patience and diplomacy.

Field relations and observation

Essentially ethnography entails a learning role in which the observer is attempting to understand a world by encountering it first-hand. Once access to a setting has been achieved, the success of observational work depends on the quality of the relations with the people under study. Firstly the researcher needs to consider the initial responses of people in the field and how to gain their trust. People will inevitably try to place the researcher within their own experience because they need to know how to deal with him or her. If they know nothing about research, they are likely to be suspicious and wonder if the researcher is acting as some kind of agent or spy for an outside body. For example, Kaplan (1991) reports that the New

England fishermen she studied thought she was a government inspector at first. On the other hand, if people are familiar with research and so view the researcher in a favourable light, there may be a mismatch between their expectations of what a researcher should do and the eventual research product. This can lead to a challenge to the legitimacy of the research and the credentials of the researcher. For example, Keddie (1971), although originally welcomed by teachers to do research within classrooms, was denounced later by them when her findings conflicted with their claims not to have streamed pupils in their mixed-ability curriculum. In the face of this the researcher needs to create a professional front.

But this raises a second issue in field relations, concerning **impression management** by the researcher. What is needed is an impression that facilitates observation and avoids producing obstacles. This, in turn, will require dress that is familiar to the people in the setting and the cultivation of demeanour, speech and habits that fit. The researcher must be able to create different self-presentations for different settings. Above all, the researcher must establish a large degree of ordinary sociability and normal social intercourse. Without this, pumping people for information can become threatening. Most anthropological field studies show that the researcher must meet local customs and decorum before research can be done at all. Yet the researcher must prevent sociability, rapport and trust from deteriorating into exploitation or 'going native'. This means some degree of frankness and self-disclosure on the part of the researcher is needed. This is not easy. The researcher will have to suppress some things as he or she will have to interact with people whose views he or she disagrees with but cannot challenge. Rapport, then, is a delicate matter to be decided by progressive initiation into the field.

Thirdly, the researcher will not be able to negotiate all aspects of his or her personal front and these non-negotiable characteristics of identity will have to be monitored for their effects on the research. Such characteristics are largely the *ascribed* ones of gender, age, ethnicity and race which tend to be institutionalized in society in terms of style and expected forms of social interaction. Chapter 5 showed how the constitution of these matters of identity can be explored in ethnographic research.

In the early stages of research, the researcher will simply be like any other stranger in the setting who watches and asks questions to make sense of it. But gradually the researcher will establish a version of himself or herself as a naive participant. In doing this, he or she must retain a self-conscious position in which incompetence is progressively substituted by an awareness of what has been learned, how it has been learned and the social transactions that inform the production of knowledge. Complete participation in the situation is impossible; such immersion would risk going native, and so a degree of **marginality** in the situation is needed to do research. Marginality is a poise between a strangeness which avoids over-rapport and a familiarity which grasps the perspectives of people in the situation. Thus the researcher can be understood to be a *marginal native*. This position creates considerable strain on the researcher as it engenders insecurity, produced by living in two worlds simultaneously, that of participation and that of research. The researcher will be physically and emotionally affected by this.

Finally, the researcher has to take a decision as to when to leave the field. This can be decided on the basis of the necessary data having been collected. Glaser and Strauss (1967) offer the concept of **theoretical saturation** to indicate the state of affairs that suggests that it is time to leave the field. As a part of their scheme for generating theory they say that saturation occurs when no new ideas are generated by empirical inquiry, after the researcher has made strenuous efforts to find instances in the field which might contradict, or help develop further, the emergent theory. Leaving the field will have to be negotiated, as it entails closing relations with participants that may have been firmly established and which they may not wish to relinquish.

Interviewing

Interviewing has a particular character in ethnography. Some ethnographers, following the dictates of *naturalism*, argue that people's accounts should always be unsolicited, so as to avoid the *reactivity* of formal interviews. But interviewing may be the only way of collecting certain data, in which case the researcher needs to decide who to interview. People in the field may select themselves and others as interviewees because the researcher has used them to update himself or herself on events. Or again gatekeepers may try to select interviewees, either in good faith or to manipulate the research. The researcher may have to accept both because access to data is not available otherwise. The researcher may consider that conventional notions of representativeness should dictate the selection of interviewees. Alternatively, informants may be selected on the basis of their particular value to the investigation: people who are outsiders, naturally reflective, or who have strong motives to reveal 'inside stories' for a variety of personal reasons. Another principle may be that based on *theoretical sampling* (see Chapter 11): the selection of informants whose information is more likely to develop and test emerging analytical ideas.

Largely speaking, *depth interviews* are done (Chapter 16), requiring active listening on the part of the researcher to understand what is being said and to assess its relation to the research. The ethnographic analysis of interviews should focus on the context in which the interview occurred. All of the considerations about the analytic status of interview data raised in Chapter 16 apply.

Documents

Most settings in contemporary society are literate and much of everyday life in them is organized around the production and use of documents. These are a valuable resource for ethnographic study. Official statistics, for example, are documents. But from an ethnographic point of view they are often understood in terms of their social production rather than their truth. Another kind of key document is the official record. Records are central to work in large organizations and are made and used in accordance with organizational routines. Such records construct a 'privileged' reality in modern society because they are sometimes treated as the objective documentation of it. But like official statistics, such records should be interpreted by the ethnographer in terms of how they are written, how they are read, who writes them, who reads them, for what purposes, with what outcomes and so on.

Yet other documents, too, of a literate society are relevant for the ethnographer. Fiction, diaries, autobiographies, letters, media products can all be useful. These can be a source of sensitizing concepts and suggest foreshadowed problems largely because they recount the myths, images and stereotypes of a culture. But as accounts biased by social interests and personal prejudices such documents can be used only to sensitize the ethnographer and open up potential worlds for scrutiny. (Approaches to the analysis of literary texts are described in Chapter 21.)

Recording data

The typical means for recording observational data in ethnography is by making **field notes** which consist of fairly concrete descriptions of social processes and their contexts and which set out to capture their various properties and features. The initial principle of selection in this will be the foreshadowed problems of the research, and in the beginning of inquiry this requires a wide focus in selection and recording. The systematic *coding* of observations into analytical categories comes later (see also Chapter 12). The central issues for making good field notes concern *what* to write down, *how* to write it down and *when* to write it down.

In terms of *when*, field notes should be written as soon as possible after the events observed. Leaving this to a later point produces the problem of memory recall and the quality of the field notes deteriorates. But note-taking has to fit in with the requirements of the setting under study, so the researcher must develop strategies for doing this. Buckingham (Buckingham et al., 1976), for instance, who adopted a secret observational role in a hospital by posing as a terminally ill patient, told anyone who inquired that he was 'writing a book' to explain his note-taking activities.

As to *how* to write down observations, field notes must be meticulous. This raises simultaneously the issue of *what* to write down. As social scenes are inexhaustible, some selection has to be made. At the beginning this must be wide, but as research progresses the field notes need to be relevant to emerging concerns. This requires focusing on the concrete, the detailed and the contextual. So the researcher should try to record speech verbatim and to record non-verbal behaviour in precise terms. Notes can then later be inspected in the secure knowledge that they give an accurate description of things. Field notes should also, wherever possible, record speech and action in relation to who was present, where the events occurred and at what time. Final analysis of data will draw on this knowledge of context. With interviewing, audio recording, and with observation, visual recording can be used as an additional and valuable aid. But audio and visual recording are still selective and so is the transcription of tapes. This is partially resolvable by following the now well-established rules of transcription that conversation analysis has produced (see Chapter 20). But to transcribe at this level of detail is really only practical for very short extracts. Documents can be collected and photocopied but they too will involve note-taking in terms of indexing, copying by hand and summarizing. In all, the primary problem of recording is always the same: as literal data are reduced, more information is lost and the degree of interpretation is increased.

Additionally, the researcher should write down any analytical ideas that arise in the process of data collection. Such **analytic memos** identify emergent ideas and sketch out research strategy. They provide a reflexive monitoring of the research and how ideas were generated. Ultimately analytic memos may be best assembled in a fieldwork journal which gives a running account of the research.

All data recording has to be directed towards the issue of storage and retrieval. This usually begins with a chronological record, but then moves to the conceptualization of data in terms of themes and categories to create a coding system that actively fosters discovery (see Chapter 12). This provides an infrastructure for searching and retrieving data, providing a basis for both generating and testing theory. Here, computers often prove useful.

Data analysis and theorizing

In ethnography the analysis of data can be said to begin in the pre-fieldwork phase with the formulation and clarification of research problems. It continues through fieldwork into the process of writing up reports. Formally it starts to take place in analytic memos and fieldwork journals but, informally, it is always present in the ideas and hunches of the researcher as he or she engages in the field setting and seeks to understand the data being collected.

The fragmentary nature of ethnographic data introduces problems. Checking the *reliability* of a particular interpretation may be difficult because of missing data. *Representativeness*, the typicality of crucial items of data, may be hard to establish. It may not be possible to investigate comparative cases in order to demonstrate *validity*. The generation of theories may not be the main aim of the researcher: many early Chicago school ethnographers (see Chapter 3), for example, were theory-free, at least in the explicit sense. The procedures of *coding*, whereby devices like *typologies* or *careers* may be developed, is the start of generating theory from data. Thus ideally theories are *grounded* in the data. Highly abstract theorizing, where concepts are not exemplified with data extracts, goes against the spirit of most ethnography.

In the funnel structure of this type of research, the initial task in the analysis of fieldwork data is to establish some preliminary concepts that make analytic sense of what is going on in the social setting. These can arise in a variety of ways. One is a careful reviewing of the corpus of the data in which the researcher seeks patterns to see if anything stands out as puzzling or surprising, to see how data relate to social theory, organizational accounts or common-sense expectations, and to see whether inconsistencies appear between different people's beliefs in the setting or between people's beliefs and their actions. Concepts can be generated in terms of *observer categories* derived from social theory, or from *folk categories*, terms used by participants in the field. But this initial conceptualization cannot be anything but sensitizing, a loose collection of orienting categories which gives a general sense of reference and guidelines in approaching the field.

The second stage is to turn such *sensitizing* concepts into *definitive* concepts, a stable set of categories for the systematic coding of data. These will refer precisely to what is common to a class of data and will permit an analysis of the relations between them. Glaser and Strauss (1967), describing the 'discovery of grounded theory', argue that the method for this in fieldwork should be that of **constant comparison** in which an item of data that is coded as a particular category is examined and its similarities with and differences from other items in the category are noted. In this way categories can be differentiated into new and more clearly defined ones and subcategories established. So this method, through its systematic sifting and comparison, comes to reveal and establish the mutual relationships and internal structure of categories.

An example of the use of the constant comparative method can be taken from their work (Glaser and Strauss, 1967). They found, as they observed nurses talking about the care of patients who had died, that these nurses would sometimes generate what Glaser and Strauss called 'social loss stories'. These were comments made that indicated the extent to which nurses felt a particular death constituted a serious loss or not. The *category* 'social loss story', though, contained some variable examples, whose properties Glaser and Strauss were able to explore by comparing different incidents where nurses spoke about the deaths of patients. Thus a nurse might regretfully say of a 20-year-old man, 'he was to be a doctor', or of a 30-year-old mother, 'who will look after the children?', or of an 80-year-old widow, 'oh well, she had a good life.' They concluded that the age of a patient was a key factor in determining the properties of social loss stories, as well as the educational and occupational class of the person who died. Additionally, they found that 'composure' (itself a category with variable properties) was often lost at moments of high social loss. Thus relationships between two categories were mapped out. Eventually Glaser and Strauss were to incorporate this into a general theory of relationships between professionals and their clients, suggesting that clients of high social value were more likely to receive rapid attention from professionals.

The discovery of grounded theory supplies a logic for ethnographic research, helping it gain scientific status. But whether this process of systematization is an entirely *inductive* and exclusively data-based method of theory generation, as Glaser and Strauss argue, is problematic. If the role of theory in structuring observation is recognized (see Chapter 2) then theory, common sense and other various assumptions precede theory generation, so grounded theory has a constructive character and not simply a data-based one. Whatever level of systematization takes place in the direction of theory construction, it is of value only if it offers a revealing purchase on the data.

Validation and verification

Ethnographic research has produced two suggested forms of validation: respondent validation and triangulation. **Respondent validation** consists of the ethnographer showing findings to the people studied and seeking verification in which the actors recognize a correspondence between the findings and what they, the actors, say and do. Thus verification is largely reduced to a matter of authenticity. But there are problems with this. Actors may not know things; they may not be privileged observers of their own actions or consciously aware of what they do and why. They may have an interest in rationalizing their beliefs and behaviour and so reject the ethnographic account of these, or indeed they may have no interest at all in the ethnographic account! So respondent validation cannot be a simple test of ethnographic findings, but it can be, as Bloor (1983) argues, a stimulus to generate further data and pursue new paths of analysis. Bloor, in his study of specialist doctors, found that sometimes they agreed with his description of their practices and sometimes not. This allowed him to reassess his analysis in various ways.

The alternative method of **triangulation** is to compare different kinds of data from different sources to see whether they corroborate one another. So data relating to the same phenomenon are compared but derive from different phases of fieldwork, different points in time, accounts of different participants, or using different methods of data collection. West (1990) demonstrates this form of triangulation in his account of what mothers said to him in interviews about medical consultations. Unlike Baruch (1981), whose research was described in Chapter 16, West wanted to know whether the accounts given in interviews were true or not. He therefore observed actual consultations and compared these with the interview accounts. Broadly speaking, he found the mothers' criticisms of the doctors to be supported. But this method of triangulation has its problems too. West's validation exercise is potentially limitless, as the next question to ask is whether his observations were 'true'. Lever's (1981) study of sex differences in children's play showed that different methods of data collection widened or narrowed the differences because they affected the play. At most, if different data tally, the observer can feel a bit more confident in his or her inferences.

However, *reflexive* triangulation is of value in working towards more plausible accounts. Hammersley (1983) advocates a subtle form of realism which comes close to the Popperian argument that validity involves confidence in our knowledge but not certainty (see Chapter 2). This involves a view that reality can be taken as independent of the claims researchers make about it. The production of truth rests on three things: the *plausibility* of the claim given our existing knowledge; the *credibility* of the claim given the nature of the phenomena; and the *circumstances* of the research and the characteristics of the researcher.

CONCLUSION

Ethnography presents both problems and opportunities for social and cultural research because of its largely qualitative character and its essential basis in the participant observer as the research instrument itself. The problems are not entirely analytical but are ethical too. The fact that ethnographic research depends on building up relations of rapport and trust with people in the field, whilst using this to generate and collect data from them, raises issues of manipulation, exploitation and secrecy. These are maximized in covert research but exist even in overt research because of the degree to which the researcher must withhold disclosure about his or her activities in order to maintain sociability in the situation and to gain access. These ethical considerations also affect the publication of research. There may be political implications which damage the people whose lives have been investigated. Yet ethnography, through participant observation of the social and cultural worlds, opens out the possibility of an understanding of reality which no other method can realize.

Further reading

Becker (1970) is an account by a leading Chicago school ethnographer based on his experience of the method. Glaser and Strauss (1967) contains their account of a method for generating theory from ethnographic data. Hammersley and Atkinson (1995) is the best textbook-length account of the ethnographic method, theoretically sophisticated and packed with examples, and written by two leading British ethnographers.

18

Analysing cultural objects: content analysis and semiotics

Don Slater

CONTENTS

Cultural objects present considerable methodological difficulties to social researchers. At the same time, they are increasingly found at the centre of their analyses. This is partly because of the enormous growth in the sociology of culture and its many associated subdisciplines such as cultural and media studies, and the sociology of the body, consumption and so on. It is also because many current theoretical debates focus on matters of language and cultural interpretation (for example the debates about *post-structuralism* and *post-modernity* reviewed in Chapter 3).

Researchers need to be able to analyse cultural objects in a way that can be treated as more than the arbitrary and subjective musings of a particular researcher. They need to be grounded in methodological controls that can justify a particular reading (or at least see it as a sensible possibility), that permit other researchers to replicate or disprove it, and that can approach different texts with enough consistency to allow comparability and generalization. As shown in Chapter 3, the *interpretive* tradition of cultural inquiry was a significant formative influence on European social thought in the nineteenth century. But the main line of development of (particularly Anglo-Saxon) social science was structured by the ideals of quantification and natural science methodology. In this context, social research which relied on cultural meanings as data was seen as shaky and subjective, incapable of rigorous control. Moreover, whereas interpretive, qualitative approaches to social *action* secured footholds in social science, cultural *texts* seemed to belong in the domain of literary or art criticism, which were irredeemably woolly and had more to do with refined 'cultural appreciation' than with any tradition of sustained analysis and investigation.

To make matters possibly more complicated, there has also been a decisive broadening over recent decades in our sense of what *is* a cultural object and what we might want to do with it as researchers. This broadening is indicated by the now-conventional use of the phrase 'reading **cultural texts**' to indicate the methodological task at hand. This phrase uses the metaphor of reading a book to argue that we can treat a vast range of social artefacts and events as if they were readable texts. The same methodology can be applied to objects as divergent as an opera, a family dinner, techno music, a television soap opera, radio news or indeed a Balinese cockfight (see Chapter 17). *Text* in this sense includes visual, aural and tactile structures of meaning, and combinations thereof. It is not confined to artefacts deemed cultural in an elite aesthetic sense (art, literature or dance) but includes any expressive form, indeed anything that can be construed as interpretable, as capable of bearing a meaning for someone. Moreover, a cultural text need not be an *object* consciously produced to bear and communicate specific meanings. Hence the way people dress, the foods they choose to eat and the way they prepare them, the pattern and structure of the meal itself can all be read as cultural texts. There need not even be an intention to communicate meaning (indeed neither of the methods under discussion here involves any necessary reference to the intentions of the text's author).

Content analysis and **semiotics** represent two important attempts to introduce consistent methods to the interpretation of culture. Both are forms of textual analysis, aiming to provide convincing readings of cultural texts, and to draw various conclusions from them, by looking at the texts themselves rather than at the ways in which people actually consume these texts. In fact, following the high-water mark of semiotics in the 1980s, there has been a decisive turn away from textual analysis towards ethnographic research into cultural consumption and a major revival of audience research (for example, Ang, 1991; Morley, 1992). Content analysis, as an old and rather positivist-inclined method, characteristic of mid-century American sociology, tends to fairly mechanistic readings and conclusions; semiotics, on the other hand, seeks to draw out the full complexity of textual meaning, as well as the act of reading texts, but with little rigour in a conventional sense.

CONTENT ANALYSIS

Content analysis clearly represents an attempt to apply conventional, and indeed positivist, notions of rigour to the unruly and ostensibly subjective field of cultural meaning. The central aim is to render issues of interpretation as controllable and non-contentious as possible in order to move quickly on to the more 'scientific' process of counting things. At bottom, content analysis simply measures frequency, and typical research questions might be: 'how prevalent in soap opera are sexist images of women?' or 'how often are women depicted in soap operas as mothers, as opposed to sex objects, workers or mainstays of the community?' or 'to what extent do women characters become less important in soap operas as they get older?' (see, for example, Cantor and Pingree, 1983). The content analyst might aim to identify instances of 'sexist images' or roles in which women might be portrayed, and count the number of cases in a well-defined sample. The controlled and replicable counting of elements of cultural texts should allow comparison and generalization across a cultural field, so that one could speak about the role of women within a clearly defined population of images (for example, all soap opera, or American versus Mexican soap opera). Trends over time can also be identified. For example, an analysis of samples drawn from a particular soap opera once a month from 1960 to 1997 might reveal much about changing representations of women not only in that soap opera, or soap operas in general, but by extension across much popular televisual culture. The point of such exercises is descriptive, but often takes the form of statements either about the accuracy with which the media represent aspects of the world, or about the kind of world that the media expose their viewers to. For example, the Glasgow University Media Group's (1976; 1980; 1982) extensive analyses of television news reporting drew conclusions about bias in the coverage of political events such as industrial action. Their careful counting up of the linguistic and visual terms used to depict strikes concluded that the media generally depicted strikers as threats to the 'national interest'.

A content analysis is rather like a social survey of a sample of images, rather than of people, using a tightly structured and closed questionnaire. The stages are much the same. Content analysis firstly involves suitably defining a population and drawing a sample from it. For example, Leiss et al.'s (1986) research for *Social Communication in Advertising* aimed to investigate how certain features of advertising have changed over the twentieth century. Specifically they were interested in looking at how new communicative strategies have altered the ways in which representations of people, products and their relationship have changed over time. To this end, they took a sample of advertisements for several product types (smoking products, cars, clothing, food, personal care items, alcohol products and corporate advertisements) that appeared in two Canadian magazines, one primarily directed at men, the other at women, over the period 1910 to 1975. In terms of sampling, content analysis is subject to the same rigours and statistical limits as any survey method: samples must be drawn in such a way as to be both representative and significant, while still small enough to be analysed in depth. Content analysis however is generally unable to draw a truly random sample. For example, a historical study like that of Leiss or studies of television news normally draw samples at periodic intervals (for example, two magazine issues per year over a given number of years) or intensively analyse a shorter period (every news broadcast over two weeks). In either case, the researcher has to think about what specific factors might have influenced their sample and how to allow for them.

The second major component of content analysis involves deciding on categories for *coding* the data and carrying out the coding. Suppose, following our earlier example of women in soap operas, we wanted to see how images of women have changed in soap operas from 1980 onwards. We might categorize these images in terms of roles: what changes have there been in the kinds of social roles that women characters have been allocated in soap opera over this period? We need to draw out of this research question a set of concepts by which to categorize the data in a relevant manner. For example, we might look at the women represented in each soap opera in our sample and ask whether they are presented as mothers, girlfriends, housewives, workers, career women and so on. The aim would be to be able to assign each represented woman to those categories and see how the frequencies change: for example, is it the case that career woman have become more common and housewives less common in soap operas?

Much of the apparent rigour of content analysis rests on the structure of categories used. Firstly, they must be exhaustive, in the sense that we must be able to assign every representation of a woman in every soap opera in our sample to one category (even if that category is 'other'). Secondly, they must be mutually exclusive (that is, the categories must not overlap). The development of coding frameworks like these involves hard conceptual work and usually a great deal of piloting or trial and error. Beyond the formal criteria (that they be exhaustive and mutually exclusive), the categories must also be enlightening, producing a breakdown of imagery that will be analytically interesting and coherent. (See also Chapter 12 for a discussion of coding.)

There is another aspect to developing categories for content analysis which shows up clearly at the coding stage: the issue of *reliability* (see also Chapter 11). Deciding on what kind of role a woman is playing in a soap or what kind of relations between people and objects are depicted in an advertisement would seem to involve a great deal of interpretation, and an unremovable residue of ambiguity or disagreement between readers. Content analysis takes a very pragmatic approach to this. Instead of a theory of textual meaning or of reading (such as semiotics invokes, as discussed below), content analysis relies on **inter-coder reliability**. This means that a number of different researchers are asked to code the same selection of images, without reference to each other, using the same set of categories and the same definitions and guidelines for assigning images to categories. This will be done at many stages, such as during pilot research and as checking exercises during the main project. The research is said to be reliable, the categories to work and the coding to be consistent to the extent that the researchers all assign the same texts to the same categories. It is obviously important to note that high inter-coder reliability can be achieved in at least two uninteresting or misleading ways: by making the categories so obvious and superficial that all ambiguity and with it all interesting features are removed from the research; and when coders agree with each other because of shared but not necessarily acknowledged common-sense assumptions. For example, the fact that the coders in a content analysis agreed with each other does not mean that anyone else (such as members of the television audience) would. The generation of reliably invalid data is also discussed in Chapter 11.

An example of the first of these problems can be found in the Leiss et al. research, although they use an otherwise very sophisticated and interesting approach. They wanted to see whether, over the period studied, advertising had come to rely more on visual than verbal techniques. This is obviously a complex interpretive issue involving questions about the structure and meaning of a vast range of images. The authors get round this by measuring the proportion of space, in square inches, taken up by text versus image in every advertisement in their sample. Of course, the measurement of image space gives a very crude sense of the 'importance' of image versus text, paying no attention for example to the structural position (as opposed to size) of each, or of the importance that the text might have in actual readers' readings of these advertisements. There are many advertisements (indeed, they may have become increasingly important) in which the very small amount of text is memorable and crucial. One can also think of advertisements in which the text *is* an image: for example, logos like Coca-Cola are both words and images. It could be argued that Leiss et al., in order to give the impression of objectivity and to avoid interpretive ambiguity or unreliability, ignored the interesting aspects.

However, once a rigorously chosen sample has been coded by the application of a clear framework of categories and to a reasonable degree of intercoder reliability, analysis of the results can then take a fairly quantitative form, departing in no significant way from the statistical routines that would be applied to any survey results. The advantages and disadvantages of content analysis are also similar to those for survey research: because methodological controls have been used all along the way, and because a significantly sized sample has been drawn to represent a coherently defined universe, comparisons and generalizations can be made across a social field and represented in meaningful numerical terms. However, to the extent that this objectivity is suspect, or limited to only the most uninteresting features of the object of study, these advantages are reduced.

SEMIOTICS

Semiotics represents the exact opposite to content analysis along every dimension. It is closer to interpretive methodologies than to quantitative and survey methods and is utterly open-ended rather than closed in its questions and investigations. It is strong on rich interpretations of single texts or codes but offers almost no basis for rigorous generalization outwards to a population. It argues that elements of a text derive their meaning from their interrelation within a code rather than looking at them as discrete entities to be counted. Where content analysis is all method and no theory, hoping that theory will emerge from observation, semiotics is all theory and very little method, providing a powerful framework for analysis and very few practical guidelines for rigorously employing it. Above all, semiotics is essentially preoccupied with precisely that cultural feature which content analysis treats as a barrier to objectivity and seeks to avoid: the process of interpretation.

Theoretical background

Semiotics starts from Saussure's structural linguistics, mentioned also in Chapter 3. As against earlier approaches to language, Saussure argued that meaning should be studied as a system of **signs**. Words do not derive their meaning either from the psychological intentions of individual speakers, or from the things the words describe. Rather their meanings arise from their place in a system of signs and their relations of difference or sequence with other terms in the system. The meaning of the word 'cat' does not arise as an expression of an individual's thoughts or as a label for an object (there is nothing about four-legged animals that miaow that produces the word 'cat' in English) but rather arises from the relation of the word to others such as 'dog', 'lion', and so on. Different languages divide up the same object world in different ways, using different systems of terms (*découpage*). These different systems of signs are neither natural objects nor intentional acts but rather *social facts*, in the Durkheimian sense: external to and constraining on the individual (see Chapter 2).

Saussure's (1974) method therefore aimed to isolate the system of signs as an object of study. It did this through a series of concepts and distinctions that form the basis of semiotics. Firstly, Saussure distinguished between diachronic analysis and synchronic analysis. **Diachronic analysis**, which is the proper method of structural linguistics, looks at the arrangement of elements in a system at a single point in time. By contrast, **synchronic analysis** (represented in the discipline of *etymology* which looks at how the meanings of words change over time) examines the historical development of the elements. Secondly, he distinguished between **language** (*langue*), the system of signs, and **speech** (*parole*), individual instances of the use of language resources to make particular utterances. Structural linguistics did not aim to account for either the historical development of languages or the particular things that individuals said (**speech acts**); it aimed solely to analyse the systems of meanings within which words could signify. Finally, Saussure methodologically 'bracketed' the question of reality or the truth of meaning: the relation between words and things (their *referents*) is treated as arbitrary, as is the relation between a word and its meaning. In terms of the distinctions made in Chapter 16, Saussure was committed to seeing language as a *topic* rather than a *resource*.

The basic building block of linguistics, and later semiotics, then, is the sign and its position within languages and language-like systems. Saussure argues that the sign comprises two components, a **signifier** which is the sound or the image of a word like 'cat', and a **signified**, which is a concept that we attach to the signifier ('four-legged furry beast that miaows'). Together they make a **sign**. The signifier, 'cat', stands for the concept we have of the animal. Saussure argued that these two were like the two sides of a sheet of paper or a coin, aspects of the same entity which can only be analytically separated. Nonetheless, the relationship between the two is arbitrary. There is nothing cat-like about the signifier 'cat', no reason why this sound-image ('cat') should bring to mind the concept we have of a furry animal that miaows. Meaning, then, is not the result of any positive qualities of a signifier. There is no natural correspondence between signifiers and signifieds: other languages will use different words for the same animal; one language, like English, can use alternative words ('tom'); and the same signifier 'cat' can have other signifieds (such as a 'cool dude' circa 1955, or slang for 'a woman who gossips maliciously'). The relationship between signified and signifier is a conventional social or cultural one, one that is internal to the systems of meaning operating in a particular culture at a particular time.

There is also a third aspect to the sign: the **referent**. That would be the 'real' cat as an object in the world, but, as noted above, Saussure brackets this off. Meaning comes about not because of the relationship between the sign and the referent but because of the relationship between the signifier and the signified. I can sound the word 'cat' to you and you understand me; I do not have to bring my actual cat into our conversation and point to him. The meaning of 'cat' is understood by its relation to other words in the system, and specifically in terms of a system of *differences*: you understand the word 'cat' by what it is not, not 'dog' and not 'person' and not 'mouse'. Language is a system of differences with no positive terms.

Not only is the sign I use not determined by its referent, but my sense of what is out there in the world – my sense of the referent – is clearly structured by words and images through which I come to represent the world. Language as a system of difference constructs or produces our idea of the objective world, of referents. Languages do not neutrally reflect or mirror or correspond to the objective world, but rather different languages produce a different sense of the world. A classic example has to do with environments: whereas an English person looking at the Australian outback may be able to name one or two things ('scrub', 'bush'), an Aborigine will have a great many words by which he or she differentiates, distinguishes and names a vast range of objects, conditions, events and so on. A central implication of Saussure's work, then, is to treat language as a social construct and to **denaturalize** it: to treat it as an active *construction* of the world rather than a passive reflection of it (see also Chapter 3). This goes against the grain of everyday usage of sign systems where we tend to take meaning for granted and treat the organization of language as identical to the organization of real objects in the world. We treat language as natural rather than cultural in much everyday life, whereas Saussure emphasized the constructed and arbitrary meaning of signs.

In sum, Saussure's structural linguistics offered a theoretical framework and concepts which focused on two central research issues. The first is the description and analysis of cultural signs in relation to the sign systems through which they get their meaning. The central task is to trace the sign back to its system or code and to analytically reconstruct that system, the full set of terms and their relationships. The second is the task of understanding how a particular sign system divides up the world (*découpage*), indicating how that culturally arbitrary division comes to be experienced as nature rather than culture, and analysing the social and ideological implications of dividing the world up in one way rather than another.

From structural linguistics to semiotics

Although Saussure's own work was entirely focused on language, he himself indicated that this entire apparatus could be extended beyond language to become a general science of signs: semiology or **semiotics**. In the event this involved extending his model in two ways. Firstly, structural linguistics was applied, as he himself suggested, to the study of any sign system or any set of objects that can be treated as signs. Indeed, the assumption has generally been that all meaning arises from the relationships between signs within systems of signs, and that therefore anything that has meaning – a traffic light, a photograph, a meal – can be analysed in terms of the system in which that meaning arises. At a descriptive level, then, semiotics as a method focuses our attention on to the task of tracing the meanings of things back to the systems and codes through which they have meaning and make meaning. Hence, for example, Roland Barthes (1977a; 1986; see also Masterman, 1986) in his seminal works looked at objects as diverse as wrestling matches, the French landscape and various articles of clothing as signs or elements of larger sign systems.

Secondly, given that systems of meaning are considered to be socially arbitrary and conventional, semiotics has focused on how particular systems of meaning divide up the world. This has involved extending the model of the sign in order to look at higher orders of meaning, usually denoted by terms such as 'codes' or 'ideologies'. A crucial step involved Barthes's (1977b; 1986) distinction between **denotation** and **connotation**. In his famous example, a magazine cover photograph of a black soldier saluting the French flag could be analysed at the *denotative* level of meaning to see how the photograph operates at a basic perceptual level: for example, we identify the figure as male rather than female, as black rather than white, the flag as French rather than English, through systematic distinctions between signs. Denotation, as Barthes originally defined it, is the perceptual, 'first-order' level of signification, the level at which we might talk about what the photograph is literally a picture *of*. However, Barthes argues that the image not only denotes particular things in the world, but also *connotes* a range of higher-level ideological meanings: the photograph (published during the Algerian struggle for independence against the French) 'means' that colonial troops are loyal to France and are part of the French nation, *la patrie*; the image conjures up a mythology of 'Frenchness', of France as essentially inclusive of a diverse but loyal population. The photographic sign, 'black soldier', an image of an identifiable object in the world, becomes a signifier within a higher-order ideological system of meanings about nationality, colonialism, and patriotism. What concerns Barthes is how, within a photograph or other representation, such cultural and indeed ideological notions as patriotism or Frenchness can come to appear as natural attributes of the real world: the viewer seems easily to accept that this photograph is not just of 'a black soldier saluting the French flag', but of 'the loyalty commanded by the French nation of its colonial subjects'. Semiotics was for Barthes not simply the description of sign systems but the analysis of this process of 'mythologization' whereby conventional social systems of meaning come to appear natural.

A classic example of this kind of analysis is provided by Judith Williamson (1978) in *Decoding Advertisements*. Williamson takes a simple advertisement that juxtaposes a pack shot of a bottle of Chanel No. 5 perfume with an image of the face of French film actress Catherine Deneuve. Deneuve's face is (denotatively) identifiable as that of a particular female celebrity. However, 'Deneuve' is also a signifier within a system of images of the feminine: she represents sophisticated, cool, elegant 'French' femininity (and was even voted to be the face on the statue representing France on the bicentennial of the French Revolution). Williamson juxtaposes this advertisement with a similarly structured advertisement for the perfume Babe which featured the American model Margaux Hemingway doing a high-kicking judo move. Hemingway occupied a quite different position in the system of signs of femininity: she is American, brash, athletic, active. These meanings make sense in relation to each other, as part of a system of differences, different signifiers of different concepts of 'femininity'. Moreover, each is anchored, via connotation, in identifiable signs (Deneuve and Hemingway). Williamson further argues that the meanings connoted by these signs are carried over by association to the images of the perfume bottles, so that sophisticated Frenchness appears to be denoted by the perfume Chanel, and brash Americanness by Babe. Indeed, the implication is that these are properties not only of the models but of the products, whereas of course a smelly liquid (and even an actress's face) is not 'naturally' feminine but is feminine within particular systems of cultural signs. Indeed we can see, through this analysis, that 'femininity' itself is not a natural property of anything but is rather constructed within these sign systems. Williamson is clear that this semiotic approach is important not only for allowing her to follow these flows of meaning between codes of femininity, a system of actresses as signs and a system of cosmetic products, but also for allowing her to see how a conventional system of signs can appear natural: cool, sophistication or Americanness are no more natural properties of smelly liquids than of women but the interplay between systems of meanings makes it seem so.

It might be worth briefly comparing this example with content analysis. On the one hand, it is obvious that because it is based on a theory of meaning and of reading, semiotics allows a much deeper analysis of the images. It is unlikely for example that any method of counting women's faces or product shots in a sample of advertisements would identify codes of femininity, the dynamics of ideology and so on. The crucial connotative level of codes has to be approached through processes of interpretation, by seeing how signs *relate*, not just how frequently they occur. Yet this is precisely what content analysis tends to avoid as too nebulous, subjective or unquantifiable. On the other hand, one can get the impression that semiotics is not just informed by theory, but spends most of its time illustrating and supporting rather than challenging its theory. It is also hard to feel very confident that Williamson's analysis of these advertisements, however clever and plausible, is anything more than one person's analysis. It is very hard to see what assurances of *reliability*, let alone *replicability*, could be put forward here. Moreover, the doubt goes beyond whether other researchers would or should concur with her analysis; one also wonders how it relates to that of lay readers of the advertisements (a worry that applies to content analysis as well). Both methods attempt to produce accounts of social meanings without offering any evidence as to what meanings people might arrive at after actual encounters with these texts.

Semiotic analysis of television

The same semiotic methodology can be applied to more complex cultural texts. For example, in *Television Culture* John Fiske (1987; see also 1989) maps out the great range of codes that need to be analysed and interrelated in order to understand the structure and meaning of a television text. He divides these into three levels starting from the level of *reality*. 'Reality', in this account, does not mean that semiotics can treat anything as intrinsically meaningful, as a brute reality that precedes systems of meaning. Fiske is pointing to the fact that anything to be televised is always already encoded through social codes such as dress, speech, gestures, expressions. In analysing, say, a news report of a politician being interviewed, we might look at how codes of dress, posture and gesture operate to represent the man as presidential or oppositional or whatever. We also know that these codes are consciously used by politicians, their handlers and TV personnel to generate particular impressions.

At the same time, different meanings arise depending on whether we encounter a politician on television as opposed to real life or radio or via written reports in the press: Fiske isolates a second level of semiotic analysis here, a level of *representation*. For example, there are televisual codes of camera angle and position in which, much as in language, different elements have different meanings in relation to each other. The camera can shoot upwards at the politician's face so that he looks down powerfully on to the viewer as opposed to shooting his profile in tight close-up to create a sense of intimacy. Other codes of representation that a semiotic approach would attend to include lighting, editing and sound, each of which provides complex choices and means for constructing different representations and meanings. Indeed, becoming a programme maker involves learning what is often called the 'grammar' of editing or lightening, the 'language' of television.

These codes of representation themselves however make sense in terms of still higher level codes: the camera angles, lighting, editing, sound and so on used to represent the politician would build up a sense of narrative, character, interaction and event, for example an image of the politician as an independent character rapidly rising through the ranks of his party and in conflict with its traditionalist wing. That is to say, all the codes so far discussed are deployed to present one particular story as opposed to the multitude of possible other stories. Semiotic analysis is basically asking us to attend to the way in which that story is constructed using all these codes of meaning at all these levels. Beyond this point, however, Fiske maps out another level of *ideological* codes (corresponding to Barthes's notion of connotation) at which the individual story takes its place within higher conceptual levels: the politician's story fits within broader systems of meaning and belief concerning the nature of individuals and individualism, nation, power and so on.

Structuralism and post-structuralism

The account of semiotics up to this point has not described the many variants and developments of the broad tradition. The most important distinction within semiotics has been between *structuralism* and *post-structuralism* (see also Chapter 3). Saussure's original work was developed into a general semiotics firstly in dialogue with literary analysis but later in relation to the idea of structuralism, most notably as developed by Claude Lévi-Strauss in anthropology. Lévi-Strauss investigated cultural systems both within and across social groups, treating individual instances of cultural texts as possible permutations within an overarching code. For example, his many analyses of myths seemed to demonstrate that the elements and relationships within individual myths made sense as oppositions, inversions, transformations and other metamorphoses within a system. He believed, therefore, that it was possible to identify general principles or 'structures' which determined the surface appearance of the particular myths current in a culture. Barthes heavily relied on this approach in developing semiotics and shared its strongly scientific bent. The assumption during the structuralist phase of semiotics (not unlike that of content analysis) was that the analyst could produce 'correct' readings of cultural texts without reference to either the intentions of the author or the interpretive acts of actual social readers. That is to say, by finding the 'deep structure' of the text the analyst finds its 'real meaning'. This 'real' meaning may be different from the individual reading that a particular person may produce, and indeed may be invisible to him or her. In fact, it was often taken to be the task of semiotics to unearth and reveal to people the real meaning of texts that they could not see but which unconsciously and ideologically structured their cultural understandings.

The second, *post-structuralist*, phase of semiotics rests on a critique of several structuralist assumptions. The methodological upshot of this critique is that cultural texts cannot be reduced to single, fixed and unitary (uncontradictory) meanings by either analysts or social subjects. The relational structure of meaning – in which terms have no positive meanings in and of themselves, but only meanings derived from their relations to other items in a code or system – is such that no final meanings are ever arrived at. Moreover, whereas earlier structuralism and semiotics assumed a singular and coherent reader, post-structuralism focused on the constitution of contradictory subject positions within contradictory texts. Thus there was a shift in aims, from the scientific and objective to the rhetorical and relative. There was also a shift in focus from the internal organization or structure of the text to the processes of reading texts and the contexts in which they were read. This in turn opens up possibilities for using methods such as interviewing and ethnography to expose how people, in practice, actually understand the cultural objects in their everyday lives.

CONCLUSION

As noted above, semiotics and content analysis are opposites in almost every way. More constructively, however, they could be construed as complementary: for example, Leiss et al. (1986), whose work was discussed at some length earlier in this chapter, try to combine the rigour of content analysis with the depth of semiotics. To a large extent, this takes the form of trying to develop coding categories which have real theoretical power and interest but which can be sufficiently refined to allow reliability between coders and comparison across cases. For example, instead of measuring extremely superficial features of their advertisements, they spent a long time building up descriptions of 'codes', values and strategies through which relationships between people and products can be represented in advertisements. The development of this framework was significantly informed by semiotic theory and the more complex analysis of texts that it affords.

Further reading

Leiss et al. (1986) show how semiotic and content analysis can be combined, in a study of advertisements. Barthes (1986) and Williamson (1978) are classic examples of semiotic analysis. Some helpful introductions to semiotic analysis are Coward and Ellis (1979), Eagleton (1983) and Hawkes (1992).

Analysing discourse

Fran Tonkiss

Contents

This chapter examines how techniques for analysing texts and documents provide useful and effective methods for social research. Specifically, it approaches the study of language and texts as forms of *discourse* which help to create and reproduce systems of social meaning. This entails taking up a critical and interpretive attitude towards the use of language in social settings. Discourse analysts do research into a wide range of subjects, studying the use of language in such fields as public policy, social work, law, education, psychiatry, media and advertising. They also research individual accounts, especially through the analysis of interview materials. Discourse analysts collect their data from a number of sources: these might include official documents, legal statutes, political debates and speeches, media reports, policy papers, maps, pictorial and exhibition materials, expert analyses, publicity literature and press statements, historical documents, tourist guides, interviews, diaries and oral histories.

The discussion in this chapter begins by outlining varieties of discourse analysis in the social sciences and related disciplines. I define what is meant by 'discourse' and describe how it fits into different social contexts. The chapter goes on to outline methods of discourse analysis in relation to three key stages of the research process: selecting and approaching data; sorting, coding and analysing data; and presenting the analysis.

APPROACHES TO DISCOURSE

Discourse analysis can sometimes seem a difficult method to pin down because it is used in different ways within different disciplines. While its origins lie most firmly in the fields of linguistics and psychology, the method has in recent years been widely taken up within sociology, socio-linguistics, social psychology, management and organization studies, politics and social policy, communications studies, cultural studies and social anthropology. The focus in this chapter is on these more 'social' approaches to discourse analysis.

Discourse analysis takes its place within a larger body of social and cultural research that is concerned with the production of meaning through talk and texts. As such, it has affinities with approaches such as semiotics, which is primarily concerned with visual texts (see Chapter 18), ethnomethodology and conversation analysis (see Chapter 20). A further important precedent for a sociological approach to discourse analysis derives from research within the sociology of science. Studies such as those by Latour and Woolgar (1979) and Gilbert and Mulkay (1984) examined the way in which scientific 'facts' and conventions are established through processes of argument and dispute which rely heavily on the presentation of plausible accounts and the rejection of alternative explanations (for a more extended discussion of Gilbert and Mulkay's work, see Chapter 16). Such processes of knowledge construction are not simply concerned with raw facts or scientific truths, but involve the skilful use of language and artful strategies of argument. These studies sought to demystify the process of scientific discovery by probing the social context in which this takes place – a social context, furthermore, that is mediated by language.

The sociology of science offers a good example of how language is viewed by discourse analysts. Language is seen not simply as a neutral medium for communicating information, but as a domain in which our knowledge of the social world is actively shaped. Anyone who has been in an argument with a skilled or slippery debater will be aware of the way that language can be used to compel certain conclusions, to establish certain claims and to deny others. Discourse analysis involves a perspective on language which sees this not as *reflecting* reality in a transparent or straightforward way, but as *constructing* and organizing that social reality for us. In these terms, discourse analysts are interested in language and texts as sites in which social meanings are created and reproduced, and social identities are formed.

An example might help to make this point clearer. In recent years there has been an increasing sensitivity to the language used to talk about disability, both in everyday speech and in such fields as social policy, health and care services, education and the media. This has been due to a perception that certain terms, such as 'mental handicap', have represented people in an inaccurate and negative way, so that such people are now referred to as experiencing 'learning difficulties'. A shift in language forms an important part of efforts to raise public awareness of disability issues and to change popular perceptions and stereotypes. This example is part of a growing social awareness of the way that language works to divide up, stereotype and categorize different groups and individuals. That is, there is a greater sensitivity to the power of *discourse* to shape people's attitudes and identities. The way that we use language is rarely innocent, and discourse analysis can help to reveal how talk and texts are ordered to produce specific meanings and effects.

This critical approach to language is closely associated with *post-structuralist* social theory, and in particular the work of the French theorist Michel Foucault (see also Chapter 3). In his historical investigations into the social organization of madness, medicine, crime and sexuality, Foucault used documentary evidence in a distinctive way. His approach was backed by a theoretical understanding of discourse as a realm in which institutions, norms, forms of subjectivity and social practices are constituted and made to appear *natural* (see Foucault, 1984). Following Foucault one might ask, for example, how our understanding and even our experience of sexuality is shaped by a set of moral, medical and psychological discourses. How does deviance (for example, 'mad' or 'delinquent' behaviour) become an object of psychiatric discourse, or repression (for example, of childhood trauma) an object of psychological discourse, or poverty an object of sociological discourse? While these may be seen as rather abstract questions, Foucault's accounts go further to ask: how are these discursive constructions linked to the shaping of social institutions and practices of social regulation and control? In this way Foucault's work provides an important conceptual backdrop to a great deal of social research currently undertaken in the form of discourse analysis.

WHAT IS DISCOURSE?

So far, I have used the terms 'language' and 'discourse' interchangeably. At this point it will be useful to specify more clearly what is meant by 'discourse' within social and cultural research. **Discourse**, then, can refer both to a single utterance or specific speech act (such as a private conversation) and to a more systematic ordering of language (such as legal discourse). The important thing to think about here is not so much what sorts of language 'count' as discourse, as how discourse analysts approach language as data. Within discourse analysis, language is viewed as the *topic* of the research (see Chapter 16 for a discussion of language as *topic* and *resource*). Rather than gathering accounts or texts so as to gain access to people's views and attitudes, or to find out what happened at a particular event, the discourse analyst is interested in how people use language to construct their accounts of the social world. For the discourse analyst, language is both active and functional in shaping and reproducing social relations, identities and ideas.

While 'discourse' may be used loosely to refer to any text or utterance, in this discussion I will be employing it in a more formal way. In this context, 'discourse' refers to a *system* of language which draws on a particular terminology and encodes specific forms of knowledge. The easiest way to understand this idea is to think about the example of 'expert' languages. Doctors, for example, do not simply draw on their practical training when doing their job; they also draw on an expert medical language that allows them to identify symptoms, make diagnoses and prescribe remedies. This language is not readily available to people who are not medically trained.

Such an expert language has three important effects: it marks out a field of knowledge; it confers membership; and it bestows authority. Firstly, medical discourse establishes a distinct domain of expertise, carving out the field of medical practice and the issues with which it is concerned. Recently, there has been a debate in British medical circles over whether chronic fatigue syndrome or ME should be considered to be primarily a physical or a psychological problem; and, to an extent, whether such a condition can be said to exist at all. One aspect of this debate concerns the language used to describe the condition. The term 'myalgic encephalomyelitis' clearly *medicalizes* the condition, while such terms as 'overwork' or 'yuppie flu' do not. In this instance, the use of discourse plays an important part in recognizing a condition as a 'proper' illness, and therefore as a suitable case for medical treatment.

Secondly, medical discourse allows doctors to communicate with each other in coherent and consistent ways. Language in this sense represents a form of tacit or backstage knowledge which professionals draw on in their everyday practice and which they tend not to reflect upon. The internal conventions and rules of medical discourse act as a way of *socializing* doctors into the medical profession, and enabling them to operate competently within it. On this level, the notion of discourse has parallels with Kuhn's concept of *paradigms* (see Chapter 2).

Thirdly, medical discourse *authorizes* certain speakers and statements. Doctors' authority is perhaps most obviously expressed by their access to an expert language from which most of their patients are excluded. On an everyday level, while we may at times be frustrated by the use of obscure medical language to describe our symptoms, we may also be reassured that our doctor is an authority on these matters. More generally, medical authority is asserted through the use of an expert discourse to dismiss competing accounts, such as those associated with homeopathic and alternative remedies.

Expert languages provide an obvious and a very fruitful area for discourse analytic research; however, as I have indicated in the introduction to this discussion, discourse analysis is by no means confined to this domain.

Rather, discourse analysts use a common set of tools to examine how different discourses present their versions of the social world. In all cases, the analyst is concerned not so much with getting at the truth of an underlying social reality through discourse, but with examining the way that language is used to present different 'pictures' of reality.

An example here would be different explanations of juvenile crime, and how these are constructed within discourses of 'delinquency' or 'deviance'. Different actors might explain juvenile crime by drawing on accounts of moral decline, poor parenting, the absence of positive role models, inadequate schooling, individual pathology, poverty, lack of prospects, rebelliousness, and so on. This is not to say that the issue – juvenile crime – does not exist or has no meaning, but asserts that different social actors make sense of this reality in various, often conflicting ways. This point goes beyond semantics. The reason why these conflicting accounts are interesting and important is because the meanings and explanations that are given to different social factors shape the practical ways that people and institutions respond to them. If a common understanding of juvenile crime rests on discourses of individual pathology (for example, crimes arise from the personal failings of the individual), it is likely that this problem will be tackled in a quite different way than if it was commonly understood in terms of a discourse of poverty (for example, crimes arise as a result of material deprivation).

DISCOURSE IN A SOCIAL CONTEXT

This example directs us to a primary point about discourse analysis in social and cultural research. Language is viewed as a *social practice* which actively orders and shapes people's relation to their social world. In considering discourse in its social context, it is useful to highlight two central themes. The first of these concerns the *interpretive context* in which the discourse is set. The second concerns the *rhetorical organization* of the discourse.

The term **interpretive context** refers to the social setting in which a particular discourse is located. Discourse analysis, while stressing close textual work, aims to analyse language use in its larger social context. It is therefore more likely to 'go beyond' the text than are ethnomethodological approaches. For example, a discourse analyst may develop an argument about the power relations implied by different speaking positions (such as the gender of the speaker) by reference 'outward' to external social relations, whereas a conversation analyst would tend to look for only those clues that appear in the text itself.

When thinking about the social context in which discourses are set, the analyst is concerned not only with the large scale (gender inequalities in society, say), but with the small-scale context of particular interactions. People modify their discourse to suit the context in which it takes place. A manner of speaking which would be appropriate in a doctor's surgery may not be right for a social gathering. Similarly, the way in which you speak to friends, partners, employers or police officers may vary in both form and content – even when you are describing the same event. This is to say not that any particular version is true and the others are therefore false, but that your account may alter so that it 'fits' each context. Indeed, getting your story straight can be hard when you have to remember what you said to different people, and how you said it! For the discourse analyst, this means it is necessary to be sensitive to the small-scale interpretive context of the data, including the type of interaction, the relations between the actors, and the immediate discursive aims of the speaker.

The second theme concerns the **rhetorical organization** of discourse. Rhetorical approaches are concerned with the argumentative schemes which organize a text and which work to establish the authority of particular accounts while countering alternatives (see Billig, 1987). Rhetorical analysis is not simply about the way statements are put together, but is also – and perhaps more importantly – about the effects that these statements seek and their insertion into a larger rhetorical context within which certain forms of knowledge will be privileged, certain modes of argument will be persuasive, and certain speakers will be heard as authoritative. We might think here of the rhetorical skills that prosecution and defence lawyers use to present their accounts of the same case, each seeking to counter and discredit the other; or the manner in which parliamentary debates are constructed by opposing parties. In both senses, 'rhetoric' refers to situations where discourse can shape (modify, constrain, elicit) outcomes: rhetorical discourse is persuasive to action. Rhetorical organization in this respect implies larger principles of social order and regulation and rhetorical analysis becomes a critical enterprise.

Certain discourses such as legal defences or political speeches are obviously rhetorical, in the sense that the speaker is clearly using language in an effort to persuade others to believe their version of events. However, rhetorical analysis is also relevant to more everyday accounts. Wherever a speaker aims to use language persuasively, to dismiss alternative claims, and to produce certain outcomes (forgiveness, agreement, apology, a purchase, and so on), attention to the rhetorical or argumentative organization of their account will be fruitful.

DOING DISCOURSE ANALYSIS

Discourse analysis is a messy method. Because it is largely 'data-driven' it is difficult to formalize any standard approach to it. However, while there are no strict rules of method for analysing discourse, it is possible to isolate certain key themes and useful techniques which may be adapted to different research contexts. In this section I will consider some of these in terms of three stages of the research process: selecting and approaching data; sorting, coding and analysing data; and presenting the analysis.

Selecting and approaching data

I have stressed the 'special' character of discourse analysis as a method of research – its distinctive approach to language and its resistance to any formulaic rules of method. However, the discourse analyst is faced with a common set of questions that arise within any research process. What is the research *about*? What are my data? How will I select and gather the data? How will I handle and analyse the data? How will I present my findings?

Formulating a research problem is one of the most difficult moments in social research. Sometimes it can seem like a very artificial exercise: qualitative research is often data-led and the researcher cannot be certain quite what the research will be 'about' until they have begun their analysis (see also Chapter 10). In other forms of research, in particular social surveys and structured interviewing, it is more important to formulate a clear research problem which will direct the process of data collection. If you don't know what you are looking for, you won't know which questions to ask. Discourse analysis shares with other types of qualitative research a certain wait-and-see attitude to what the data 'throw up'. This is underlined by the fact that this form of research is not so much *looking for* answers to specific questions ('What are the causes of juvenile crime?') as *looking at* the way meanings are constructed ('How is juvenile crime explained and understood within political or media discourse?')

As with other forms of social and cultural research, discourse analysis generally begins with a broad – and often vague – interest in a certain area of social life. You may, for example, be interested in researching the topic of immigration. There are a number of different ways of approaching such a topic. You might analyse statistical data relating to the number of people entering Britain in each year, their countries of origin, and patterns of change over time. Or you might select a sample of people who have settled in Britain, and use an interview method to research various aspects of their experiences of immigration. From a discourse analytic perspective, you might choose to examine political debates surrounding the passage of immigration legislation through Parliament. Alternatively, you might analyse press reports of such debates, or anti-immigration literature published by right-wing organizations.

In each of these cases, the research problem that you are setting up will be rather different. A statistical analysis will be asking about the number and origins of people entering Britain in any one year, and will be seeking to trace whether patterns of immigration are changing in these respects. The researcher could gather data from official statistics. In an interview study, the researcher will be more concerned with the subjective experience of immigration, which could focus on a number of different angles, such as different people's experience of immigration bureaucracy, the process of integration, questions of cultural difference, the notion of 'home', and so on. A discourse analysis, meanwhile, might be concerned with how immigration is constructed as a political issue or 'problem', the ways in which immigrants are represented within public discourses, the manner in which certain conceptions of immigration are warranted in opposition to alternative ways of thinking. A starting point for such a study might be as simple as: 'How is immigration constructed as a "problem" within political discourse?' The analytic process will tend to feed back into this guiding question, helping to refine the research problem as you go along.

Having set up the problem which you wish to investigate, the next step is to collect data. In some cases, a discourse analyst will actually *begin* with a promising set of data, out of which they then seek to generate fruitful research questions. This happens, for example, when a researcher gains access to an archive, or a set of official records or personal papers which have not previously been analysed. But it can also happen on a smaller scale when the researcher comes across a press report or political speech which appears especially interesting to them. Mostly, however, researchers begin with an area of concern for which they then have to gather relevant data. Say that you are interested in researching issues about immigration, to pursue this example. What data should you draw on? This will in part be determined by how you are defining the issue. Do you want to look at immigration policy? Or do you want to look at aspects of immigrant identity? Are you interested in media representations of immigration issues? Or do you want to explore attitudes towards immigration within sections of the public?

Depending on how you are conceptualizing the research problem, you could collect data from a number of sources. These might include parliamentary debates, political speeches, party manifestos, policy documents, personal accounts, press or television reports, and campaigning literature. A discourse analyst can draw on a wide range of data. For example, in a piece of discourse research which I undertook into urban policy in England (Tonkiss, 1995), I collected policy statements from a number of central government departments; Treasury guidance notes; oral and written parliamentary questions; local government agency action plans, evaluations and annual reports; reports from voluntary organizations; ministerial speeches; government press releases; local development plans, zoning details and other urban planning documents; reports from policy 'think-tanks' and corporatist associations; maps and exhibition materials; reports from non-departmental public bodies; annual reports and company memoranda from private firms. This large data set marked out a policy domain which was shaped by a range of different and often competing discourses.

It is not, however, necessary to assemble such a large 'archive' of materials. Indeed, it is possible to do so only if one has a significant amount of time to undertake a large-scale study. I use this example simply to indicate the wide variety of materials that are available to the discourse analyst. The most important consideration in selecting your data is not the amount of material you gather; I certainly don't think I read everything that was written, said or depicted about contemporary urban policy in England, in spite of collecting a large data set. Rather, the primary concern of the discourse analyst is to find data that will provide insights into a problem. In this sense, a single speech or newspaper report or conversation can generate very fruitful themes for analysis. What matters is the richness of textual detail, rather than the number of texts analysed.

It is particularly important to stress this idea in relation to the analysis of interview accounts. Many types of both quantitative and qualitative interviewing draw on representative sampling techniques in gathering data (see Chapter 11). However, a discourse analyst does not approach interview data in the same way. As the primary interest which the discourse analyst has in personal accounts is not so much the views being expressed, but how different views are established and warranted, questions of representativeness are not so crucial. Researchers who are new to discourse analysis often worry about whether they have done *enough* interviews, or chosen a sufficiently representative sample. As a discourse analyst, however, you are not necessarily aiming to give a representative overview of public attitudes towards immigration, for instance, but seeking to examine how particular attitudes are shaped, reproduced and legitimized through the use of language.

When analysing data, it is not necessary to provide an account of every line of the text under study. It is often more appropriate and more informative to be selective in relation to the data, extracting those sections which provide the richest source of analytic material. This does not mean that one simply 'selects out' the data extracts that support the argument, while ignoring more troubling or ill-fitting sections of the text. As I will discuss in the following section, contradictions within a text (including and perhaps especially those parts that contradict the researcher's own assumptions) can often provide the most productive point of an analysis. While it has been argued that discourse analysis is not centrally concerned with 'some general idea that seems to be intended' by a text (Potter and Wetherell, 1987: 168), it is good research practice to aim to be 'faithful' to a text's overall meaning, even when analysing its detail. Indeed, the overall discursive effect of a text provides a framework in which to consider its inconsistencies, internal workings and small strategies of meaning. While a discourse analyst always includes the extracts that they are interpreting in their writing up, it can also be useful (given space) to append the whole text to the research report, so that the reader can evaluate the argument in relation to the data, and perhaps offer alternative readings of their own.

Sorting, coding and analysing data

Different commentators have referred to the idea that discourse analysis is a 'craft skill' (Potter and Wetherell, 1994: 55). Potter and Wetherell compare it to the skill involved in riding a bike: a process that one picks up by doing it, and perfects by practising it, and which is difficult to describe in a formal way. As, when learning to ride a bike, it is helpful to watch someone else do it, the best way to learn how to do discourse analysis is to read other research reports which use this method, and then to have a go yourself. Doing effective discourse analysis has much to do with getting a real feel for one's data, working closely with them, trying out alternatives, and being ready to reject analytic schemes that do not work.

Indeed, if there is one rule of method that we might apply to discourse analysis, it would be Durkheim's first principle: abandon all preconceptions! At times it can be tempting to impose an analytic schema on a piece of discourse, but if this is not supported by the data then it will not yield an adequate analysis. We cannot *make* the data 'say' what is simply not there. As an individual I frequently have views, often very critical, of the political discourses which I analyse, and it can be personally frustrating not to find themes I 'know' are going on in a larger discursive context in the specific data with which I am dealing. However, as with other forms of social and cultural research, the researcher enters a different space in undertaking analysis, one in which it is best to suspend one's own assumptions. While we may have to set aside some closely held beliefs at this point, we have as a trade-off the common experience of surprise and satisfaction at finding things in the data we had not expected to encounter.

In this respect discourse analysis shares with other research methods a commitment to challenging common-sense knowledge and disrupting easy assumptions about the organization of social life and social meanings. It follows that the discourse analyst should take as broad an approach to the data as possible. That is, the process of analysis begins in a very inclusive way, selecting a number of themes and sections of data which appear relevant to the research question. While the problem you have set yourself as a researcher will guide this process of selection and coding, the categories of analysis which emerge from the data may well feed back into the way the research question has been set up, causing you to modify your domain of interest.

Discourse analysis is, then, a fluid, interpretive process which relies on close analysis of specific texts, and which therefore does not lend itself to setting up hard-and-fast 'rules' of analysis. Nevertheless, we can pick out certain pointers which may be useful in any discourse analysis. In this section I will consider: the selection of key words or themes; looking for variation in the text; reading for emphasis and detail; and paying attention to silences.

Using key words and themes

One primary approach to coding and analysis is to organize the data into key categories of interests, themes and terms. While the most obvious elements of a discourse are not always the most interesting for analysis, identifying recurrent themes or terms can help you to organize the data and bring a more systematic order to the analytic process. On this level, discourse analysis uses techniques similar to those of qualitative interviewing, and draws on more general approaches to handling and coding data (see Chapters 16 and 12). Analysis then becomes a process of sifting, comparing and contrasting the different ways in which these themes emerge within the data. What ideas and representations cluster around them? What associations are being established? Are particular meanings being mobilized? Is a certain reading implied by the organization of the text?

In my analysis of urban policy, I was interested in the way that a specific set of economic solutions was put forward to address problems of social deprivation and environmental blight in the inner city. One of the ways in which this worked was through the association of economic discourses with other, more qualitative ways of thinking about urban life. For example, one central government document produced by the Department of the Environment spoke of the importance of creating a 'climate of environmental quality and enterprise culture likely to attract people to live and work in the area' (see Tonkiss, 1995: 121). We can see here that an economic language of 'enterprise' has become bound up with a discourse about the quality of urban life. The association of 'enterprise' with 'culture' is a strategic move in this context, lending itself to the highly *natural* language of an attractive urban 'climate' or 'environment'. Within a policy programme that advocated market solutions to urban problems, a set of associations was mobilized around a notion of 'enterprise', linking this to the ambience of the urban environment. Such an association leaves out perhaps obvious questions of whether enterprise culture is always conducive to environmental quality in the inner city.

Looking for variation in the text

Another useful way to analyse a piece of discourse is to look for patterns of *variation* within the text. Differences within an account point us to the work that is being done to reconcile conflicting ideas, to cope with contradiction or uncertainty, or to counter alternatives. By paying attention to such variations the analyst disrupts the appearance of a 'smooth', coherent piece of discourse, allowing for an analysis of two different processes at work. The first concerns the text's internal hesitations or inconsistencies. The second concerns the way that the discourse aims to combat alternative accounts.

To illustrate the first use of variation within a text, I draw on another aspect of my research into policy discourse in inner city areas. In analysing these texts, I was concerned to examine (among other things) how an image of 'the community' was being constructed within local regeneration strategies. Reading through a range of documents from different local government bodies in England, I was struck by the curious 'double life' that inner city populations seem to lead within them. On one side, statistics were used to represent local populations in terms of consistent and severe patterns of poverty, inadequate housing, unemployment, crime, illness and premature mortality. On the other side, more descriptive accounts celebrated the same populations for their vitality, resourcefulness and civic pride. A stark contrast appeared between the detailed social problems outlined by social statistics, and the strongly asserted but rather abstract community qualities promoted in the descriptive passages of the policy documents.

Such a contradiction was an important aspect of the work these policy discourses were doing. That is, they were bringing together a discourse of 'deprivation' with one of 'development'. In order to apply for financial help from central government it was necessary to show that public money was needed in these areas, but also to guarantee that it would not be wasted and would have real beneficial effects. This deprivation–development couplet ran through the documents. Consider, for example, the patterns of variation in the following policy extract from a local regeneration agency in the north of England, where the stated aim is

> to reverse the negative perceptions of the area; make it a part of the City where, increasingly, people will choose to live, rather than leave; an area which business will see as one of opportunity, rather than decline; a community which is confidently developing its own solutions, rather than passively accepting those of others. (quoted in Tonkiss, 1995: 307).

The discourse is shaped around a set of oppositions: choose to live versus leave, opportunity versus decline, confidently developing versus passively accepting. These oppositions work both to justify the need for policy intervention, and to create a vision of what the transformed inner city area (given funding) will become.

To consider the second way that variation can be examined within a text – in terms of how alternative accounts are countered – I can take an example from today's newspaper. In it, a politician has written an article defending the construction of a major new road through a historic city in south-west England, and close to a declared Site of Special Scientific Interest (Key, 1996). The road proposal has met with angry opposition from environmental protesters and some sections of the local population. In his account, the politician establishes his own claims to the city and the area. He writes 'I love Salisbury. I love it passionately. It is an awesome place' and refers to the fact that he 'was only two' when he moved there in 1947. This has the effect of *warranting* the author's account on the basis of his long-term association with and attachment to the city. In contrast, those opposing the road programme are constructed as newcomers whose interest in the place comes from a particular political agenda, rather than a long-standing attachment: they are an alliance of 'Johnny-come-latelys and greens'. Such a contrast is more clearly stated in the following extract:

> But what an irony that the respect for history, heritage and countryside that motivates so many of the real citizens of Salisbury has been hijacked by an odd collection of the politically correct, the emotional and the fanatical.

Here, the claims of 'real citizens', with their association with timeless qualities of 'history, heritage and countryside', are depicted as being under threat (consider the violent connotations of the word 'hijacked'). The threat comes from an 'odd collection' of people motivated by their political correctness, their emotion and their fanaticism. The effect of these patterns of contrast is to undermine the validity of the environmentalists' claims, reducing them to a brand of fanaticism which has little to do with the authentic concerns of local people.

In both of the examples I have briefly discussed here, I have been concerned to look for patterns of contrast. However, looking for *consistency* within and between texts can also provide a useful analytic tool. On a simple level, the repetition of key words, phrases and images reveals most clearly what the speaker or author is trying to put across in their discourse. In the policy discourses I analysed, the words 'competition' and 'partnership' echoed through the texts, underlining a shift to market solutions in urban policy. It was in fact striking, as I trawled through a large set of documents from more than a dozen different local government agencies, how similar their accounts were. Given that the documents were drawn from all over England, from inner city and outer city sites, from old industrial areas and the inner urban core, from places with very different local histories, it was notable that the documents drew on a very limited range of discourses to represent their local places and communities. This led me to argue that, while recent academic and policy discourse in this field has stressed the importance of locality, the fact that political and financial decisions remain highly centralized means that local areas fall into line with a set of centrally agreed standards for what constitutes both 'urban problems' and valid solutions to them.

Reading for emphasis and detail

The process of looking for patterns of variation within a text is part of a more general attention to emphasis and detail within discourse analysis. As discourse analysts are concerned not simply with the surface or manifest meanings of a text, but with the often intricate ways in which these meanings are put together, they aim to examine the twists and turns through which data are shaped. While not all discourse analysts will work at the level of detail involved in conversation analysis (see Chapter 20) – discourse analysis does not always involve the reading of hesitations, pauses or slips, for example – they nevertheless look for clues in the detail.

Specific methodological tricks of the trade look for patterns of emphasis within a discourse, or the use of taken-for-granted notions. Favourites with analysts include the use of such tactics as the *three-part list*. This device creates emphasis by building up a sequence to create a 'crescendo' effect. Both the local policy text and the newspaper article on the proposed road-building programme in Salisbury shown earlier make use of the three-part list to emphasize their arguments. The policy extract imagines a city where 'people will choose to live, rather than leave; an area which business will see as one of opportunity, rather than decline; a community which is confidently developing its own solutions, rather than passively accepting those of others'. Similarly, the author of the media text emphasizes the contrast between those with a respect for 'history, heritage and countryside' and the 'politically correct, the emotional and the fanatical'.

Another common device which discourse analysts look for is the use of vague but difficult to challenge formulations. References to 'the community' or 'family life' in political discourses are hard to rebut, because they seem to embody values which no one would want to dispute, but at the same time fail to specify precisely who or what they are talking about. Note that both of these examples represent devices or tools for opening up a text to analysis, rather than forming part of any fixed set of analytic strategies. The tactics which you adopt as an analyst come from the data themselves, rather than from any textbook method of approach.

Attending to silences

This kind of analysis requires the researcher to adopt a rather 'split' approach to the text. That is, it is necessary to read *along* with the meanings that are being created, to look to the way the text is organized and to pay attention to how things are being said. At the same time, discourse analysis often requires the researcher to read *against* the grain of the text, to look to silences or gaps, to make conjectures about alternative accounts which are excluded by omission, as well as those which are countered by rhetoric. While I have argued that we cannot force our data to 'say' things that are not there, we can as critical researchers point out those places where the text is silent. Such a move can help to place the discourse in a wider interpretive context.

A further example from the field of urban policy may serve to illustrate this point. While urban policy in England has since the late 1960s focused on local areas which include a high concentration of minority ethnic populations, any direct discussion of racial issues has been relatively absent. The documents which I studied, while noting the proportion of minority ethnic residents in each area, limited their discussion of race to an economic discourse of enterprise, noting, for example, 'low rates of entrepreneurship especially amongst ethnic minorities'. While this may identify an important problem, it is developed in a discursive context where other issues – such as racial violence and harassment, institutional discrimination in housing and employment, and police–community relations – are simply ignored. 'Race' enters this discourse in a particular economic way, while alternative accounts are excluded.

Presenting the analysis

The final stage of the research process involves developing and presenting an argument on the basis of your discourse analysis. It is at this point that the researcher is concerned with using language to construct and warrant their own account of the data. This aspect of the process provides a useful context in which to consider the relation of discourse analysis to issues of *validity*, writing and *reflexivity* (see Chapter 22 for a discussion of the reflexive writing of research reports).

Social researchers think about research validity in terms of both **internal** and **external validity** (see also Chapter 11). **Internal validity** refers to the coherence and consistency of a piece of research, and in particular how well the data presented support the researcher's conclusions. **External validity**, on the other hand, refers to whether the findings are generalizable to other research or social settings. Discourse analysis has a particular concern with issues of internal validity. Its reliance on close textual work means that it generates arguments on the basis of detailed interpretation of data. We might think about this in terms of the following 'rules of evidence'. How coherent is the interpretive argument? Is it soundly based in a reading of the textual evidence? Does it pay attention to textual detail? How plausible is the movement from data to analysis? Does the researcher bring in arguments from outside the text, and if so how well supported are these claims?

Discourse analysis is concerned with the examination of *meaning*, and the often complex processes through which social meanings are produced. While I have argued that this process is 'fluid' and difficult to model on a general scale, at the same time discourse analysts aim to be systematic in their approach to specific data. In evaluating discourse research we should therefore be looking for interpretive rigour and internal consistency in argument. Research claims need always to be supported by a sound reading of data. In this sense, good discourse analyses stand up well to the demands of internal validity. However this is not to say that discourse research aims to offer a 'true' or objective account of any text. Meaning, for the discourse analyst, is contestable, and specific texts are always open to alternative readings. The discourse analyst, like other social actors, aims to provide a *persuasive* account, which in this case offers an insightful, useful and critical interpretation of a research problem.

This critical function within discourse analysis makes it difficult to advance claims to external validity. The discourse analyst seeks to open up statements to challenge, interrogate taken-for-granted meanings, and disturb easy claims to objectivity in the texts they are reading. It would therefore be inconsistent to contend that the analyst's own discourse was itself wholly objective, factual or generally true. Additionally, discourse analysts tend to deal with relatively small data sets emerging from specific social settings which are unlikely to be more widely representative. This raises problems regarding generalization. Why should we, as readers of social and cultural research, be interested in small-scale studies which do not claim to be representative, and anyway offer only one possible account of the problem under investigation? I think this is a fair question to ask of discourse analysis, and one which this method must address along with other qualitative approaches.

The response to such a question goes back to the argument that discourse analysis requires a distinct way of looking at social research. This involves an interpretive commitment to processes of meaning in social life, a certain modesty in our analytic claims, and an approach to knowledge which sees this as open rather than closed. By adopting such an approach to knowledge, the analyst and the reader can be convinced of the validity and usefulness of a particular account while remaining open to other critical insights. Discourse analysis fits into a broad range of social research methods which between them seek to analyse general social patterns but also to examine the devil in the detail.

A critical and open stance towards data and analysis may also be understood as a **reflexive** approach to social research. In aiming to be reflexive in their research practice, social researchers question their own assumptions, critically examine their processes of inquiry, and consider their effect on the research setting and research findings – whether in terms of their presence in a fieldwork situation, the way they select their data, or how their theoretical framework shapes the process of data collection and analysis. Reflexivity also involves attention to the writing strategies that researchers employ to construct a research account (see Chapter 22), and here the insights of discourse analysis are very useful.

In writing this chapter, for example, I have drawn on various discursive strategies in an effort to make my account fit into a methods textbook (and doubtless everyone else in the book has too!). While stressing that discourse analysis does not sit easily with any hard-and-fast rules of method, I have at the same time drawn on a particular language (validity, representativeness, data, evidence, analysis) and on particular forms of textual organization (moving from theory to data, using subheadings and lists) so as to explain discourse analysis in the form of a fairly orderly research process. An attention to the way that language is put to work is a useful tool for any reader or researcher who wants to think critically about social research processes and to evaluate research findings.

Further reading

For clear and helpful introductions to doing discourse analysis, Gill (1996) and Potter and Wetherell (1994) are invaluable. Both provide detailed examples of the use of discourse analysis in media research.

Analysing conversation

David Silverman

CONTENTS

Although you may be inclined to think of conversation as trivial ('merely' talk), it is worth reflecting that conversation is the primary medium through which social interaction takes place. In households and in more 'public' settings, families and friends relate to one another through talk (and silence!). At work, we converse with one another and the outcome of this talk (as in meetings or job selection interviews) is often placed on dossiers and files.

As social scientists, even if our aim is to search data for supposedly non-linguistic, social 'realities' (for example, social class, gender, power), our raw material is often the words written in documents or spoken by interview respondents. Even if we are just 'observing' what people do, observations have to be recorded in some way, for example, through field notes or pre-coded schedules. But sophisticated field notes still cannot offer the detail found in transcripts of recorded talk. Even if some people are able to remember conversations better than others, we are unlikely to be able to recall such potentially crucial details as pauses and overlaps. Indeed, even with a tape recording, transcribers may tidy up the 'messy' features of natural conversation, such as length of pauses or overlapping or aborted utterances.

Features like pauses matter to all of us, not just to analysts of conversations. Indeed, they are one basis on which, as Sacks (1992a) has pointed out, reading somebody else's mind, far from being some paranoid delusion, is both routine and necessary in everyday life. Look at Extract 1.

Extract 1
1 C: So I was wondering would you be in your office on Monday by any chance?
2   (2.0)
3 C: Probably not. (Levinson, 1983: 320, simplified)

The numbers in brackets on line 2 indicate a two-second pause. The presence of this pause gives us a clue to how C can guess that the person he is questioning might indeed not be in his office on Monday (line 3). This is because when there is a pause when it is someone's turn to speak, we can generally assume the pause will foreshadow some difficulty. Hence C is able to read the pause as indicating that the other person is unlikely to be in his office on Monday and say 'Probably not' in line 3.

Now consider Extract 2. This is taken from an interview between a health adviser (H) and a patient who has requested an HIV test. H is offering a piece of advice about condom use and her patient is a young woman who has just left school.

Extract 2
1 H: it's <u>important</u> that you tell them to (0.3) use a condom (0.8) or to practise
2   safe sex that's what using a condom means.
3   (1.5)
4 H: okay? (Silverman, 1996: 118)

In Extract 2, line 4, H asks 'okay?', which may be heard as a request for the patient to indicate that she has understood (or at least heard) H's advice about condom use. As with Extract 1, we can see that a pause in a space where a speaker might have taken a turn at talk (here at line 3) has indicated some difficulty to the previous speaker. Indeed, it is likely that H heard an earlier difficulty. Note that in line 1 there is a pause of 0.8 seconds at a point where H may be heard to have completed her turn. It is not unreasonable to assume that since the patient has not used this space to indicate some understanding of what H has just said (for instance, by saying 'mm'), H's explanation of what 'using a condom means' (lines 1–2) is given precisely in (what turns out to be) an unsuccessful attempt to overcome this difficulty.

At this point, you may be asking yourself 'why should any of this matter?' Indeed, what is the point of such detailed attention to such apparently minor matters as pauses in talk? In fact, it turned out that this form of analysis proved crucial in my attempt to understand the circumstances in which the clients of HIV counsellors showed interest in the advice that they were being given, including condom use, as in Extract 2. For instance, where, as in this extract, H has delivered a piece of advice without attempting to find out anything about her patient's knowledge or interest in the subject, the usual response is minimal or, as here, non-existent. Conversely, advice sequences built after prior questioning of clients are much more likely to receive acknowledgments like 'Oh really' which show interest in the advice given. In the context of debates about effective health promotion, such findings are of no little importance (see Heritage and Sefi, 1992; Silverman, 1996: Chapter 6).

The rest of this chapter will tell you how to transcribe conversations and will offer an insight into fundamental concepts relating to how certain responses to invitations and the like are produced, how turns at talk are taken and repaired and how the openings of telephone conversations are organized. Finally, we will look at how these and other features are used or revised when people talk as members of formal organizations. This way of analysing conversation is a method derived from the concerns of *ethnomethodology* (see Chapter 3), having links, therefore, with a body of social theory about the ways in which people construct their social worlds as well as having a number of practical outcomes.

PREPARING TRANSCRIPTS

At this point, you may still be wondering how these transcripts can give such precise lengths of pauses. In fact, you do not need any advanced technology for this. Although transcribers may use complicated timing devices, many others get into the habit of using any four-syllable word which takes about a second to say. If you then say this word during a pause, you can roughly count each syllable as indicating a one-quarter of a second pause. However, pauses are not the only features that you may need to record. In Table 20.1 I provide a simplified set of **transcription symbols**.

It should not be assumed that the preparation of transcripts is simply a technical detail prior to the main business of the analysis. As Atkinson and Heritage (1984) point out, the production and use of transcripts are essentially research activities. They involve close, repeated listenings to recordings which often reveal previously unnoted recurring features of the organization of talk. The convenience of transcripts for presentational purposes is no more than an added bonus.

As an example, try examining Extract 3, based on the transcribing conventions listed in Table 20.1, which report such features as overlapping talk and verbal stress as well as pauses (in parts of a second):

Extract 3
(S's wife has just slipped a disc)
1 *H*:   And we were <u>w</u>ondering if there's <u>a</u>nything we can do to help

2 S: [Well 'at's
3 H: [I mean can we do any shopping for her or something like tha:t?
4   (0.7)
5 S: Well that's <u>most</u> ki:nd Heather<u>ton</u> .hhh At the moment
6   no:. because we've still got two bo:ys at home. (Heritage, 1984)

In Extract 3, we see S refusing an offer made by H. Heritage shows how S's refusal (lines 5–6) of H's offer displays three interesting features. Firstly, when S does not take an early opportunity to accept H's offer (after 'anything we can do to help', line 1), H proceeds to revise it. Secondly, S delays his refusal via the pause in the slot for his turn at line 4. Thirdly, he justifies it by

Table 20.1 *Simplified transcription symbols*

Symbol	Example	Explanation
[	C: quite a [while M: [yea	Left brackets indicate the point at which a current speaker's talk is overlapped by another's talk
=	W: that I'm aware of = C: = Yes. Would you confirm that?	Equal signs, one at the end of a line and one at the beginning, indicate no pause between the two lines
(0.4)	Yes (0.2) yeah	Numbers in parentheses indicate elapsed time of silence in tenths of a second
(.)	to get (.) treatment	A dot in parentheses indicates a tiny gap, probably no more than one-tenth of a second
————	What's <u>up</u>?	Underlining indicates some form of stress, via pitch and/or amplitude
::	O:<u>kay</u>?	Colons indicate prolongation of the immediately prior sound. The length of the row of colons indicates the length of the prolongation
WORD	I've got ENOUGH TO WORRY ABOUT	Capitals, except at the beginnings of lines, indicate especially loud sounds relative to the surrounding talk
.hhhh	I feel that (0.2) .hhh	A row of h's prefixed by a dot indicates an inbreath; without a dot, an outbreath. The length of the row of h's indicates the length of the in- or outbreath
( )	future risks and ( )	Empty parentheses indicate the transcriber's inability to hear what was said
(word)	Would you see (there) anything positive	Parenthesized words are possible hearings
(( ))	confirm that ((continues))	Double parentheses contain author's descriptions rather than transcriptions
?	What do you think? That's it.	Rising intonation Falling intonation

invoking a contingency about which H could not be expected to know (the existence of two boys at home who can provide such help).

Why should S and H bother with these complexities? The answer lies in the way in which they end up by producing an account which blames nobody for the refusal of an offer of help – an offer which now might, in these circumstances, even appear to be 'intrusive'. In an early paper, Erving Goffman (1955) similarly suggested that a persistent consideration of people as they interact is to protect one another's public self-esteem, or 'face'. In doing whatever people are doing, they take into consideration the moral standing of themselves and their co-interactants that their doings project. In the ordinary course of events, this consideration entails the *protection* of the positive moral standing of the self and of others.

We can develop Goffman's observation by noting that certain actions – typically actions that occur in response to other actions, such as invitations, offers or assessments – can be marked as **dispreferred actions**, that is, problematic in one way or another. Thus, rejections of invitations or offers, or disagreements in response to assessments, can be performed in such a way that marks their problematic status. Conversely, an acceptance of an invitation or offer, or an agreement with an assessment, can be performed in a way that does not exhibit such problematic status.

Subsequent research has identified a number of practices through which the dispreferred status of an action can be marked. According to Heritage (1984: 265–80), these practices include four things: firstly, the action is *delayed* within a turn or across a sequence of turns; secondly, the action is commonly *prefaced* or qualified within the turn in which it occurs; thirdly, the action is commonly accomplished in *mitigated* or indirect form; and fourthly, the action is commonly *accounted* for by providing reasons or justifications for the action. These actions together constitute what has been called **preference organization**. But note that the concept of 'preference', when used in this sense, does not refer to inner experiences of the actors about 'problems' or the lack of them involved in performing certain actions (Levinson, 1983). Furthermore, conversation analysts are not saying that actors have entered the conversation having decided beforehand what actions they will prefer. Rather, people categorize actions as 'preferred' and 'dispreferred' according to the strategic demands that appear as a conversation develops. We can see how conversationalists can prevent problems arising if we return to Extract 1.

C's question (at line 1) is one of those kinds of questions that we hear as likely to precede some other kind of activity. For instance, we all know that, if somebody asks if we will be free on Saturday night, an invitation is in the offing. Here we can guess that if C had got a positive reply, he would then have gone on to offer a request or an invitation.

Why should speakers proceed in this indirect way? The answer is to do with what Goffman called 'face' and what we have called *preference organization*. By asking a question about someone's whereabouts or plans, speakers avoid others having to engage in the dispreferred act of turning down an invitation. If we reply that we are busy, the invitation need never be offered. The prior question thus helps both parties: the recipient is not put in the position of having to turn down an invitation and, if the question elicits negative information or a meaningful pause (as in Extract 1), the questioner is saved from losing face by being able to avoid offering an invitation doomed to be declined.

ELEMENTS OF CONVERSATION ANALYSIS

The detailed transcription symbols in Extract 3 derive from the approach called **conversation analysis** (CA). CA is based on an attempt to describe people's methods for producing orderly social interaction. These methods include what we have called preference organization. As we shall see, CA's concern with the *sequential* organization of talk means that it needs precise transcriptions of such (commonsensically) trivial matters as overlapping talk and length of pauses. As Sacks once put it:

> What we need to do . . . is to watch conversations . . . I don't say that we should rely on our recollection for conversation, because it's very bad . . . One can invent new sentences and feel comfortable with them (as happens in philosophy and linguis-tics). One cannot invent new sequences of conversation and feel happy with them. You may be able to take 'a question and answer', but if we have to extend it very far, then the issue of whether somebody would really say that, after, say, the fifth utterance, is one which we could not confidently argue. One doesn't have a strong intuition for sequencing in conversation. (1992b: 5)

However, without a way of defining a research problem, even detailed transcription can be merely an empty technique. Thus we need to ask: what sort of features are we searching for in our transcripts and what approach lies behind this search? For reasons of space, I will briefly describe just three features of talk with which CA is concerned. These are turn-taking and *repair mechanisms*; conversational openings and *adjacency pairs*; and some basic features of 'institutional' talk. All three features relate to what Sacks refers to as 'sequencing in conversation'.

Turn-taking and repair

Turns at talk have three aspects. These involve, firstly, how a speaker makes a turn relate to a previous turn (for example, 'Yes', 'But', 'Uh huh'); secondly, what the turn accomplishes in the interaction (for example an invitation, a question, an answer); thirdly, how the turn relates to a succeeding turn (for example, by a question, request, summons, and so on).

Where turn-taking errors and violations occur, *repair mechanisms* will be used. For instance, where more than one party is speaking at a time, a speaker may stop speaking before a normally possible completion point of a turn. Again, when turn transfer does not occur at the appropriate place, the current speaker may repair the failure of the sequence by speaking again (as happened in Extracts 1 and 2). Finally, where repairs by other than the current speaker are required (for instance because another party has been misidentified), the next speaker typically waits until the completion of a turn. Thus the turn-taking system's allocation of rights to a turn is respected even when a repair is found necessary.

There are three consequences of this which are worth noting. Firstly, speakers *need to listen*. The turn-taking system provides an intrinsic motivation for listening to all utterances in a conversation. Interest or politeness alone is not sufficient to explain such attention. Rather, every participant must listen to and analyse each utterance in case (s)he is selected as next speaker. Secondly, turn-taking organization controls some of the ways in which utterances are *understood*. So, for instance, it allows 'How are you?', as a first turn, to be usually understood not as an inquiry but as a greeting. Thirdly, speakers will often *display understanding*. When someone offers the 'appropriate' form of reply (for example, an answer to a question, or an apology to a complaint), he or she displays an understanding of the significance of the first utterance. The turn-taking system is thus the means whereby actors display to one another that they are engaged in *social* action – action defined by Weber as involving taking account of others (see Chapter 3).

Thus CA is an empirically oriented research activity, grounded in a basic theory of social action and generating significant implications from an analysis of previously unnoticed interactional forms. As the next section shows, one such unnoticed form is the structure of questions and answers.

Conversational openings and adjacency pairs

In the 1960s, the American sociologist Emmanuel Schegloff studied data drawn from the first five seconds of around 500 telephone calls to and from an American police station. Schegloff began by noting that the basic rule for two-party conversation, that one party speaks at a time (in other words, providing for a sequence *a–b–a–b–a–b* where *a* and *b* are the parties), does not decide who is going to be the first and second speakers (*a* and *b*). Telephone calls offer interesting data in this regard because non-verbal forms of communication – apart from the telephone bell – are absent. Somehow, despite the absence of visual cues, speakers manage an orderly sequence in which both parties know when to speak. Schegloff suggests that this can be done because 'A first rule of telephone conversations which might be called "a distribution rule for first utterances" is: *the answerer speaks first*' (1967: 351).

In order to see the force of the 'distribution rule', consider the confusion that occurs when a call is made and the phone is picked up, but nothing is said by the receiver of the call. Schegloff cites an anecdote by a woman who adopted this strategy of silence after she began receiving obscene telephone calls. Her friends were constantly irritated by this practice, thus indicating the force of the rule 'the answerer speaks first.' Moreover, her tactic was successful: 'However obscene her caller might be, he would not talk until she had said "hello", thereby obeying the requirements of the distribution rule' (1967: 355).

Although answerers are expected to speak first, it is callers who are expected to provide the first topic. Answerers, after all, do not normally know who is making the call, whereas callers can usually identify answerers and answerers will assume that callers have initiated a call in order to raise a topic: hence the embarrassment we feel when somebody we have neglected to call, calls us instead. Here we may convert ourselves from answerers to hypothetical callers by using some formula like: 'Oh, I'd been trying to reach you.' Having reallocated our roles, we are now free to introduce the first topic.

On examining his material further, Schegloff discovered only one case (out of 500) which did not fit the rule that the answerer speaks first. He concluded that the person who responds to a telephone bell is not really answering a *question*, but responding to a *summons*. A summons is any attention-getting device (a telephone bell, a term of address – 'John?' – or a gesture, like a tap on the shoulder or raising your hand). A summons tends to produce answers. Schegloff suggests that **summons–answer (SA) sequences** have three features which they share with a number of other linked turns (for example, questions–answers, greetings) classed as **adjacency pairs**.

The first of these Schegloff describes as *non-terminality*. This means that they are preambles to some further activity; they cannot properly stand as final exchanges. Consequently, the summoner is obliged to talk again when the summoned completes the SA sequence. Secondly, Schegloff identifies their *conditional relevance*, whereby further interaction is conditional upon the successful completion of the SA sequence. And lastly, there is an *obligation to answer*. Answers to a summons have the character of questions (for example, 'What?', 'Yes?', 'Hello?'). This means that, as in question–answer (QA) sequences, the summoner must produce the answer to the question he or she has elicited. Furthermore, the person who has asked the question is obliged to listen to the answer he or she has obligated the other to produce. Each subsequent nod or 'uh huh' recommits the speaker to attend to the utterances that follow. Through this 'chaining' of questions and answers 'provision is made by an SA sequence not only for the coordinated entry in a conversation but also for its continued orderliness' (1967: 378–9).

Schegloff was now able to explain his deviant case as follows: summons (phone rings), no answer; further summons (caller says 'Hello'). The normal form of a telephone call is: summons (phone rings), answer (recipient says 'Hello'). In the deviant case, the absence of an answer is treated as the absence of a reply to a summons. So the caller's use of 'Hello' replaces the summons of the telephone bell. The failure of the summoned person to speak first is heard as an uncompleted SA sequence. Consequently, the caller's speaking first makes sense within the conditional relevance of SA sequences.

The power of these observations is suggested by two examples. The first is mentioned by Cuff and Payne: 'The recipient of a summons feels impelled to answer. (We note that in Northern Ireland, persons still open the door and get shot – despite their knowledge that such things happen)' (1979: 151). The second example arises in Schegloff's discussion of a child's utterance first discussed by Sacks (1974): 'You know what, Mommy?' This establishes an SA sequence, where a proper answer to the summons is 'What?' This allows the child to say what it wanted to at the start, but as an obligation (because questions must produce answers). Consequently, this utterance is a powerful way in which children enter into conversations despite their usually restricted rights to speak.

As Heritage points out, this should not lead us to an over-mechanical view of conversation: 'conversation is not an endless series of interlocking adjacency pairs in which sharply constrained options confront the next speaker' (1984: 261). Instead, the phenomenon of adjacency works according to two non-mechanistic assumptions. Firstly, it is assumed that an utterance which is placed immediately after another one is to be understood as produced in response to or in relation to the preceding utterance. Secondly, this means that, if a speaker wishes some contribution to be heard as *unrelated* to an immediately prior utterance, he or she must do something special to lift the first assumption – for instance by the use of a prefix (like 'by the way') designed to show that what follows is unrelated to the immediately prior turn at talk.

BASIC FEATURES OF INSTITUTIONAL TALK

As noted at the start of this chapter, talk is a feature of both formal and informal interactions, ranging from a courtroom to a casual chat. In a courtroom, for instance, who can speak when is usually clearly defined and, unlike casual chatter, one can be ruled to be speaking 'out of order' and even held to be 'in contempt of court'. However, it is dangerous to assume that just because talk is occurring in some formal setting, it necessarily has a different structure to such chat. As we all know, people still chatter in the course of doing their jobs and some formal move may be needed for the talk to take on a formal (or institutional) character, for instance by the chair of a meeting calling the meeting to order. In any event, as Sacks et al. (1974) suggest, ordinary conversation always provides a baseline from which any such departures are organized and recognized. This means that, in the study of institutional talk, we need carefully to examine how the structures of ordinary conversation 'become specialised, simplified, reduced, or otherwise structurally adapted for institutional purposes' (Maynard and Clayman, 1991: 407). I will use research on the organization of TV news interviews as an example before attempting a brief summary of what is known so far about institutional talk.

TV news interviews

Clayman (1992) characterizes TV news interviewing as a site for much caution given that news interviewers are supposed to be neutral or objective. How is this achieved? When interviewers (IVs) come on to relatively controversial opinion statements, they distance themselves, creating what Clayman calls a different **footing**. This is seen in Extract 4:

Extract 4
1 *IV*: Senator, (0.5) uh: <u>P</u>resident Reagan's elected thirteen months ag<u>o</u>:
2   an en<u>o</u>rmous landslide.
3   (0.8)
4 *IV*: It is s::<u>aid</u> that his <u>p</u>rograms are in trouble. (1992: 5)

In lines 1–2, a footing is constructed whereby IV is the author of a factual statement. However, at line 4, the footing *shifts* to what 'is said': here IV is no longer the author and the item is thereby marked as possibly 'controversial'. Footing shifts are also *renewed* during specific 'controversial' words as IVs avoid showing their own evaluations of the statements they report. They also may comment on the authority of the source of an assertion or mention the range of important persons associated with it. However, the achievement of 'neutrality' is a locally accomplished and co-operative matter. Thus interviewees (IEs) 'ordinarily refrain from treating the focal assertion as expressing the IV's personal opinion' (1992: 180). For instance, they do this by attributing the assertion to the same third party.

As Clayman remarks, this is unlike ordinary conversation, where it seems unlikely that speakers are expected to be neutral. Like Clayman, Greatbatch (1992) notes the specific ways in which participants produce their talk as 'news interview' talk. He shows how the maintenance of IVs' neutrality ties in with the mutual production of the talk as aimed at an overhearing *audience*. Both parties maintain a situation in which it is not problematic that IEs properly limit themselves to responses to IVs' questions. IVs confine themselves to asking questions and avoid responding to IEs' answers in any way which would make them a report recipient rather than just a report-elicitor. So IVs typically avoid responses like 'mmm hm', 'uh huh', 'yes', 'oh', 'really?', 'did you?' (1992: 269–70). In this context, 'neutrality' is not the only feature which contrasts with talk in other settings. Greatbatch shows that 'disagreements' have features specific to news interview talk. In ordinary conversation, agreements, like acceptance of invitations or advice, are marked as *preferred* activities.

Conversely, disagreements are not necessarily marked as dispreferred in news interviews. Take Extract 5, where one interviewee interrupts another:

Extract 5
1 *IE1*: the government advertising campaign is h <u>high</u>ly irresponsible. h It's
     being given

2   [u n d e r hug]e
3 *IE2:* [Utter rubbish]. (1992: 12)

This extract departs from the conversational rules of preference organization (which, as we have seen, show speakers to be more cautious about expressing their disagreement with one another). It also seems to clash with the normal production of a news interview format (because they are not produced as an answer to an IV's question). However, Greatbatch argues, such disagreements display an underlying adherence to the news interview format. First, IE2 can still be heard as responding to the question that produced IE1's answer. Second, IE2 directs his answer to the IV *not* to IE1 and this is quite different from ordinary conversation where the person being disagreed with is also the addressee of the disagreement. Greatbatch found that such disagreements are routinely followed by IV intervening to manage an exit from the disagreement without requiring them to depart from their institutional roles as IEs rather than becoming, for instance, combatants, mutual insulters and so on.

Greatbatch summarizes his findings as follows. In news interviews, many of the features of preference organization are rendered redundant, replaced by the interview turn-taking system. Within news interviews, 'the structure of turn-taking and its associated expectancies provide simultaneously for the *escalation* and *limitation* of overt disagreement' (1992: 299, my emphasis). As Greatbatch suggests, this may explain why panel interviews are so common and assumed to produce 'lively' broadcasting.

Institutional talk

Drew and Heritage (1992: 22–5) distinguish some dimensions according to which we can analyse institutional talk including TV news interviews. Firstly, institutional talk is usually *goal-oriented* in institutionally relevant ways; thus people design their conduct to meet various institutional tasks or functions. For example, emergency calls to the police need to be rapidly but accurately accomplished (Zimmerman, 1992). Alternatively, the goals of interactions can be ill-defined, creating a need for the participants to fashion a sense of what the interaction will be about (Peräkylä and Silverman, 1991; Heritage and Sefi, 1992). Secondly, institutional talk is associated with particular ways of reasoning or inference-making (for example, the assumption that news interviewers are meant to be neutral). Lastly, although institutional talk is usually shaped by certain constraints (for example, what can be done in a court of law or news interview), in other situations, like counselling or doctor–patient interaction, participants may negotiate or ignore such constraints.

SUMMARY: CONVERSATION ANALYSIS

Let us pull together what we have been saying about CA, drawing upon Heritage's (1984) standard text, which points out the *structural organization of talk*, meaning that talk exhibits stable, organized patterns, demonstrably oriented to by the participants. These patterns 'stand independently of the psychological or other characteristics of particular speakers' (1984: 241–4). This has two important implications. Firstly, it is illegitimate and unnecessary to explain that organization by appealing to the presumed psychological or other characteristics of particular speakers. Secondly, nonetheless, it is always necessary to examine the local activities through which speakers assemble the 'here and now' meaning of their talk (as both 'context-dependent' and 'context-renewing'). So, while a concern with the social organization of talk rules out analysts' speculations about mental phenomena like 'minds', intentions' and 'motives', it demands an analysis of how people attend to these and other matters.

Heritage notes too the *sequential organization* of talk: 'a speaker's action is *context-shaped* in that its contribution to an on-going sequence of actions cannot adequately be understood except by reference to its context ... in which it participates' (1984: 242). However, this context is addressed by CA largely in terms of the preceding sequence of talk: 'in this sense, the context of a next action is repeatedly renewed with every current action' (1984: 242). He also stresses the need for an *empirical grounding of analysis*. The properties of talk need to be identified in precise analyses of detailed transcripts. It is therefore necessary to avoid premature theory construction and the 'idealization' of research materials which use only general, non-detailed characterizations. Heritage sums up as follows:

> Specifically, analysis is strongly 'data-driven' – developed from phenomena which are in various ways evidenced in the data of interaction. Correspondingly, there is a strong bias against *a priori* speculation about the orientations and motives of speakers and in favour of detailed examination of conversationalists' actual actions. Thus the empirical conduct of speakers is treated as the central resource out of which analysis may develop. (1984: 243)

In practice, Heritage adds, this means that it must be demonstrated that the regularities described can be shown to be produced by the participants and attended to by them as grounds for their own inferences and actions. Further, deviant cases, in which such regularities are absent, must be identified and analysed (as in Schegloff's study of telephone calls, discussed above).

DOING CONVERSATION ANALYSIS

Despite the battery of concepts found in this chapter, doing CA is not an impossibly difficult activity. As the founder of CA, Harvey Sacks, once

---

Things to strive for
1 Always try to identify sequences of related talk.
2 Try to examine how speakers take on certain roles or identities through their talk (for example, questioner–answerer or client–professional).
3 Look for particular outcomes in the talk (for example, a request for clarification, a repair, laughter) and work backwards to trace the trajectory through which a particular outcome was produced.

Things to avoid
1 Explaining a turn at talk by reference to the speaker's intentions.
2 Explaining a turn at talk by reference to a speaker's role or status (for example, as a doctor or as a man or woman).
3 Trying to make sense of a single line of transcript or utterance in isolation from the surrounding talk.

Figure 20.1   *How to do conversation analysis*

pointed out, in doing CA we are only reminding ourselves about things we already know:

> I take it that lots of the results I offer, people can see for themselves. And they needn't be afraid to. And they needn't figure that the results are wrong because they can see them ... [It is] as if we found a new plant. It may have been a plant in your garden, but now you see it's different than something else. And you can look at it to see how it's different, and whether it's different in the way that somebody has said. (1992a: 488)

However, the way in which CA obtains its results is rather different from how we might intuitively try to analyse talk. It may be helpful, therefore, if I conclude this section by offering a crude set of prescriptions about how to do CA and point to some common errors. These are set out in Figure 20.2. If we follow these rules, as Sacks suggests, the analysis of conversations does not require exceptional skills. All we need to do is to 'begin with some observations, then find the problem for which these observations could serve as ... the solution' (1992b: xlviii).

CONCLUSION

The last thing I want to do is to impose conversation analysis as the only acceptable method of doing social research. As noted elsewhere in this volume, everything will depend upon the research problem being tackled. Moreover, thoughtful researchers will often want to use a combination of methods. However, this benevolent neutrality towards the varying logics of research coexists with an appeal to two very strong principles. Firstly, researchers always need to address the analytic issues that may lie concealed behind apparently straightforward issues of method. Secondly, a concern for an 'in-depth' focus on people's activities (or representations of those activities) is no warrant for sloppy thinking or anecdotal use of 'telling' examples. We owe it to ourselves and our audiences to generate reliable data and valid observations. If there is a 'gold standard' for social and cultural research, it should be: have the researchers demonstrated successfully why we should believe them? And does the research problem tackled have theoretical and/or practical significance?

Further reading

Silverman (1997) provides three very valuable, straightforward chapters on conversation analysis. 'Conversation analysis and institutional talk: analysing data' by John Heritage uses one conversation to show how to do CA; 'Analysing activities in face to face interaction using video' by Christian Heath shows how one can transcribe and analyse video data; and finally, 'Reliability and validity in research based upon transcripts' by Anssi Peräkylä demonstrates how one can generalize using CA methods. An excellent but more theoretical introduction to CA is provided by John Heritage (1984). Paul Drew and John Heritage's (1992) reader includes important papers on institutional talk.

21

Analysing literary texts

Paul Filmer

CONTENTS

The literary critic F.R. Leavis believed that the study of literature was necessary for those engaged in social and cultural research. He wrote, for example, that:

> Without the sensitizing familiarity with the subtleties of language, and the insight into the relations between abstract or generalizing thought and the concrete of human experience, that the trained frequentation of literature alone can bring, the thinking that attends social and political studies will not have the edge and force it should. (1952: 194)

His view of the social relevance of literature is echoed in his later assertion that 'it is the great novelists above all who give us our social history; compared with what is done in *their* work – their creative work – the histories of the professional social historian seem empty and unenlightening (1972: 81–2).

Both statements offer a clear justification for treating literary texts as socially relevant, but their adequacy as data for research remains an important issue. Leavis's statements can be read as implying that the novelist or poet might be better equipped to do the work of social history than the historian, or that people engaged in social and political studies would benefit from the study of literature. But he does not go so far as to say that literature constitutes data for researchers.

There is in fact little systematic study of literature as a social phenomenon in the classical traditions of social research. The few studies of the relations between social structure and literature that have been done (described in Laurenson and Swingewood, 1972: 23–31) have tended to be quite unsystematic, sometimes being **reductive** in character. An example of the reductive study of literature is found in the work of the French positivist philosopher and critic Hippolyte Taine, who argued in his encyclopaedic *History of English Literature* (1906) that literature was a product of three essential, determining elements: *race, milieu* and *moment*. These are, respectively, the ethnic or national character of the work, the cultural context from which it arose, and the specific historical occasion to which the work relates. Taine believed that all literature could be *reduced* to these elements. Taine's thesis is also an example of the main difficulty of treating literature as a source of data for social and cultural research: this can involve treating the context of literary production as more significant than the literary text itself.

This may lead to a lack of attention to the language of the text and the range of its possible meanings, in favour of using it as a resource for illustrative material about the society in which it is produced or to which it refers. In Chapter 3 you saw that a shift occurred in social theory and in methodology around the middle of the twentieth century. Socio-linguistic and structuralist methods began to require attention to the relations between language and social structure as constitutive features of all texts – not only literary texts, but interviews, documents and images as well, indicating a shift towards treating texts as topics. Semiotic analysis (Chapter 18) involves this approach to language, as does discourse analysis (Chapter 19).

This chapter will consider the analysis of literary texts in two distinct but related ways. Firstly, it will show how researchers can examine the social context in which such texts are produced. Secondly, it will show how researchers can analyse the structures of relations within the text, and between its linguistic contents and the social conditions to which they refer.

THE SOCIAL STUDY OF LITERATURE

Why the social study of literary texts has tended to reductive explanations is not easy to explain, but may be a legacy of positivism. By contrast, Loewenthal has defined the 'essential task' of such study as being

> to find that core of meaning which, through artistic images, expresses the many facets of thought and feeling ... permitting us to develop an image of a given society in terms of the individuals who composed it ... what the individual felt about it, what he could hope from it, and how he thought he could change it or escape from it ... The social meanings of this inner life of the individual are related to the central problems of social change. (1961: xv)

This involves seeking knowledge that is available both *in* and *about* literature. On the one hand this is knowledge about the social and cultural contexts in which literature is produced. On the other hand, it is knowledge that is contained within literature about the society in which it is produced and that to which it refers. Historical novels, for example, are likely to contain at least as much about the society in which they are written, and its sense of history at the time that they are written, as they contain about the past condition of the society that is their topic. The same principle can reasonably be assumed to hold for novels that are written in one society about another, different society and its culture, and for works of science fiction also. Nevertheless, the social study of literature remains concerned primarily with knowledge *about* literature. It is seen still as

> a specialized area of study which focuses upon the relation between a work of art, its public, and the social structure in which it is produced and received. It seeks to explain the emergence of a particular art work in a particular form of society, and the ways in which the creative imagination of the writer is shaped by cultural traditions and social arrangements. (Coser, 1963: 4)

Analysis of literary texts, by contrast, is concerned with knowledge of society contained within literature on the grounds that

> Literary artists often convey very involving descriptions of society. They are sometimes able to show the direction a given society is taking, and to describe inconsistencies within it – they are often prophets of the future. The literary artist does not avoid value judgements, for in portraying the lives of members of society, he is able to show that life *is* value judgements. The literary artist is not a passive reporter, an 'objective' observer; he swims through the mud with the characters he creates. Many literary artists have taken it upon themselves to . . . assume responsibility for commenting upon the social issues of which they are a part. (Gliner and Raines, 1971: ix–x)

There are two clear differences between these approaches: firstly, the relative significance that each awards to the literary text, namely whether it is central to the relations between literature and society, or whether it provides the occasion for studying the social determination of literature and the social role of the writer; secondly, the relevance of the engagement of the writer with the society that he or she is writing about and the critical significance for society of the literary text.

Extrinsic and intrinsic approaches

Both sociology and cultural studies have been important institutional locations for the social study of literature. There are two principal approaches used which can be termed the **extrinsic** and the **intrinsic**. The extrinsic approach is designed to provide sociological knowledge *about* literature; the intrinsic approach is to analyse the sociological knowledge to be found *within* literary texts. The extrinsic approach involves the view that, because literature is produced in a societal context, it is determined by society and so can be treated as a reflection of the social conditions of its production. It is, in a sense, a mirror of social life which presents society with some image of itself. Such analysis has examined the backgrounds of authors and readers, and investigated the circumstances of literary production and distribution.

A major problem with this approach is that it pays relatively little attention to the literary text, except as a resource for illustrating social conditions. The nineteenth century European novel, for example, might be used as a source of illustrations of urbanization and industrialization. As an approach it is criticized both by social researchers and by literary critics. Firstly, literature offers an unrepresentative account of society because its authors are unrepresentative of typical social positions and experiences; they are often drawn from elites or classes of high social status, socialized and educated in minority cultures, and to some extent reflect the values and interests of those groups in their work. They are therefore an unreliable guide to the reality of the social life that they write about (Filmer, 1969). Literary critics argue that to treat the contents of literature as illustrations of social life is to misrepresent both literature and its relation to language. Literature is about the subjective consciousness of the individual characters created by the writer's imagination. Some of these may be created to represent recognizable types of individuals and their social practices but only, from the literary critical viewpoint, as a function of the narrative structure of the text and not as an illustration of society. Thus, from both points of view, the relations between literature and society are much more complex and subtle than can be conveyed by the idea of straightforward, mirror-like reflection.

The intrinsic approach operates rather differently, therefore, on the grounds that, although literature is produced in society, it is a *reflexive* feature of the society in which it is produced, engaging with it through critical reflection on social practices. It is designed to release literature from the reduction to illustration that is a problem of the extrinsic approach. It has its own problems of representativeness though, particularly when applied to popular literature. The intrinsic method is applied more effectively either to traditional minority cultural literary works, or to avantgarde modernist literature. The two approaches are not incompatible, however, since each emphasizes different aspects of the relations between literature and society and so both can be applied to the same text. This can be demonstrated in an analysis of some aspects of Charles Dickens's novel *The Pickwick Papers*.

The Pickwick Papers

Dickens wrote *The Pickwick Papers* for publication in 20 monthly parts (which numbered 19 in the event) between April 1836 and November 1837. The success of this novel was to make part publication the characteristic form of publication of novels in Britain for the next half-century. Prior to publication of the first part, the novel had been advertised as '*The Posthumous Papers of the Pickwick Club*; containing a faithful record of the perambulations, perils, travels, adventures, and sporting transactions of the corresponding members. Edited by "Boz"' (Patten, 1972: 899).

There are three points to note about this advertisement, all of which raise questions about issues *intrinsic* to its text. The first is the full title of the advertised work, indicating that what quickly become known as *The Pickwick Papers* are, at the outset, 'posthumous' papers of the Pickwick 'club', containing records of its *corresponding members*. We might ask in what sense the papers are posthumous (perhaps because the club is no longer in existence?) and the members are 'corresponding' (perhaps because they are unable to attend meetings of the club?). Secondly, the papers are 'edited'. This indicates that they may be the faithful record that they claim to be, though we know that what became *The Pickwick Papers* will also come to be acknowledged as a work of fiction authored by Dickens. Thirdly, the editor's name ('Boz') is the pseudonym, indicated by its abbreviated form and its enclosure in inverted commas, of 'a gentleman who the publishers consider highly qualified for the task of arranging these important documents and placing them before the public in an attractive form' (1972: 900). The editor, who comes later to acknowledge himself author of the work of fiction is even, at the outset, himself a fiction, by name. All of these questions indicate a distancing of the *Papers*: from their authors, the corresponding members presumably unable to attend the club; from their editor, who is not an author and is not named, only nicknamed; and from the club itself, which is posthumous.

Some light is thrown on some of these questions by the following statement, which opens Chapter 4 of the *Papers*:

> Many authors entertain, not only a foolish, but a really dishonest objection to acknowledge the sources from whence they derive much valuable information. We have no such feeling. We are merely endeavouring to discharge, in an upright manner, the responsible duties of our editorial functions; and whatever ambition we might have felt under other circumstances to lay claim to the authorship of these adventures, a regard for truth forbids us to do more than claim the merit of their judicious arrangement and impartial narration. The Pickwick papers are our New River Head; and we may be compared to the New River Company. The labours of others have raised for us an immense reservoir of important facts. We merely lay them on, and communicate them in a clear and gentle stream, through the medium of these numbers to a world thirsting for Pickwickian knowledge. (1972: 116)

In the context of a general statement about authorial honesty, an attempt is made here to justify the editing rather than authoring of the papers by claiming no more than 'the merit of their judicious arrangement and impartial narration'. Others – the corresponding members of the club – are acknowledged to 'have raised for us an immense reservoir of important facts' which have made the papers analogous to the 'New River Head' and the editor to the 'New River Company'. At this point, a complex metaphor is introduced with both *extrinsic* references and related *intrinsic* images. The New River was a fresh water supply brought to London early in the seventeenth century, with its head located in Islington where it filled reservoirs. It remains of central importance to the provision of fresh water to that area of north London and the city. Early in the nineteenth century the New

River Company was formed successfully as a joint stock company to develop the facility for the increasing population of the city. This would certainly have been known to Londoners amongst Dickens's readers and the river would have been a familiar yet still compelling image for the 'clear and gentle stream' in which the 'important facts' were communicated 'through the medium' of the papers.

The image of the papers communicating a clear and gentle stream of important facts, though it is derived ingeniously from the *extrinsic* references to the fresh water of the New River, is however *intrinsic* in character, in two distinct ways. Firstly, it establishes a distinct version of language – one which is a clear medium of communication, composed of transparent signs capable of conveying the much vaunted facts contained in the metaphorical reservoir constituted by the papers. Yet the use of the New River and of water itself, as metaphors, is done in order to sustain the fiction that *The Pickwick Papers* is not a fiction! Secondly, the clear and gentle stream of important facts is communicated 'to a world thirsting for Pickwickian knowledge'. Readers, at the point at which they encountered this piece of text, knew that Pickwickian 'knowledge' was really something of a joke. Pickwick, for example, was 'the man who had traced to their source the mighty ponds of Hampstead, and agitated the scientific world with his Theory of Tittlebats' (1972: 68). The Hampstead ponds are fed by underground springs, knowledge not difficult to establish; 'tittlebat' is a variant form of stickleback, the most common freshwater fish in the British Isles and so scarcely likely to require speculative theorizing. The term originates in childish pronunciation of the fish's name. At the meeting at which Pickwick delivers a paper on these topics his fellow members recommend, amusingly, 'carrying the speculations of that learned man into a wider field ... extending his travels, and consequently enlarging his sphere of observation, to the advancement of knowledge, and the diffusion of learning' (1972: 67)

This leads to the formation of a Corresponding Society of the Pickwick Club consisting of Pickwick and three other members. One sense of the posthumousness of the club arises from this, since no further meetings of it are recorded, only its dissolution in the final chapter. It continues to exist until then only through its corresponding members, which enables their papers to become both *the* Pickwick papers and posthumous. Pickwick delivers an oration in acceptance of this commission, in the full flow of which he is interrupted by another member, 'Mr Blotton (of Aldgate)', who refers to Pickwick as a 'humbug'. He is asked by the Chairman to withdraw and, when he refuses, is asked

> whether he had used the expression ... in a common sense. Mr Blotton had no hesitation in saying that he had not – he had used the word in its Pickwickian sense ... He was bound to acknowledge that, personally, he entertained the highest regard and esteem for the honourable gentleman; he had merely considered him a humbug in a Pickwickian point of view. (1972: 72)

Pickwick accepts this explanation and by doing so, in the light of what we have already learned about Pickwick's version of science, he gives us a clear indication of what is meant by Pickwickian knowledge. It is a knowledge which claims the obvious as a discovery, and which is expressed in a language which appears to mean the opposite of what is conventionally understood – a language, that is, which is anything but a clear and gentle stream, and which communicates the opposite of facts as conventional representations of truth (Marcus, 1972). In effect, it negates them, together with the claim to their judicious editorial arrangement and impartial narration. But what this negation does, in turn, is to allow for the reconstitution of the papers as a work of literary fiction on intrinsically constructed terms.

Ironically, though, Dickens was almost too successful in his attempt to pass off the novel as an edition of 'real' papers. After the fourth part, in which the fiction of editorial responsibility was explicitly stated, sales began to increase substantially. By the spring of 1837, within a year of publication of the first part, its circulation had increased 40 times to more than 20,000 copies each month. At the conclusion of the 10th part in December 1836, when the sequence was at its halfway point, Dickens was moved to add an announcement of the 'author' (no longer an editor), *extrinsic* to the text, that 'He has long been desirous to embrace the first opportunity of announcing that it is his intention to adhere to his original pledge of confining this work to twenty numbers' (Patten, 1972: 902). His reasons are 'to keep the strictest faith with his readers' and that 'the book may not have to contend against the heavy disadvantage of being prolonged beyond his original plan'. The intention was realized, but in apparently bad humour on Dickens's part. The final part is concluded by a chapter entitled 'In which the Pickwick Club is finally dissolved, and everything concluded to the satisfaction of everybody'. Every character in the novel, that is, but not Dickens himself, who begins the final passage of the chapter thus:

> It is the fate of most men who mingle with the world, and attain even the prime of life, to make many real friends, and lose them in the course of nature. It is the fate of all authors or chroniclers to create imaginary friends, and lose them in the course of art. Nor is this the full extent of their misfortunes; for they are required to furnish an account of them besides. In compliance with this custom – unquestionably a bad one – we subjoin a few biographical words, in relation to the party at Mr Pickwick's assembled. (1972: 896)

This is a markedly different account of the novel when compared with the passage at the opening of Chapter 4. Whereas the earlier passage sought deliberately to confuse the distinction between representations of nature and art (between editor and author), Dickens is now concerned to reinforce a fundamental difference between them by identifying the double misfortune suffered by authors. They have not only to suffer the loss of imaginary friends created in the course of art, but also to account for them, and thus keep them alive after they are lost to the conclusion of the fiction – an option not available to those who lose friends in the course of nature. The custom of furnishing an account of imaginary friends, moreover, is announced by Dickens to be 'unquestionably a bad one'. Yet it is only in response to an extrinsic factor – the phenomenal success of *The Pickwick Papers* – that it is required at all. Therefore, Dickens writes his final chapter to satisfy a readership who demand to know more of the (now admitted to be) fictional characters.

Dickens, then, gives a number of indications to readers on how to read *The Pickwick Papers*. Initially he encourages readers to read them as a chronicle, in the sense of a true record of actual social events kept by those involved in them and subsequently edited for publication. Later, he encourages readers to perceive them as the imaginative fiction created by the art of their author, who invented all the events and characters that they contain except some of the places in which the imaginary events occurred, though these could have been invented also.

Though he begins with the first set of instructions, Dickens changes to a clear preference for the second. Yet his readers at the time stubbornly preferred the first way of reading the *Papers*. Hence Dickens's complaint at having to comply with the 'unquestionably bad' custom of furnishing an account of a hypothetical history of his characters after the conclusion of the fiction for which he has invented them. The text has, in effect, taken on a life of its own for its readers which, despite acknowledging it as his invention, he can no longer control. Together with his readers, Dickens has created an autonomous social world *within* the text, which can be seen to have two sources. The first is intrinsic, and can be termed **intratextual** (Altman, 1981), since it occurs in part as a result of the credibility of the fictional reality that the text has created, the world of the corresponding members of the Pickwick club and their associates, their travels and the adventures that befall them. Secondly, the text has been given an extrinsic, **extratextual** reality, through its reception by its readers, as a result of its credibility. This is both as a result of the real existence of the extrinsic places and social practices to which it refers and because of its readers' reactions to its plausibility in treating the invented events and characters as if they are real. This took the form, amongst the first readers of *The Pickwick Papers*, of travelling the same stagecoach routes as Pickwick and his colleagues, of visiting the same inns and hotels at which they dined and lodged, and of purchasing and wearing the shrewdly retailed clothing which Dickens described them as wearing, with a careful detail enhanced by the illustrations that were included with the published parts of the text (Steig, 1978). Additionally, other writers came to refer to Pickwick and his colleagues as recognizable social types, so that fiction and reality became progressively intertwined. The significance of this interrelation that can occur with works of fiction has been summarized as follows:

> The capacity of works of fiction to present us with dense, detailed and suggestive canvasses ... of the imagination, constitutes fiction's advantage over history or reportage. We can allow ... that our novelists evoke something like a full range of facts, events and human reactions, so as to give us a sense of experience. For ... we do not have to worry about the literal truth of what we are being told, only about

its plausibility ... We invent sufficient detail to suggest the density of real experience. The constructed referents of fiction therefore differ from the real referents of history in that (1) the latter have to be historically accurate, and can contain only what is known. But (2) when we can *construct* our referents, we can inject more reality into them. (Martin, 1975: 91)

This type of relation, between the factual realities of a social world *extrinsic* to literature and the invented realities that are *intrinsic* to works of literary fiction, holds for all literature.

RELATIONS BETWEEN LITERARY TEXTS AND SOCIAL CONTEXTS

The reflexivity of the relations between literary texts and social contexts is accessible, as the example drawn from *The Pickwick Papers* suggests, from within the texts themselves through the indications that the texts offer on how they can be read. This presents an interesting methodological problem since in part it requires an approach to the text that is open to its ability to invent, as it proceeds, both itself and the reality outside itself to which it refers. Cicourel indicates that this can be difficult, since 'The interpretation of any ... novel ... is continually subject to the possibility of reinterpretation in light of "second thoughts" or additional information' (1964: 154–5).

There are, however, four distinct approaches on which social and cultural researchers can draw in analysing literary texts which address the difficulties outlined by Cicourel. Firstly, there is the approach of *semiotics* and *structural linguistics* which provide theories of signs required to make sense of the language of the literary text and its relation to everyday language (see Chapter 18). This approach is demonstrated by Eco (1981; 1989). Secondly, there is the *phenomenological* approach (see Chapter 3). This makes possible analysis of the relations between the specific (intrinsic) meanings of the text and those (extrinsic to it) of the realities experienced by readers. Schutz (1964) provides an illustration of this. Thirdly, as is shown in the work of Williams (1977), the researcher can investigate *structures of feeling*; literary texts are then seen in their social and historical contexts as expressions of social change, perhaps pointing to the possibility of new social structures. Lastly, Goldmann (1964; 1975) has shown how literary works can be read as the articulation of an emerging social consciousness – a world vision. This is analysed for its potential in enabling the social group who develop it to provide for future change to the institutional and political order of their society.

There are overlaps between these four approaches. All are concerned with the potential of the language of literary texts to constitute meanings – that is, with language's ability to express and communicate new experiences. They are all, therefore, centrally concerned with the structure and contents of the literary text itself and thus avoid the problems already noted of extrinsic sociologies of literature which use the text as a source of illustrative reflections of social conditions, or as a site for analyses of the institutional processes of literary production. This is especially the case for semiotic, linguistic and phenomenological approaches, all of which are committed to some extent to the analysis of social structure as itself a linguistic phenomenon. We acquire our knowledge of social structure and the ways in which it constrains us through language; and by offering us alternative versions, literature can offer one way of considering how to change it (Skinner, 1980).

The approaches of Williams and Goldmann take this a stage further by implicating literature in the process of change itself. Both suggest that writers of literature can articulate collective experience which is at odds with the beliefs and values of the dominant social groups of the time. The structure of certain literary works thus parallels the emerging structure of a future condition of society and a future shared consciousness on the part of those individuals who may bring about this new condition. Literary texts can then be seen as ideological, since they offer persuasive and coherent accounts which can endorse or challenge societies and social processes of which they are themselves a part.

CONCLUSION

These approaches to the analysis of literary texts offer ways of establishing the adequacy of literature as a source of data for researchers. Thus they refute the rather narrow conception of Leavis expressed at the beginning of this chapter. Literature can be used by researchers to examine the structure of relations between the individual and society, the processes of social change and, perhaps most important, the ways in which these are to be studied systematically by taking account of the meanings, as well as the causes, of social action. Literature is more than a reflection of social life; it is a reflexive engagement with it which is undertaken by writers and readers in a conscious awareness of the essentially reflexive relation between language, subjective imagination and social structure. The force of this engagement is its ability to transcend the limits of personal biographies, specific cultures and particular historical periods. For these reasons, its systematic development within the range of research methods remains vital to the contemporary study of culture.

Further reading

Coser (1963) is an early introduction to ways of using literature for social research. Laurenson and Swingewood (1972) is also a useful general guide, as are Burns and Burns (1973) and Hall (1979). Eagleton (1983) offers a relevant introduction to literary theories and concepts. For an excellent recent treatment of different approaches, see Milner (1996).

Reading and writing research

Les Back

CONTENTS

At its most fundamental the process of doing research involves reading and writing. This seems obvious. Yet, it was not until relatively recently that researchers paid serious attention to the social, linguistic and rhetorical structures of the texts which form the ultimate product of the research act. Beyond this very little has been written about the nature of our audience. We have few insights into the impact of social research on the societies within which it is conducted. Glance at any newspaper and one finds an extraordinary amount of information, and a fetish for social measurement. The appetite for social commentary seems almost infinite. But what place does social science occupy within these circuits of facts and figures? Who is listening and why?

A cynic might reply that the low social standing of some branches of social and cultural research means that no one cares and no one is interested. If this is true, and I must say I am not entirely convinced, then we equally need to ask what has produced a situation where a society, almost pathologically preoccupied with information, demonstrates such little interest in academic research. Writing of sociology, for example, Silverman cautions that 'We do our subject no service if we assume that our low status is simply the result of a cruel world. If in Britain, sociologists are often little more than figures of fun, then the activities of sociologists themselves may have something to do with this' (1990: 1). We therefore need to think carefully about the products of research and how they enter the social world beyond academic circles.

Research is inherently a **rhetorical** activity (Atkinson, 1990). In its common usage 'rhetoric' is often associated with insincere oratory or sloganeering. However, philosophically and historically this notion has another meaning. Here it is defined as the art of persuasion or effective communication, connected with speaking with propriety, elegance and force. Concerns about the lack of status within the social sciences reflect a rhetorical failure on the part of researchers to convince their non-academic audiences of the relevance of research.

This chapter looks in turn at the ways in which social research has been *read* critically and examines new strategies for *writing* research. My aim here is to think through, in a non-programmatic way, a strategy that more closely connects writing with identifying particular audiences. At the same time, the forms of textual critique discussed in the chapter have in common an insistence that forms of power and history affect the process of writing in ways that the authors of research only partly understand and control.

READING RESEARCH

One of the core paradoxes of social and cultural research is that the writer or researcher is inside the very thing that she or he wishes to understand, in other words, society and culture. In this sense research texts are social products. This is equally true of the natural sciences; the cool remoteness of scientific papers is in many ways a kind of rhetoric. It is this apparent lack of style that gives scientific accounts their authority. Yet even natural science can be seen as being 'inside' language. Yearley (1981) has shown this through examining the forms of rhetoric found within just one scientific paper and suggests that close scrutiny reveals particular modes of accounting, argument and persuasion. The audience is as much convinced by the rhetoric of scientific texts as it is by the 'facts' that are represented through these means.

Science writing, in both natural and social sciences, attempts to achieve what Latour and Woolgar (1979) refer to as 'literary inscription'. This refers to their success in having the correctness or **facticity** of a given argument accepted as true. Latour and Woolgar point out that this is accomplished when the reader accepts the facts without seeing rhetorical processes at work. The 'scientific message' is composed of conventions of textual performance. I believe that we need to identify and unlock these processes of literary inscription in order to see through the technical mystifications of research texts. In order to achieve this it is necessary to suspend the taken-for-granted assumptions to which readers submit when reading a monograph or research paper. The reader needs to remove prior assumptions and attend to how 'facts' and 'social realities' are constructed through language.

This is an attitude towards text rather similar to that of the discourse analyst (Chapter 19).

I will discuss two genres of critical reading that have examined the textual nature of research writing, namely feminist critiques of male bias in social research, and what I will refer to as the *literary turn* in the social sciences. Firstly, I will look at the ways in which feminist writers have criticized the gendered nature of research texts.

Feminism, writing and androcentrism

One of the themes of feminist criticism is that accounts of social life produced by male researchers are presented through a male-centred or **androcentric** viewpoint (see also Chapter 4). Lofland (1974), for example, has argued that the portrayals of women within the American urban studies literature either completely ignore the presence of women or portray them through the eyes of male social actors. She argues that these representations of urban life do not give women a voice or any sense of social agency. This literature presents the men as the generic representatives of the society or subculture as a whole. At the simplest level, this is done by use of the male pronoun ('he') to refer to both men and women. Morgan points out that this also renders significant parts of male social experience invisible: 'men were there all the time but we did not see them because we were looking for mankind' (1980: 93). Missing out the effect of gender on the experience of social life thus disadvantages both sexes.

Feminist responses to this have not been uniform (as was shown in Chapter 4). There are a range of positions on the relationship between research, writing and a political commitment to feminism. Harding, in *The Science Question and Feminism*, identifies a key problem for feminist knowledge:

> The epistemological problem for feminism is to explain an apparently paradoxical situation. Feminism is a political movement for social change. How can such politicized research be increasing the objectivity of enquiry? On what grounds should these feminist claims be justified? (1986: 24)

Subsequently, Harding (1987) outlined a number of broad responses to this paradox. I want to look in detail at what she refers to as *feminist empiricism* and *feminist post-modernism*. Both of these broad areas have addressed issues of rhetoric, modes of writing and the role of research.

Harding maintains that the central tenets of **feminist empiricism** are that the existing methodological tools of social science are fundamentally sound. The problem is the issue of male bias and this can be corrected by a stricter, less gender-loaded adherence to the methodological norms of scientific enquiry. One of the features of feminist epistemology is the premise that personal experiences should be admissible within feminist knowledge. However, feminist empiricists have been sceptical of the way in which this has involved a dismissal of the potential use of reason and objectivity. Thus, with regard to the biological sciences Birke concludes:

> the association of objectivity with masculinity has sometimes led feminists to reject objectivity and to glorify subjectivity in opposition to it. While it is necessary to re-value the subjective ... we do ourselves a disservice if we remove ourselves from objectivity and rationality; we then simply leave the terrain of rational thought ... to men, thus perpetuating the system which excluded us in the first place. (1986: 157)

If, as some have argued, scientific rationality is inevitably compromised with male intellectual models, then how do feminist researchers convince a potentially hostile audience of the power of their critique? It is precisely the *rhetorical* power of social science and objectivity that some feminist empiricists have found appealing. Jayaratne and Stewart comment that 'The greatest benefit of apparent objectivity lies in its power to change political opinion. Thus traditional research methods can be used to our advantage to change sexist beliefs or to support progressive legislation' (1991: 100). Sara Arber's work in the secondary analysis of official statistics, described in Chapter 15, demonstrates the appeal of this. Jayaratne and Stewart quote an example of a study of maternal death rate conducted in Chicago, which showed a much higher death rate amongst black women than amongst whites. As a result of the research a new programme was initiated by the Illinois health commissioner and the Chicago Health Department allocated $35 million to improve prenatal care. It was precisely the rhetoric of science and the allure of statistical evidence that made the case so compelling. Jayaratne and Stewart conclude that 'Feminist researchers must be critical of both quantitative and qualitative research which is used against women and must be able to marshal the richest and most persuasive evidence in the service of women' (1991: 100). They suggest that the political commitments of feminism are best served by this pragmatic or instrumental approach. Although they do not labour this point, such an approach also subscribes to established forms of research writing which include striving for objectivity, the use of reasoned argument and establishing truth empirically.

The second response identified by Harding is **feminist post-modernism**. Inspired by French thinkers like Derrida and Foucault and the deconstruction movement (see Chapter 3) this strand within feminist thought is profoundly sceptical about the power of reason and the universalizing claims of scientific discourse. The project of science is seen as fundamentally flawed; the knowledge produced through empirical means is little more than a regime of power and an effect of the desire to know. The rhetoric of social science is viewed as irrevocably harnessed to oppressive ways of knowing and governing people's social experience.

This critique completely breaks with the established conventions of empirical research writing. This is not just a matter of critically engaging with the gender distortion present in male social science; rather, research texts are viewed as little more than the embodiment of male desire, in which power forges representations of social reality through discursive means. The truth-telling power of research texts is reduced to patterns of discourse enshrined in writing. Deconstructivist criticism has been influential in other areas of social thought. Here, I want to look in particular at this perspective as applied to anthropological writing.

'True fictions': the poetics of ethnography

Renato Rosaldo, in his ground-breaking book *Culture and Truth: The Remaking of Social Analysis* (1989), pointed out that classical modes of ethnographic reporting seem farcical parodies when applied to familiar social settings. To demonstrate this Rosaldo describes a breakfast scene at his prospective parents-in-law:

> Every morning the reigning patriarch, as if just in from the hunt, shouts from the kitchen, 'How many people would like a poached egg?' Women and children take turns saying yes or no. In the meantime, the women talk among themselves and designate one among them the toast maker. As the eggs near readiness, the reigning patriarch calls out to the designated toast maker, 'The eggs are about ready. Is there enough toast?' 'Yes,' comes the deferential reply. 'The last two pieces are about to pop up.' The reigning patriarch then proudly enters bearing a plate of poached eggs before him. Throughout the course of the meal, the women and children, including the designated toast maker, perform the obligatory ritual praise song, saying, 'These sure are great eggs, Dad.' (1989:47)

This account of the family breakfast is rendered in the present tense favoured in ethnographic writing. It is framed as a drama of generational domination and gender deference, and uses both direct quotes and 'anthropological' categories (such as 'reigning patriarch' and 'ritual praise song'). Yet it reads as a humorous parody and a gross caricature. Rosaldo's in-laws laughed as they listened to him recite his anthropological contemplations. He reflected: 'The experience of having gales of laughter greet my microethnography made me wonder why a manner of speaking that sounds like the literal "truth" when describing distant cultures seems terribly funny as a description of "us" '(1989:50).

But this is not to say that ethnographic accounts of social life are without merit. They may produce insightful observations. The father in his breakfast ritual was approaching retirement and his adult daughters had successful careers. Rosaldo's caricature shows how gender roles were being maintained, even where the 'ruling patriarch's' status was fast being undermined by professional changes in status amongst his daughters. But until recently these modes of anthropological description were taken to be objective characterizations. It is only when one applies them to social contexts with which we are familiar that they strike us as **objectifying** caricatures. This brings into focus the importance of examining the **poetics** of ethnographic writing.

Here the notion of poetics means the analysis of the conventions whereby ethnography, or any other form of research, is constructed and interpreted.

The publication in 1986 of *Writing Culture* by Clifford and Marcus marked an important moment in what I want to refer to as the **literary turn** in anthropology. One of the features of this movement is the application of perspectives from literary criticism to ethnographic writing. The book is a collection of essays produced from a discussion forum on the 'making of ethnographic texts' held at the School of American Research in Santa Fe, New Mexico. The fundamental starting point of this collection is that ethnography possesses a rhetorical structure, modes of authority and processes of suppression and omission.

In his introduction to the book Clifford argues that the poetics of ethnography are structured in at least six ways:

Contextual	It fashions and creates particular social situations and in doing so creates an object of study. In its classical period ethnographers created 'the tribe' as their unit of analysis.
Rhetorical	Ethnographic writing demonstrates particular conventions of expression. Rosaldo exemplifies one of the most common (the use of the ethnographic present). This way of describing society constructs social relations as if they are enduring facts that are almost timeless.
Institutional	Ethnographers write within (and sometimes against) specific traditions, disciplines and their audiences. The ethnographic monograph itself is shaped institutionally. It is an unwritten rite of passage that the anthropologist must write long research monographs which provide the space for them to recount the fruits of participant observation.
Generic	Ethnographies are a particular genre of texts distinguishable from travel writing and other types of research writing.
Political	This form of writing monopolizes the authority to represent cultural realities.
Historical	All these conventions and constraints are shifting and changing through time.

These various elements act collectively as ethnographers write. It is as if all of these inherited conventions sit at the shoulder of the writer as he or she commits descriptions, observations and analysis to paper. Clifford uses this analysis to argue that ethnographic truths are inherently partial, committed and imperfect: 'Even the best ethnographic texts – serious, true fictions – are systems, or economies, of truth. Power and history work through them, in ways their authors cannot fully control' (1986: 7). Crapanzano (1986), one of the book's contributors, argues that ethnographers are like tricksters who promise not to lie but on the other hand never tell the whole truth. His point is that their rhetoric of absolute truth both empowers and subverts the message. The task of critical reading is then to read against the grain of the text, to identify the exclusions and the trickery of ethnographic writing and authority. Clifford comments:

> 'Cultures' do not hold still for their portraits. Attempts to make them do so always involve simplification and exclusion, selection of a temporal focus, the construction of a particular self–other relationship, and the imposition or negotiation of a power relationship. (1986: 10)

The point here is that in order to evaluate ethnographic writing more accurately its *discursive* nature needs to be specified. In simple terms this means posing a number of questions in relation to the text. Who speaks? Who writes? What modes of description are used? What is the relationship between the style of writing and the reality which is represented through these means?

In order to understand the significance of the literary turn one needs to see anthropology in its historical context. In many respects modern anthropology was the child of colonialism. Yet the anthropologists of the 1940s and 1950s were often 'reluctant imperialists' caught between the expectations of colonial bureaucrats and a desire to construct a cross-cultural science (Asad, 1973). With the emergence of independence movements in the 1960s there was a move to reinvent anthropology (Hymes, 1974) and combine the ethnographic enterprise with politicized perspectives drawn from Marxism, feminism and anti-colonialism. The significance of the literary critique developed by people like Clifford is the argument for a reconfiguring of the relationship between the Western anthropologist and the colonial or post-colonial world. Clifford suggests that anthropologists need to share authorship to produce collaborative accounts of the social world. Even so, he warns against the view that such 'cultural insiders' will tell 'the real story'. Accounts from the 'inside' are equally rhetorical performances with conventions and constraints.

Ethnographic writing, though, can allow more than one voice to be represented. This is appropriate because

> Culture is contested, temporal, and emergent. Representation and explanation – both by insiders and outsiders – is implicated in this emergence. The specification of discourses I have been tracing is thus more a matter of making carefully limited claims. It is thoroughly historicist and self-reflexive. (Clifford, 1986: 19)

Although these points have been illustrated by arguments from anthropologists, they can be applied equally to other forms of research writing. Atkinson (1990), for example, applies this perspective to sociologists writing ethnographic accounts. Reading any research text from this point of view is helpful in promoting a more reflexive, self-aware style when the time comes to begin writing research for yourself.

WRITING RESEARCH

The literary turn in feminism, anthropology and sociology offers new insights into the processes that affect the textual production of research-based knowledge. What implications does this have for writing research? Atkinson in his discussion of ethnographic writing in sociology concludes:

> The fully mature ethnography requires a reflexive awareness of its own writing, the possibilities and limits of its own language, and a principled exploration of its modes of representation. Not only do we need to cultivate a self-conscious construction of ethnographic texts, but also a readiness to *read* texts from a more 'literary critical' perspective. Sociologists and their students must cultivate the discipline of reading their own and others' arguments for their stylistic and rhetorical properties. (1990: 180)

The bottom line seems to be that researchers should be aware of their rhetorical strategies because of the tautological notion that self-knowledge is good. There is a real danger, though, that the preoccupation with reflexivity will degenerate into solipsism and self-absorption, where social researchers are continually examining their own discrete and sometimes stale professional cultures. It would be a disaster, in my view, if these insightful perspectives resulted in little more than a self-referential endo-professionalism, where research is reduced to endless textual deconstruction.

Students and young researchers seem to be bewildered by this insistence on complexity and contingency. One of the unintended consequences of the literary turn is that all claims to describe reality are placed in inverted commas. Any kind of research in this scenario appears to be compromised by the fact that it involves a textual practice that can be subjected to the kinds of deconstruction discussed in this chapter. This can result in a kind of intellectual vertigo, where the level of analysis is abstracted to such a degree that the social world with which we are familiar – and which for many provided the basis for an interest in social research in the first place – seems to disappear into a tangle of obfuscating jargon, pathos and uncertainty as to how to write anything at all about social life.

In order to avoid this we might think of ways in which attention to the textual and rhetorical nature of our writing might be used to improve the ways in which we communicate our ideas beyond the boundaries of academia. It is this question that I want to address in the final part of this chapter. Here I want to look at the work of W.E.B. Du Bois and the relationship between research writing, literary form and audience in his early work.

W.E.B. Du Bois, racial terror and social science

William Edward Burghardt Du Bois was an extraordinary intellectual figure. I want to look at his writing career in some detail because he is an example of someone who wrote in a variety of styles depending on the context and audience. Du Bois was a sociologist who both used and broke free from the rhetorical conventions of social science. He was also one of the first African American intellectuals to conduct extensive empirical research. In many respects Du Bois was tackling and resolving some of the issues discussed in this chapter almost 100 years ago. In his work, I would argue, we can find some clues as to how contemporary researchers might develop more creative writing strategies.

He was born on 23 February 1868 and died on 27 August 1963 on the eve of the first civil rights march on Washington. In large part Du Bois has been left out of the canon of American sociology despite the fact that his work and thought influenced figures like Robert Park, Horace Cayton, St Clair Drake and Gunnar Myrdal. He was also a personal friend of Max Weber whom he met while studying in Germany. During his long life he wrote an immense amount, close to 2,000 bibliographical entries which span a wide range of genres including research monographs, social histories, novels, poems, pamphlets and newspaper articles. It is the eclecticism of Du Bois that I want to address, particularly in relation to the way he switched genres in order to make public interventions.

Du Bois was first exposed to the emerging forms of social enquiry which came to be associated with sociology at Harvard and then the University of Berlin. In 1896 Du Bois became the first black person to receive a doctorate from Harvard. This was also the year that he began working on what became *The Philadelphia Negro*, the first serious social investigation of an urban black community. His vision of social science was both utopian and pragmatic: 'The Negro problem was in my mind a matter of systematic investigation and intelligent understanding. The world was thinking wrong about race, because it didn't know. The ultimate evil was stupidity. The cure for it was knowledge based on scientific investigation' (1940: 58).

The Philadelphia Negro was published in 1899. It was met with considerable acclaim and some disquiet from white reviewers. It is an incredible compendium of quantitative and qualitative information on black life and race relations in Philadelphia. In many respects the book provides a blueprint for the kind of urban sociology that was later developed famously at the University of Chicago under the guidance of Park and Burgess (see Chapter 3). What is striking is the way the text is couched within a rhetoric of pragmatism and scientific method. Equally, there is a strong moral discourse that runs through this text with regard to certain indigent sections of the black community. The book in many ways exemplifies an almost contemptuous scientific fairness and Du Bois subscribed to this way of writing the 'race problem' in a very self-conscious way. At this point in his life reason and science provided the cornerstone of his attack on racism and white supremacy.

By the 1890s a range of black southern educational institutions had started to conduct research into the conditions of rural black communities. After finishing his work in Philadelphia Du Bois was invited to head a research centre at the University of Atlanta. In his autobiography he reflects that at Atlanta:

I laid down an ambitious program for a hundred years of study ... I proposed gradually to broaden and intensify the study, sharpen the tools of investigation and perfect our method of work, so that we would have an increasing body of scientifically ascertained fact, instead of the vague mass of so-called Negro problems. And through this laboratory experiment I hoped to make the laws of social living clearer, surer and more definite. (1968: 217)

For 18 years Du Bois oversaw the Atlanta studies. It is worth emphasizing that this sophisticated work was conducted in a period when American sociology was in its infancy. Du Bois, at least initially, had a faith that white scholars shared his vision of an intellectual culture that could move beyond the racial divide. He saw the University of Atlanta as having a cultural mission with regard to the politics of academic freedom and social criticism. But in the violent years at the end of the century one incident had a lasting affect on Du Bois's faith in the role of science and reason in achieving social progress. It involved the plight of an illiterate black farm labourer called Sam Hose.

Sam Hose had killed his white landlord's wife. Du Bois set about the task of committing to paper appropriate evidence and the mitigating circumstances of Hose's crime. In *The Autobiography of W.E.B. Du Bois* he describes that:

I wrote out a careful and reasoned statement concerning the evident facts and started down to the Atlanta Constitution Office, carrying in my pocket a letter of introduction to Joel Chandler Harris. I did not get there. On the way news met me: Sam Hose had been lynched, and they said his knuckles were on exhibition at a grocery store farther down Mitchell Street along which I was walking. I turned back to the University. I began to turn aside from my work. (1968: 222)

This experience brought home the barbarism of white supremacy. He could not be a cool, calm and detached social scientist while people like Sam Hose were being lynched, brutalized and starved. The research which he was conducting constituted in his words 'so small a part of the sum of occurrences'; it was too far from the 'hot reality of real life'. He began to re-evaluate the role of science:

I regarded it as axiomatic that the world wanted to learn the truth and if the truth were sought with even approximate accuracy and painstaking devotion, the world would gladly support the effort. This was, of course, but a young man's idealism. (1968: 222)

While these experiences shifted Du Bois away from his commitment to science, this was not total. He would return to Atlanta in the 1930s to write perhaps the definitive history of the Black Reconstruction (Du Bois, 1934). But it was at this point that he became a man of letters, an essayist and a contributor to popular journals. He is thrust into the realm of politics and leadership struggles within the emerging movement for the advancement of black Americans. What is significant for my purpose here is that he did this through *writing*.

On 18 April 1903 the Chicago-based company A.C. McClung published a collection of Du Bois's essays entitled *The Souls of Black Folk* (1989). With the exception of one piece written especially for the book, these articles had appeared in a wide range of popular journals. Between 1903 and 1905 there were no less than six printings of the book. The demand for the work was extraordinary. One of the things that immediately strikes one when reading *The Souls* is its interdisciplinary nature and the variety of genres of writing in the book, which combine fiction, history, sociology and autobiography. The aesthetic of the book is totally engaging and Du Bois's use of language verges on the sublime. This forms a sharp contrast to *The Philadelphia Negro* which is in the style of a sociological monograph (examples from both books are given in a workshop exercise associated with this chapter: see Part IV of the book). It is the combination of fact and moving testimony which stimulated *The Times* reviewer in England to write that *The Souls* 'is an extraordinary compound of *emotions* and *statistics*' (my emphasis).

Gates (1989) has argued that no other text (except possibly the King James Bible) has had more impact on the shaping of the African American literary tradition. Du Bois as a master craftsperson of language manages to rise above the veil of colour to communicate the violence and injustice of segregation and racism to white audiences. Gates suggests that rather than reflecting history, *The Souls* makes history:

> How can a work be 'more history-making than historical?' It becomes so when it crosses the barrier between mainly conveying information, and primarily signifying an act of language itself, an object to be experienced, analysed and enjoyed aesthetically. (1989:xvi–xvii)

Clearly, then, Du Bois had made a choice to change the rhetorical nature of his writing, leaving the rhetoric of the sociological monograph and using a whole range of representational strategies to convey social criticism and make social commentary. The literary critique of research writing points to the quite rigid writing conventions which determine the form of academic research writing. Du Bois shows us the potential for developing a range of rhetorical strategies.

It is beyond the scope of this chapter to suggest in a programmatic fashion what such a multiple writing strategy might look like. But rather than relying on the academic formats of publishing (for example, books, chapters and journal articles) one might think of a variety of ways to disseminate research findings. It still seems to be the case that social researchers view popular genres of writing like journalism to be simplistic, intellectually inferior and somehow beneath them. Yet having dabbled in journalism myself, I realize the skill involved in expressing sometimes complicated arguments in clear and accessible ways. It is my feeling that as researchers we need to be more promiscuous with regard to the genres of writing that we use to convey our message. Equally, autobiographical and fictional modes of writing might be used in productive ways to represent research findings. An attention to the literary critique of social science writing may help in providing rhetorical ways to supplement, rather than replace, the poetics of social research.

CONCLUSION

Roland Barthes (1977b: 148) once commented that the unity of texts lies not in authorship and writing but in the destination of written work, in other words the creative process of reading. I am not so convinced that as active researchers we should submit completely to this notion of the 'death of the author'. Barthes indicates that one can never control completely the ways in which texts are read. Yet there are possibilities for researchers to exercise a greater influence over how their messages are interpreted. One of the problems in the relationship between social research and wider society is the addiction of some social and cultural researchers to relativistic forms of discourse, and a resistance to making conclusive, absolute statements. This is often interpreted as showing a lack of clarity. The public allure of science and research can itself be used rhetorically in a self-conscious fashion. This point is made well by Jayaratne and Stewart (1991) who offer an instrumental strategy to use the social authority of research, fact and science to achieve feminist outcomes. The literary turn in the social sciences offers us fresh insights into the textual dimensions of social investigation. We must seek to turn these insights into useful tools, whereby we can think again about the way in which we express and disseminate our ideas and findings. Developing the rhetoric of writing will help researchers find new ways of intervening within public life and may enable us to reach wider audiences in a more effective way.

Further reading

Clifford and Marcus (1986) is a classic text which introduced the literary turn to anthropological writing. Atkinson (1990) shows how sociological ethnographies can be understood as deploying rhetorical strategies. Yearley (1981) applies this perspective to the production of texts in natural science.

Part IV

WORKSHOP AND DISCUSSION EXERCISES

INTRODUCTION

These exercises are based on the experience of the contributors (and others in the Department of Sociology at Goldsmiths) teaching research methods to students at both undergraduate and postgraduate levels. They are intended to improve understanding of the ideas expressed in the chapters, and give practice in the techniques described. In many cases they are suitable for group work, where students can join together to do the exercises. They are not intended to be wholly prescriptive: they can be modified to suit particular learning needs. In many cases there is no 'right answer', but the exercises will nevertheless enable you to form a deeper and more practical understanding of the material.

Chapter 2: Selected issues in the philosophy of social science

2.1 What, in your view, are the major features of a *science*?

2.2 Explain the arguments for:

(a) treating social sciences as analogous to natural sciences and

(b) rejecting the notion of the methodological unity of natural and social sciences.

2.3 What do you understand by the terms *value freedom* and *objectivity*?

2.4 Why do certain theorists (for example, Stanley and Wise, Rosaldo) criticize the idea that emotions are best kept out of social science?

Chapter 3: Developments in social theory

3.1 Take each of the following theoretical perspectives in turn: functionalism, action theory, symbolic interactionism, phenomenology, ethnomethodology, structuralism, post-structuralism and post-modernism. Answer the following questions for *each* perspective:

(a) How could researchers working within this perspective use *quantitative* methods (for example, social surveys, official statistics, content analysis, counting events)?

(b) How could researchers working within this perspective use *qualitative* methods (for example, participant observation, qualitative interviews, semiotics, discourse and conversation analysis)?

(c) Are there any theoretical perspectives where it is not possible to think of examples?

3.2 Why is interpretive social theory said to draw upon *idealism*?

3.3 Which theoretical perspectives illustrate a *realist* approach?

3.4 How can the method of deconstruction help researchers who want to alleviate human suffering?

Chapter 4: Feminist methodology

4.1 What are the chief feminist criticisms of other forms of social and cultural research? Describe the variety of ways in which feminists have tried to remedy these problems.

4.2 Outline two research projects designed to achieve feminist objectives, one using qualitative methods, the other using quantitative methods.

4.3 Why has positivist methodology been described as androcentric?

4.4 How should feminist researchers approach the issues of objectivity and value freedom?

4.5 Is any single research method distinctively 'feminist'?

Chapter 5: Gender, ethnicity and fieldwork: a case study

5.1 In the light of the chapter, assess the claim that only women researchers can get authentic accounts of women's lives, black researchers of black people's lives, and so on.

5.2 What does the chapter demonstrate about the relationship between theory and 'reality'?

5.3 In what way does the chapter illustrate the political nature of social research?

5.4 What does the chapter tell us about the possibilities of objective, value-free social science?

5.5 In which area(s) of social theory (outlined in Chapter 3) can this research study be located?

Chapter 6: The history of the social survey

6.1 What were the chief methodological innovations developed by Booth, Rowntree and Bowley?

6.2 In what ways did the surveys of Booth and Rowntree participate in the Victorian social construction of poverty?

6.3 Assess the argument that the production of social statistics is inevitably linked with the mentality of government.

6.4 Explain the difference between descriptive and explanatory social surveys.

Chapter 7: Historical and comparative research

7.1 Outline a research study investigating any of the following phenomena in which the advantages of the historical and comparative method are maximized: childhood, dying and mourning, housing, the marketplace, money, educational systems, health care, childbirth. Specify the sources of data you will use.

7.2 What are the characteristics, the strengths and the limitations of the experimental method when used in historical and comparative research?

7.3 How can a sensitivity to historical and cross-cultural comparison help researchers?

Chapter 8: Research and social policy

8.1 In the context of any social problem you choose (for example, homelessness, racism, sexism), outline what you think to be a relevant research problem. Now discuss the following questions:

   (a) How does your research topic differ from the common-sense version of your selected social problem?

   (b) If your research topic sticks very closely to this common-sense version of the problem, how does it benefit from the insights of social science?

   (c) If your research problem differs from how we usually see this social problem, how can your proposed research contribute to society?

8.2 This exercise gives you an opportunity to think through the various ways researchers have answered Becker's question: 'Whose side are we on?' You are asked to imagine that research funding is available for whatever topic and research design you prefer.

   (a) Suggest a research topic and outline a methodology using one or more of the methods set out in Part III of this book.

   (b) Justify the topic and methodology from the point of view of (i) the scholar and (ii) the partisan.

   (c) Now select any one article which reports research findings in a social science journal. Which of the positions referred to in (b) does it adopt?

(d) Set out how this position might be criticized from the point of view of (i) the other position and (ii) your own views on the relevance of social science research.

Chapter 9: Research and social theory

9.1 This exercise asks you to think further about the different research strategies used by Moerman and Douglas.

(a) How far do (i) Moerman and (ii) Douglas make use of the five points listed towards the end of the chapter to help them theorize about data? (These were *chronology, context, comparison, implications* and *lateral thinking*.)

(b) Imagine that you were carrying out a study of a small group already known to you (for example, a family, a friendship group or club). How could you use either Moerman's or Douglas's ideas to help you work out a research problem and to theorize about your data?

9.2 This exercise encourages you to think further about the different ways of conceiving family life. Imagine that you wish to do an observational study of the family. Now consider the following questions:

(a) What are the advantages and disadvantages of obtaining access to the family household?

(b) In what ways may families be studied outside the household setting? What methodology might you use and what questions could you ask?

(c) What might observation tell you about the 'family' in each of the following settings: law courts, doctor–patient consultations, television soap operas?

(d) Either do a study of one of these settings or write hypothetically about all three.

9.3 What does it mean to say you are studying the 'family' (that is, within inverted commas)?

Chapter 10: Writing a research proposal

10.1 With a partner or a small group, choose *one* of the following topics: students who are in paid employment; men who stay at home to look after children while wives or partners go out to work; youth crime.

Individually draft an outline research proposal in line with the areas discussed in this chapter, paying particular attention to the aims and objectives, method, data analysis, and dissemination. You can use any of the methods in the book.

Discuss your outline proposal with other(s), who should ask questions to clarify the reasons for planning a study in this area, what the study aims to achieve, how it will be done, and whether the findings will be useful. Take note of the questions which you would ask others in order to be convinced of their proposal.

Chapter 11: Doing social surveys

11.1 Pick one or more of the sampling frames listed in Figure 11.5 (p. 136). Discuss the adequacy of these lists in covering the populations concerned. What omissions are there likely to be? What problems of access might there be in getting these lists, and in approaching people listed on them? What stratifying factors are likely to be present and useful for each sampling frame?

11.2 The questionnaire in Figure IV.1 was distributed to passengers on an overnight car train arriving in Brive, France as they left the train early in the morning. Piles of the questionnaires were left at the entrance to a hall where a breakfast was being served. A notice asked for passengers to help by completing a questionnaire, and a box was provided in which people could place their completed questionnaires.

(a) Discuss the issues of external validity involved in this exercise.

(b) Discuss the adequacy of the questionnaire design.

(c) How would you design and carry out a survey of tourists visiting a specified geographical area? Make sure you state the aims of the survey, design an interview or questionnaire, and describe your sampling strategy.

11.3 In a group of three or more, design a short interview schedule, containing some open, some closed and some pre-coded questions. The topic may be anything of which people in the group can reasonably be expected to have some experience (for example, watching or participating in sports events, studying research methods).

One person should use the interview schedule to interview another person in the group, while others observe, considering the following issues:

(a) What difficulties were there in doing the interview?

(b) Did the interviewer appear or feel at ease?

Trains Auto-Couchettes

Please fill in this questionnaire by circling the answers that apply and indicate your name and address in the space below. Thank you.

Name:
Address:

1 What is your country of origin?
0 No answer	1 England	2 Belgium	3 Denmark	4 Scotland
5 Finland	6 France	7 Ireland	8 Netherlands	9 Wales
10 West Germany	11 Sweden	12 Other		

2 What is your destination?
0 No answer	1 Brive	2 Corrèze	3 Lot
4 Dordogne	5 Limousin	6 Auvergne	7 Atlantic coast
8 Mediterranean coast	9 Pyrenees	10 Spain	11 Tarn

3 Have you heard of Corrèze before?
0 No answer   1 Yes   2 No

4 How often have you been to Brive?
0 No answer   1 Never   2 Once   3 Twice   4 Three times
5 More than three times

5 Who helped you choose and book your stay?
0 No answer   1 Travel agency   2 Tourist authority   3 Local reservation service
4 Friends   5 Yourself   6 French Motorail   7 Other

6 How did you find information about our region?
0 No answer   1 Press advertisement   2 Exhibition/fair   3 Travel agency
4 Tourist authority   5 By word of mouth

7 Was the documentation on this region of any use to you while planning your trip?
0 No answer   1 Yes   2 No

8 What kind of holidays do you prefer?
0 No answer   1 Organized tours   2 Self-planned itinerary   3 Gastronomic tour
4 Sporting holiday   5 Other

9 If you appreciate active holidays, which are the sports you would like to do in Corrèze?
0 No answer	1 Canoeing 2 Fishing 3 Hiking		4 Horse riding
5 Golf	6 Tennis 7 Rock climbing		8 Rafting
9 Hunting	10 Mountain biking	11 Water sports	12 Hang gliding

10 What kind of accommodation would you prefer for your holidays?
0 No answer	1 Furnished	2 Camping*	3 Camping**
4 Camping***	5 Camping****	6 Gîtes France	7 Holiday camp
8 Hotel*	9 Hotel**	10 Hotel***	11 Hotel****
12 Holiday home	13 Bed and breakfast	14 Other	

11 Briefly, what does Corrèze evoke for you?
0 No answer   1 Pleasant climate   2 Lakes and reservoirs   3 Mountains
4 Cultural and historical heritage   5 Gastronomy
6 Beautiful countryside/places of interest

12 Would you consider spending your holidays here?
0 No answer   1 Yes   2 No

13 Would you like to be kept informed about holiday breaks and round trips in our region?
0 No answer   1 Yes   2 No

14 Observations:

Figure IV.1: *Questionnaire distributed to train passengers*

(c) Did the respondent appear or feel at ease?

(d) Did the respondent find the questions unambiguous and easy to answer?

(e) Did he or she find them relevant to his/her life experience?

Swap roles, until everyone has had a go at interviewing, replying, and observing.

How would you now redesign the interview schedule?

11.4 Imagine that you are engaged in a small-scale interviewing survey, designed to discover how people feel about balancing the demands of home life with those of their work life. You have the resources to interview about 20 people. How would you select people to interview?

11.5 Examine the questions in Figure 11.6 (p. 143), taken from Bruce and Filmer's (1983) survey of craftspeople. How well do they indicate the concepts which they are designed to indicate (level of involvement in craftwork, income, and level and usefulness of training)?

Imagine that you are to survey members of another occupational group (say, doctors, teachers, shopkeepers, road sweepers, painters and decorators, people doing housework). Design questions to indicate the same concepts and discuss their adequacy with other members of your group.

Chapter 12: Coding and analysing data

12.1 For this exercise you will need some questionnaire items, some of which are *pre-coded*, others *closed* and others *open*. Examples of these are in Figure 11.1. There are other examples of questions in Figures 11.3 (p. 130), 11.6 (p. 133), 16.1 (p. 143) and IV.1 (p. 206). You are also likely to have an interview schedule, and some data, if you have carried out Exercise 11.3.

Having chosen a number of items you will need to generate answers to the questions, either by asking them of at least five people, or by using your imagination. Now you have some data and can prepare it for quantitative analysis.

Draw up a coding scheme which indicates the variable names and the value labels. Using a square grid of boxes, fill in the values of the data matrix. If you are learning SPSS or some other statistical software package you can try entering these data and producing some frequency counts.

12.2 Examine the transcript of a taped interview between Jocelyn Cornwell and one of her interviewees (Wendy) reproduced below. This is from a study reported in Cornwell (1981). Then do the following:

(a) Consider what themes you can 'find' in this extract. How would you interpret the meanings in this extract? Mark your transcript down the right-hand margin.

(b) Consider what assumptions you have made. What have you found difficult? Are you drawing on a feminist theory of gender? If not, would coding from a feminist perspective affect what you could 'find' in the data? Why? Why not?

(c) Make a list of possible codes for this passage. Are these codes objective? What decisions have you taken in choosing particular codes to characterize particular words or phrases in particular ways? How do you account for similarities and differences in coding between other people in your group who have coded the extract? What has been left out? Can the use of such codes give us agreed interpretations of these data? If codes are not agreed, what use are our interpretations?

(d) Report back to the rest of the workshop. Can interviews of this sort be used as a basis for generalizing about the beliefs, practices and feelings of women? Does this interview raise any ethical issues?

(e) If you are using a computer package for analysing qualitative data such as NUD • IST or ETHNOGRAPH you may find it helpful to enter the data and your codes and use the computer to search for coded segments, or segments where codes overlap.

(f) You could repeat this Exercise using the speech in Exercise 19.1.

Interview transcript

Jocelyn:	Last time we met, you told me that between the times	1
	that we'd seen each other, you'd been in hospital, and	2
	had had an operation.	3
Wendy:	That's right, I had er the hysterectomy done last year.	4
Jocelyn:	Can you tell me about that, about, take me back to the	5
	beginning with what happened. Were you unwell, what	6
	happened?	7
Wendy:	It was mainly cos I'd been on the pill for twelve years,	8
	and because of my age and the fact I smoked. I was	9
	reaching what they classed as erm a risk barrier, at risk	10
	age, and they wanted me to come off the pill. I'd been	11
	using the pill mainly to regulate my periods all that time.	12
	So I knew that if I come off, I'd be having a lot of	13
	problems, and basically the doctor suggested other forms	14
	of contraceptive, but it wouldn't have helped me as far as	15
	the bleeding was concerned.	16

Jocelyn:	What was the bleeding about?	17
Wendy:	My periods had never regulated from the time I'd started,	18
	so I used to bleed heavily, and maybe lose for ten, fifteen	19
	days at a time. The only thing that really regulated it was,	20
	was the pill. But it was getting to a stage that that wasn't	21
	easing it off any more.	22
Jocelyn:	Right.	23
Wendy:	It was unusual. I used to bleed for just five days while I	24
	was on the pill. I used to know exactly when my periods	25
	would start. It used to be sort of like 3.30 on a Wednesday	26
	afternoon, and then it started to change. I was starting to	27
	lose maybe on the Tuesday, heavier and for longer. And	28
	I found that strange considering all them years it had	29
	stayed the same.	30
Jocelyn:	Did you talk to anyone about it before you went to see	31
	the doctor?	32
Wendy:	No, no.	33
Jocelyn:	No one at all?	34
Wendy:	No, I was just worried myself that there might be	35
	something wrong.	36
Jocelyn:	Did you ever talk about anything of that kind with either	37
	Sandra or with your mother?	38
Wendy:	No.	39
Jocelyn:	No, or with friends?	40
Wendy:	No, no. I would, I would tell them after I'd already sorted	41
	it out myself. But I would just automatically follow through	42
	on something myself. Go to my own doctor, or the family	43
	planning clinic.	44
Jocelyn:	And did they talk to you about that sort of thing or not?	45
Wendy:	No, no, it was never discussed. When I was younger nothing	46
	like that was ever discussed. Something that you just . . .	47
	well I've always dealt with it on my own, I suppose I could	48
	talk to my mum about it, I just never did. Something I never	49
	spoke to her about.	50
Jocelyn:	So you went to see the doctor, and she said, she sent you	51
	to the hospital.	52
Wendy:	She suggested, well she said it was my body, and it was my	53
	choice. Cos, they said I could go on for quite a few years like	54

	it. But they did want me off the pill, and that I wasn't willing	55
	to do, just come off the the pill and take a chance on what	56
	would happen.	57

Jocelyn: Who was it who first mentioned having a hysterectomy then, 58
you or them? 59

Wendy: Me. 60

Jocelyn: You? 61

Wendy: Yes, on the, erm the second occasion when I went to the 62
hospital, that was my suggestion. He asked me what I 63
wanted done and I said I wanted the lot taken away, and 64
he said fine. The first doctor didn't want to know, he 65
said I wasn't old enough. There was nothing they could do. 66

Jocelyn: How old, how old were you? 67

Wendy: About 33, 32 or 33. And then they wasn't willing to do it. 68

Jocelyn: What made you think of that as an option? Were you, you 69
were given other options, were you given the option of 70
being sterilized, or anything like that? 71

Wendy: No, sterilization wouldn't have made any difference to the 72
bleeding. 73

Jocelyn: Right. 74

Wendy: That's just a form of contraception. As far as the bleeding's 75
concerned, it's a matter of trial and testing different drugs. 76
And I know other women that have maybe done that for 77
four years. Tried drugs, don't work. Tried a different one, 78
it doesn't work, try another one, it doesn't work. And they 79
still end up having the hysterectomy done anyway. I don't 80
see why I should go through all that hassle for two, three, 81
four years, just for the same end result anyway. Makes you 82
feel rather like a guinea pig, just testing out the drugs for 83
them to see if they work. It's annoying, most of the 84
gynaecologists are men anyway, so they don't know what 85
you're going through. It's fine for a doctor to sit there and 86
say you can go on for another ten years. He doesn't have 87
that problem every month. 88

Jocelyn: You see I think that um a great many people would find it 89
shocking that you chose that as an option. 90

Wendy: Well. No not really. I've got my children. If you want to 91
look at it that way, that's what the womb is for. The 92
womb is for reproduction, I've done my bit! I've got my 93

two, I didn't want any more, so it was fine for me to have   94
it taken away.   95

Jocelyn: Did you have any idea, have you ever had any idea   96
           about why you have always bled so much, why, why your   97
           periods haven't ever been regulated?   98

Wendy: No, I'd never, from the time mine started when I was at   99
           school, I never knew when I would start, I never knew   100
           how heavy I would lose. I used to be at home maybe for   101
           three or four days in bed. I was that ill. And the only time I 102
           wasn't was when I was on the pill. The doctor at the family 103
           planning said like they will regulate. I said I'm thirty! If they 104
           haven't regulated in fifteen years I said I don't think they're 105
           going to now. But she just didn't want me to have it no   106
           more cos I smoked. That was it. She wanted me to stop   107
           smoking and I wouldn't. So I got my pills from my doctor   108
           instead! Just changed.   109

Jocelyn: Did she give you any explanation for why you needed to   110
           stop smoking that was connected to whether or not she   111
           would prescribe the pill?   112

Wendy: Because as you get older your blood thickens, you're more 113
           susceptible of getting thrombosis etc., etc. Smoking also 114
           thickens the blood. And taking the pill also does the same, 115
           so for me I had three factors.   116

Jocelyn: Getting older, taking the pill, smoking.   117

Wendy: Getting older, taking the pill, smoking. I can't stop getting 118
           older! I wanted to stay on the pill, but I could give up   119
            smoking, you know what I mean, so that was it, you cut   120
           out the smoking and you can keep the pill.   121

Jocelyn: And what's the consequence of this been? You had the   122
           operation a year ago?   123

Wendy: Yes, I had it done last year. And I felt fine, never had no 124
           problems. Obviously same problems as anyone has after   125
           an operation, but nothing drastic.   126

Jocelyn: Um, has it made any difference to your sense of yourself? 127

Wendy: Err, no. I mean some, some women sort of say they feel   128
           less of a woman for it, I don't. Not at all. I'm same as I   129
           was before. Just can't have children. That's it. I feel better 130
           in myself healthwise, because I don't have them problems   131
           every month that I had before.   132

Chapter 13: Statistical reasoning: from one to two variables

13.1 (a) Using the data matrix in Table 13.1 (p. 166) draw a frequency distribution for the variable *Working*. Do the same for *Age*, recoding it into three broad categories. Draw a bar chart of these distributions. Calculate the mean, median and mode for each variable.

(b) Now construct contingency tables that show the relationship between: *Sex* and *Working*; *Sex* and *Jobsat*; *Working* and *Jobsat*. Ensure that each cell contains a count and column and row percentages. Describe the character of the relationships which you find.

(c) Now, draw a scattergram, plotting *Age* against *Jobsat*. Describe the character of this relationship.

(d) Using the recoded version of *Age* construct contingency tables showing the relationship between this variable and each of the other three variables. Describe the character of the relationships you find.

(e) If you are learning SPSS or another statistical package and have entered these data, you will find it easier to get the computer to do these things. You can also generate tests of association and significance and consider the meaning of these.

13.2 Table IV.1 consists of four contingency tables demonstrating different types of relationship between the two variables of social class and home ownership. Below each is a *p*-value and the result of a test of association

Table IV.1   *Tables showing different relationships between social class and home ownership (column %)*

(a)

Home ownership	Social class		
	Lower	Middle	Upper
Owner	20	30	50
Private, rented	30	40	30
Council, rented	50	30	20

$p < 0.01$, $Q = 0.6$.

(b)

Home ownership	Social class		
	Lower	Middle	Upper
Owner	60	40	3
Private, rented	35	35	45
Council, rented	5	25	52

$p < 0.01$, $Q = -0.8$.

(c)

Home ownership	Social class		
	Lower	Middle	Upper
Owner	33	32	36
Private, rented	30	28	33
Council, rented	37	40	31

$p < 0.05$, $Q = 0.04$.

(d)

Home ownership	Social class		
	Lower	Middle	Upper
Owner	56	10	59
Private, rented	23	20	22
Council, rented	21	70	19

$p < 0.01$, $Q = -0.02$.

(*Q*). For each table, describe the character of the relationship and explain why the *p*-values and tests of association vary.

Chapter 14: Statistical reasoning: causal arguments and multivariate analysis

14.1 Choose any article or book that reports the results of a *qualitative* research study. What sort of causal propositions does the author assume to be true? What sort of causal arguments are contained in the text? How could these be tested in quantitative data analysis? What would the independent and dependent variables be?

14.2 Table 14.2 and the discussion that accompanies it suggests that hospice care may cause people to want euthanasia. What plausible objections might there be to this causal argument? How could they be tested in further research? How could qualitative research be used to investigate this proposition?

14.3 Take Table IV.1(a) to be a zero-order table. Draw hypothetical conditional or first-order tables that you might expect to find by entering the test variable of *income*, measured as low or high. The pairs of tables should, in turn, illustrate (a) the existence of a *spurious* or *intervening* relationship between social class and home ownership; (b) *replication* of the original relationship; (c) *specification* of the original relationship; (d) *suppression* of a stronger relationship.

Chapter 15: Using official statistics

15.1 This is a structured exercise in reading a statistical table that aims to give you a general strategy for perceiving the main messages of such tables. You could apply this approach to Table 15.2 in this book, or find tables suggested in Exercise 15.2 (p. 200). You will find that not all of the questions are relevant to every table, but experience has shown that these steps, if followed carefully, enable a deeper understanding of any statistical table.

(a) Read the title before you look at any numbers. What does this reveal about the content of the table?

(b) Look at the source: who produced the data, with what purpose? Was it a census or a sample?

(c) Look at any notes above or below the table. How will they influence its scope and your interpretation?

(d) Read the column and row titles. They indicate which variables are applied to the data.

(e)   How many variables are there and what are they? Can any be considered independent or dependent?

(f)   How are the variables measured? Are there any omissions or peculiarities in the measurement scale? How else might such a measure have been constructed?

(g)   What units are used – percentages, thousands, millions? If you are dealing with percentages, then which way adds up to 100%?

(h)   Look at the 'All' or 'Total' column. These are usually found on the right-hand column and/or the bottom row (the 'margins' of a table). What do variations in the row or column tell you about the variables concerned?

(i)   Now look at some rows and/or columns *inside* the table. What do these tell you about the relationships between variables? What social processes might have generated the trends you find?

(j)   Is it possible to make causal statements about the relationship between variables? If so, do any of these involve the interaction of more than two variables?

(k)   What are the shortcomings of the data in drawing conclusions about social processes?

(l)   What other enquiries could be conducted to take this analysis further?

(m) Finally, consider the issue of whether the table reveals something about social reality, or creates a particular way of thinking about reality.

15.2 Choose a topic of interest to you, for example, ethnicity, gender differences, class inequalities, educational inequalities, family structure, health differences. Find some tables of official statistics on your chosen topic in the reference section of your library. Do not choose data that are already presented in graph form. Some examples of UK statistical series that you are likely to find are: *Social Trends; General Household Survey; Annual Abstract of Statistics; Population Trends; Mortality Statistics; Decennial Census; Marriage and Divorce Statistics.*

Present an analysis of up to four tables of data from such publications relevant to your chosen topic. Consider questions like: what do the tables tell you about the topic? What might explain the patterns you see? How might the way in which the statistics were collected affect the conclusions that can be reached? How would the tables need to be modified (in other words, broken down by other variables) in order to take your enquiry further? What further data would need to be collected in order to take your enquiry further?

You may find it relevant to recalculate and re-present data in simpler or graph form to clarify the main messages of the tables analysed. Speculate on the links between the tables chosen: conduct an *enquiry* into the topic by analysing the data from the various tables. Make sure you consider critically the measurement validity of the variables involved.

Chapter 16: Qualitative interviewing

16.1 Examine the section 'Criticisms of the classical approach' in this chapter. Look back to Figure 11.1 (p. 130) or 11.3 (p. 133) or any structured questionnaire or interview schedule, especially one using fixed-choice items. Do the criticisms seem justified? Do some items seem more problematic than others? Could the problems be solved by reformulating the questions?

16.2 Read the transcript of a taped interview between Jocelyn Cornwell and Wendy used in Exercise 12.2. Then consider the following questions:

   (a) To what extent is Wendy's account a 'public' one, rather than the sort of thing she might have said 'privately'? How might the account have been different if the interviewer had been a man, or had not known Wendy well already?

   (b) What, in Wendy's speech, suggests that she was concerned to display particular qualities of character during the interview? How does she make her account persuasive?

   (c) What does this interview tell us about what has happened to Wendy in her medical consultations and in her talks with other people? Can we infer anything about the quality of these relationships from this interview?

16.3 The aim of this exercise is to produce interview data on students' experiences of studying and thus to experience some of the problems of asking questions and understanding answers in an unstructured interview.

   (a) The workshop should be divided into groups of three or four.

   (b) Each group should draw up a short *topic guide* for unstructured interviews with other students. Focus on a specific aspect of experience (for example, reasons for coming to university, financial problems, reactions to lectures and classes) and work out some questions.

   (c) Each group should choose an interviewer, an interviewee and one or two observers.

   (d) The interviewer should interview the interviewee using the topic guide. The observer should write down as much as they can of what the interviewee says. Then change roles, and do another interview.

(e) Compare the two interviews and discuss what you have found out. Consider the language of the questions. What do these take for granted? How far is the interviewer sharing understandings with the interviewee? How could the interview be improved?

Chapter 17: Doing ethnography

17.1 This discussion exercise involves thinking again about the methods used by Fortier in her study of Italian social life (Chapter 5). When you have read her account, try to answer the following questions:

(a) To what extent was Fortier a stranger in this social setting? How did this influence what she 'saw'?

(b) In terms of Junker's four observer roles, which of these best characterizes the research? What were the advantages and disadvantages of the role adopted?

(c) How did Fortier gain access to the setting? What obstacles did she face? Did she find herself 'sponsored' by anyone? What did her access negotiations reveal about the power relations within the setting?

(d) How did Fortier use her relations in the field as a source of data? What personal strains did this entail? What ethical issues did this raise? Did her 'ascribed characteristics' (for example, her gender), dictate what she observed?

(e) What issues of reliability, validity and representativeness were entailed in the research?

(f) What role did social theory play in the research? Was it generated from data, or did theory guide observation?

(g) Whose 'side' was Fortier on?

17.2 This is a field-based exercise in ethnographic methods using observation techniques.

(a) Choose a social setting where you can act as an observer more than a participant. Examples of suitable settings are: council meetings; student union meetings; libraries; interaction between people providing a service (shop workers, doctors' receptionists and so on) and clients; pubs; launderettes; public transport.

(b) Record what you see and hear as fully and as neutrally as possible, that is without making inferences about why people are doing whatever they are doing. Note the sequence of events, the frequency, any patterns you can discern as well as groupings and non-verbal behaviour. Briefly describe the physical setting of the room. You may find it necessary to concentrate on a particular group, or person.

(c) Write on-the-spot observations on one side of a double-sided page of a notebook; on the opposite side of the page write down your own thoughts about what is going on so that you separate your observation from your interpretation. Write down any difficulties you experience and note any instances of when your observing seems to be affecting the scene you are observing. If you are doing this with a partner, you may find it interesting to compare notes, looking for any similarities and differences in what you recorded.

(d) Then try to interpret what you have seen. You should be concerned with trying to explain what you have been observing and hearing, and to a degree participating in. Your interpretation should try to understand what has been going on from the perspective of those you have been observing.

(e) Consider whether there are any aspects or themes which seem worth exploring further. Discuss what you have learned about the problems and possibilities of participant observation as a method of data collection.

Some advice: people beginning this sort of research often have difficulty in 'seeing' the unusual in situations which initially seem pretty routine. To avoid producing a purely descriptive account of 'what happened' try observing two contrasting examples of the setting (for example: compare an academic library with a public one; compare queuing at a bus stop with queuing in a takeaway shop). This can often help you see the underlying rules of interaction that are being used by participants. If you are observing a social situation that is strange to you, see if you can find a person to 'guide' you through it; such an informal sponsor can help by explaining the underlying rules of the situation, as well as showing you how to pass successfully as a member.

17.3 Below is an extract from the field notes of a practising ethnographer, Daniel Miller, who did fieldwork in Trinidad in 1988. This was published in Miller (1994). These sections of the notes contain records of conversations, observations and other techniques relevant to how Trinidadians liked to view and talk about a US-made soap opera 'The Young and the Restless', which in Miller's words concentrated 'on the domestic life and turmoil of wealthy families in a generalised American city' (1994: 247–8). In his final research report Miller argues that Trinidadians use their viewing of this programme to express a spirit which they call 'bacchanal', which 'can refer to [a] general level of excitement and disorder, [but also involves] the emergence into light of things which normally inhabit the dark ... directed against the pretensions of

various establishment forms, revealing their hollow or false nature.'
(Miller, 1994: 246–7).

Examine these field notes and answer the following questions:

(a) Which of them describe people's actions, and which their words?

(b) What details of the context of actions and words are given? Are there
any notes that suggest what Miller was doing? For example, is there
any evidence of him having questioned people?

(c) Is any counting involved? Where do the numbers appear to come
from, and what do they tell us?

(d) Are there any *analytic memos*, in which Miller reflects on what the
observations mean to him?

(e) How objective and representative do these observations appear to
be?

(f) How could notes like this be improved?

Field notes extract

507:    Longdenville women, both addicts of Y&R, since view it daily, say – it's
about young people, about relations between rich and poor, tend
always to go back to the first person you loved, eg in own family elder
sister went with moslem boy, married off by parents to hindu man but
she left husband, gone back to first man and had child by him.

614:    result of my survey of all media: note 70% watched Y&R, news just less
but then nothing else over 30%, asking who watched (I guess regularly
50% women, 30% men)

622:    even panmen watch Y&R

641:    Rene: I discuss TV with sister, neighbours or with people in the health
centre – have to get back by 12 to see it, when my neighbour gets back
from her friends where she watches – we discuss, very exciting right
now. Where Brad's first wife taken him away but he doesn't know why
he's doing it; people who come from America saw it already.

(Me: most Trinidadians asked to describe the character of their islands in one
word would say 'bacchanal' with a smile that suggests affectionate pride
triumphing over shame.)

EY18: Women talk about Y&R: 'I prefer that, you see it is safer to talk about
the celebrities business than to talk about people business, you won't
get into trouble, nobody won't cuss you if you say Chancellor was with
this one's husband you just won't get into trouble. Although it is gossip
won't be anybody's personal life … but it is just bacchanal, all them

soaps is just bacchanal ... even if you don't like what is happening on the show you could even admire their earrings or their pearl necklaces; their hairdressing is exotic ... I would copy Brad's wife although I won't like to have a husband like Brad. I like Cricket, I like Tracy and I like Lauren.' Talking about marriage in Trinidad: 'I find it should be 50–50 not 30–70. The woman have to be strong, she have to believe in her vows no matter what ... that make me remember Y&R – Vickie want her marriage to work but Victor is in love with somebody else, but she is still holding on.'

ET21: Everybody does watch Y&R, 'when they tell me Mamy they like so and so's clothes in the picture, so I would sit down on Friday evenings and watch it to see the style. I don't have ties during the day. If watch it from TV I can copy the style. The last style copied was a style Ashley had – low cut across with a frill and a mini.' It is a black and white TV so she buy a black skirt, don't know what colour it really was. Copied Cassandra's jacket with the gathers on top; got the T shirt from Young and Restless.

Chapter 18: Analysing cultural objects: content analysis and semiotics

18.1 This exercise involves doing a content analysis of a women's magazine to answer the question: 'What are the main attributes in terms of which women are represented?' It is helpful to do this with another person, though you can work on your own.

(a) *Defining categories*   Look through the magazine, image by image, and discuss the images (look at both advertisements and editorial images to get a large enough selection). Develop a limited list of categories (about four to eight) which you think describe the main attributes ascribed to women in the images: for example, 'active', 'passive', 'looked at', 'looking', 'sexual', 'professional', 'nurturing', 'in leisure activity'. At this stage, you simply want to be able to assign each image to at least one category. If an image does not fit the categories already defined, think of another.

(b) *Assigning images to categories*   Once your list is complete, go through the magazine, image by image, assigning the categories that apply to each one. Where there are disagreements over assignments, discuss these. Keep a tally of how many images are assigned to each category.

(c) *Analysis*   Look at the overall distribution of images across the various categories and try to draw some conclusions about how women are portrayed in this magazine. Which attributes predominate? Why do you think this is? Have your categories worked well? What different story would other categories have told? Do you think your findings can be generalized to other magazines or other media?

(d) You can apply this process to a variety of other media and to topics other than images of women. It is often illuminating to make statistical comparisons of different media, or to compare a medium in the past (say, 1960s children's comics) with the same genre today.

18.2 In this exercise you will do a semiotic analysis for which you will need to have collected a number of advertisements featuring women. For instance, select from a women's magazine all the advertisements for perfume. The overall concern is to gain knowledge of how meanings about gender are used, organized and produced within visual texts. For example, questions you might ask are: how are women portrayed? How is sexual difference represented? How are relationships between men and women depicted? Use semiotic concepts *(sign, signifier, signified, connotation, denotation)* to consider the following questions for each image (these are suggestions):

(a) What are the elements of the sign (the advertisement)? Look at images of people, settings, products, written text. Consider what they *signify:* what kinds of meanings and associations do they bring into the image? What kinds of codes of meaning do they draw on? How are these elements organized and related to each other (do they support or contradict each other, do they comment on each other)?

(b) How are the different meanings in the text related to the product advertised, and what meaning is thereby given to the product?

(c) Is there an overall ideological structure of meaning which emerges from the advertisement? (For example, what conclusions about gender do you think the advert leads the reader to?)

(d) In comparing the different advertisements, what can you infer about the range of possible constructions of gender available within advertising?

(e) You can apply this approach to other types of image too – say images of men in cigarette advertisements, or images of children in clothes catalogues.

Chapter 19: Analysing discourse

19.1 The extract below is from a 1994 British parliamentary debate concerning a move to lower the age of consent for homosexual intercourse from 21 to 16 years of age, which is the age of consent for heterosexual intercourse. You should read it and consider the following questions.

(a) Consider the different *discourses* that are being drawn upon to construct the speaker's arguments: for example, which moral, medical, 'expert' and political theories and ideas are being mobilized in order to support the speaker's position?

(b) How does the speaker construct a particular 'identity' or 'authority' for himself?

(c) How does the speech use variation and patterns of emphasis to create its rhetorical effect?

(d) Note the instances where the speaker draws on abstract ideals that are difficult to challenge, for example 'wisdom' or 'justice'. Are there alternative ways in which these ideals could have been drawn upon to create an argument *against* equalizing the age of consent?

Extract from a speech made in the House of Commons

Mr Neil Kinnock (Islwyn): I shall do my best to respond positively to your appeal, Mr Morris, in the interests of the Committee and in defiance of my record.

I support new clause 3, moved by the Hon. Member for Derbyshire, South (Mrs Currie), and I pay tribute to the way in which she has worked to ensure this debate. I hope that she will have the reward of achieving a necessary reform to the law.

I support the new clause, which provides for an age of consent for sexual relations common to both men and women, on three main grounds. First, it is equitable to treat both sexes the same. Secondly, it is rational to legislate for equal treatment, in terms of both sexual orientation and enforcement of the law. Thirdly, it is wise to decriminalise consensual sexual activity above the age of 16 at a time when the fearful disease AIDS has to be fought with all the information, counselling and promotion of greater safety in sexual relationships that we can muster or bring to bear as a consequence of our activities in the House.

I shall develop each of those arguments, but I must first emphasise an essential general principle: all that I say and all that is said by everyone who favours reform, whatever the age and the amendment that they prefer, refers to consensual sexual relations. The essential purpose of supporting change in the law is to remove the threat of prosecution and punishment for engaging in sexual activity, which to them is natural, from homosexual males above the age of 16. The purpose is emphatically not to provide any opportunity or excuse to anyone – heterosexual or homosexual – who seeks to impose his or her sexual will on anyone else.

I arrived at the decision that I should support the new clause and the common age of consent of 16 in two stages. It became obvious to me, as it did to many Hon. Members, that the age of consent, which was fixed at 21 in

1967, has long failed to deal with the realities of sexual orientation and civil liberties. There are significant difficulties in enforcing the law credibly and injustices and dangers inherent in continuing a system that criminalises male homosexuals before the age of 21.

Having reached that conclusion, I was faced with the question, 'What is the most appropriate age of consent if it is not 21?' The compromise of 18 automatically suggested itself. It is the age of majority and the age at which young men seem most able to decide for themselves about their sexual orientation. In short, it is not only the legal age of majority, but the biological age of maturity. It seemed to me to be a view that was sensible as an alternative to the current legal provision, liberal in terms of the accommodation of personal convictions and sexual orientation and realistic in terms of an individual's right to privacy.

Then, just when I was comfortable with that, the facts began to intervene. I had made the assumption that young men and young women were somehow more able to determine their sexuality at 16 if they were heterosexual. Because of that, I assumed that the heterosexual age of consent could reasonably remain lower than the homosexual age of consent. On reflection, however, it became difficult for me to convince myself that there was a difference in the capacity to decide among 16-year-olds.

If I and the majority of other heterosexual men knew our sexual orientation by the age of 16, why should not homosexuals be equally sure of their sexual orientation? The evidence has long existed to prove that people are sure, as the Hon. Member for Derbyshire, South said. The Wolfenden report, published 37 years ago, concluded: 'The main sexual pattern is laid down in the early years of life and ... usually fixed by the age of 16.'

More recently, the Royal College of Psychiatrists reported its long-held view: 'there is no developmental reason to treat young men and young women differently' in the law relating to the age of consent. Project Sigma, jointly financed by the Department of Health and the Medical Research Council, proffered strong evidence that homosexual orientation was fixed and understood by homosexuals by their mid teens. The British Medical Association holds the same view.

That evidence and other reliable, responsible material persuaded me that it would be wrong to continue to discriminate in the law between men who are homosexual and those who are heterosexual. It would also be wrong to continue to discriminate in the law between young men who are homosexual and young women who are heterosexual.

As a father, I must say that I was equally exercised about the prospect of my daughter and son engaging in heterosexual relations at 16. No father could think otherwise. Frankly, I just hope that had it been the case that either of my children had proved to be of homosexual orientation, I could have shown them the love, and understanding, as their parent, as several parents already do to their children in similar circumstances. I was not offered that test, for which I frankly give thanks. Faced with that prospect, however, as children grow up, who could conclude that we should discriminate in the law between different kinds of young people of different sexes on the basis of sexual orientation? How could we do that when we know that heterosexual relationships carry at least as much danger, as much menace and as much threat to young people's moral values as homosexual relationships? (Hansard, 1994: 81–2)

Chapter 20: Analysing conversation

20.1 This is a task designed to help you familiarize yourself with the transcription conventions used in conversation analysis. As a consequence, you should start to understand the logic of transcribing this way and be able to ask questions about how the speakers are organizing their talk.

Tape record no more than five minutes of talk in the public domain. One possibility is a radio call-in programme. Avoid using scripted drama productions as these may not contain recurrent features of natural interaction (such as overlap or repair). Do not try to record a television extract as the visual material will complicate both transcription and analysis.

Now go through the following steps:

(a) Attempt to transcribe your tape using the conventions in Table 20.1 (p. 264). Try to allocate turns to identified speakers where possible but don't worry if you can't identify a particular speaker (put ? at the start of a line in such cases).

(b) Encourage a friend to attempt the same task independently of you. Now compare transcripts and relisten to the tape recording to improve your transcript.

(c) Using this chapter as a guide, attempt to identify in your transcript any features in the organization of the talk (for example, adjacency pairs, preference organization, institutional talk and so on).

20.2 Examine Extracts I and II below (drawn from Atkinson and Drew, 1979: 52 and discussed in Heritage, 1984: 248–9):

(a) Why does Heritage argue that these extracts demonstrate that 'questioners attend to the fact that their questions are framed within normative expectations which have sequential implications' (1984: 249)? Use the concept of 'adjacency pairs' in your answer.

(b) In Extract II, What are the consequences of Ch. naming the person to whom his utterance is addressed? Why might children often engage in such naming? Use the concept of 'summons–answer'.

Extract I

1 *A*: Is there something bothering you or not?
2 (1.0)
3 *A*: Yes or no.
4 (1.5)
5 *A*: Eh?
6 *B*: No.

Extract II

1 *Ch*: Have to cut the:se Mummy.
2 (1.3)
3 *Ch*: Won't we Mummy?
4 (1.5)
5 *Ch*: Won't we?
6 *M*: Yes.

Chapter 21: Analysing literary texts

21.1 For this exercise you should select a work of literary fiction which you
have read and enjoyed. Consider the following questions:

(a) What signs does the book show of having emanated from a particular social or cultural context? What can it tell us about that context?

(b) Are there any indications about the social background of the author
(for example, social status, educational level, ethnic identity,
gender)? In what ways can you show that these have influenced the
content of the text?

(c) Are there any instructions, either explicit or implicit, about how the
book should be read? For example, are there any attempts to inter-
twine fiction and 'reality'?

(d) In what ways is the work ideological? Are there any political or
moral messages contained in the narrative or the ways in which
characters are presented?

Chapter 22: Reading and writing research

22.1 These two extracts from Du Bois's writing discuss the issue of infant
mortality within African American life. The first is taken from his
sociological monograph *The Philadelphia Negro* and the second is an

excerpt from his autobiographical essay 'On the passing of the first born' taken from *The Souls of Black Folk*. Here Du Bois writes about the death of his son and its significance to him as a black man living under segregation and racism. Compare and contrast the narrative voice, textual quality and 'empirical facts' in these two extracts. How, in each case, does the writer achieve authority and persuasiveness? What are the rhetorical aspects of each extract?

From The Philadelphia Negro *(1996)*

Separating the deaths by the sex of the deceased, we have:

Total death rate of Negroes, 1890 (still-births included)	32.42 per 1,000
For Negro males	36.02 " "
For Negro females	29.23 " "

Separating by age, we have

Total death rate, 1890 (still-births included)

All ages	32.42 per 1,000
Under fifteen	69.24 " "
Fifteen to twenty	13.61 " "
Twenty to twenty-five	14.50 " "
Twenty-five to thirty-five	15.21 " "
Thirty-five to forty-five	17.16 " "
Forty-five to fifty-five	29.41 " "
Fifty-five to sixty-five	40.09 " "
Sixty-five and over	116.49 " "

The large infant mortality is shown by the average annual rate of 171.44 (including still-births), for children under five years of age, during the years 1884 to 1890.

The statistics are very instructive. Compared with modern nations the death rate of Philadelphia Negroes is high, but not extraordinarily so: Hungary (33.7), Austria (30.6), and Italy (28.6) had in the years 1871–90 a larger average than the Negroes in 1891–96, and some of these lands surpass the rate of 1884–90. Many things combine to cause the high Negro death rate: poor heredity, neglect of infants, bad dwellings and poor food. On the other hand the age classification of city Negroes with its excess of females and young people of twenty to thirty-five years of age, must serve to keep the death rate lower than its rate would be under normal circumstances. The influence of bad sanitary surroundings is strikingly illustrated in the enormous death rate of the Fifth Ward – the worst Negro slum in the city, and the worst part of the city in respect to sanitation. On the other hand the low death rate in the Thirtieth Ward illustrates the influence of good houses and clean streets in a district where the better class of Negroes have recently migrated. (Du Bois, 1996: 150–1)

From The Souls of Black Folk *(1989)*

Blithe was the morning of his burial, with bird and song and sweet-smelling flowers. The trees whispered to the grass, but the children sat with hushed faces. And yet it seemed a ghostly unreal day – the wraith of Life. We seemed to rumble down an unknown street behind a little white bundle of posies, with the shadow of a song in our ears. The busy city dinned about us; they did not say much, those pale-faced hurrying men and women; they did not say much – they only glanced and said, 'Niggers!'

We could not lay him in the ground there in Georgia, for the earth there is strangely red; so we bore him away to the northward, with his flowers and his little folded hands. In vain, in vain! – for where, O God! beneath thy broad blue sky shall my dark baby rest in peace – where Reverence dwells, and Goodness, and a Freedom that is free?

All that day and all that night there sat an awful gladness in my heart – nay, blame me not if I see the world thus darkly through the Veil – and my soul whispers ever to me saying, 'Not dead, not dead, but escaped; not bound, but free.' No bitter meanness shall sicken his baby heart till it die a living death, no taunt shall madden his happy boyhood. Fool that I was to think or wish that this little soul should grow choked and deformed within the Veil! I might have known that yonder deep unworldly look that ever and anon floated past his eyes was peering far beyond this narrow Now. In the poise of his little curl-crowned head did there not sit all that wild pride of being which his father had hardly crushed in his own heart? For what, forsooth, shall a Negro want with pride amid the studied humiliations of fifty million fellows? Well sped, my boy, before the world had dubbed your ambition insolence, had held your ideals unattainable, and taught you to cringe and bow. Better far this nameless void that stops my life than a sea of sorrow for you . . .

If one must have gone, why not I? Why may I not rest me from this restlessness and sleep from this wide waking? Was not the world's alembic, Time, in his young hands, as is not my time waning? Are there so many workers in the vineyard that the fair promise of this little body could lightly be tossed away? The wretched of my race that line the alleys of the nation sit fatherless and unmothered; but Love sat beside his cradle, and in his ear Wisdom waited to speak. Perhaps now he knows the All-Love, and needs not to be wise. Sleep, then, child – sleep till I sleep and waken to a baby voice and the ceaseless patter of little feet – above the Veil. ['The Veil' refers to Du Bois's notion of the 'veil of colour'.] (Du Bois, 1989: 149–50)

Glossary

Action theory: social theory in which action, its purposive nature and its meaning to people, is taken to be of central importance. Action theory is often associated with the name of Max Weber, who developed the interpretive tradition in social science.

Androcentrism: ideas or methods of research which prioritize men's views of the world, excluding the experience of women.

Career: used, primarily, by symbolic interactionists and ethnographers to describe a person's progress through a social setting, as where marijuana users progress through various stages in learning how to experience the drug, or mental patients pass through a series of institutional settings.

Census: a count of the characteristics of every member of a given population (as opposed to a survey of a selected sample from that population).

Coding: this is done when observations or responses to a questionnaire or interview are collected into groups which are like one another, and a symbol is assigned as a name for the group. Data may be 'coded' as they are collected, as where respondents are forced to reply to fixed-choice questions. Alternatively, the coding of qualitative data can form a part of theory building.

Comparative method: the comparison of people's experiences of different types of social structure or social setting in terms of historical points in time, or across cultures at a single point in time. This is an approach which can shed light on the particular arrangements of both sides of the comparison.

Connotation: used in semiotics to indicate the interpretive meanings of signs, which may be ideological. Thus a picture of a soldier saluting a flag connotes nationhood and patriotism as well as the more straightforward things such as 'soldier' and 'flag' that it denotes.

Contingency table: a table of numbers in which the relationship between two variables is shown. Contingency tables can usefully be broken down into rows and columns. Percentages placed in the cells of the table, giving the proportion which each cell contributes to the sum of particular rows or columns, are often helpful in detecting the strength and direction of relationships.

Cultural scripts or texts: terms used by those concerned to analyse cultural objects, such as pictures, films, sports events, fashions, food styles, to indicate that these can be viewed as containing messages in a manner comparable to a piece of written text.

Data: is the plural of datum, which refers to a record of an observation. Data can be numerical (and hence quantitative) or consist of words or images (hence qualitative). A distinction is sometimes made between naturally occurring data – such as tape recordings of conversations that would have occurred whether a researcher was present or not – and data generated in research settings, as in interviews or on questionnaires. Quantitative data are often arranged in a data matrix for ease of analysis.

Deconstruction: is an approach to social analysis that undermines claims to authority by exposing rhetorical strategies used by social actors, including the authors of research reports themselves. It has been promoted in particular by the post-modernist Derrida.

Determinism: is the view that everything that happens is caused. When applied to human action, it suggests that our perception of having a free will is an illusion, and that the task of social research is to expose the true causes of action.

Discourse: has come to refer, under the influence of Foucault, to systems of knowledge and their associated practices. More narrowly, it is used by discourse analysts to refer to particular systems of language, with a characteristic terminology and underlying knowledge base, such as medical talk, psychological language, or the language of democratic politics.

Elaboration paradigm: a structured approach to the exploration of causal relationships between variables through the examination of contingency tables. By introducing third variables to bivariate tabulations, arguments about causal direction and spuriousness are tested. The logic of this approach underlies most multivariate statistical analysis.

Empiricism: the view that knowledge is derived from sensory experience, for example visual observation. More loosely, it is often used to describe research that contains little in the way of reflection or theory, preferring to report 'facts' as they appear to be.

Epistemology: refers to the philosophical theory of knowledge, consisting of attempts to answer questions about how we can know what we know, and whether this knowledge is reliable or not. Debates about the adequacy of empiricism, for example, are epistemological debates.

Essentialism: is now increasingly used in order to explain why anti-essentialism is preferable, though in more purely philosophical discussion the term has greater usefulness. Amongst social and cultural researchers, anti-essentialism involves the rejection of a scientific quest for universal essences, such as the discovery of a universal psychological makeup, or generally applicable sex differences, in preference for a view that human 'nature' is a social construction.

Ethnocentrism: refers to the practice of judging a different society by the standards and values of one's own. This is seen, particularly by ethnographers, as inhibiting understanding of other ways of life.

Ethnomethodology: involves the examination of the ways in which people produce orderly social interaction on a routine, everyday basis. It provides the theoretical underpinning for conversation analysis.

Facticity: is the process whereby certain perceptions or phenomena achieve the status of uncontroversial fact. Phenomenological analysis attempts to reduce facticity, as does the method of deconstruction, by exposing the social practices which generate it.

Frequency distribution: a count of the number of times each value of a single variable occurs. Thus, the proportion of the population fitting into each of six categories of social class may be given as a frequency distribution. The distribution can be presented in a variety of ways, including for example a raw count, percentages or a pie chart.

Functionalism: is an approach to explaining social phenomena in terms of their contribution to a social totality. Thus, for example, crime is explained as necessary for marking the boundary of acceptable behaviour, reinforcing social order. Prominent functionalists include Durkheim and Parsons.

Grounded theory: a term coined by Glaser and Strauss to describe the type of theory produced by their methods of ethnographic data collection and analysis. The approach emphasizes the systematic discovery of theory from data, by using methods of constant comparison and theoretical sampling, so that theories remain grounded in observations of the social world, rather than being generated in the abstract. This they propose as an inductive alternative to hypothetico-deductive approaches.

Hypothetico-deduction: is the view that science proceeds by deriving hypotheses from theories, which are then tested for truth or falsity by observation and experimentation. It is the opposite of induction, which proposes that theories can be derived from observations.

Idealism: often opposed to realism, this term describes the view that the world exists only in people's minds.

Interpretivism: refers to approaches emphasizing the meaningful nature of people's participation in social and cultural life. The methods of natural science are seen as inappropriate for such investigation. Researchers working within this tradition analyse the meanings people confer upon their own and others' actions.

Intersubjectivity: the common-sense, shared meanings constructed by people in their interactions with each other and used as an everyday resource to interpret the meaning of elements of social and cultural life.

Linguistic repertoire: a term used in discourse analysis to refer to the resources (discourses, intersubjective meanings, etc.) on which people draw in order to construct accounts.

Marginality: Used to describe the typical position of the ethnographer, who exists on the margins of the social world being studied, in that he or she is neither a full participant nor a full observer. Also used to describe groups of people living outside mainstream culture.

Measures of central tendency: statistics such as the mean, median or mode which in various ways indicate the central point in a frequency distribution.

Methodology: concerns the theoretical, political and philosophical roots and implications of particular research methods or academic disciplines. Researchers may adopt particular methodological positions which establish how they go about studying a phenomenon.

Multivariate analysis: analysis of the relationships between three or more variables (as opposed to bivariate analysis, which involves two variables, or univariate analysis which involves one).

Naturalists: take the view that the methods of the natural sciences are appropriate to the study of the social and cultural world. This should be distinguished from another meaning of the term *naturalism* which is sometimes used to refer to the claim of ethnographers to collect naturally occurring data.

Naturalizing: is the process whereby matters which are in fact socially constructed and were once fluid and changeable come to be perceived as a part of the natural order and therefore fixed, inevitable and right. Social researchers often wish to de-naturalize phenomena (such as sexual identity for example) by exposing the human processes whereby they are constructed.

Paradigms (Kuhnian): the overall conception and way of working shared by workers within a particular discipline or research area. In this view, paradigm shifts occur from time to time as scientific communities experience revolutions of thought.

Participant observation: used to describe the method most commonly adopted by ethnographers, whereby the researcher participates in the life of a community or group, while making observations of members' behaviour.

Positivism: in its looser sense has come to mean an approach to social enquiry that emphasizes the discovery of laws of society, often involving an empiricist commitment to naturalism and quantitative methods. The word has become almost a term of abuse amongst social and cultural researchers, losing its philosophical connotations where its meaning is both more complex and precise.

Post-modernism: a social movement or fashion amongst intellectuals centring around a rejection of modernist values of rationality, progress and a conception of social science as a search for over-arching explanations of human nature or the social and cultural world. By contrast, post-modernists celebrate the fall of such oppressive 'grand narratives', emphasizing the fragmented and dispersed nature of contemporary experience.

Randomized controlled trial: an experimental method whereby subjects are randomly allocated to either a group receiving a 'treatment' or another which acts as a 'control', so that the effects of the treatment can be established. The method is effective in ruling out spurious causation.

Reactivity: the reactions of people being studied to the presence of an observer, seen by some to be a source of bias, in that behaviour may become artificial as a result.

Realism: is the view that a reality exists independently of our thoughts or beliefs. The language of research is seen to refer to this reality, rather than purely constructing it, though more subtle realists recognize constructive properties in language as well. The term is also used to characterize an approach to art and literature analysing the accuracy with which these reflect social life.

Reductionism: the identification of a basic explanation for a complex phenomenon. Thus sexual identity may be explained by reference to genetic determinants alone, or social life explained in terms of economic relations alone.

Reflexivity: in its broad meaning this is used to refer to the capacity of researchers to reflect upon their actions and values during research, whether in producing data or writing accounts. More narrowly, ethnomethodologists use the term to describe a property of language, which reflects upon actions to make them appear orderly.

Regression: a statistical technique for using the values of one variable to predict the values of another, based on information about their relationship, often given in a scattergram. Multiple regression involves the prediction of an interval-level variable from the values of two or more other variables. Logistic regression does this too, but predicts the values of nominal or ordinal variables.

Relativism: can be epistemological (or 'conceptual'), cultural or moral. The first of these involves the rejection of absolute standards for judging truth. The second suggests that different cultures define phenomena in different ways, so that the perspective of one culture cannot be used to understand that of another. The third implies that perceptions of good and evil are matters of social agreement rather than having universal validity.

Reliability: the capacity of a measuring device, or indeed of a whole research study, to produce the same results if used on different occasions with the same object of study. Reliability enhances confidence in validity, but is insufficient on its own to show validity, since some measurement strategies can produce consistently wrong results.

Replication: is closely linked with reliability, involving the repetition of a study to see if the same results are obtained on both occasions. (The term has a narrower meaning within the context of the elaboration paradigm.)

Rhetoric: the linguistic strategies used by speakers or authors of text to convey particular impressions or reinforce specific interpretations, most commonly in support of the authority of the text to speak the truth.

Sampling: the selection of units of analysis (for example, people or institutions) for study. Sampling can involve attempts to statistically represent a population, in which case a variety of random methods are available. Alternatively, sampling can be opportunistic, or formed by emerging theoretical concerns of a researcher.

Secondary analysis: analysis of data by researchers unconnected with the original purposes of the data collection, as where academic researchers use data sets gathered as a part of government social surveys.

Social constructionism: the view that the phenomena of the social and cultural world and their meanings are created in human social interaction. Taken further, social constructionism can be applied to phenomena ordinarily thought to constitute the natural world, at which point the perspective verges on relativism. The approach often, though not exclusively, draws on idealist philosophical orientations.

Social facts: regularities of social life that appear to have an independent existence, acting to determine or constrain human behaviour. Norms of conduct or religious rules are examples. The concept is of particular importance in relation to functionalism and positivism.

Social structure: ordered interrelationships that are characteristic of particular societies, such as its class structure or system of economic or political relations.

Statistical inference: the generalization of findings from a sample to the broader population from which the sample has been randomly drawn. A variety of statistical tests, such as the chi-square, help in estimating the level of probability that such inferences about the population are true, given the sample size. This is expressed as the statistical significance of the finding.

Structuralism: the view that behind the social and cultural realities we perceive, such as clothes or food fashions, kinship organization and even language itself, deep structures exist which, through combinations of their elements, produce the surface complexity of the relevant phenomena.

Validity: at its most simple this refers to the truth status of research reports. However, a great variety of techniques for establishing the validity of measuring devices and research designs has been established, both for quantitative and qualitative research. More broadly, the status of research as truth is the subject of considerable philosophical controversy, lying at the heart of the debate about post-modernism.

Variables: qualities on which units of analysis vary. Thus, if a person is the unit of analysis in, say, a social survey, examples of variables might be their social class, gender, attitudes to politics, and so on. Variables can be measured at a variety of levels, according to which they can be subjected to specific mathematical operations. In considering relationships between variables it is important to define which is a causal (or independent) variable, and which is an effect (dependent) variable.

References

Abel-Smith, B. and Townsend, P. (1965) *The Poor and the Poorest*. London: Bell.

Abrams, P. (1968) *The Origins of British Sociology 1834–1914*. Chicago: University of Chicago Press.

Abrams, P. (1982) *Historical Sociology*. Somerset: Open Books.

Addleson, K.P. (1993) 'Knowers/doers and their moral problems', in Alcoff, L. and Potter, E. (eds) *Feminist Epistemologies*. London: Routledge.

Altman, C. (1981) 'Intratextual rewriting: textuality as language formation', in Steiner, W. (ed.) *The Sign in Music and Literature*. Austin, TX: University of Texas Press.

Ang, I. (1991) *Desperately Seeking the Audience*. London: Routledge.

Antaki, C. and Rapley, M. (1996) '"Quality of life" talk: the liberal paradox of psychological testing', *Discourse and Society*, 7(3): 293–316.

Arber, S. and Ginn, J. (1991) *Gender and Later Life: A Sociological Analysis of Resources and Constraints*. London: Sage.

Asad, T. (ed.) (1973) *Anthropology and the Colonial Encounter*. London: Ithaca Press.

Atkinson, J.M. (1978) *Discovering Suicide*. London: Macmillan.

Atkinson, J.M. and Drew, P. (1979) *Order in Court: The Organisation of Verbal Interaction in Judicial Settings*. London: Macmillan.

Atkinson, J.M. and Heritage, J. (eds) (1984) *Structures of Social Action*. Cambridge: Cambridge University Press.

Atkinson, P. (1990) *The Ethnographic Imagination: Textual Constructions of Reality*. London: Routledge.

Back, L. (1996) *New Ethnicities and Urban Culture: Racisms and Multiculture in Young Lives*. London: UCL Press.

Barthes, R. (1977a) *Image Music Text*. New York: Hill and Wang.

Barthes, R. (1977b) *Elements of Semiology*. New York: Hill and Wang.

Barthes, R. (1986) *Mythologies*. London: Paladin.

Baruch, G. (1981) 'Moral tales: parents' stories of encounters with the health professions', *Sociology of Health and Illness*, 3(3): 275–96.

Baruch, G. (1982) 'Moral tales: interviewing parents of congenitally ill children'. PhD dissertation, Goldsmiths College, University of London.

Bauman, Z. (1987) *Legislators and Interpreters*. Cambridge: Polity.

Becker, H.S. (1963) *Outsiders: Studies in the Sociology of Deviance*. New York: Free Press.

Becker, H.S. (1967) 'Whose side are we on?', *Social Problems*, 14: 239–48.

Becker, H.S. (1970) *Sociological Work: Method and Substance*. Chicago: Aldine.

Becker, H.S. and Geer, B. (1957) 'Participant observation and interviewing: a comparison', in McCall, G. and Simmons, J.L. (eds) (1959) *Issues in Participant Observation*. New York: Addison-Wesley.

Bell, D., Caplan, P. and Karim, W. J. (eds) (1993) *Gendered Fields: Women, Men and Ethnography*. London: Routledge.

Bell, J. (1993) *Doing Your Research Project: A Guide for First-time Researchers in Education and Social Science*. Buckingham: Open University Press.

Berger, P. and Luckmann, T. (1966) *The Social Construction of Reality*. New York: Doubleday.

Bhaskar, R. (1989) *Reclaiming Reality*. London: Verso.

Billig, M. (1987) *Arguing and Thinking: A Rhetorical Approach to Social Psychology*. Cambridge: Cambridge University Press.

Birke, L. (1986) *Women, Feminism and Biology*. New York: Methuen.

Blaxter, M. (1990) *Health and Lifestyles*. London: Routledge.

Bloor, B. (1983) 'Notes on member validation', in Emerson, R. (ed.) *Contemporary Field Research: A Collection of Readings*. Boston: Little, Brown.

Bowley, A.L. and Burnett-Hurst, A.R. (1915) *Livelihood and Poverty: A Study in the Economic Conditions of Working-Class Households in Northampton, Warrington, Stanley and Reading*. London: Bell.

Bowley, A.L. and Hogg, M.H. (1925) *Has Poverty Diminished? A Sequel to 'Livelihood and Poverty'*. London: Ling.

Brown, G. and Harris, T. (1978) *Social Origins of Depression*. London: Macmillan.

Bruce, A. and Filmer, P. (1983) *Working in Crafts*. London: Crafts Council.

Bryman, A. and Cramer, D. (1994) *Quantitative Data Analysis for Social Scientists*. London: Routledge.

Buckingham, R.W., Lack, S.A., Mount, B.M., Maclean, L.D. and Collins, J.T. (1976) 'Living with the dying: use of the technique of participant observation', *Canadian Medical Association Journal*, 115: 1211–15.

Burns, E. and Burns, T. (eds) (1973) *Sociology of Literature and Drama*. Harmondsworth: Penguin.

Cain, M. and Finch, J. (1981) 'Towards a rehabilitation of data', in Abrams, P., Deem, R., Finch, J. and Rock, P. (eds) *Practice and Progress: British Sociology 1950–1980*. London: Allen and Unwin.

Cantor, M.G. and Pingree, S. (1983) *The Soap Opera*. London: Sage.

Cartwright, A. (1964) *Human Relations and Hospital Care*. London: Routledge and Kegan Paul.

Cartwright, A. and Seale, C.F. (1990) *The Natural History of a Survey: An Account of the Methodological Issues Encountered in a Study of Life before Death*. London: King's Fund.

Centre for Contemporary Cultural Studies (ed.) (1982) *The Empire Strikes Back*. London: Hutchinson.

Chambliss, W. (1975) 'On the paucity of original research on organized crime', *American Sociologist*, 10: 36–9.

Cicourel, A. (1964) *Method and Measurement in Sociology*. New York: Free Press.

Clayman, S.C. (1992) 'Footing in the achievement of neutrality: the case of news-interview discourse', in Drew, P. and Heritage, J. (eds) (1992) *Talk at Work*. Cambridge: Cambridge University Press.

Clifford, J. (1986) 'Introduction: partial truths', in Clifford, J. and Marcus, G.E. (eds) *Writing Culture: The Poetics and Politics of Ethnography*. Berkeley, CA: University of California Press.

Clifford, J. and Marcus, G.E. (eds) (1986) *Writing Culture: The Poetics and Politics of Ethnography*. Berkeley, CA: University of California Press.

Coffey, A. and Atkinson, P. (1996) *Making Sense of Qualitative Data: Complementary Research Strategies*. London: Sage.

Collins, R. (1994) *Four Sociological Traditions*. Oxford: Oxford University Press.

Committee of Enquiry into the Crafts in Australia (1975) *The Crafts in Australia*. Canberra: Australian Government Publishing Service.

Cornwell, J. (1981) *Hard Earned Lives*. London: Tavistock.

Corsaro, W. (1981) 'Entering the child's world: research strategies for field entry and data collection in a pre-school setting', in Green, J.L. and Wallats, C. (eds) *Ethnography and Language in Education Settings*. Norwood, NJ: Ablex.

Coser, L. (ed.) (1963) *Sociology through Literature: An Introductory Reader*. Englewood Cliffs, NJ: Prentice-Hall.

Coward, R. and Ellis, J. (1979) *Language and Materialism*. London: Routledge and Kegan Paul.

Coxon, A.P.M. (1996) *Between the Sheets: Sexual Diaries and Gay Men's Sex in the Era of AIDS*. London: Cassell.

Crapanzano, V. (1986) 'Hermes' dilemma: the masking of subversion in ethnographic description', in Clifford, J. and Marcus, G.E. (eds) *Writing Culture: The Poetics and Politics of Ethnography*. Berkeley, CA: University of California Press.

Cressey, D.R. (1953) *Other People's Money: A Study in the Social Psychology of Embezzlement*. Belmont, CA: Wadsworth.

Cuff, E.C. and Payne, G.C.F. (1979) *Perspectives in Sociology*. London: Allen and Unwin.

Dale, A., Arber, S. and Proctor, M. (1988) *Doing Secondary Analysis*. London: Unwin Hyman.

Davies, P.M., Hickson, F.C.I., Weatherburn, P. and Hunt, A.J. (1993) *Sex, Gay Men and AIDS*. London: Falmer.

De Vaus, D.A. (1991) *Surveys in Social Research*. London: Routledge.

Denzin, N. (1970) *The Research Act in Sociology*. London: Butterworth.

Denzin, N. (1989) *The Research Act: A Theoretical Introduction to Sociological Methods*. Englewood Cliffs, NJ: Prentice-Hall.

Dingwall, R. and Murray, T. (1983) 'Categorisation in accident departments: "good" patients, "bad" patients and children', *Sociology of Health and Illness*, 5(12): 121–48.

Douglas, J. (1967) *The Social Meanings of Suicide*. Princeton, NJ: Princeton University Press.

Douglas, M. (1975) 'Self-evidence', in Douglas, M. (ed.) *Implicit Meanings*. London: Routledge.

Drew, P. and Heritage, J. (eds) (1992) *Talk at Work*. Cambridge: Cambridge University Press.

Du Bois, B. (1983) 'Passionate scholarship: notes on values, knowing and method in feminist social science', in Bowles, G. and Duelli Klein, R. (eds) *Theories of Women's Studies*. London: Routledge and Kegan Paul.

Du Bois, W.E.B. (1934) *The Black Reconstruction*. New York: Harcourt, Brace.

Du Bois, W.E.B. (1940) *The Dusk of Dawn*. New York: Henry Holt.

Du Bois, W.E.B. (1968) *The Autobiography of W.E.B. Du Bois: A Soliloquy on Viewing my Life from the Last Decades of its First Century*. New York: International Publishers.

Du Bois, W.E.B. (1989) *The Souls of Black Folk*. New York: Bantam (first published 1903 in Chicago by A.C. McClung).

Du Bois, W.E.B. (1996) *The Philadelphia Negro: A Social Study*. Philadephia: University of Philadephia Press (first published 1899).

Duelli Klein, R. (1983) 'How to do what we want: thoughts about feminist methodology', in Bowles, G. and Duelli Klein, R. (eds) *Theories of Women's Studies*. London: Routledge and Kegan Paul.

Durkheim, E. (1915) *The Elementary Forms of the Religious Life: A Study in Religious Sociology*. London: Allen and Unwin.

Durkheim, E. (1970) *Suicide: A Study in Sociology*. London: Routledge and Kegan Paul (originally published 1897).

Durkheim, E. (1972) *Selected Writings* (ed.: A. Giddens). Cambridge: Cambridge University Press.

Durkheim, E. (1982) *The Rules of Sociological Method*. London: Macmillan.

Eagleton, T. (1983) *Literary Theory: An Introduction*. Oxford: Blackwell.

Eco, U. (1981) *The Role of the Reader: Explorations in the Semiotics of Texts*. London: Hutchinson.

Eco, U. (1989) *The Open Work* (trans. by Anna Cancogni). London: Hutchinson Radius.

Economic and Social Research Council (1996) *Priorities News*, Spring. Swindon: ESRC.

Elias, N. (1978) *The Civilising Process Part 1: The History of Manners*. Oxford: Blackwell.

Elias, N. (1982) *The Civilising Process Part 2: State Formation and Civilisation*. Oxford: Blackwell.

Evans-Pritchard, E.E. (1940) *The Nuer*. Oxford: Oxford University Press.

Feyerabend, P. (1975) *Against Method*. London: New Left Review.

Feyerabend, P. (1978) *Science in a Free Society*. London: New Left Review.

Feyerabend, P. (1981) 'How to defend society against science', in Hacking, I. (ed.) *Scientific Revolutions*. Oxford: Oxford University Press.

Fielding, N. (1981) *The National Front*. London: Routledge and Kegan Paul.

Filmer, P. (1969) 'The literary imagination and the explanation of socio-cultural change in modern Britain'. *European Journal of Sociology.*, X(2): 271–91.

Finch, J. (1984) ' "It's great to have someone to talk to": ethics and politics of interviewing women', in Bell, C. and Roberts, H. (eds) *Social Researching: Politics, Problems, Practice*. London: Routledge.

Fiske, J. (1987) *Television Culture*. London: Methuen.

Fiske, J. (1989) *Reading the Popular*. Boston: Unwin Hyman.

Fortier, A.-M. (1991) *Langue et rapports sociaux: analyse des langues d'usage chez des italiens de deuxième génération*. Québec: Centre International de Recherche en Aménagement Linguistique/Les Presses de l'Université Laval.

Fortier, A.-M. (1996) 'Gender, ethnicity and power: identity formation in two Italian organisations of London'. PhD dissertation, Goldsmiths College, University of London.

Foucault, M. (1977) *Discipline and Punish*. Harmondsworth: Penguin.

Foucault, M. (1979a) 'On governmentality', *Ideology and Consciousness*, 6: 17–35.

Foucault, M. (1979b) *The History of Sexuality: Volume 1*. Harmondsworth: Penguin.

Foucault, M. (1984) 'The order of discourse', in Shapiro, M. (ed.) *Language and Politics*. Oxford: Blackwell.

Game, A. (1991) *Undoing the Social: Towards a Deconstructive Sociology*. Buckingham: Open University Press.

Game, A. and Metcalfe, A. (1996) *Passionate Sociology*. London: Sage.

Gans, H. (1968) 'The participant observer as human being: observations on the personal aspect of fieldwork', in Becker, H.S., Geer, B., Reisman, D. and Weiss, R. (eds) *Institutions and the Person*. Chicago: Aldine.

Garfinkel, H. (1967) *Studies in Ethnomethodology*. Englewood Cliffs, NJ: Prentice-Hall.

Gates, H.L. (1989) 'Darkly, as through the veil', introduction to Du Bois, W.E.B. *The Souls of Black Folk*. New York: Bantam.

Geer, B. (1964) 'First days in the field', in Hammond, P. (ed.) *Sociologists at Work*. New York: Basic Books.

Geertz, C. (1973) *The Interpretation of Cultures*. London: Fontana.

Gilbert, G.N. and Mulkay, M.J. (1984) *Opening Pandora's Box: A Sociological Analysis of Scientists' Discourse*. Cambridge: Cambridge University Press.

Gilbert, N. (1993) *Researching Social Life*. London: Sage.

Gill, R. (1996) 'Discourse analysis: practical implementation', in Richardson, J. (ed.) *A Handbook of Qualitative Methods for Social Psychologists and Other Social Scientists*. Leicester: British Psychological Society.

Glaser, B.G. and Strauss, A.L. (1966) *Awareness of Dying*. London: Weidenfeld and Nicolson.

Glaser, B.G. and Strauss, A.L. (1967) *The Discovery of Grounded Theory: Strategies for Qualitative Research*. Chicago: Aldine.

Glasgow University Media Group (1976) *Bad News*. London: Routledge and Kegan Paul.

Glasgow University Media Group (1980) *More Bad News*. London: Routledge and Kegan Paul.

Glasgow University Media Group (1982) *Really Bad News*. London: Writers and Readers.

Gliner, R. and Raines, R. (eds) (1971) *Munching on Existence: Contemporary American Society through Literature*. New York: Free Press.

Goffman, E. (1955) 'On face-work: an analysis of ritual elements in social interaction', *Psychiatry: Journal for the Study of Inter-Personal Processes*, 18(3): 213–31.

Goffman, E. (1968) *Stigma: Notes on the Management of Spoiled Identity*. Harmondsworth: Pelican.

Goldmann, L. (1964) *The Hidden God: A Study of Tragic Vision in the Pensées of Pascal and the Tragedies of Racine* (trans. P. Thody). London: Routledge and Kegan Paul.

Goldmann, L. (1975) *Towards a Sociology of the Novel* (trans. A. Sheridan). London: Tavistock.

Goodman, N. (1982) 'The fabrication of facts', in Krausz, M. and Meiland, J. W. (eds) *Relativism: Cognitive and Moral*. Notre Dame, IN: University of Notre Dame Press.

Greatbatch, D. (1992) 'On the management of disagreement among news interviewers', in Drew, P. and Heritage, J. (eds) *Talk at Work*. Cambridge: Cambridge University Press.

Gubrium, J. (1988) *Analyzing Field Reality*. Qualitative Research Methods Series 8, Newbury Park, CA: Sage.

Gubrium, J. and Holstein, J. (1987) 'The private image: experiential location and method in family studies', *Journal of Marriage and the Family*, 49: 773–86.

Hacking, I. (1990) *The Taming of Chance*. Cambridge: Cambridge University Press.

Hall, J. (1979) *The Sociology of Literature*. London: Longman.

Hall, S. (1992) 'The question of cultural identity', in Hall, S., Held, D. and McGrew, T. (eds) *Modernity and its Futures*. Cambridge: Polity.

Hall, S., Critcher, C., Jefferson, T., Clarke, J. and Roberts, B. (1978) *Policing the Crisis: Mugging, the State, and Law and Order*. London: Macmillan.

Hammersley, M. (1983) *Reading Ethnographic Research: A Critical Guide*. London: Longman.

Hammersley, M. (1992) *What's Wrong with Ethnography: Methodological Explorations*. London: Routledge.

Hammersley, M. (1995) *The Politics of Social Research*. London: Sage.

Hammersley, M. and Atkinson, P. (1995) *Ethnography: Principles in Practice* (2nd edn). London: Routledge.

Hansard (1994) *Criminal Justice and Public Order Bill*. House of Commons, 21 February. London: HMSO.

Hansen, E.C. (1977) *Rural Catalonia under the Franco Regime*. Cambridge: Cambridge University Press.

Harding, S. (1986) *The Science Question and Feminism*. Bloomington, IN: Indiana University Press.

Harding, S. (ed.) (1987) *Feminism and Methodology*. Milton Keynes: Open University Press.

Hawkes, T. (1992) *Structuralism and Semiotics*. London: Routledge.

Hempel, C. (1966) *Philosophy of Natural Science*. Englewood Cliffs, NJ: Prentice-Hall.

Heritage, J. (1984) *Garfinkel and Ethnomethodology*. Cambridge: Polity.

Heritage, J. and Sefi, S. (1992) 'Dilemmas of advice: aspects of the delivery and reception of advice in interactions between health visitors and first time mothers', in Drew, P. and Heritage, J. (eds) *Talk at Work*. Cambridge: Cambridge University Press.

Hesse, M. (1972) 'In defence of objectivity', *Proceedings of the British Academy*, LVIII.

Hindess, B. (1973) *The Use of Official Statistics: A Critique of Positivism and Ethnomethodology*. London: Macmillan.

Hirschi, T. and Selvin, H.C. (1967) *Delinquency Research: An Appraisal of Analytic Methods*. New York: Free Press/Collier-Macmillan.

Holdaway, S. (1982) 'An inside job: a case study of covert research on the police', in Bulmer, M. (ed.) *Social Research Ethics: An Examination of the Merits of Covert Participant Observation*. London: Macmillan.

Hollis, M. (1994) *The Philosophy of Social Science: An Introduction*. Cambridge: Cambridge University Press.

Holmes, T.H. and Rahe, R.H. (1967) 'The social readjustment rating scale', *Journal of Psychosomatic Research*, 11: 213–18.

Holmwood, J. (1995) 'Feminism and epistemology: what kind of successor science?', *Sociology*, 29(3): 411–28.

Homan, R. (1991) *The Ethics of Social Research*. London: Longman.

Home Office (1983) *The British Crime Survey*. London: HMSO.

Hughes, J. (1976) *Sociological Analysis*. London: Nelson.

Humphreys, L. (1970) *Tearoom Trade: A Study of Homosexual Encounters in Public Places*. London: Duckworth.

Hyman, H. (1955) *Survey Design and Analysis*. New York: Free Press.

Hymes, D. (1974) *Reinventing Anthropology*. New York: Vintage.

Irvine, J., Miles, I. and Evans, J. (eds) (1979) *Demystifying Social Statistics*. London: Pluto.

Jackson, B. and Marsden, D. (1962) *Education and the Working Class*. London: Routledge and Kegan Paul.

Jayaratne, T.E. (1983) 'The value of quantitative methodology for feminist research', in Bowles, G. and Duelli Klein, R. (eds) *Theories of Women's Studies*. London: Routledge and Kegan Paul.

Jayaratne, T.E. and Stewart, A. (1991) 'Quantitative and qualitative methods in the social sciences: current feminist issues and practical strategies', in Fonow, M.M. and Cook, J.A. (eds) *Beyond Methodology: Feminist Scholarship as Lived Research*. Bloomington and Indianapolis, IN: Indiana University Press.

Jeffery, R. (1979) 'Normal rubbish: deviant patients in casualty departments', *Sociology of Health and Illness*, 1(1): 90–107.

Jones, S. (1985) 'Depth interviewing', in Walker, R. (1985) (ed.) *Applied Qualitative Research*. Aldershot: Gower.

Junker, B. (1960) *Fieldwork*. Chicago: University of Chicago Press.

Kaplan, A. (1991) 'Gone fishing, be back later', in Shaffir, W.B. and Stebbins, R. (eds) *Experiencing Fieldwork*. Newbury Park, CA: Sage.

Keddie, N. (1971) 'Classroom knowledge', in Young, M. (ed.) *Knowledge and Control*. London: Collier-Macmillan.

Kelly, L., Burton, S. and Regan, L. (1994) 'Researching women's lives or studying women's oppression? Reflections on what constitutes feminist research', in Maynard, M. and Purvis, J. (eds) *Researching Women's Lives from a Feminist Perspective*. London: Taylor and Francis.

Kent, R.A. (1981) *A History of British Empirical Sociology*. Aldershot: Gower.

Key, R. (1996) 'Dual carriageway', *The Guardian*, 15 October.

Knott, C. (1994) *Crafts in the 1990s*. London: Crafts Council.

Krathwohl, D.R. (1988) *How to Prepare a Research Proposal: Guidelines for Funding and Dissertations in the Social and Behavioural Sciences* (3rd edn). Syracuse, NY: Syracuse University Press.

Kuhn, T. (1970) *The Structure of Scientific Revolutions* (2nd edn, enlarged). Chicago: University of Chicago Press.

Laslett, P. (1979) *The World We Have Lost*. London: Methuen.

Latour, B. and Woolgar, S. (1979) *Laboratory Life: The Social Construction of Scientific Facts*. Beverly Hills: Sage.

Laurenson, D. and Swingewood, A. (1972) *The Sociology of Literature*. New York: Schocken.

Layder, D. (1994) *Understanding Social Theory*. London: Sage.

Lazarsfeld, P.F. and Rosenberg, M. (1955) *The Language of Social Research: A Reader in the Methodology of Social Research*. Glencoe, IL: Free Press.

Leavis, F.R. (1952) *The Common Pursuit*. London: Chatto and Windus.

Leavis, F.R. (1972) *Nor Shall My Sword: Discourses on Pluralism, Compassion and Social Hope*. London: Chatto and Windus.

Leiss, W., Kline, S. and Jhally, S. (1986) *Social Communication in Advertising: Persons, Products & Images of Well-Being*. London: Methuen.

Lever, J. (1981) 'Multiple methods of data collection: a note on divergence', *Urban Life*, 10(2): 199–213.

Lévi-Strauss, C. (1969a) *Totemism*. Harmondsworth: Penguin.

Lévi-Strauss, C. (1969b) *Elementary Structures of Kinship*. London: Eyre and Spottiswood.

Levinson, S.C. (1983) *Pragmatics*. Cambridge: Cambridge University Press.

Levitas, R. and Guy, W. (1996) *Interpreting Official Statistics*. London: Routledge.

Little, D. (1991) *Varieties of Social Explanation*. Boulder, CO: Westview.

Livingston, E. (1987) *Making Sense of Ethnomethodology*. London: Routledge.

Loewenthal, L. (1961) *Literature, Popular Culture and Society*. Englewood Cliffs, NJ: Prentice-Hall.

Lofland, J. (1971) *Analysing Social Settings: A Guide to Qualitative Observation*. Belmont, CA: Wadsworth.

Lofland, L. (1974) 'The "thereness" of women: a selective review of urban sociology', in Millman, M. and Kanter, R.M. (eds) *Another Voice: Feminist Perspectives on Social Life and Social Science*. New York: Anchor.

Longino, H. (1990) *Science as Social Knowledge: Values and Objectivity in Scientific Inquiry*. Princeton, NJ: Princeton University Press.

MacIntyre, S. (1977) *Single and Pregnant*. London: Croom Helm.

Malseed, J. (1987) 'Straw men: a note on Ann Oakley's treatment of textbook prescriptions for interviewing', *Sociology*, 21(4): 629–31.

Marcus, S. (1972) 'Language into structure: Pickwick revisited', *Daedalus: Journal of the American Academy of Arts and Sciences*, 101(1): 183–202.

Marris, P. (1958) *Widows and their Families*. London: Routledge and Kegan Paul.

Marsh, C. (1982) *The Survey Method: The Contribution of Surveys to Sociological Explanation*. London: Allen and Unwin.

Marsh, C. (1984) 'Problems with surveys: method or epistemology?', in Bulmer, M. (ed.) *Sociological Research Methods*. London: Macmillan.

Martin, G. (1975) *Language, Truth and Poetry: Notes towards a Philosophy of Literature*. Edinburgh: Edinburgh University Press.

Martin, M. and McIntyre, L.C. (eds) (1994) *Readings in the Philosophy of Social Science*. Cambridge, MA: MIT Press.

Masterman, L. (ed.) (1986) *Television Mythologies: Stars, Shows and Signs*. London: Comedia/MK Media.

May, T. (1996) *Situating Social Theory*. Buckingham: Open University Press.

Maynard, D. and Clayman, S. (1991) 'The diversity of ethnomethodology', *Annual Review of Sociology*, 17: 385–418.

Maynard, M. (1994) 'Methods, practice and epistemology: the debate about feminism and research', in Maynard, M. and Purvis, J. (eds) *Researching Women's Lives from a Feminist Perspective*. London: Taylor and Francis.

Maynard, M. and Purvis, J. (eds) (1994) *Researching Women's Lives from a Feminist Perspective*. London: Taylor and Francis.

McCall, G.J. and Simmons, J.L. (eds) (1969) *Issues in Participant Observation: A Text and Reader*. Reading, MA: Addison-Wesley.

McLennan, G. (1995) 'Feminism, epistemology and postmodernism: reflections on current ambivalence', *Sociology*, 29(3): 391–409.

McWhinney, I.R., Bass, M.J. and Donner, A. (1994) 'Evaluation of palliative care service: problems and pitfalls', *British Medical Journal*, 309: 1340–2.

Mies, M. (1983) 'Towards a methodology for feminist research', in Bowles, G. and Duelli Klein, R. (eds) *Theories of Women's Studies*. London: Routledge and Kegan Paul.

Miles, M. and Weitzman, E. (1995) *Computer Programs for Qualitative Data Analysis*. Beverly Hills, CA: Sage.

Milgram, S. (1963) 'Behavioural study of obedience', *Journal of Abnormal Psychology*, 67: 371–8.

Mill, J.S. (1973) *A System of Logic Ratiocinative and Inductive: Being a Connected View of the Principles of Evidence and the Methods of Scientific Investigation: Books I–III and Appendices*. London: Routledge and Kegan Paul.

Mill, J.S. (1976) *A System of Logic*. London: Longmans.

Miller, D. (1994) *Modernity: An Ethnographic Approach*. Oxford: Berg.

Mills, C.W. (1959) *The Sociological Imagination*. Oxford: Oxford University Press.

Milner, A. (1996) *Literature, Culture and Society*. London: UCL Press.

Mitchell, J.C. (1983) 'Case and situational analysis', *Sociological Review*, 31(2): 187–211.

Mitchell, R.G. (1991) 'Secrecy and disclosure in fieldwork', in Shaffir, W.B. and Stebbins, R.A. (eds) *Experiencing Fieldwork*. London: Sage.

Moerman, M. (1974) 'Accomplishing ethnicity', in Turner, R. (ed.) *Ethnomethodology*. Harmondsworth: Penguin.

Morgan, D. (1980) 'Men, masculinity and the process of sociological enquiry', in Roberts, H. (ed.) *Doing Feminist Research*. London: Routledge and Kegan Paul.

Morley, D. (1992) *Television, Audiences and Cultural Studies*. London: Routledge.

Moser, C.A. and Kalton, G. (1971) *Survey Methods in Social Investigation* (2nd edn). Aldershot: Gower.

Najman, J.M., Morrison, J., Williams, G.M. and Andersen, M.J. (1992) 'Comparing alternative methodologies of social research: an overview', in Daly, J., McDonald, I. and Willis, E. (eds) *Researching Health Care: Designs, Dilemmas, Disciplines*. London: Routledge.

Nelson, B. (1984) *Making an Issue of Child Abuse: Political Agenda Setting for Social Problems*. Chicago: University of Chicago Press.

Newton-Smith, W.H. (1981) *The Rationality of Science*. London: Routledge.

Oakley, A. (1972) *Sex, Gender and Society*. London: Maurice Temple Smith.

Oakley, A. (1974) *The Sociology of Housework*. New York: Pantheon Books.

Oakley, A. (1981) 'Interviewing women: a contradiction in terms?', in Roberts, H. (ed.) *Doing Feminist Research*. London: Routledge.

Oakley, A. (1989) 'Who's afraid of the randomised controlled trial? Some dilemmas of the scientific method and "good" research practice', *Women and Health*, 15(4): 25–59.

Oakley, A. and Oakley, R. (1979) 'Sexism in official statistics', in Irvine, J., Miles, I. and Evans, J. (eds) *Demystifying Social Statistics*. London: Pluto.

Oakley, A., Rigby, A.S. and Hickey, D. (1994) 'Life stress, support and class inequality', *European Journal of Public Health*, 4(2): 81–91.

Pan American Health Organization (1989) *Health Profile of the Elderly in Trinidad and Tobago*. Technical Paper 22, Washington, DC: Pan American Health Organization.

Parkes, C.M. and Parkes, J. (1984) 'Hospice versus hospital care: re-evaluation after ten years as seen by surviving spouses', *Postgraduate Medical Journal*, 60: 120–4.

Parsons, T. (1937) *The Structure of Social Action*. New York: Free Press.

Parsons, T. (1966) *Societies: Evolutionary and Comparative Perspectives*. Englewood Cliffs, NJ: Prentice-Hall.

Parsons, T., Naegele, K., Pitts, J. and Shils, E. (eds) (1961) *Theories of Society* (2 vols). New York: Free Press.

Patten, R. (ed.) (1972) *Charles Dickens: The Pickwick Papers*. Harmondsworth: Penguin.

Peräkylä, A. and Silverman, D. (1991) 'Reinterpreting speech-exchange systems: communication formats in AIDS counselling', *Sociology*, 25(3): 627–51.

Polanyi, K. (1957) *The Great Transformation: The Political and Economic Origins of our Time*. Boston: Beacon.

Popper, K.R. (1957) *The Poverty of Historicism*. London: Routledge and Kegan Paul.

Popper, K.R. (1963) *Conjectures and Refutations*. London: Routledge and Kegan Paul.

Popper, K.R. (1972) *Objective Knowledge*. Oxford: Clarendon Press.

Popper, K.R. (1994) *The Myth of the Framework*. London: Routledge.

Potter, J. and Mulkay, M. (1985) 'Scientists' interview talk: interviews as a technique for revealing participants' interpretative practices', in Brenner, M., Brown, J. and Canter, D. (eds) *The Research Interview: Uses and Approaches*. London: Academic Press.

Potter, J. and Wetherell, M. (1987) *Discourse and Social Psychology: Beyond Attitudes and Behaviour*. London: Sage.

Potter, J. and Wetherell, M. (1994) 'Analyzing discourse', in Bryman, A. and Burgess, R.G. (eds) *Analyzing Qualitative Data*. London: Routledge.

Probyn, E. (1993) *Sexing the Self: Gendered Positions in Cultural Studies*. London: Routledge.

Probyn, E. (1996) *Outside Belongings*. London: Routledge.

Ragin, C. (1987) *The Comparative Method*. Berkeley, CA: University of California Press.

Ramazanoglu, C. (1989) 'Improving on sociology: the problems of taking a feminist standpoint', *Sociology*, 23(3): 427–42.

Ramsay, K. (1996) 'Emotional labour and qualitative research: how I learned not to laugh or cry in the field', in Lyon, E.S. and Busfield, J. (eds) *Methodological Imaginations*. London: Macmillan.

Rayner, G. and Stimson, G. (1979) 'Medicine, superstructure and micropolitics: a response', *Social Science and Medicine*, 13A: 611–12.

Reason, P. and Rowan, J. (1981) *Human Inquiry: A Sourcebook of New Paradigm Research*. Chichester: Wiley.

Riessman, C.K. (1990) 'Strategic uses of narrative in the presentation of self and illness: a research note', *Social Science and Medicine*, 30(11): 1195–200.

Rosaldo, R. (1989) *Culture and Truth: The Remaking of Social Analysis*. London: Routledge.

Rose, D. and Sullivan, O. (1993) *Introducing Data Analysis for Social Scientists*. Buckingham: Open University Press.

Rose, G. (1982) *Deciphering Social Research*. London: Macmillan.

Rosenberg, M. (1968) *The Logic of Survey Analysis*. New York: Basic Books.

Rosenblatt, P.C., Walsh, R.P. and Jackson, D.A. (1976) *Grief and Mourning in Cross-Cultural Perspective*. Human Relations Area File Press.

Rowntree, B.S. (1901) *Poverty: A Study of Town Life*. Basingstoke: Macmillan.

Rowntree, B.S. (1941) *Poverty and Progress: A Second Social Survey of York*. London: Longmans.

Rowntree, B.S. and Lavers, G.R. (1951) *Poverty and the Welfare State: A Third Social Survey of York Dealing Only with Economic Questions*. London: Longmans.

Russell, D. (1975) *The Politics of Rape: The Victim's Perspective*. New York: Stein and Day.

Russell, D. (1986) *The Secret Trauma: Incest in the Lives of Girls and Women*. New York: Basic Books.

Sacks, H. (1974) 'On the analyzability of stories by children', in Turner, R. (ed.) *Ethnomethodology*. Harmondsworth: Penguin.

Sacks, H. (1992a) *Lectures on Conversation, Volume 1*. Oxford: Blackwell.

Sacks, H. (1992b) *Lectures on Conversation, Volume 2*. Oxford: Blackwell.

Sacks, H., Schegloff, E. and Jefferson, G. (1974) 'A simple systematics for the organization of turn-taking in conversation'. *Language*, 50(4): 696–735.

Saussure, F. de (1974) *Course in General Linguistics*. London: Fontana.

Schegloff, E. (1967) 'The first five seconds: the order of conversational openings'. PhD dissertation, University of California, Berkeley.

Schutz, A. (1962) *Collected Papers, Volume 1*. The Hague: Martinus Nijhoff.

Schutz, A. (1964) *Collected Papers, Volume 2*. The Hague: Martinus Nijhoff.

Schutz, A. (1970) 'Concept and theory formation in the social sciences', in Emmet, D. and MacIntyre, A. (eds) *Sociological Theory and Philosophical Analysis*. London: Macmillan.

Scott, S. (1984) 'The personable and the powerful', in Bell, C. and Roberts, H. (eds) *Social Researching: Politics, Problems, Practice*. London: Routledge.

Seale, C.F. and Addington-Hall, J. (1994) 'Euthanasia: why people want to die earlier', *Social Science and Medicine*, 39(5): 647–54.

Seale, C.F. and Addington-Hall, J. (1995a) 'Euthanasia: the role of good care', *Social Science and Medicine*, 40(5): 581–7.

Seale, C.F. and Addington-Hall, J. (1995b) 'Dying at the best time', *Social Science and Medicine*, 40(5): 589–95.

Seale, C.F. and Cartwright, A. (1994) *The Year before Death*. Aldershot: Avebury.

Seale, C.F. and Kelly, M. (1997a) 'A comparison of hospice and hospital care for people who die: views of surviving spouse', *Palliative Medicine*, 11: 93–100.

Seale, C.F. and Kelly, M. (1997b) 'A comparison of hospice and hospital care for the spouses of people who die', '*Palliative Medicine*, 11: 101–6.

Seidel, J., Friese, S. and Leonard, D.C. (1995) *The ETHNOGRAPH Version 4.0: A User's Guide*. Amherst: Qualis Research Associates.

Shaffir, W.B. (1985) 'Some reflections on approaches to fieldwork in Hassidic communities', *Jewish Journal of Sociology*, 27(2): 115–34.

Shaffir, W.B. (1991) 'Managing a convincing self-presentation', in Shaffir, W.B. and Stebbins, R.A. (eds) *Experiencing Fieldwork*. London: Sage.

Silverman, D. (1984) 'Going private: ceremonial forms in a private oncology clinic', *Sociology*, 18: 191–202.

Silverman, D. (1985) *Qualitative Methodology and Sociology*. Aldershot: Gower.

Silverman, D. (1987) *Communication and Medical Practice: Social Relations in the Clinic*. London: Sage.

Silverman, D. (1990) 'Sociology and the community: a dialogue with the deaf?'. Inaugural lecture, Goldsmiths College, University of London, 24 October.

Silverman, D. (1993) *Interpreting Qualitative Data: Methods for Analysing Talk, Text and Interaction*. London: Sage.

Silverman, D. (1996) *Discourses of Counselling: HIV Counselling as Social Interaction*. London: Sage.

Silverman, D. (ed.) (1997) *Qualitative Research: Theory, Method, Practice*. London: Sage.

Skinner, Q. (1980) 'Language and social change', in Michaels, L. and Ricks, C. (eds) *The State of the Language*. Berkeley, CA: University of California Press.

Smart, B. (1993) *Postmodernity*. London: Routledge.

Stanley, L. and Wise, S. (1983) *Breaking Out: Feminist Consciousness and Feminist Research*. London: Routledge and Kegan Paul.

Stanley, L. and Wise, S. (1993) *Breaking Out Again: Feminist Ontology and Epistemology*. London: Routledge.

Steig, M. (1978) *Dickens and Phiz*. Bloomington, IN: Indiana University Press.

Strong, P. (1979) 'Sociological imperialism and the profession of medicine', *Social Science and Medicine*, 13A: 199–215.

Strunk, W. and White, E.B. (1979) *The Elements of Style* (3rd edn). Boston: Allyn and Bacon.

Sudnow, D. (1968) *Passing On: The Social Organization of Dying*. Englewood Cliffs, NJ: Prentice-Hall.

Sydie, R.A. (1987) *Natural Women, Cultured Men: A Feminist Perspective on Sociological Theory*. Milton Keynes: Open University Press.

Taraborrelli, P. (1993) 'Becoming a carer', in Gilbert, N. (ed.) *Researching Social Life*. London: Sage.

Taylor, C. (1994) 'Interpretation and the sciences of man', in Martin, M. and McIntyre, L.C. (eds) *Readings in the Philosophy of Social Science*. Cambridge, MA: MIT Press.

Tilly, C. (1984) *Big Structures, Large Processes, Huge Comparisons*. New York: Russell Sage Foundation.

Tonkiss, F. (1995) 'Economic government and the city'. PhD dissertation, Goldsmiths College, University of London.

Townsend, P., Corrigan, P. and Kowarzik, U. (1987) *Poverty and Labour in London*. London: Low Pay Unit.

Waitzkin, H. (1979) 'Medicine, superstructure and micropolitics', *Social Science and Medicine*, 13A: 601–9.

Walkerdine, V. and Lucey, H. (1989) *Democracy in the Kitchen: Regulating Mothers and Socialising Daughters*. London: Virago.

Warren, C.B. (1988) *Gender Issues in Field Research*. London: Sage.

Warren, C.B. and Rasmussen, P.K. (1977) 'Sex and gender in fieldwork research', *Urban Life*, 6: 359–69.

Weber, M. (1930) *The Protestant Ethic and the Spirit of Capitalism*. London: Allen and Unwin.

Weber, M. (1946) 'Science as a vocation', and 'Politics as a vocation' in Gerth, H. and Mills, C.W. (eds) *From Max Weber*. Oxford: Oxford University Press.

Weber, M. (1949) *The Methodology of the Social Sciences*. New York: Free Press.

Weber, M. (1978) *Economy and Society* (2 vols). Berkeley, CA: University of California Press.

Wellings, K., Johnson, A.M., Wadsworth, J., Bradshaw, S. and Field, J. (1994) *Sexual Behaviour in Britain*. London: Penguin.

Wells, A.F. (1935) *The Local Social Survey in Great Britain*. London: Allen and Unwin.

West, P. (1990) 'The status and validity of accounts obtained at interview: a contrast between two studies of families with a disabled child', *Social Science and Medicine*, 30(11): 1229–39.

Whyte, W.F. (1943) *Street Corner Society: The Social Structure of an Italian Slum*. Chicago: University of Chicago Press (3rd edn 1981).

Williams, M. and May, T. (1996) *Introduction to the Philosophy of Social Research*. London: UCL Press.

Williams, R. (1977) *Marxism and Literature*. Oxford: Oxford University Press.

Williamson, J. (1978) *Decoding Advertisements: Ideology and Meaning in Advertising*. London: Marion Boyars.

Winch, P. (1970) 'Understanding a primitive society', in Wilson, B.R. (ed.) *Rationality*. Oxford: Basil Blackwell.

Wolcott, H. (1990) *Writing Up Qualitative Research*. Qualitative Research Methods Series 20, Newbury Park, CA: Sage.

Wright, P. and Treacher, A. (1982) *The Problem of Medical Knowledge: Examining the Social Construction of Medicine*. Edinburgh: Edinburgh University Press.

Wrigley, E.A. and Schofield, R.S. (1989) *The Population History of England 1541–1871: A Reconstruction*. London: Edward Arnold.

Wrong, D. (1961) 'The oversocialized conception of man in modern sociology', *American Sociological Review*, 26: 183–93.

Yearley, S. (1981) 'Textual persuasion: the role of social accounting in the construction of scientific arguments', *Philosophy of Science*, 11: 409–35.

Young, M. and Cullen, L. (1996) *A Good Death: Conversations with East Londoners*. London: Routledge.

Young, M. and Willmott, P. (1957) *Family and Kinship in East London*. London: Routledge and Kegan Paul.

Zimmerman, D. (1992) 'The interactional organization of calls for emergency assistance', in Drew, P. and Heritage, J. (eds) *Talk at Work*. Cambridge: Cambridge University Press.

Zorbaugh, H. (1929) *The Gold Coast and the Slum*. Chicago: University of Chicago Press.

Index

The page numbers of terms in **bold** in the text (normally where a definition of that term is given), are in bold type.